THE ON~YOUR~OWN
GUIDE TO ASIA
REVISED FIFTH EDITION

JAPAN
SOUTH KOREA
TAIWAN
HONG KONG
MACAU
PHILIPPINES
THAILAND
MALAYSIA
SINGAPORE
INDONESIA

Edited by
John Doll and Terry George

Published by Charles E. Tuttle Co., Inc.
and Volunteers in Asia, Inc.

REPRESENTATIVES

For Continental Europe:
BOXERBOOKS, INC., Zurich

For the British Isles:
PRENTICE-HALL INTERNATIONAL, INC., London

For Australasia:
BOOK WISE (AUSTRALIA) PTY., LTD.
104 Sussex Street, Sydney

For Thailand:
BOOKS FOR ASIA
221 Sukhumvit Road, Bangkok

Published jointly by:
Volunteers in Asia, Inc. Stanford, California
Charles E. Tuttle Co., Inc. Rutland, Vermont & Tokyo, Japan

**Copyright © 1981
By Volunteers in Asia, Inc.**
All rights reserved, including the right of
reproduction in whole or in part in any form.

**Library of Congress Catalog Card No. 77-90889
International Standard Book No. 0-8048-1353-1**

**First Printing, 1981
Printed in the U.S.A.**

CREDITS

Cover by Winnie Lum.

Cartography by Ken Kreshtool and Anne Huckins.

Chinese calligraphy for Taiwan chapter by Wang Sang and Wang Ke-wen.

Drawings for Thailand chapter borrowed with illustrator's permission from **Little Things**, written by Prajuab Thirabutana and illustrated by Jamlong Busadee.

Table of Contents

PREFACE 5
BEFORE YOU GO 6
   Tips for Travelers
   Working in Asia
   Health
   Contacts for Travel Information
HONG KONG & MACAU 20
INDONESIA 50
JAPAN 118
MALAYSIA. 180
PHILIPPINES 222
SINGAPORE. 270
SOUTH KOREA 288
TAIWAN 314
THAILAND 350

Maps

East and Southeast Asia 19
Hong Kong Territory 20
   Downtown Hong Kong. 32
   Kowloon. 36
Macau 46
Indonesia 50
   Jakarta. 68
   Java 74
   Bali 96
   Denpasar 98
   Kuta 101

Japan	118
Tokyo Trains	138
Malaysia	180
Kuala Lumpur	200
East Malaysia	214
Philippines	222
Manila	234
Singapore	270
Downtown Singapore	283
South Korea	288
Seoul	301
Taiwan	314
Taipei	328
Taipei Train/Bus Stations	331
Thailand	350
Bangkok	364
Chiang Mai	375
Phuket	381

Preface

On Your Own draws upon the experience of dozens of young travelers who as members of Volunteers in Asia (VIA) have lived and worked in Asian countries for extended periods of time. VIA is a small, non-profit organization which sends students from Stanford University and the University of California at Santa Cruz to fulltime work positions in seven Asian nations.

The most exciting aspect of travel revolves as much around the people we meet as the scenic sights we see. Yet those traveling off the well-worn tourist paths can still be as far away from the people as travelers who opt for package tours. Knowing a few words in the local language, remembering not to point your feet at someone in Thailand or use your left hand in Indonesia, can open doors to a rich array of personal experiences and discoveries about your host culture that most tourists would never see, and make your travels more meaningful and exciting.

It would be impossible to list all the Asian friends and fellow travelers who have been kind enough to contribute information to this guide; we owe them an enormous thanks. Researchers and consultants for this edition of **On Your Own** include: Hong Kong—Carmen Pe Siu-pik, Rowena Chow; Indonesia—Astrid R. Hutapea, Marcus Kaufman, Eric Kettner, Kusnarjono, Kate Littleboy, Mary Anna Maloney, Mark Nelson, Bob Simons, Drs. T. Subyarno, Jill Tucker; Japan—Bob Bagwill, Tim George, Alice Hill, Yoko Kondo, Matt Lippert, George Prince, Liz Rankin, Paul Yoshimura and the San Francisco JNTO office; Macau—Rose Marie Chan; Malaysia—Halim Abdullah, Abdul Halim Md. Anuar, Mrs. Nalini Danker, Miss Khoo Guat Im, Noorani Yusoff; Philippines—Dan and Mila Thomas, Jello and Howdy Bouis; Singapore—Doug Aden, Goh, Fokke von Knobloch; South Korea—Kathy Tormey, Sam Schwartz; Taiwan—Cindy Fong, Eugene Gregor, Rich Macdonald, Liz Morrison, Karin Pascoe, Jeff Ryan, Karen Salter, Linda Shaw, David Woo; Thailand—Buzz and Doug Thompson. Special thanks to Dan Fietkiewicz for contributions to the Indonesia chapter. Alison Davis, editor of the last two editions of this guide, and Anne Huckins, did a tremendous job updating the Hong Kong, Indonesia, Macau, Malaysia, and Singapore chapters, and provided invaluable editorial advice. Thanks to Mahesh Shrestha for typesetting. Many thanks to Rich Rawson, who edited the first edition of the guide, and to Ken Darrow, who designed it. A warm personal thanks to Linda Shipley, Dave Tuffs, and the VIA staff for proofreading the manuscript. Finally, neither this book nor Volunteers in Asia would be possible without the inspirational leadership of Dwight Clark.

—The Editors

BEFORE YOU GO

On Your Own is written for the traveler who doesn't want to experience Asia through the tinted glass of tour bus windows. It offers detailed information which will help make it possible for people who have time and energy to explore Asia independently and inexpensively. Such travel is more exciting, more meaningful—and also more demanding; you must be willing to get lost periodically, to make mistakes, to be confused.

While traveling off the beaten track can be challenging for you, it also has an impact on the people you come in contact with. Though you can't completely avoid making mistakes, and generally people will be quite tolerant of unintentional errors, you do have some obligation to be minimally disruptive in the places you visit. Many inns in Japan no longer accept foreign guests who don't speak Japanese because previous visitors have caused great consternation by putting cold water and soap in the bath (which is supposed to remain hot and clean for all the inn's guests). People in many parts of Indonesia and Malaysia (especially strongly Moslem areas) have been offended by the excessively casual dress of some visiting foreigners. To the extent that you can adapt to different local situations you'll get along much better with the people you meet, and you'll make it a lot easier for the travelers who come after you. With this in mind, we've provided cultural cues for each country, as well as details on language, food, accommodations, and transportation.

Tips for Travelers

PASSPORT

Application for a passport can be made through a central post office, the office of the county clerk, or U.S. State Department offices in major cities. You will need: 1) proof of citizenship (certified copy, not xeroxed copy, of your birth certificate or naturalization certificate, or a previous passport), 2) identification (e.g. a valid driver's license, with signature and photograph to be verified by the person handling the application), 3) two identical photographs (2'' x 2'') taken within six months of the date of application and signed on the left-hand side, and 4) an application fee of US$14 (or US$10 if your proof of citizenship is a previous passport issued in the last 8 yrs.). Allow 10-14 days for processing of the application.

You can **register your passport** at U.S. embassies upon arrival in a foreign country. In case your passport is lost or stolen this will greatly simplify the process of having a new one issued. Otherwise you will have to pay a cable charge and wait until verification of your passport is obtained from the U.S. State Department.

Carry about two dozen **extra passport photos**, if you're traveling through many countries; you'll use more than you expect for visa applications and other purposes. A low-cost source of extra prints: Pictures—U.S.A., Box 455, San Francisco, CA 94101. Send a print or negative—US$1.60 plus $.50 postage/handling for 20 black-and-white prints. Also bring a negative with you to Asia to have prints made there at low cost.

VISAS

A visa is official permission to visit a country, obtained from an embassy or consulate of that country (it's stamped in your passport). The governments of some countries don't require visas for short stays; others grant them for varying lengths of time. Visas must be used within a specified period from the date of issue—usually 3 months—so it may be easier (and cheaper) to get some of them along the way rather than all at once before you leave.

INTERNATIONAL DRIVER'S LICENSE

American Automobile Association (AAA) offices throughout the country issue this license for US$3; two photos are required.

LUGGAGE

An airline bag and small- or medium-sized suitcase or a lightweight bag with a shoulder strap should suffice. Buy sturdy luggage that won't disintegrate on you in the Sumatran highlands at the height of the rainy season. Backpacks are convenient for hiking, but are not recommended for traveling in most of Asia due to their association with 'hippies' ('hippie' = scroungy, dirty, untrustworthy).

Every piece of luggage should have a **name and address label** both inside and outside the bag. Other distinguishing marks will help you identify your things quickly at baggage claim counters in crowded airports. Remove old baggage tags before check-in to avoid possible confusion over the destination of your luggage.

CLOTHING & TOILETRIES

Travel light! The usual tendency is to take too much, which you'll regret later when you try to wrestle your gear onto a

8 BEFORE YOU GO

jam-packed Indonesian bus or sprint with it through the Hong Kong Airport. The ultimate test: pick your bags up and walk 100 meters. You'll likely reconsider how much you 'need.'

Prepare for hot, humid weather; permanent press clothing is highly recommended. You can have clothes made at low cost in many Asian countries, and almost anything you might need is available—with the possible exceptions of shoes (large sizes) and underwear.

Women. Several lightweight dresses (to at least middle of the knee) or blouse/skirt combinations, made of material that won't wrinkle easily or show dirt. One or two pairs of pants (jeans can be hot; shorts are OK for beaches). Cotton (never nylon) underwear. Nightclothes (light pajamas help keep the mosquitoes off). Bathing suit (not too skimpy or clingy). One or two pairs of socks. Tampons are hard to find; sanitary napkins are more widely available.

Men. Two pairs of lightweight pants (jeans can be hot). 3-4 short-sleeved shirts. Lightweight underwear (boxer shorts are cooler and may help prevent jock rash). Several undershirts. Pajamas (they help keep the mosquitoes off). Swim trunks. 3-4 pairs of socks.

General. Two pairs of sturdy shoes and/or sandals (keep them dry—metal parts will quickly rust and leather will get moldy); if you're going to spend much time in Japan, take shoes that are easy to slip in and out of. One sweater or light jacket (it can get quite chilly at higher altitudes, even in equatorial countries). One towel (a thin one that will dry quickly and pack easily). Handkerchiefs (for mopping your sweaty brow). Folding umbrella (cheap in Japan and Hong Kong). Inflatable hanger (for drying hand-washed clothes). Sunglasses. Deodorant (available in Asia, but expensive). If you're sexually active, bring birth control supplies with you; they're not always easily obtainable in Asian countries.

It always pays off to dress neatly when entering or leaving any country; customs and immigration officials are much more likely to let you through quickly.

GIFTS

Travelers will find giving gifts a good way (sometimes the only way) to return the kindness and hospitality which one so often encounters in Asia. A few suggestions of **small gifts** you can take for Asian friends you meet along the way: school Tshirts, decals, picture calendars, pens, hair clips, attractive postcards, stamps, toys, hard candies, anything distinctive to your home area. Gifts such as chocolate bars or special brands of coffee are greatly appreciated because they are expensive or hard to find in most Asian countries. Cigarettes and liquor can be purchased in the tax-free shops in airport departure lounges or on planes for last-minute gifts. Instant Polaroid snapshots will make you a hit in any village or town.

ACCOMMODATIONS

• YWCAs and YMCAs once offered cheap and clean accommodations in major cities throughout Asia. They're still spotless but prices at many of the Ys have nearly doubled in the last two years, putting them in the same price range with some fairly nice hotels. A few remaining bargains: M$5 dorm beds at the YMCA in Kuala Lumpur; singles and doubles at the YWCA on MacDonnell Rd. in Hong Kong which start at HK$35 and HK$40 respectively; and the Salisbury Rd. YMCA in Hong Kong offers dorm beds for HK$20. All of these rooms are available for both women and men.

• In Chinese hotels, 'singles' often have double beds.

• Avoid keeping food in your hotel room or stash it with care—otherwise it's a standing invitation for visits from cockroaches, ants, and other assorted animal life.

• Cheap hotels are often located on busy streets; try to get a room at the back if you don't want to listen to motorcycles all night.

• If you plan to stay in **youth hostels**, get a **membership card from the American Youth Hostels** (AYH), a member of the International Youth Hostel Federation. Cards are US$14 and are issued on a calendar year basis except for the card which is issued on and after Oct. 1 and is valid for up to 15 months. Information on hostel regulations and a listing of hostels by country can be found in the annually-published **International Youth Handbook**, Vol. 2: Asia, Australia, Africa, and the Americas (US$5.00). For AYH membership, a handbook, and more information, write to American Youth Hostel, Inc., Delaplane, VA 22025.

• **Hotel reservations** may be made in advance by sending a postcard indicating your date of arrival. This is highly recommended for YW/YMCAs (and youth hostels) during the summer months.

• Always obtain the **name card** of your hotel after you check in so you can telephone the hotel or show the card to a taxi driver if you get lost.

• **Inexpensive hotels** can generally be found within a few blocks of train and bus stations; occasionally these areas will also be red light districts. Airport tourist information centers usually don't have listings of low-cost places to stay, but they can help arrange for accommodations in a moderately-priced hotel for your first night if you arrive after dark.

THEFT

Beware of rip-offs; travelers are favored targets for thieves and pickpockets around the world. Some common sense precautions:

• Be especially careful in train stations, bus stations, and airports; also on crowded buses.

• Bring along a small padlock to double lock your hotel door if you suspect your cheap hostel is not really safe. Latches are often provided for this purpose on hotel doors.

• In Bangkok and Penang particularly, watch out for thieves on motorcycles. They work in pairs—the guy in front eases the motorcycle up beside you while the one in back clamps an iron grip on your shoulder bag, purse, etc. Then they roar off. This strategy works especially well when you're distracted watching the traffic and trying to cross a busy street (a 5-minute undertaking in some cases). Women are the most common victims.

Although people in most areas of Asia are usually very friendly, there are a few places which can be rough at times. Use your common sense, be aware, and stay away from places where you don't feel comfortable at night.

MONEY

Carry **travelers' checks**—ten and twenty-dollar denominations allow you to exchange a small amount when that's all you need; American Express and First National City Bank checks can be cashed most easily throughout the world. Be sure to keep the receipts separate from the checks; to be extra safe make a xerox copy of your receipts and leave it with a friend for reference in case your checks are lost or stolen. New travelers' checks will not be issued unless you have a record of the serial numbers of all checks lost.

Exchange money at authorized moneychangers and save receipts so that you can convert extra local currency back to U.S. dollars upon leaving the country. The exchange rates are reasonably good at most Asian airports (one notable exception is Hong Kong, where you should exchange only the amount you will need before getting to a local bank). Remember to bring your passport when exchanging money.

All prices in this guide are given in the local currency. We encourage you to think in those terms rather than in U.S. dollar equivalents. We also suggest that you carry two wallets or a wallet and a coin purse so you can keep small amounts of the local currency separate from the rest of your money; nothing is so awkward as bargaining for a low price and then pulling out a wad of large bills. Just before you leave a country, cut back on your coin supply, because banks (always) and money changers (usually) will not change coins into another currency.

INTERNATIONAL MONEY TRANSFERS

The following procedures can be used in an emergency to have money transferred on your behalf from a U.S. bank to an Asian bank. Don't use them unless absolutely necessary because they're generally complicated and time-consuming.

The **Cable Remittance Order** is the fastest way to send money overseas. The home bank transfers funds to a foreign bank which notifies the payee. U.S. dollars or foreign currencies may be transferred.

The **Mail Remittance Order** offers the same service as the Cable Remittance Order but is sent via airmail, relying on normal mail delivery.

An **International Money Order** is prepared by a bank but mailed by the customer. The maximum amount transferable by this method is US$500; for larger amounts ask for a Foreign Draft.

International money transfers handled by mail can be registered as a safety precaution. This makes for slower delivery (because each carrier handling the letter must sign for it), but the letter can easily be traced if lost or delayed.

CUSTOMS

American citizens can bring back US$300 worth of foreign goods for personal use of for gifts without paying duty. Under the GSP (Generalized System of Preferences) which went into effect in 1976 you may also bring back certain products (including cameras, musical instruments, tapes, wood carvings, etc.) from 'beneficiary developing countries' free of duty. All countries covered in this book qualify, except Japan. For a more complete list of eligible goods, write to the nearest U.S. Customs office or to the Dept. of the Treasury (see address below) for the pamphlet "GSP and the Traveler." All articles acquired abroad, whether duty-free or not, must be declared upon your return.

Register foreign-made items, such as cameras and watches, before leaving the U.S. to certify that you didn't buy them during your travels. This can be done at the customs office in any international airport in the U.S. For more information, write to the nearest U.S. Customs office or to the Dept. of the Treasury, U.S. Customs Service, Washington, D.C. 20229 for the pamphlets "Know Before You Go (Customs Hints for Returning U.S. Residents)" and "Pocket Hints (Capsule Information for Returning U.S. Residents)."

12 BEFORE YOU GO

STUDENT DISCOUNTS

An **International Student Identity Card** entitles the student traveler to discounts on accommodations, transportation, etc. To get an ISIC you need certification of your student status from the registrar at your school. Submit this certification, along with one passport photo and the application fee of US$6, to Council on International Educational Exchange (CIEE), Student Travel Services, 205 East 42nd St., New York, New York 10017, or a Student Travel Center at the university in your area. The new 1981 card includes travel insurance; check with CIEE for details.

INTERNATIONAL AIRPORTS

Immigration may include inspection of your yellow International Certificate of Vaccination (see Health section), so be sure to carry this with your passport rather than in your baggage. Your passport and visa are also inspected before you enter the baggage claim area and customs.

Look for **tourist information centers, banks,** and other travelers' aids immediately after customs inspection, often before entering the airport lobby where the public greets arriving passengers.

You can **bond baggage** inexpensively in most Asian airports. Check in early at the airport if you have to pick up bonded baggage upon leaving the country.

Reconfirm your airline reservation if you break your journey. Take care of this at the airport before you go into town, if possible; otherwise, call the local airline office, ideally at least 72 hours before departure in view of the frequency of overbooked flights. Try to get to the airport a good two hours before your scheduled flight time (to allow for security checks, standing in line at the check-in counter etc.).

Travelers leaving Asian countries by plane should be prepared to pay an **airport departure tax**, usually equivalent to US$2-3. Put aside the necessary amount in the local currency (listed in the General Information section of each chapter) soon after your arrival so you won't be caught short. (Or keep a small supply of U.S. one dollar bills so you can exchange small sums of money to take care of this and other last-minute expenses.)

LOCAL TRANSPORTATION

• Hang on to your tickets (bus, train, whatever)—you never know when they will be punched, collected, inspected, or torn nearly in half and handed back to you.

• Keep a supply of small change handy—paying for 20 cent rides with $10 bills will make you unpopular with bus conductors. Either that or it will be an expensive trip because in many Asian cities you have to put the correct amount in the fare box—no change given.

BEFORE YOU GO 13

• In large cities keep track of rush hours so you can avoid using public transportation at those times. Public transport to popular amusement parks, etc. will often be jammed on weekends and holidays (in some places, e.g. Hong Kong, prices go up as well).

• Beware of taxi drivers who claim their meter is broken. To avoid getting a roundabout tour to your destination, have at least an idea of the most direct route before you take a taxi.

• Ask someone at your hotel/hostel or at the tourist information office to write destinations down for you in the local language; then if you can't find anyone who speaks English, people will at least be able to point you in the right direction.

LANGUAGE

Knowing just a few words in the local language will surely open doors for you, and will surprise and please Asian friends you meet (all the more so since so few tourists bother to learn any words at all). However, don't be afraid to venture onto the rural backroads of Asia just because your language ability is virtually nil. A combination of grunts, hand signals, patience and a warm smile, along with a few stock phrases in the local language will get you anywhere you want to go.

BARGAINING

Bargaining, an art developed through much practice and many bad deals, is common in many Asian countries and indispensable in markets and in any shop that doesn't post fixed prices. If you think of bargaining as a game or an adventure, rather than a life-or-death struggle, the process will be more pleasant for shopper and shopkeeper alike. Here are some general rules to keep in mind:

• Don't start bargaining unless you sincerely want to buy.

• Know the general price you want to pay. Ask a third person (like your hotelkeeper) and look in several shops beforehand to determine the going price.

• Establish some rapport by asking about the merchandise and just chatting a little. Don't look too interested in buying, or the price may never come down.

• Unless you have shopped around, let the salesperson state the first price. Begin bargaining well below the price you hope for, and see how low the seller will go.

• If, in the course of bargaining, you counter with a price and the shopkeeper accepts, you're obligated to buy.

• When you get to the highest price you're willing to pay, thank the salesperson and leave (keeping your ears perked—you may be called back).

14 BEFORE YOU GO

Working in Asia

Working can be a way to become more involved in another culture than is possible for the transient visitor. Though it may lack some of the excitement of traveling, a job can give you a sense of 'belonging' and a more intimate exposure to different ideas and values.

Employment opportunities are sometimes listed in the "Help Wanted" sections of local English-language newspapers in the capital cities of Asia. University bulletin boards, student unions, and embassies are other sources of information. Though there is still a fairly widespread demand for English teachers and private tutors, travelers who hope to subsidize their stay in Asia by finding such jobs should be aware of several major difficulties. In most countries regulations regarding work permits, visas, and payment of taxes are getting stricter each year; a law was recently passed in Japan requiring all English teachers to have a college degree. You must have an employer to act as a sponsor in order to apply for a work permit and appropriate visa. In some countries (e.g. Japan) you cannot exchange your tourist or entry visa for a work visa unless you leave the country and apply for re-entry.

Work camps and volunteer service projects offer an alternative to full-time paid employment, though a long-term commitment is often required.

For more information on opportunities for working in Asia, contact:

Council on International Educational Exchange (CIEE), 205 East 42nd St., New York, NY 10017. **Whole World Handbook** (A Student Guide to Work, Study, and Travel Abroad). Provides extensive information on short- and long-term employment opportunities, work camps, and voluntary service projects. $4.95 plus postage and handling for the 1981-82 edition, due to be published in spring 1981.

Coordinating Committee for International Voluntary Service, UNESCO, 1 rue Miollis, Paris 75015, France. Best source of information on non-governmental overseas service programs. They also publish a **Workcamps Programme**, listing work camps in more than 50 countries. Order it from COTRAVAUX, 11 rue de Clichy, Paris 75009, France, or directly from the CCIVS Secretariat; enclose four international postal reply coupons.

U.N. Headquarters NGO Youth Caucus, c/o Social Development Division, Rm. DC-977, United Nations, New York, NY 10017. **International Directory for Youth Internships**. A biennial publication listing

BEFORE YOU GO 15

about 400 intern/volunteer positions that relate directly to work with the U.N. or other international programs sponsored by non-governmental organizations. US$2.

LAOS, 4920 Piney Branch Rd., N.W., Washington, DC 20011. Places volunteers in both church-related and secular service projects in the U.S. and abroad. They help publish **Invest Yourself**; order this catalog of service opportunities from Nancy Duryea, 418 Peltoma Rd., Haddonfield, NJ 08033. US$2 (3rd class postage), US$2.25 (1st class).

Overseas Service Corps Project, International Division, National Council of YMCAs, 291 Broadway, New York, NY 10017. For information on English teaching positions in YMCA language schools in Taiwan (1-2 years) and Japan (2 years, minimum). Summer programs are also available. A basic salary and housing provided.

AIPT, Inc. (Association for International Practical Training), the U.S. branch of IAESTE (International Association for the Exchange of Students for Technical Experience), American City Building, Suite 217, Columbia, MD 21044. A reciprocal exchange program providing on-the-job practical training for students in a variety of fields in 46 member countries (including Japan, South Korea, and the Philippines).

Health

IMMUNIZATIONS

The **International Certificate of Vaccination** (yellow card) is no longer required in most countries since there are few required immunizations. However, you **must** carry the card if you are going to a country or countries which require a certain immunization. Plan ahead in order to get all the necessary shots in the required sequence.

If you will be traveling only on **major tourist routes**, you should be immunized against **tetanus** and **polio**, and take **malaria pills** where needed (see p. 16).

If you will be traveling **off the major tourist routes**, get immunized against: **tetanus, polio**, and **typhoid**, take **malaria pills** if needed (see p. 16), and receive a dose of **gamma globulin** immediately before departure as protection against infectious hepatitis. Also have a **tuberculosis skin test** done before your trip to establish that you have a negative reaction. Then get retested about 2 months after you return home.

You should get immunized against **cholera** if you are going to an area where it is endemic (ask your doctor); and possibly **typhus** (necessary only for certain remote highland areas—check with your local health department) and **measles** (if you've never had measles or were vaccinated against them before 1969).

When deciding which immunizations you need, remember

16 BEFORE YOU GO

that it's better to be over-protected. A prolonged sickness can ruin your trip. The entire series need never be repeated, but you should get a booster dose for any immunization for which the effective period has passed. Local public health departments often give these shots free of charge, but a fee of US$5 may be charged for the International Certificate of Vaccination card.

RECOMMENDED HEALTH SUPPLIES

• **For wounds and skin problems:** disinfectant soap, bandaids, sterile gauze pads, adhesive tape, tweezers, needles, scissors.

• **For sun and insects:** hat and sunglasses, sunscreen cream or lotion, insect repellent (Cutter's is good), caladryl lotion.

• **For infections and rashes:** antibiotic ointment (e.g. Bacitracin, Neosporin), baby or medicated powder, powder or cream for fungus infections (e.g. Desenex, Tinactin, Kwell).

• **For rinsing wounds or gum and tooth infections:** hydrogen peroxide (H_2O_2). Available worldwide and cheap. Dilute with equal parts water and rinse for 3 minutes 3 times/day.

• Sodium bicarbonate ($NaHCO_3$)—soap, deodorant, and toothpaste all in one cheap box.

• Thermometer in hard case, dental floss, aspirin, multiple vitamins (iron supplement for women). Water purification: Globulin (iodine) tablets or 2% tincture, 5-10 drops per quart of water. (Note: halazone and other chlorine compounds are ineffective against amoebas.)

• **Medications:** anti-diarrheal* (e.g. Lomotil, paregoric, charcoal tablets), motion sickness pills (e.g. Dramamine—note the side-effect of drowsiness which occurs 3-4 hours later), antibiotics (e.g. penicillin, tetracycline), antihistamine (e.g. Promethazine—which may have the side-effect of blurring vision temporarily) for itching and vomiting. Your doctor or health center can help you assemble these medications.
*Note: Enterovioform, which is sold over the counter as an anti-diarrheal in parts of Asia, may cause serious neurological damage.

• If there is any specific medicine which you need regularly, you should carry an adequate supply which is well-labeled, with a physician's letter explaining the importance of the medication.

• **Malaria:** According to the U.S. Public Health Service, the following are malaria risk areas: Indonesia (except Jakarta and Surabaya), South Korea (from June to September), Malaysia, Philippines (except Cebu and Leyte), Singapore (except city district), and Thailand (except most urban areas). The most common malaria pills are chloroquine phosphate (brand names: Aralen, Avloclor, Resochin). However, some areas are known to have chloroquine-resistant strains: East Kalimantan and Irian Jaya in Indonesia; all of Malaysia; Luzon, Basilan, Sulus, Mindoro, and Palawan in the Philippines; and all malarious areas of Thailand. For these areas, the recommended drug is pyrimethamine-sulfadoxine (brand names: Fansidar, Falcidar, Antemal, and Methipox). Ask your doctor for specific instructions on how to take malaria pills and follow them carefully. You may meet travelers, resident Americans, and Asians who will scoff at the need for malaria pills, but our experience strongly suggests that malaria prevention should be taken seriously.

BEFORE YOU GO 17

• A copy of your lens prescription or other important information regarding your medical history (allergies, reactions to medication, etc.).

SOURCES OF INFORMATION ON HEALTH FOR TRAVELERS

Health Hints for the Tropics, Harry Most, M.D. (ed.), The American Society for Tropical Medicine and Hygiene, 1980. Available from Editor, Tropical Medicine and Hygiene News, 3307 Harrell St., Wheaton, MD 20906. US$1.

International Association for Medical Assistance for Travelers, Empire State Bldg., 350 fifth Ave., Suite 5620, New York, NY 10001. The IAMAT provides a list of recommended doctors throughout the world. Membership is free; voluntary donations are requested.

Staying Healthy in Asia, Anne Huckins, ed., 1979. Available from Volunteers in Asia Press, Box 4543,, Stanford, CA 94305. Packed with Asia-specific information on nutrition, illnesses, first aid, and preventive health. US$2.50 plus $.75 postage/handling (California residents add $.15 sales tax).

Contacts for Travel Information

Hong Kong:
Hong Kong Tourist Association, 160 Sansome St., Suite 1102, San Francisco, CA 94104 **or** 510 W. Sixth St., Suite 1217, Los Angeles, CA 90014 **or** 1411 Fourth Ave., Suite 1327, Seattle, WA 98101 **or** Alexander Young Bldg., Suite 473, Honolulu, HI 96813 **or** 333 N. Michigan Ave., Chicago, IL 60601 **or** 548 Fifth Ave., New York, NY 10036 **or** 1000 Connecticut Ave., NW, Washington, DC 20036. Also has offices in London, Paris, Rome, Frankfurt, Sydney, Perth and the capital cities of most Asian countries.

Macau:
Macau Tourist Information Bureau, 177 Post St., Penthouse, San Francisco, CA 94108 **or** 60 East 42nd St., New York, NY 10017 **or** 3133 Lake Hollywood Dr., Los Angeles, CA 90068. Also has offices in London, Vancouver, Sydney, Bangkok, Tokyo, Osaka and Manila.

Indonesia:
Indonesian Tourist Promotion Board, 323 Geary St., Suite 305, San Francisco, CA 94102. Also has offices in Tokyo, Frankfurt, London, Singapore, and Sydney.

18 BEFORE YOU GO

Japan:
Japan National Tourist Organization, 1737 Post St., San Francisco, CA 94115 **or** 624 S. Grand Ave., Los Angeles, CA 90017 **or** 2270 Kalakaua Ave., Honolulu, HI 96815 **or** 1516 Main St., Suite 200, Dallas, TX 75201 **or** 333 N. Michigan Ave., Chicago, IL 60601 **or** 630 Fifth Ave., New York, NY 10111. Also has offices in Toronto, Mexico City, Sao Paulo, London, Paris, Geneva, Rome, Frankfurt, Sydney, Hong Kong, and Bangkok.

Malaysia:
Malaysia Tourist Information Center, 36th floor, Transamerica Pyramid Bldg., 600 Montgomery St., San Francisco, CA 94111. Also has offices in Sydney, Singapore, Bangkok, Hong Kong, Tokyo, London, and Frankfurt.

Philippines:
Philippines Ministry of Tourism, 447 Sutter St., Suite 409-411-413, San Francisco, CA 94108 **or** FIC Bldg., Suite 606, 3325 Wilshire Blvd., Los Angeles, CA 90010 **or** 30 N. Michigan Ave., Suite 111, Chicago, IL 60602 **or** 556 Fifth Ave., New York, NY 10036. Also has offices in Tokyo, Osaka, Sydney, Singapore, Hong Kong, Madrid and Frankfurt.

Singapore:
Singapore Tourist Promotion Board, 251 Post St., San Francisco, CA 94108 **or** Suite 1008, 342 Madison Ave., New York, NY 10017. Also has offices in Sydney, Perth, Auckland, Tokyo, London, Frankfurt, and Zurich.

South Korea:
Korea National Tourism Corporation, Korea Center Bldg., Suite 628, 460 Park Ave., New York, NY 10022 **or** Suite 1500, 230 N. Michigan Ave., Chicago, IL 60601 **or** 510 Bldg., Suite 323, 510 W. Sixth Ave., Los Angeles, CA 90014 **or** 1501 Kapiolani Blvd., Honolulu, HI 96814. Also has offices in London, Paris, Frankfurt, Zurich, Stockholm, Sydney, Singapore, Hong Kong, Fukuoka, Nagoya, Osaka, and Tokyo.

Taiwan:
Republic of China Tourism Bureau, Suite 705, 210 Post St., San Francisco, CA 94108 **or** Suite 1060, 3660 Wilshire Blvd., Los Angeles, CA 90010 **or** 1 World Trade Center, Suite 86155, New York, NY 10048.

Thailand:
Tourist Authority of Thailand, 3440 Wilshire Blvd., Los Angeles, CA 90010 **or** 5 World Trade Center, Suite 2449, New York, NY 10048. Also has offices in Tokyo, Singapore, Sydney, London, Paris and Frankfurt.

General:
Council on International Educational Exchange (CIEE), 205 East 42nd St., New York, NY 10017. **Whole World Handbook** (A Student Guide to Work, Study, and Travel Abroad), 1981-82 ed. An excellent resource. US$4.95.

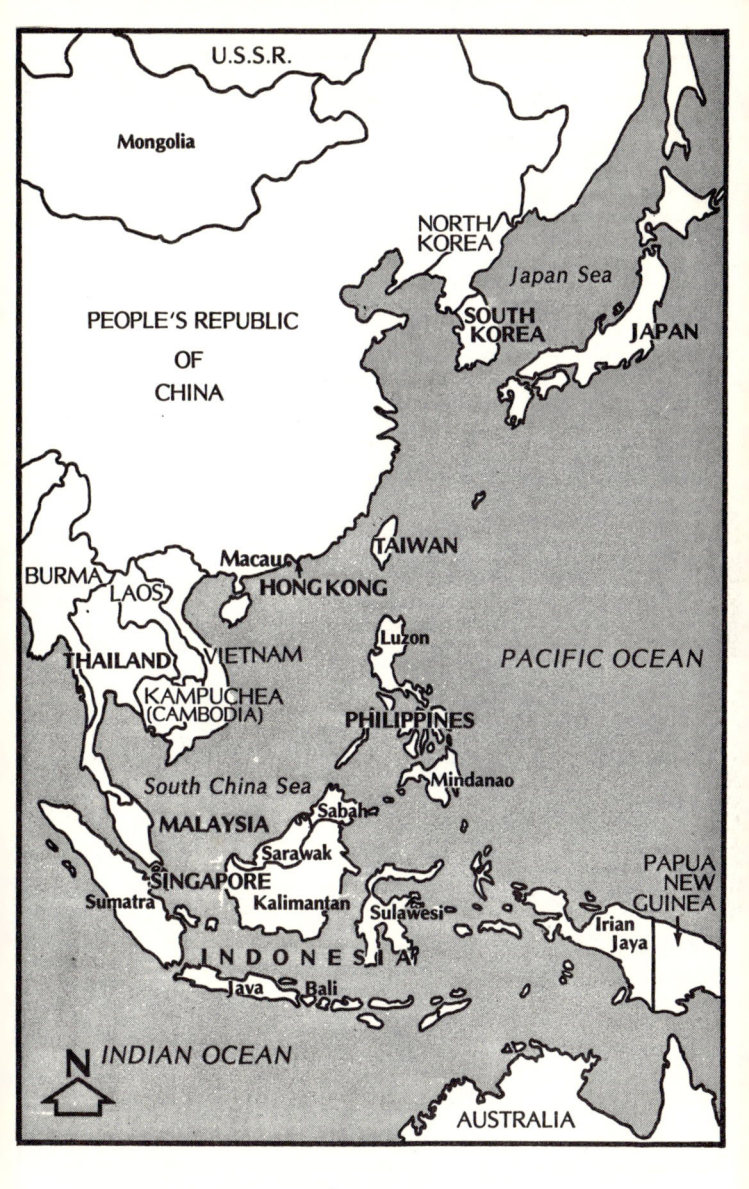

East and Southeast Asia

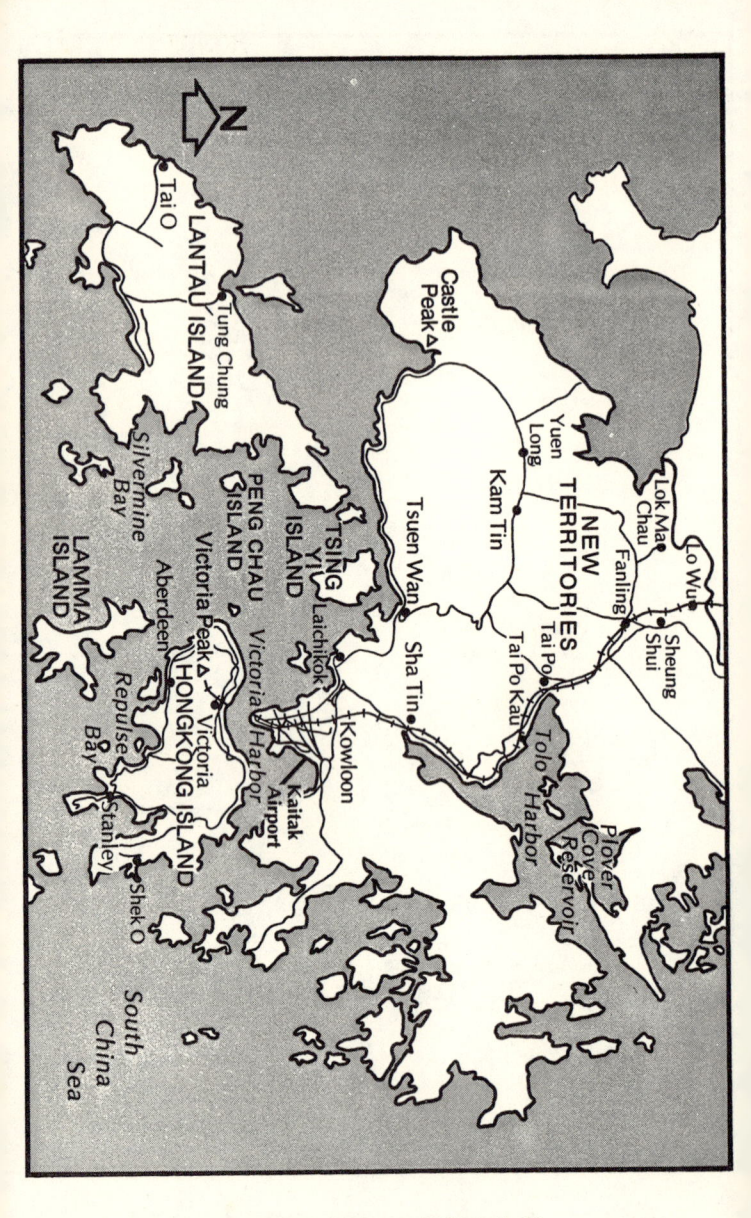

HONG KONG

General Information

Arrival: Kai Tak International Airport sits on reclaimed land in northeastern Kowloon, 15 min. by car from the Star Ferry Terminal at the tip of the peninsula. After clearing customs you will find yourself in a buffer lounge, which people greeting arriving passengers are not allowed to enter. Change a minimal amount at the money exchange counter here because the money changers downtown give better rates. Then pick up a free map and brochures at the Hong Kong Tourist Assn. (HKTA) counter. If you arrive late at night or without definite lodging plans, talk with the people at the hotel reservations desk (open until 11:30 pm). They have listings of relatively inexpensive rooms as well as more plush accommodations, and can call ahead for you to make sure there's a vacancy. Or choose a hotel from the HKTA pamphlet "Hotels in Hong Kong," and call ahead yourself to make reservations, using the free phones located just in front and to the left of the HKTA counter. There are three exits from the buffer lounge: one for tour groups, one for hotel guests, and one for general arrivals.

Luggage can be left at the airport at the Left Luggage counter, 2nd floor, at HK$5 per piece for the first day and HK$3/day from then on.

From the airport, several bus routes serve the downtown area. Most convenient are the airport coaches which link Kai Tak with major hotels in Kowloon (route 201, HK$1.50) and on Hong Kong Island (route 200, HK$2.50). These buses have baggage racks, which regular buses lack. Route 201 and 200 buses leave every 15 min., 8:30 am-11 pm and 7:25 am-10:30 pm respectively. (Route 201 buses stop quite near the most popular hostels and guest houses.) The hard-core budget traveler can take a regular city bus. Buses #9 and #5 go to the Star Ferry, the former via Nathan Rd., the latter via Chatham Rd. (fare: HK$.50). Ask how to get to the bus stop at the HKTA counter. Taxi fare from the airport to destinations in downtown Kowloon is HK$11-12, to Hong Kong Island about HK$25 (this includes the HK$10 charge for the cross-harbour tunnel). Finally, the YMCA/YWCAs provide their guests with transportation from the airport for less than taxi fare, though a public bus would still be cheaper.

Telephone numbers have a prefix depending upon geographical location: "5" for numbers on Hong Kong Island, "3" for Kowloon, and "12" for the New Territories. The prefix numbers are like area codes in that they are dropped when dialing within an area.

22 HONG KONG

Departure: As of mid-1980 many airlines were limiting carry-on hand baggage to a single piece with a maximum size of 9" x 14" x 22". American carriers going to destinations in the U.S. were allowing two pieces of hand baggage. Ask about current regulations when you reconfirm your plane reservation.

The airport departure tax is HK$20.

Visas: Americans and nationals of many other countries can stay in Hong Kong for up to 30 days without a visa if they have proof of transportation out of the colony; citizens of Commonwealth nations and some other countries can stay up to three months without a visa. Tourist visas good for a 90-day stay are available at British consulates, but must be obtained before arrival in Hong Kong.

Currency: In November 1980 the exchange rate was 5.03 Hong Kong dollars (HK$5.03) to the U.S. dollar.

Climate: Subtropical. Summers are hot and humid, winters cool and less humid; rain falls mainly in spring and summer. Typhoons sometimes hit Hong Kong between June and October.

Sources of Information

In addition to its airport desk (open 10-10 daily), the **Hong Kong Tourist Association** (HKTA) has an office in Kowloon on the Star Ferry concourse. On Hong Kong Island there are HKTA offices on the 35th floor of the Connaught Centre Bldg., and in the Government Publications Centre in the Central Post Office Bldg. (near the Star Ferry). Hours: Star Ferry (Kowloon) and Connaught Ctr., 8-6 Mon.-Fri., 8-1 Sat.; Gov't Publications Ctr., 9-6 Mon.-Fri., 9-1 Sat. The Star Ferry Office is also open 8-1 on Sunday.

The HKTA Official Guidebook, free of charge at HKTA offices and hotels, lists ferry and train schedules along with some of the most frequently used bus routes. The free HKTA weekly newspaper "Orient" lists upcoming concerts, Chinese opera performances, exhibits, etc. Of the numerous free brochures which the HKTA puts out, the "Six Walks," "See for Yourself," and "Hong Kong Beaches" pamphlets are particularly useful for budget travelers. The HKTA also offers a Telephone Information Service; just dial 3-671111.

Hong Kong Student Travel Bureau, 1024 Star House (near the Star Ferry), Kowloon; tel. 3-694847. Open 9-6 on weekdays and 9-4 on Saturday. Helpful, friendly staff. A small "Student Guide to Hong Kong" is available for HK$3.

NOTE: Although the maps provided by the HKTA are quite useful, not all of the streets are marked. If you expect to explore off the main streets, you may want to pick up street maps of Hong Kong Island and Kowloon, available at Swindon's Books in Ocean Terminal Bldg., near the Star Ferry Pier in Kowloon.

Background

The British Colony of Hong Kong perches precariously on the southeastern coast of China. While its giant neighbor tries to leap into the 21st century, this thriving anachronism remains as a symbol of the best and the worst of 19th-century British colonial Asia.

Hong Kong can be divided into four geographical areas: mountainous Hong Kong Island, with the capital city of Victoria (usually referred to as Hong Kong or 'Central') on its northern edge; Kowloon, the densely populated, flat, mainland peninsula; the New Territories, a rural-but-industrializing region stretching north from Kowloon to the border with China; and the Outlying Districts (technically part of the New Territories), consisting of about 235 islands, most of which are tiny and uninhabited. Between Hong Kong Island and Kowloon lies Victoria Harbour, which ranks with San Francisco and Rio de Janeiro as one of the three best natural harbors in the world.

Pottery and other objects unearthed in archeological digs on Lantau and Lamma Islands indicate that the first settlers came to Hong Kong during the Han Dynasty (207 B.C.-220 A.D.). China was forced to cede Hong Kong Island to the British in 1842, at the end of the first Opium War. With its excellent harbor and location close to the port of Canton, Hong Kong provided British merchants with a convenient and easily-defended base of operations. The British extracted the Kowloon Peninsula and Stonecutter's Island from China in 1860 under the First Convention of Peking, following the second Opium War. In 1898 the New Territories were secured under a 99-year lease (and are thus due to revert to China on July 1, 1997), bringing the colony to its present size.

Hong Kong continued to serve as a trans-shipment center for trade between China and Europe under British rule until it was occupied by the Japanese during WWII. In the confusion following the end of the war, England was able to reestablish its rule by maintaining a stable economy and efficient administration. It presently exists only at the sufferance of the People's Republic of China, which supplies much of the colony's fresh water and food.

Immigration and a high birth rate have boosted the colony's population from ½ million in 1945 to more than 5 million today, living on a mere 400 square miles of land. In the past most of the people crowded into Victoria and Kowloon (about 12% of the colony's total land area), but recently there has been a pronounced population shift towards 'New Kowloon,' the southernmost 12 square miles of the New Territories. Over half the colony's residents live in government-subsidized accommodations, mostly high-rise housing estates. Housing remains a severe problem, with the increasing flow of legal and illegal immigrants from China (250,000 in the last two years) and the unwelcome arrival of 75,000 Vietnamese refugees contributing to a 6% population growth rate.

With few resources of its own (most of the colony is mountainous and unproductive), Hong Kong's thriving economy was first built around commercial activity, but since the early 1950s—when the Korean War and a U.N. embargo on the export of strategic goods to China severely cut back trade—a versatile manufacturing sector has also developed. Leading exports include textiles and clothing, toys, plastics, electronics, and digital watches. Hong Kong's bustling laissez-faire economy would surely make Adam Smith proud, though the price of success has been paid in low wages, long hours, and cramped working conditions for much of the workforce.

Culture and Customs

Though Hong Kong has the same cultural foundation as Taiwan, its history and location at the crossroads of east and southeast Asia have made it a much more cosmopolitan society. Citizens of Hong Kong have grown accustomed to almost every manifestation of the human phenomenon and can get along with most of them.

Buddhism and Taoism are the most widely practiced religions in the colony. Most households have ancestral shrines and many shops have a 'god shelf' with images of several of the hundreds of deities. Since Hong Kong has always depended on the sea—originally for fishing and later for trade—the most popular deities are those connected with the sea and the weather. Tin Hau, the Taoist Queen of Heaven and protector of seafarers, is worshipped by ¼ million people. About 10% of the total population is Christian, and there are also small Moslem and Hindu communities.

All Chinese celebrate the five major festivals of the Chinese (lunar) calendar. First and foremost is the Lunar New Year (Feb. 5, 1981; Year of the Rooster), when friends and relatives exchange visits and gifts. Ancestral graves are visited during the Ching Ming Festival (April 5, 1981). The Dragon Boat Festival (June 6, 1981) is celebrated with dragon boat races throughout the colony. Gifts of mooncakes, wine, and fruit are exchanged during the Mid-Autumn Festival (Sept. 12, 1981), and everyone goes moongazing. During Chung Yeung (Oct. 6, 1981) large crowds climb Victoria Peak and the hills of the New

Territories to commemorate an ancient Chinese family's escape from disaster by fleeing to the tip of a high mountain. There are plenty of local festivities too. The people of Cheung Chau, for example, hold a four-day "Bun Festival" every year, usually in May, to appease the gods angered by the misdeeds of the pirates who once used the island as a hideout. For details on these and other Chinese festivals, see the HKTA pamphlet "Chinese Festivals in Hong Kong." Christmas, Easter, and New Year's Day are also public holidays.

If you're in Hong Kong for very long the odds are good you'll be able to see **Cantonese opera**, a traditional Chinese art form which combines music, singing, dance, speech, and mime. Though the sets are simple, the costumes are brilliant and elaborately differentiated. Make-up, stylized gestures, and costume color peg each player by age, rank, and personality the moment s/he steps on stage. Much use is made of symbolic representation: a waving blue banner stands for water, a man carrying a whip is understood to be on horseback. Since Cantonese opera has a huge following in Hong Kong, local audiences already know most of the plots. During festivals informal theaters for open-air performances are put up in public places all around the city.

Language

Chinese and English are the official languages of government and business, but the farther you venture from the tourist trail the more helpful a few words of Cantonese will be. Cantonese is the most widely spoken dialect of Chinese, as different from Mandarin—the dialect usually studied in the U.S. and Europe—as German is from English. However, all dialects are written with the same system of characters; newspapers in Hong Kong can be read by a Chinese from Canton, Taipei, or Beijing.

The fact that Cantonese is a tonal language—the sound "si" can mean poem, private, city, time, the verb "to be," or try, depending on the tone—will cause some problems for English-speaking foreigners, but the following words and phrases may be understood even without perfect tonal pronunciation:

good morning	**dzhou sahn**
thank you (for a favor)	**m goi**
You're welcome ("it's not important")	**m gan yiu**
how much?	**gay do chin?**
(make it) cheaper	**peng di la**
too expensive	**gwai gwo tauh**
Where is———?	**Pin sue hai——— a?**
Is this the bus to———?	**Min ga ba si hai m hai hui——— a?**

HONG KONG

Bus/Bus station	**Ba si/Ba si xan**
Train/Train station	**Foh che/Foh che xan**
Excuse me	**Tai mju**
Goodbye	**Jai yi** or **bai bai**

Food

Though food is not as cheap as in some parts of Asia, eating out in Hong Kong doesn't have to be an expensive affair. You can eat well for HK$25-30 a day, and the really impecunious can shave that figure to HK$15 without risking scurvy or the willy-willies.

Here are some general tips:

- If you're satisfied with a light breakfast, you can take care of this meal for HK$2-3. Great rolls (try the brown bread ones with raisins) are available in small bakeries for HK$.50-1.00; then add an orange or an apple. If you buy fruit at sidewalk stands, be sure to bargain or at least comparison-shop; prices fluctuate wildly depending on the season and one's appearance.

- Get to know the cheap dishes on a Chinese menu. (Almost all Chinese restaurants have at least one copy of the menu with English equivalents of the Chinese dishes pencilled in.) Even restaurants in the middle and upper-middle price range hide some excellent buys under the 'rice' and 'noodles' columns. Sample the great variety of noodle dishes; 'ho fun' isn't a punch line, it's a thick rice noodle, often served in soups.

- The check won't come until you ask for it ('mee-don' in Cantonese); if the waiter isn't within earshot, try to catch his eye and then make a scribbling motion across your left palm.

- If a service charge isn't added to the bill, leave a 10% tip, which will be pooled among the waiters. (Even when a service charge is added, locals often leave small change as well.)

- Cantonese cooking is the most common Chinese cuisine in Hong Kong, but there are numerous other kinds. For a description of the best-known varieties, see the **Food** section of the Taiwan chapter.

- Try **dim sum** (means 'little heart') for breakfast or lunch; it's served in many restaurants, especially in the Central District and along Nathan Rd. in Kowloon, between 11 am and 2 pm. Dim sum could be called "the-cafeteria-that-comes-to-you." A wide variety of foods, mostly steamed and bite-sized, are either carried or wheeled around the room on a cart. You choose the ones you want, and at the end of the meal the waiter counts the empty serving dishes and charges accordingly. Most dim sum dishes cost HK$2-2.50. Tea is often free; invert the teapot lid to signal the waiter for a refill. Dim sum restaurants are jammed during the noon hour, so go early.

HONG KONG

- Little fast food counters have sprung up all over Hong Kong offering hamburgers, hot dogs, soft drinks, etc. for just a few HK dollars. They cater mainly to local students, not necessarily tourists. Sometimes you have to buy tickets for the food you want from a cashier, then redeem the tickets at the counter.
- If you dare to venture where there aren't any menus and the waiters (if there are any) don't speak English, you can rub elbows with the Chinese working class and eat inexpensively at the street stalls set up along side streets and in night markets. Chinese food is almost always well-cooked, so the main danger to your health would originate with the dish-washing procedure used in the stall. In Hong Kong, water taken off the main system is supposed to be potable, so use your own judgment. Usually the simplest way to order is to point at a dish being eaten by another customer or to point out the ingredients you want. And smile. Occasionally vendors will try to charge a ridiculously high price, so it's best to pay when you order. Good outdoor stall food is available every night at the **Poor Man's Nightclub** in front of the Macau Ferry Pier, 8 pm-midnight, where various steamed and fried dishes can be sampled for HK$2-5. Fat slices of watermelon cost HK$1.
- Hong Kong offers an endless variety of cuisines. The area east of Nathan Rd. in Tsimshatsui in particular is crowded with Indonesian, Malaysian, Vietnamese, Filipino, Japanese, Korean, Russian, and French restaurants, in addition to the ones serving regional Chinese foods from Shanghai, Hunan, Szechwan, etc.

Restaurants:

Choi Kun Heung Vegetarian Restaurant, 219E Nathan Rd., Kowloon (near intersection of Nathan and Austin Rds.).

Tasty, moderately-priced food: rice dishes, HK$7-11; noodle dishes, HK$6-20; most vegetable dishes, HK$10-18. Take-out service in front.

Ruby Bakery and Restaurant, on the 40 block of Carnavon Rd., Kowloon.

This quick-lunch counter serves Chinese dishes as well as Western 'fast food.' Try one of the noodle soups (HK$2.50). Fish and chips, HK$2.50. The restaurant is on the 2nd floor—take the staircase near the Hop Kee moneychanger.

Ritz Hotel Restaurant, Austin Rd., Kowloon.

Serves a HK$8.50 fixed-menu lunch between 12:30 and 2:15 pm which includes soup, bread, choice of entree (served with vegetables), a small dessert, and tea or coffee.

Kam Kong Restaurant, 60 Granville Rd., Kowloon.

A great Szechwan place serving those spicy dishes that bring tears to your eyes. Lots of dishes with vegetables (HK$10-35), tofu (HK$9-26), and meat (HK$12-50); also a good selection of soups (HK$10-25).

Kuala Lumpur Restaurant, 12 Observatory Rd. (east of Nathan Rd.), Kowloon.

Serves Malay dishes (e.g. curry chicken and rice, HK$10.50), plus European and Chinese food.

Accommodations

Hong Kong once offered a wide variety of low- as well as medium-priced accommodations, but today most of the former have either disappeared or joined the ranks of the latter. Room prices at some guest houses and most YW/YMCAs and small hotels have gone up sharply in the last two years. Feel free to go room shopping—most places will show you what they have and you can take it or leave it. Weekly and monthly rates can often be negotiated. The cheapest beds are in the few remaining **hostels**.

That Hong Kong phenomenon, the **guest house**, is a cross between a boarding house and a motel. It offers the privacy of your own room at a price higher than in hostels but far less than in hotels. The best-known concentration of guest houses can be found in **Chungking Mansion** (see below for details). Incidentally, not all guest houses are interested in taking guests in the form of tourists. Some establishments function as rendezvous spots for amorous encounters. They can usually be identified by an especially luxurious entryway, often with an empty bar set up with two or three stools. If these clues are not obvious, the truth will come out when a flustered Cantonese tries to explain that there aren't any rates by the week or even by the day.

Very comfortable accommodations at moderate and not-so-moderate prices can be found at the **YWCAs** and **YMCAs**. (See below for specifics.)

The **Hong Kong Student Travel Bureau** (HKSTB) can arrange discounts for students and young travelers at the YWCA on Man Fuk Rd. (singles and doubles w/private bath for HK$100 and HK$110), at the YMCA on Waterloo Rd. (singles and doubles w/private bath for HK$88 and HK$110), and at the luxurious **Shamrock Hotel** on Nathan Rd. (singles and doubles w/private bath for HK$120 and HK$146-157)*. They can also make arrangements for you to stay at the **Methodist Centre International Hostel** on Hennessey Rd. in Hong Kong Central (singles and doubles, HK$36 and HK$50) or at the **YTSC Youth Hostel** on Cameron Rd. in Kowloon (singles and doubles, HK$45 and HK$70). All bookings and payment must be made through the HKSTB, 1024 Star House (near the Star Ferry), Kowloon; tel. 3-694847. The HKSTB is open 9-6 on weekdays and 9-4 on Saturday. Write ahead for reservations.

Many travelers pass through Hong Kong, especially in the summer, and the accommodations listed below are no secret. A postcard mailed ahead, a few days before you arrive, will not guarantee you a place, but it will improve the odds.

NOTE: All the prices quoted below are subject to a 10% service charge plus a 4% government tax.

*no taxes will be added to these prices.

HONG KONG 29

ACCOMMODATIONS IN HONG KONG

Hostels:

Travellers Hostel, Block A, 16th floor, Chungking Mansion, 40 Nathan Rd., Kowloon; tel. 3-682505. HK$12 for a dorm bed (some dorms have fans, some have ac). Private rooms (presently w/fans, but may soon have some w/ac) cost HK$40-50, depending on how many people share them. Offers simple cooking facilities and lockers. Jovial management. If you take bus #201 from the airport, get off at the Imperial Hotel, almost next door to Chungking Mansion; otherwise take bus #9.

International Youth Accommodations Centre, 6th floor, 21 A Lock Rd., Kowloon. HK$14 for a dorm bed. This hostel can accommodate about 30, but usually at least half the people staying here are 'in residence,' working in HK as English teachers, etc. Has kitchen facilities. Rather close quarters. Take bus #9 or #201; get off at the Imperial Hotel or the Hyatt Regency (roughly across the street from each other). The IYAC is on Lock Rd. behind the Hyatt.

Hong Kong Hostel, 11th floor, 230 Nathan Rd., Kowloon. HK$14 a night. It has three large rooms with about 30 beds and a shared bath; ac is turned on at night. A refrigerator and simple cooking facilities are available. Despite the constant noise of traffic on Nathan Rd., this is a pleasant (and cheap) place to stay. Take bus #201 (get off at the Shamrock Hotel) or #9 from the airport; the hostel will be on the left side of Nathan Rd., opposite the Shamrock Hotel. It's hard to find; located in a drab apartment and office building, the building next to it has been demolished. Keys and a locker for valuables are given to each guest.

Guest Houses:

Chungking Mansion, 40 Nathan Rd. (just across from the Hyatt Regency), Kowloon. The bewildering maze of the Chungking Arcade conceals five sets of elevators, each of which leads to a 16-story hodgepodge of private apartments, small offices, and guest houses. Check the signs over the elevator doors to see which floors the guest houses are on. The cleaner, more obvious "A" block elevators stop at the larger and more expensive guest houses like Chungking House (4th and 5th floors), which offers rooms w/ac and private bath, dining facilities, TV rooms, laundry service, babysitters, etc. (singles HK$80-85, doubles HK$100-130). Most of the cheaper (HK$30-60), simpler guest houses can be found in the B and D blocks. Shop around, and don't be afraid to bargain—prices fluctuate with the demand and most places offer discounts for stays of a week or longer. To get to Chungking Mansion take bus #201 or #9.

Washington Guest House, 15A Austin Ave. (5th floor), Kowloon. Singles HK$40-55, doubles HK$54-75. All rooms have ac. To get there, go east on Austin Rd. and bear right onto Austin Ave.

"Y"'s:

The **Salisbury Rd. Y** has a great location at the tip of Kowloon, between the Star Ferry and the Peninsula Hotel (tel. 3-692211). Dorm beds for students only (women and men) HK$20/night. Rooms (some w/ac, some without) for men only are available for HK$30-40 (single), HK$45-55 (double). Rooms in the old building (w/ac) cost HK$60-65 (single), HK$70-80 (double), HK$105 ('family room'); new wing rooms

30 HONG KONG

are considerably more expensive. From the airport take bus #9 (or any other bus with the Star Ferry as its destination) or #201 (get off at the Peninsula Hotel). This Y and the one on Waterloo Rd. also offer transportation to and from the airport at moderate cost.

The **YWCA 'Headquarters Hostel,'** 1 MacDonnell Rd. (tel. 5-223101), faces the Botanic Garden above the Central District on Hong Kong side. Singles and doubles w/fan and shared bath cost HK$35-65 and HK$40-75; singles and doubles w/ac and private bath cost HK$60-90 and HK$65-120. No service charge. From the airport take bus #200 to the Hilton and then hike up the hill, or get off at the Mandarin and take a taxi (HK$4-5). Or take a bus to the Star Ferry on Kowloon side, cross the harbor, and then take bus #12A from the stop at the right side of City Hall.

The **YMCA International House** (also known as the **Chinese Y**), 23 Waterloo Rd. (tel. 3-319111), has an exceptionally friendly staff and is closer to the Chinese areas of Mongkok and Yaumati than to touristy Tsimshatsui. The cheapest singles are open to men only: HK$25-30 (w/fan) and HK$40 (w/ac). Doubles (all w/ac & private bath) start at HK$120. This Y has a Cantonese restaurant (w/excellent dim sum), as well as a restaurant serving Western food. Take bus #9 from the airport and get off just past the intersection of Nathan and Waterloo Rds. Walk back to Waterloo Rd. and turn right; the Y is less than a block away, on the left side of the street.

The **YWCA**, Man Fuk Rd., Waterloo Rd. Hill (tel. 3-039211), offers singles w/shared bath for HK$66 (women only), w/shared bath & ac HK$77, w/private bath & ac HK$99, doubles w/private bath & ac HK$121-143. Unfortunately, the YW's location is a little inconvenient. Take bus #9 as though you were going to the Chinese Y. Then catch bus #7 or #7A going north; it will turn onto Waterloo Rd. (passing the Chinese Y)—get off about 5 blocks later at Pui Ching Rd. You'll see the YW on your right on the side of a hill, just past a Caltex gas station. Turn right at the gas station, then left up the hill (or cut through the playground).

Hotels:
(All on Kowloon side, w/ac, private bath, restaurant.)

Chung Hing Hotel, 380 Nathan Rd. (corner of Pak Hoi St.); tel. 3-887001. Singles HK$110, doubles HK$130.

King's Hotel, 473 Nathan Rd., corner of Public Square St.; tel. 3-301281. Singles HK$110, doubles HK$130-140.

Shamrock Hotel, 223 Nathan Rd., just north of intersection with Austin Rd.; tel. 3-662271. Singles HK$105-130, doubles HK$125-150. Restaurant serves good dim sum; most waiters speak English.

Ritz Hotel, 122 Austin Rd., one-half block east of Nathan Rd.; tel. 3-672191(-6). Singles HK$100, doubles HK$120. Restaurant serves inexpensive set lunches.

Transportation

An excellent system of public transportation makes it easy to travel within and between different parts of Hong Kong.

Numerous ferries connect Kowloon and Hong Kong Island, crossing Victoria Harbour; they rank as Asia's all-time travel bargain. The 7-minute ride on the Star Ferry, which plies between the tip of Kowloon (end of Salisbury Rd.) and the Central District, costs only HK$.30 (2nd class, lower deck) or Hk$.50 (1st class, upper deck). You seldom wait more than five minutes for a Star Ferry; it operates 6 am-2 am. The Jordan Road Ferry (end of Jordan Rd., Kowloon) to Wanchai costs HK$.50 and operates 6:20 am-1 am. Another ferry runs between Hunghom (Kowloon) and Central from 7 am to 7 pm (HK$.50). Ferries also connect Hong Kong Island and some of the outlying islands; check the HKTA Official Guidebook for routes, schedules, and fares.

If you miss the last ferry across the harbor, take a **walla-walla** (motorized sampan) from the Kowloon Public Pier, next to the Star Ferry, to Queen's Pier on the island, or vice versa. The sampan will wait till it has a full load of 6-10 passengers before departing (HK$3.00/person).

Buses are the most convenient form of land transportation in the colony—they go almost everywhere, run frequently on major routes, and are inexpensive. Generally you pay a flat fare, depending on the route. Most rides in Kowloon cost HK$.50, up to a maximum of HK$2.50 for trips to the New Territories; HK$.50 covers most rides on Hong Kong Island, and HK$2.50 is the maximum fare. Keep a supply of small change handy. Most buses no longer carry ticket-sellers, in which case you must drop the exact fare into a red box as you get on. Usually the fare is clearly marked.

Some bus stops are marked by red signs which read "All Buses Stop Here." Don't be misled; **all** buses do not stop anywhere. Below the sign is a list of the buses which stop. The destination is written on the front of each bus, along with the route number. Brief descriptions of the routes can be found at the terminals. Buses with numbers between 100 and 200 (listed in red, with red signs on the bus) follow routes through the cross-harbour tunnel. Routes numbered over 200 indicate service by new, fancier buses, similar to highway buses in the U.S. Full fare for these buses is HK$1.50-2.50. Most buses operate 7 am-11 pm; a few run 6 am-midnight. One cross-harbour bus, #121, runs every 15 minutes from 12:45 am-5 am. For information on Hong Kong bus routes, call 5-616171; the number for Kowloon is 3-741822.

Minibuses—the small, cream-colored buses with red stripes on the sides—will pick up and drop off passengers anywhere along their routes. A sign on the roof indicates the final

32 HONG KONG

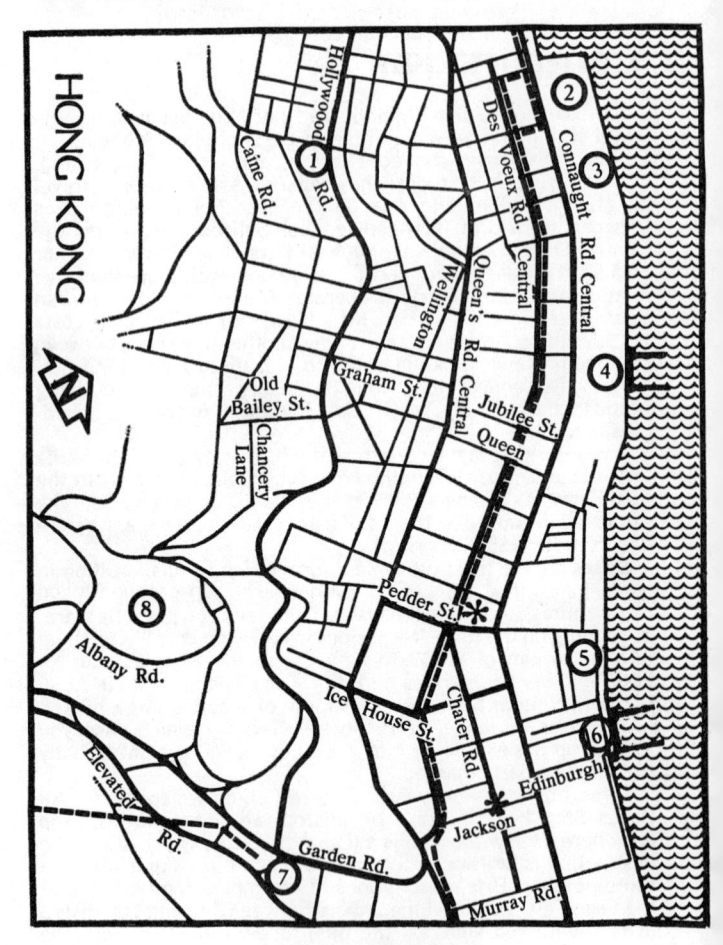

1. Man Mo Temple
2. Poor Man's Nightclub
3. Bus Terminal
4. Outlying Districts Ferry Pier
5. HKTA Information Office
6. Star Ferry Pier
7. Peak Tram Terminal
8. Botanic Garden

✱ = Subway Entrance

HONG KONG 33

destination. The main obstacles to riding minibuses: their routes are hard to figure out and the drivers usually don't speak English. Fares range from HK$.50 to HK$4.00, depending on the distance, time of day, and weather (more expensive during rush hours, late at night, and when it's raining).

Taxis on Hong Kong Island and Kowloon charge HK$2.50 for the first mile and HK$.50 for each additional fifth of a mile. A charge of HK$10 is added to the fare for trips via the cross-harbour tunnel, and locals usually tip about HK$.50, unless it's a long ride. There is a small additional charge for baggage.

In the New Territories, taxi fare is HK$1.50 for the first mile and HK$.30 for each succeeding fifth of a mile.

The only **tram line** still in use runs along the north side of Hong Kong Island, from West Point to Shaukiwan. The tram is basically a double-decker streetcar running along a track. A ride on the upper level (HK$.30) is still one of the best sightseeing deals in Hong Kong. To reach the tram line go straight out of the Star Ferry, through the underpass, and across the park towards the Hong Kong and Shanghai Bank. The tram stops are to the right or left, depending on which direction you want to go.

The first segment of the **Mass Transit Railway** (MTR)—which began operating in stages during late 1979 and early 1980—offers fast, though relatively expensive, service between Central District and the Kowloon peninsula. From Chater station under the harbor to Tsimshatsui in Kowloon costs HK$2 and takes 4-5 min.; the 6-, 8-, and 10-min. rides to Jordan, Waterloo, and Argyle stations cost HK$2.50. Trains run frequently from approximately 6 am to 1 pm daily. A guidebook with route maps, a fare chart, schedules, and lists of feeder transportation services is available for HK$1 at the information counters in MTR stations. An extension to northwestern Kowloon will begin operating by the end of 1982.

Tired of crowded, exhaust-spewing buses and trains? Riding a **bicycle** is a refreshing way to take in the sounds and sights in the New Territories, near Hong Kong beaches, and on some of the outlying islands. Look for rental stalls near beaches and in small towns; some bike rental shops are even listed in the Hong Kong phone book. A deposit is required (and returned); the rental fee depends on the bike owner's selection and location, and the client's bargaining ability (generally HK$2-3/hr.). Weekend bicyclists should get an early start, or they won't be able to find any bicycles to rent.

The **Kowloon-Canton Railway** provides excellent access to the New Territories; there are generally 22 departures a day. The train starts from the Kowloon Rail Terminus at Hunghom; you can also board at Mongkok Station on Argyle St., 3 blocks west of Waterloo Rd. Get off at University Station to see the Chinese University, and at Tai Po Kau catch the Tolo Harbour Ferry to the Sai Kung Peninsula. Visitors can ride the train as far as Sheung Shui Station, one stop short of the border with the PRC. The journey from Hunghom to Sheung Shui takes an hour (HK$4.20 1st class, HK$2.10 ordinary class).

Exploring Hong Kong

Victoria Peak offers the best view in Hong Kong. The peak tram leaves every 10-15 minutes, 7 am-midnight, rising almost straight up to an altitude of more than 400 meters (HK$2.00). To find the lower station, walk straight out of the Star Ferry Terminal on the Hong Kong side, and cross the park to the Hong Kong and Shanghai Bank. Turn left, passing the Bank of China and bear left around the Hilton, heading up the hill. The terminal is on the left side of the street. You can also get to the peak on bus #15 from the Vehicular Ferry terminus; a seat on the upper deck is well worth the HK$1.50 fare.

The walk around the Peak is level (40 min.). Walk behind the Peak Lookout House and make a right turn onto Lugard Rd. You'll be looking out over Victoria Harbour and Kowloon. Continue on, and if it's clear you'll see Green and Lantau Islands in the distance. About this time the road becomes Harlech Rd., from which you can see Cheung Chau and Lamma Islands, and later Aberdeen. If you're still up to it after completing the circle, hike up Mount Austin Rd. to some gardens and a lookout station.

City Hall, just east of the Star Ferry, contains a concert hall, the Hong Kong Museum of Art, and a library, as well as a large, moderately-priced restaurant serving excellent dim sum lunches. Large bulletin boards in the lobby advertise upcoming cultural events.

Not surprisingly, Hong Kong is well endowed with **markets**. On Kowloon, visit the poultry and produce market located around the junction of Waterloo and Canton Rds. From 10 am to 12:30 pm daily the local wholesale jade market is laid out on the sidewalks of Canton Rd., about halfway between Jordan and Waterloo Rds. Merchants barter silently, using a complicated system of hand signals. Before investing in any bargains, remember that good jade is expensive (see **Shopping**). The entire area from Waterloo Rd. to Jordan Rd. is honeycombed with markets of various types. Actually, it isn't really necessary to actively seek out a market; a walk down a side street in any area outside the main tourist districts will probably lead to one. The activity, noise, and smell are enough to make a permanent impression on anyone who grew up thinking that all foods originate wrapped in plastic on supermarket shelves. Go early in

HONG KONG 35

the morning (7-9 am) when markets are busiest. The HKTA "Six Walks" brochure has excellent suggestions on neighborhoods to explore on foot and things to look for as you walk.

For the visitor interested in learning something about Hong Kong's social problems and on-going efforts to solve them, there are **welfare project tours** which visit vocational training centers, resettlement estates, social service centers, hospitals, etc. The Hong Kong Christian Service (tel. 3-670071), ext. 222) offers tours each Friday, 10 am-1 pm, starting from the Salisbury Rd. YMCA on Kowloon. There is a set donation of HK$20.

Recreation and Entertainment

For those interested in the **fine arts**, the Urban Council publishes a monthly Cultural Programme Highlights pamphlet listing exhibits, concerts, dramas, variety shows, etc. (available at the City Hall ticket office). The HKTA newspaper "Orient" provides similar information on a weekly basis. Watch for performances of **Cantonese opera**, frequently held free of charge in parks and playgrounds. (See **Culture and Customs** for more information on Cantonese opera.)

Visiting a **museum** can offer a respite from Hong Kong's crowded sidewalks as well as a chance to brush up on your knowledge of Chinese art and history. Start at the Museum of History, on the 4th floor of the Star House (near Kowloon Star Ferry Terminal). The HKTA brochure "Hong Kong Museums" has details on types of exhibits, hours, and locations of four other museums.

Movie addicts can see anything from the most recent Hollywood releases to documentaries from China to the ever-popular kung fu thrillers. Theaters offer four shows daily; seats are generally HK$8 and HK$11.

Sports enthusiasts should consult the "Sports" section of the HKTA Guidebook for information on such activities as basketball, hiking, rowing, and horse racing.

Nightlife

There's no shortage of things to do when evening falls in Hong Kong—shake your booty at a disco, down Australian beers at a pub, wander around night markets, or just gaze at the view from the top of Victoria Peak.

The Tsimshatsui district is the center of the **bar** and **disco** scene. All the major hotels in the area have discos, usually in the basement; cover charges are not cheap, however (HK$35-85, usually including two drinks; prices are higher on weekends). A popular area on the Hong Kong side is Wanchai, once known as the hot and sleazy "Suzie Wong" district. Wanchai traditionally has been patronized by sailors whose ships are in port, and was once frequented by large numbers of American servicemen who came up from Indochina on R&R. Since the area grew up catering to men who had money to spend, prices are on the high side. There are, however, two friendly English

36 HONG KONG

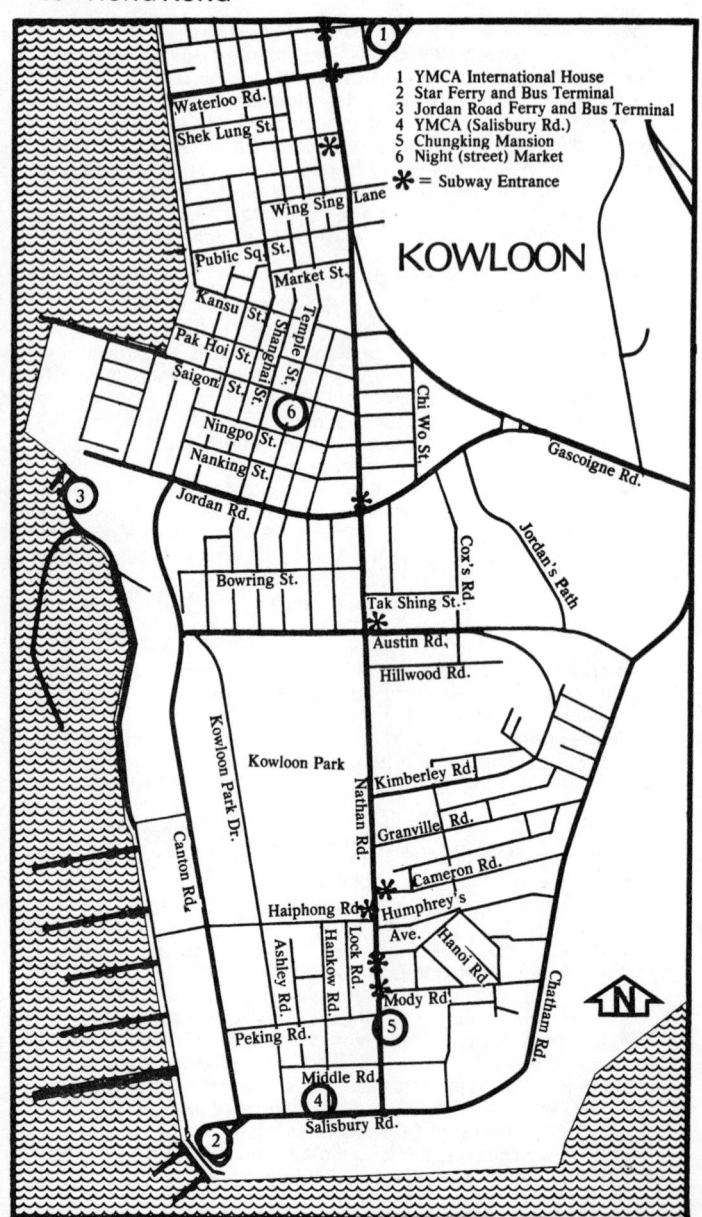

KOWLOON

1 YMCA International House
2 Star Ferry and Bus Terminal
3 Jordan Road Ferry and Bus Terminal
4 YMCA (Salisbury Rd.)
5 Chungking Mansion
6 Night (street) Market
✷ = Subway Entrance

pubs in Wanchai. **The Old China Hand Tavern**, 104 Lockhart Rd., serves San Miguel (HK$3.50/bottle) and English beers, and meat pies for HK$8. Just down the street at 126 Lockhart Rd., **The Horse and Groom** serves fish & chips for HK$6.50 and is open until 5:30 am.

The **Godown Restaurant**, located on an alley off Club St. between Connaught Rd. Central and Chater Rd. in the Central District, has live music every night until 2 am (Dixieland jazz on Wednesdays). Beer is HK$4.50/bottle, $7.50/large draft. Wine is HK$6.50/glass. Meals are expensive, but desserts and snacks are more reasonable. On Wednesday nights there is a HK$1 surcharge on drinks. Call 5-221608 to make a reservation because this place is very popular.

Ned Kelly's Last Stand, 11A Ashley Rd., Kowloon (not too far from the Star Ferry) is an Australian club featuring live music nightly 9-2:15. During the day a small draft beer costs HK$3.50, a glass of wine HK$5.50; after 7 pm the prices go up to HK$5.50 and HK$8.50. Try the meat pie (HK$5) or beef stew (HK$11.50).

There are also numerous opportunities for low- or no-cost entertainment. **Victoria Peak** is easily worth a second trip at night. Take an hour for the walk around the peak at sunset. From the top of the Peak Tram, catch a bus down (sit in the upper deck). In the evening, when the traffic is light, some bus drivers lose their inhibitions and tear madly down the hill.

At the Macau Ferry Pier, 15 minutes west of the Star Ferry in the Central District, the **Poor Man's Nightclub** offers fortune telling, music, and hot snacks from the many food stalls. Hot and sour soup sells for HK$2/bowl; mango, melon, orange, or coconut smoothies go for HK$1-2/glass.

On Kowloon, for the price of a soft drink you can spend a relaxing evening sitting in the rooftop restaurant of the Salisbury Rd. YMCA, gazing across the harbor and enjoying the cool breeze. **Temple St.** between Jordan Rd. and Public Square St. is the site of a well-patronized night market. The goods for sale run from simple household articles and clothing to cassette recordings. In the nearby public square (on Public Square St.) enterprising salesmen demonstrate their latest items while fortune tellers examine palms and medicine peddlers explain how their brand will cure any ailment, great or small.

Shopping

Department stores selling goods from the People's Republic of China can be found all over Hong Kong. Some of the arts and crafts outlets are more like museums than stores; other outlets are filled with well-made but inexpensive everyday items. Goods are sold at fixed prices which are clearly marked. The PRC stores are scrupulously honest, so you can buy things like gold, jewelry, jade, and ivory carvings without fear of getting plated brass, green plastic, or camel bone. These are the most conveniently located stores:

38 HONG KONG

Hong Kong
- Chinese Arts and Crafts, Shell House, Queen's Rd. Central
- China Products Department Store, Hennessy Rd., Causeway Bay

Kowloon
- Chinese Arts and Crafts, Star House (next to the Star Ferry)
- Chinese Arts and Crafts, 233 Nathan Rd.
- Yue Hwa Chinese Products Emporium, 54-64 Nathan Rd.
- Yue Hwa Chinese Products Emporium, 301-309 Nathan Rd.

If you're planning to shop seriously for a particuar item (e.g. watch, camera, etc.), you might find the HKTA "Bargain Guide to Shopping in Hong Kong" helpful. It lists the going prices of brand name items, and the shops at which you can get them.

The main shopping area for well-heeled tourists can be found in the **Central District**. Window-shop along Queen's Rd. Central and Des Voeux Rd. Lower prices can be found along Upper and Lower Lascar Rows (together known as Cat Street), between Hollywood St. and Queen's Rd., an area which was once even more crowded with curio shops than it is now. Redevelopment has replaced many of the old stalls with apartments, but there are still opportunities to buy interesting 'antiques,' etc. Bargain relentlessly before buying anything here.

Many local residents do their shopping in **Causeway Bay**. Though less colorful than Cat St., it does have food stalls, fortune tellers, herb shops, calligraphers, and lantern factories, in addition to large department stores. To get to this area from the Central District, pick up a tram bound for North Point and get off anywhere along Hennessey Rd.

The heart of Kowloon's shopping district is **Tsimshatsui**. The Ocean Terminal/Star House combination is touristy and expensive. The streets off Nathan Rd. are lined with stores selling stereos, cameras, jewelry, clothing, and just about anything else you can think of.

Welfare Handicraft Shops sell a variety of hand-made goods. There are three shops on Kowloon—on Salisbury Rd. near the Star Ferry, in Rm. 176 of the Ocean Terminal, and in the Hong Kong Hotel—and one on Hong Kong in the Connaught Centre.

Shopping hours are generally 9-6 in the Central District, and 10-10 in Causeway Bay and downtown Kowloon.

Here are a few tips on some of the most popular shopping items. Remember that for luxury goods, even bargain prices will not be cheap. If someone offers you an unbelievable price, follow your intuition—don't believe it. Be sure to compare serial numbers on guarantees with those on your purchase; make sure you have a world-wide guarantee.

Jade: Subtle differences between grades of jade can be difficult even for experts to see. Modern methods of producing 'bastard jade'—dyeing an inferior piece of white jade to make it resemble a more valuable green piece—can be detected only through extensive testing. The PRC department stores sell reliable pieces at fair prices.

Silk: Pure Thai silk is sold at some of the yardage shops off Nathan Rd. Check the entire piece for stains or tears, since some shops handle damaged goods. Chinese silk is sold at modest prices in the Chinese department stores.

Embroidery. Shop at the Chinese department stores or at the small shops on side streets in the Central District.

Watches: Prices in Hong Kong are roughly half of those elsewhere, so you can afford to shop in a reputable store. Both Japanese and European watches are available. In order to avoid fraud (such as a Hong Kong-made movement inside a Swiss-made case), look for shops that display the HKTA seal.

Cameras: Check lenses with extreme care. Be careful that you aren't sold a used lens on a new camera body, or vice versa.

Clothing & Shoes: A good bargain wherever you find them; try Nathan Rd. north of Tsimshatsui. For tailor-made clothing (men's and women's), don't pay too much as a down payment and don't accept hasty, overnight work. Reputable tailors will ask for several fittings. Men should make it clear whether they want a Continental or an American cut to their suits and shirts.

Books: The best selection of English-language books can be found in Swindon's Bookstores, located in Kowloon in the Ocean Terminal and on Lock Rd. behind the Hyatt Regency; the latter has an impressive collection of books on Asia.

Meeting Students

The colony's two major universities are the Chinese University in the New Territories and Hong Kong University on Hong Kong Island. To reach the Chinese U., take the train to University Station. Here, as at HKU, the canteen is the best place to meet students. To get to HKU take bus #3 in front of the Connaught Centre Bldg. in Central District.

Escaping the City

If you spend all your time exploring Kowloon and Hong Kong, you'll be missing out on 88% of the colony. The far side of Hong Kong Island, the New Territories, and many of the outlying islands are easily accessible by public transportation; the trips described below can serve as antidotes to an overdose of shopping or sightseeing in Hong Kong's congested urban areas.

Hong Kong Island

Here are two of the various possible routes:

Take bus #6 from the Central Bus Terminus to Stanley Village (HK$1.50, 40 min.). As the bus starts to climb, the Central District, Wanchai, and Happy Valley (which contains Hong Kong's race track) lie below you. After passing through the upper-class residential areas near the peak, the bus descends to the southeast side of the island, giving a view of the Tai Tam Reservoirs (constructed as part of Hong Kong's long battle to secure an ample supply of fresh water) and the islands of Lo Chan and Po Tui, sites of recent archeological discoveries. Finally, you come around to the eastern end of Deep Water Bay, Repulse Bay, and arrive in Stanley, which has a good beach for swimming and sunning.

In Stanley, transfer to bus #73 for the 30-min. ride to Aberdeen. This 'water-city' is in a stage of transition as some of its thousands of boat dwellers move ashore and the edge of the harbor is filled in for construction projects. The HKTA "Six Walks" pamphlet describes a 1-hr. tour of the market area.

From Aberdeen take bus #7 back to the Central Bus Terminus (HK$1, 30 min.). The bus passes through the campus of Hong Kong University. This route and an alternative one are described briefly in the HKTA "See for Yourself" pamphlet.

This is a variation which features an easy trek through the woods:

Take the peak tram up Victoria Peak (see p. 37), and walk a short way down Peak Rd., behind the tram station, to find Pokfulam Reservoir Rd. It's on the same side as the Peak Cafe, behind a traffic barrier. This road takes you on a downhill stroll through lush forest alive with all sorts of birds and butterflies. About 45 min. later you will pass the reservoir itself—so crucial to the chronically water-short colony—and come out onto Pokfulam Rd. Turn left and walk down to the second bus stop (buses won't always stop at the nearest one) to catch any bus bound for Aberdeen. Or cross the street and take any of the buses headed back to the Central District.

The New Territories

The rural scenery of the New Territories is a refreshing switch from the mad rush of the city, although the area is presently changing a lot as the target of a government plan which will considerably increase its population density. Buildings are springing up as if there is no tomorrow—and there may well be no tomorrow for the New Territories if the PRC takes it back in 1997 when Hong Kong's lease on the area is up.

The standard approach to touring the New Territories (described in the HKTA pamphlet "See for Yourself") is to take a series of buses, but the enterprising traveler can devise a wide variety of self-guided tours with combinations of ferries, buses, and trains. You'll need an HKTA official guidebook (for train

HONG KONG 41

schedules, general bus route chart, map) and a ferry schedule (or check with the HKTA, because the ferry schedules in the official guidebook are incomplete). The trip described below will give you an idea of the possibilities. Bus fares are not given because they change so frequently. Usually they're posted; otherwise, ask the driver. They're generally HK$.30-$2.

This tour starts at the Outlying Districts Ferries Pier in Hong Kong Central. Take the 9:30 am ferry bound for Tai O on Lantau Island, and get off at Castle Peak in the western New Territories (fare: HK$2); the ferry will call there at about 10:50 am, between stops at Ma Wan, a small island, and Tai O. It's just a short walk from the Castle Peak Bay ferry pier to the main road. Catch bus #50 or #53 for the 20-25 min. trip to Yuen Long (or Un Long), the largest town in the New Territories. From Yuen Long bus #76 continues northeast through the countryside to Sheung Shui (30-35 min.). There are numerous possible stops and side trips along this stretch; see below under "Variations." The 2:07 train from Sheung Shui to Kowloon will get you to Tai Po Kau (3 stops south, HK$.60) in plenty of time to catch the Tolo Harbour Ferry at 3:15 pm; it leaves from the wharf right next to the train stop. Buy a ticket for Tai Tan (HK$2), where the ferry will arrive shortly past 5:30 pm, after stopping at six fishing villages. See ragged green mountains and rocky promontories looming on both sides of the harbor. Bus #94 will be waiting at Tai Tan to take ferry passengers to the town of Sai Kung, a good place for a seafood dinner (also a great place to spend a whole day exploring unspoiled sandy beaches). From Sai Kung take bus #92 for the 30 min. trip to Choi Hung Estate in eastern Kowloon (HK$.70, last departure around 10:30 pm). At Choi Hung you have a wide choice of buses going to downtown Kowloon (e.g. #9, #5) or through the tunnel to Hong Kong Island.

Variations:
• Instead of taking the Tai O ferry, take bus #50 to Yuen Long from the Jordan Rd. Ferry Terminus (75-80 min.).
• Rather than going directly to Yuen Long, stop en route at Ching Chung Koon, a Taoist temple near Castle Peak Hospital with lovely bonsai (miniature trees). A few minutes past Castle Peak Bay (for those arriving by ferry), bus #50 enters Tuen Mun, a new town being built on reclaimed land which will eventually house more than half a million people. Get off at the second stop after the bus swings around a semi-circle; slightly past the stop is a bright blue bridge leading to a concrete path which will take you to the temple. In addition to hundreds of bonsai (look for the one shaped like a deer), the temple complex includes an ancestral worship hall where ceremonies for the dead are often held. The miniature paper mansions, cars, etc. you may see on the terrace in front of the hall will be burned as offerings to assure the departed an affluent after-life.

- From Yuen Long take bus #64 to Kam Tin (20 min.). The inhabitants of this walled village are all descendants of the original settlers from the Tang clan, who founded Kam Tin in the 17th century. As in most rural areas of Hong Kong, the people are sensitive about having their pictures taken; if they let you photograph them they usually expect a tip. Squeezed inside the walls which protected villages from soldiers and bandits in earlier times are traditional Chinese houses and a maze of narrow streets and alleys. Kat Hing Wai and Shui Tau are two other walled villages in the area. To get to both villages, take bus #51 from Yuen Long.
- From Yuen Long take bus #55 to Hong Kong's main oyster bed in the village of Lau Fau Shan.
- For a panoramic view of the People's Republic of China, get off bus #76 between Yuen Long and Sheung Shui at Lokmachau and walk to the border lookout. (This stop will probably become less popular as it gets easier and cheaper to actually visit China).
- Visit Sheung Shui Heung, the 600-year-old walled village of the Liu family clan just north of Sheung Shui.
- If you're tired or it's late when you reach Sheung Shui you can return directly to Kowloon by train (HK$2.10) or bus #70; both take about an hour. The last bus leaves early in the evening; the last train leaves at 9:14 pm.
- The Tolo Harbour Ferry makes two round trips a day. Early risers might consider catching the 7:25 am ferry (take the 6:21 train from Hunghow, the Kowloon Railway Station, which arrives at Tai Po Kau at 7:02). You could make the 4-hr. roundtrip or get off at Tai Tan (arrival, 9:35 am) to go on to Sai Kung. Or, get off at one of the stops to hike some of the trails traversing the rolling hills above the harbor. To get back to Tai Po Kau (or go on to Tai Tan), catch the afternoon ferry; doublecheck when the ferry arrives at the village where you plan to meet it, and don't miss it. Hikers can get around with government-published "Countryside Maps." Trails, picnic sites, roads, etc. are clearly marked. They're available at all HKTA information offices for HK$3. Most of these excursions can be done in reverse (e.g. take buses to Tai Tan, catch ferry to Tai Po Kau, and so on). Check timetables and fares with the HKTA.

Outlying Islands

The Hong Kong Yamatei Ferry Co. provides regular ferry service to some of the larger of Hong Kong's 235 islands from the Outlying Districts Ferries Pier in Hong Kong Central (schedules are available at HKTA offices). Fares are generally HK$1-2, a real bargain. The ferry ride itself is entertaining (and cool), as the boat weaves through the bustling harbor traffic, and the small villages where the ferries call offer a whole new perspective on what it might be like to live away from the constant drone and sputter of motorized vehicles.

HONG KONG

Lamma Island (sometimes called 'Stone Age Island') is just southwest of Hong Kong Island; its 6,000 inhabitants live in two small towns—Sok Kwu Wan and Yung Shue Wan—and a few coastal villages. A recommended excursion: catch an early afternoon ferry to one of the towns, take the leisurely 1-hr. hike across the island to the other (stopping at the small beaches along the way when the heat gets to you), have a seafood dinner and return to Central on an evening ferry.

The HKTA puts out a pamphlet describing five hikes (3½-9 miles in length) on sparsely-populated **Lantau**, the largest island in the colony. For a panoramic view, walk No. 4, which goes to the top of Sunset Peak, is excellent; on a clear day you can even see the Pearl River estuary in China. Walk No. 3, from Silvermine Bay (Mui Wo) to Tung Chung Pier, is also recommended. For those who want to spend the night there are several possibilities; for example, the Trappist and Po Lin Monasteries offer dormitory accommodations for HK$30, including three meals. Ask at the HKTA offices for up-to-date details. Advance booking is usually required.

Cheung Chau Island, just southeast of Lantau, is small but lively. You can see every facet of the fishing industry here—from hook making to junk building to fish processing. The island has numerous temples, some beaches, and an old pirates' cave. Cheung Chau is also the site of the annual 'Bun Festival' (see HKTA's "Chinese Festivals in Hong Kong").

Fishing is the base of **Peng Chau**'s island economy, but villagers also are involved in a variety of cottage industries, including toy making, basket weaving, and woodwork. Visit the island's porcelain factory.

Travel to The People's Republic of China

The opening up of China to large groups of foreign visitors since 1978 has proven too inviting to pass up for many travelers, including some on the tightest of budgets. Some pointers on getting yourself to China in 1981 and 1982:

Group Tours

General travel to China is still limited to group tours. These

44 HONG KONG

range from one-day jaunts to cities near Macau and Hong Kong, to 18-day tours to most of the major cities, including Peking. All tours are organized and guided by the China International Travel Service, the PRC government travel agency; however, several private travel agencies in Hong Kong are allowed to sell tickets to these tours. As of this printing, the Chinese government is working through China Travel Service (H.K.) Lt., 77 Queen's Rd. (4th floor), Central District, GPO Box 6016 (tel. 5-259121). China International Travel Service is scheduled to open up an office in Kowloon in late 1981.

Other travel agents through which to arrange tours:

- The Travel Advisors Ltd., Peninsula Hotel Lobby, Salisbury Rd., Kowloon; tel. 3-698321.
- Arrow Travel Agency, Ltd., Alexandra House, 21st floor, Des Voeux Rd., Hong Kong; tel. 5-23171. U.S. office: Arrow Tours USA Inc., 626 Wilshire Blvd., Suite 310, Los Angeles, CA 90017.
- Swire Travel Ltd., 2nd floor, Swire House, Hong Kong; tel. 5-265131.
- U.S.-China People's Friendship Association, 635 South Westlak Ave., Los Angeles, CA 90057 **or** 80 Eighth Ave., Rm. 303, New York, NY 10011.
- Hong Kong Student Travel Bureau, 1024 Star House, Kowloon; tel. 3-694847.

Prices are steep, ranging from US$40/day to US$162/day, depending on the tour. This includes all transportation, visa fees, meals, and double occupancy hotel room. Prices vary from agency to agency for the same tour, so shop around. China Travel Service and the Hong Kong Student Travel Bureau are usually cheapest. Agencies require you to pay a hefty deposit along with your reservation, usually refundable in full only if you cancel reservations more than 30 days in advance.

Tours are arranged on a first come, first served basis. Write the tour agency well in advance—one month for the shorter tours, and two months for the longer tours. All tours begin and end in Hong Kong or Macau. You must be in Hong Kong 4 working days before the beginning of your tour to obtain a visa for entry into China. Some people have shown up in Hong Kong only 5-7 days before a tour starts and have still gotten in, but this method is risky.

Spring and summer are the most popular times for going to China, although tours are fully booked the year round. Tours are not held to southern China April 15-May 15 and Oct. 15-Nov. 15, due to the Guangzhou (Canton) Trade Fair.

NOTE: If you have been to Taiwan, or would like to go there again and are worried about getting back if you have been to the PRC, not to worry. The tour is given a group visa, and individual passports are not stamped with the PRC visa.

Macau

Sole remaining symbol of a once widespread Portuguese empire in Asia, tiny Macau maintains a rhythm and style all its own—with its dog track and gambling palaces next to whitewashed rococo mansions and cobblestone streets straight from Old World Portugal. Established as a trading post with China in 1557, the territory is the oldest European settlement in Asia, and has long been a center for gold exchange (and gold smuggling). Gambling takes center stage in Macau's economy; every weekend thousands of Hong Kong Chinese come to seek instant wealth at the casinos. At other times, the city retains a quiet, if not sleepy, appearance. However, Macau is entering a new era of prosperity, largely as a result of the income generated by the casinos, greyhound racing, jai-alai and other attractions. The current construction boom—hotels, resorts, apartment and office blocks, factories, etc. are going up all over the territory—will probably speed up the pace of life in Macau in the '80s.

The Portuguese administration in Macau has less than an iron grip on affairs in Macau; corruption and smuggling illegal immigrants from China to Hong Kong by snakeboat run largely uncontrolled. Portugal has tried twice in the last six years to give Macau back to China, but both times the Chinese refused, fearing that a takeover in Macau would upset Hong Kong, fully aware that it could be next. Macau is properly termed a Chinese territory administered by the Portuguese. The territory has a population of about 350,000, more than 95% of whom are Chinese.

Arrival: Boats leave from the Macau Ferry Terminal on Connaught Rd. in Hong Kong's Central District. Fares for the 2½-hr. trip by ferry start at HK$16 and run all the way up to HK$90 for a VIP suite. Hydrofoils (65-75 min.; HK$25 weekdays, HK$35 weekends & holidays) leave every 30 min. during daylight hours. Jetfoils (HK$40 weekdays, HK$45 weekends & holidays) leave frequently during the day and reach Macau in 55 min.; as of summer 1980 several jetfoils equipped with radar were also allowed to 'fly' at night (HK$55). Buy tickets a day or two in advance—booking offices are located in the ground floor arcade of the Star House, Kowloon; on the ground floor of Manning House, Queen's Rd., Central District; and at the Macau Ferry Terminal. A Hong Kong government passenger tax of HK$8 is added to each fare.

46 MACAU

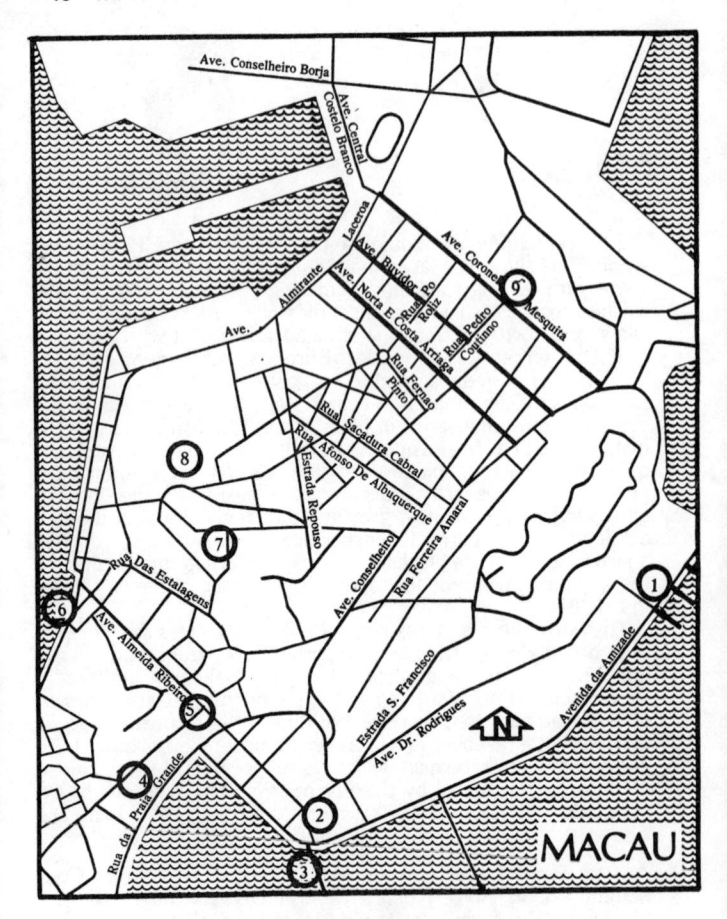

1 Ferry/hydrofoil/jetfoil Pier
2 Lisboa Hotel
3 Bridge to Taipa Island
4 Tourist Information Office
5 Leal Senado (Loyal Senate)
6 Floating Casino
7 Ruins of St. Paul's Church
8 Camoes Museum
9 Kun Iam Temple

MACAU 47

Currency: In November 1980 the exchange rate was 5.1 pataca (M$5.1) to the U.S. dollar. Though the pataca (composed of 100 avos) is worth slightly less than one Hong Kong dollar, the two currencies circulate freely and are generally interchangeable.

Visas: Visas for a stay of 20 days or two visits within 20 days can be easily obtained on arrival in Macau for M$25 (good for one individual or a married couple).

Sources of Information

Macau Tourist Information Bureau, 1729 Star House, Salisbury Rd., Kowloon, Hong Kong; tel. 3-677747. Open 9-1 & 2-5 weekdays and 9-1 Saturday.

Department of Tourism and Information, Travessa do Paira, Macau; tel. 7218. Open 9-1 & 3-5 weekdays and 9-1 Sat. To get there take bus #3 from the stop just south of the pier, get off a few blocks after it turns right off of Avenida da Amizade and then walk south on Rua da Praia Grande. Turn right just before a large pink building; the tourist office is on the right. Ask for a map and the very heplful "Guide to Macau" pamphlet.

Getting Around Town

Buses cost M$.30/ride; the tourist information office can explain bus schedules and routes (5 in all). Taxis charge M$3.00 at flagfall and M$.40 for each one-fifth mile. Pedicabs can be rented for around M$20/hour. Or rent a bicycle from one of the roadside dealers around town (about M$3/hr.). One of these is located at Avenida D. Joao IV, near the intersection of Rua da Praia Grande and Rua do Campo.

Eating in Macau

Sample the local Macau cuisine (reflecting Chinese, Iberian and African influence), as well as Chinese and Portuguese dishes. Walk up any of the cobblestone streets off the main avenues to find inexpensive Chinese restaurants and bakeries.

Exploring Macau

Macau is a good place for walking and biking, small enough to get to know in a few days. The "Guide to Macau" pamphlet describes points of interest in detail; it also explains how to tour the city by public bus (p. 10).

The **Citadel of Sao Paulo Do Monte**, built by the Jesuits in the early 17th century, overlooks the city and harbor it successfully defended against several attacks.

The magnificent hilltop ruin of **St. Paul's Church** reflects the design of a 16th century Italian Jesuit and the labor of Japanese Christians who fled from persecution in Nagasaki. The church itself burned down during a typhoon in 1835; the impressive facade remains.

The beautiful **Temple Of Kun Iam** on Avenida do Coronel

48 MACAU

Mesquita dates from the Ming Dynasty, about 400 years ago. China and the United States signed their first treaty here in 1844.

The **Luis de Camoes Museum** on the Praca Luis de Camoes has artifacts from ancient China and paintings, engravings, and prints of Macau in the 18th and 19th centuries. In summer 1980 the museum was closed for remodeling, its exhibits sent off to be displayed in Portugal. Check with the tourist office to find out if it has reopened and what its hours are.

Worth a stop in any walking or biking tour: the **Leal Senado**, or Loyal Senate Building, regarded as the most outstanding example of Portuguese architecture in the Territory; the **Sao Domingos Church**, perhaps the most beautiful of the many 17th century baroque churches in Macau; the **Lou Lim Ioc Garden**, modeled on famous gardens in Soochow, China; and three interesting Buddhist temples—**Hall of the Reclining Buddha** (behind the ruins of St. Paul's Church), **Hung Kong Miu**, and the temple and convent of **Macau-Seac**.

The islands of **Taipa** and **Coloane** are connected to Macau by a bridge 2½ km long. There are beaches on Coloane's southern shore: Cheoc Van is one of the most popular, Hac Sa (or Black Sands) is less crowded but equally good. You can take a bus from in front of Hotel Lisboa from 7 am to 11 pm (at 2-hr. intervals), costing M$1 to Taipa, M$1.50 to Coloane Village, and M$2 to Hac Sa. Catch a Macau-Taipa bus, then change to a #1 bus at Taipa if you want to go on to Coloane. The trip to Hac Sa takes about ½ hr. Refer to the "Guide to Macau" for a map of Taipa and Coloane with bus routes, which is useful if you get lost since not many people speak English.

Night Life

Night life in Macau is, not surprisingly, centered around the casinos, which stay open all night. Walking along the city's busier streets, however, can provide an evening's entertainment at no cost. Start at sunset from the Ferreira do Amaral Monument across from Hotel Lisboa, from which you get a beautiful view of the ocean and the Macau-Taipa Bridge. Walk in front of Hotel Lisboa and you will be on Avenida de Almeida Ribeiro, Macau's busiest street day or night. Several blocks past the Lisboa stands the large General Post Office, beyond which lies the civic square, flanked by the Leal Senado with its classic Portuguese architecture. In front of the building is a large fountain illuminated with colored lights; watch all the activity from nearby benches, or try some of the restaurants on the square. The most reasonable in price is the Leitaria I Son, which serves freshly squeezed orange juice, sandwiches, and superb egg custard (M$2). You may have to point, because the menu is not in English. Continue down Ave. Ribeiro, which will be crowded with shoppers. Along this stretch there are jewelry and clothing stores, Chinese herb shops, and for those who don't believe in herbs, an equal number of liquor stores. At the end of the street is the famous Floating Casino.

MACAU 49

ACCOMMODATIONS IN MACAU

There are few really inexpensive places to stay in Macau. The first five hotels listed below are on or near Avenida de Almeida Ribeiro, and can be reached by taking bus #3 from the stop south of the pier. Several offer discounts on weekdays. Most rooms have ac and private bath.

NOTE: All room rates are subject to a 10% service charge and a 5% government tax.

Hotel Central, 26-28 Avenida de Almeida Ribeiro (downtown, near the Leal Senado).
Singles M$36-59, doubles M$47-69.

Hotel Man Va (or 'Muen Va'), 30-34 Rua da Caldeira.
Room w/double bed M$60, w/twin beds M$75. Go north on Avenida de Almeida Ribeiro until you see a large blue Parker pen sign; turn left down the small street just past it.

Hotel Ko Wah, 71 Rua da Felicidade (4th floor).
Singles M$67, doubles M$82; 20% discount on weekdays. Rua da Felicidade is one block south of the upper end of Avenida de Almeida Ribeiro. Look for a tall blue sign in Chinese with 'Kou Seng Restaurante' in small letters at the top.

Hotel Grand, 146 Avenida de Almeida Ribeiro (north end, near the floating Casino).
Singles w/o ac M$45-50, w/ac M$45-70; doubles w/o ac M$55, w/ac M$65-70.

Hotel Bela Vista, 8 Rua do Comendador Kou Ho Neng.
Singles M$40-50, doubles M$60-70. A pale green, 3-story colonial 'confection'; it really does have a nice view. Located on a hill above Rua da Praia do Bom Parto in southwest Macau.

Hotel London, 4 Praca Ponte E Horta (near the Floating Casino).
Singles M$58-74, doubles M$90-120; 20% discount on weekdays. Go to the end of Avenida de Almeida Ribeiro, turn left on Rua das Lorchas, then left again on Praca Ponte E Horta.

Bibliography

Hong Kong: Borrowed Place, Borrowed Time, by Richard Hughes, a well known 'old China hand.' The book is full of interesting anecdotes about Hong Kong in the 1930s.

Hong Kong Annual Report, by the Hong Kong government.

Half-Crown Colony, by John Pope-Hennessey. This offers a somewhat less complimentary view than the report issued by the government.

INDONESIA

General Information

Arrival: Jakarta is served by two airports—Halim for international and some domestic flights (Denpasar, Yogyakarta) and Kemayoran for all other domestic flights. From Halim, 15 km from the center of the city, green Pelita Mas Jaya buses leave every 15-20 min. for Banteng Square, the central bus station (Rp50); catch the bus on the road in front of the airport, about a 5-min. walk from the terminal. If you have a lot of luggage it would be easier to take a taxi (taxis now use their meters on this run). The ride into town costs Rp2200-2500; look for some fellow travelers to split the taxi fare with. The Visitor Information Service at the airport is open 8-8 daily except Sunday.

Other points of entry are Medan in north Sumatra, Denpasar on the island of Bali, and Manado in northern Sulawesi.

Departure: The airport departure tax is Rp2000.

Currency: The exchange rate in November 1980 was 625 rupiah (Rp625) to the U.S. dollar.

Visas: When you apply for a visa you must have plane or ship tickets in and out of Indonesia (or a letter from an airline, steamship company, or travel agent confirming the purchase of those tickets). Because of this regulation, some travelers may prefer to get their visas in Singapore or Penang. Tourist visas, valid for four weeks, can be extended once for two weeks upon payment of a US$20 'landing fee.' Visitors' visas can be extended up to four months and more, but you must have a letter of invitation from Indonesia (or be traveling for business-related purposes) in order to get one. One (expensive) strategy to arrange for a longer stay is to leave the country after six weeks (go to Singapore or Penang) and apply for another tourist visa. (Tourist visas previously could be extended for much longer periods of time, but immigration regulations tightened up considerably in 1978. Since local immigration officials are given a lot of leeway, regulations, fees, etc. tend to vary from office to office. The travelers' grapevine usually carries up-to-date news on which offices are most lenient.)

Climate: Hot and humid all year round, except in the mountains (where it can get quite cold). Two seasons, wet and dry, which vary from region to region. In general, the rainy season falls between November and April.

Sources of Information

Visitor Information Center, Jakarta Theatre Building, 9 Jl. Thamrin (next to Sarinah Dept. Store); tel. 354094 & 364093.

Open Mon.-Thur. 8-3, Fri. 8-11, & Sat. 8-1. They offer maps and a variety of publications; especially useful are the "Jakarta General Information" and "Jakarta Bus Routes & Train Services" pamphlets. Very helpful.

Visitor Information Service, Halim International Airport; tel. 801817. Open 8-8 daily except Sunday.

Directorate General of Tourism, Jl. Kramat Raya 81; tel. 348428. Publishes travel information for the whole country. To get there take PPD bus #13 from Banteng (via Senopati-Salemba) and get off at 'Kenari.'

Amanda Bali International Travel Service, Jl. Wahid Hasyim 110; tel. 353748/49. Open Mon.-Fri. 9:30-4:30 & Sat. 9:30-2:30. This agency handles snazzy tours, but can provide useful information for low-budget travelers as well.

Background

The Indonesian archipelago sits astride the major sea lanes which link Europe, the Middle East, and India with China and Japan. This strategic location has played a major role in shaping Indonesia's history—economically, culturally, militarily—and continues to do so today. Of Indonesia's 13,000 islands, the best known are Sumatra, Java, Bali, Kalimantan (Borneo), the Moluccas, Sulawesi (Celebes), and Irian Jaya (formerly West New Guinea). The region is quite volcanic; many of the volcanoes which run in an arc through Sumatra, Java, and Bali are still active.

With a population of 140 million, Indonesia is the fifth largest country in the world. About two-thirds of the people live on Java (1/14 of the country's land area), making that relatively small island a very densely populated one. While the bulk of the people live on Java, most of Indonesia's income-generating resources come from the 'outer islands' of Sumatra and Kalimantan; this discrepancy between population and resources is another distinctive theme of Indonesian history.

The country contains at least 14 major ethno-linguistic groups (each with a million or more members), plus about 200 smaller ones. About 90% of the people are nominally Moslem ('statistical Moslems'), but in fact fewer than half of those are devout believers. The remaining 10% include Hindus (mainly on Bali), Protestants, Catholics, and Buddhists (mostly Chinese).

INDONESIA 53

More than 60% of the people work in agriculture, mainly rice production (although, in this mountainous country, only 12% of the land is cultivated). Indonesia has not been able to attain self-sufficiency in rice; in late 1977 it became the world's number one rice importer. The country exports no manufactured goods; foreign exchange is generated through sale of natural resources, most of which are actually extracted by American and Japanese multi-nationals. (More than 90% of Indonesian crude oil production comes from fields worked by American oil companies.)

Indian religions—Buddhism and (Shivaite) Hinduism—were the first major foreign influences in Indonesia. Small Hinduistic kingdoms in the early centuries A.D. were succeeded by two rival dynasties in Central Java during the 8th-10th centuries— one Buddhist, the other Shivaite. The great Borobudur temple was built by the Buddhist Shailendra dynasty, a branch of which developed the empire of Srivijaya (based on Sumatra). Mataram, the Shivaite dynasty which superseded the Shailendra in Java, built numerous Hindu monuments, including Prambanan. Between the 10th and 16th centuries three powerful kingdoms arose in East Java: Kediri, Singosari, and Majapahit (which ruled most of the archipelago at one point). These kingdoms were basically syncretic, combining Shivaism and Buddhism.

Conversion to Islam began in Sumatra at the end of the 13th century, then spread to the coastal regions of Java and other islands in the 15th and 16th centuries. Sultanates on Java's west and north coasts gained power during this period, successfully challenging Majapahit (most of the Majapahit court retreated to Bali, where Hindu-Buddhist ritual life has flourished ever since). At the end of the 16th century a Moslem dynasty in Central Java resurrected Mataram as a sultanate.

Portuguese, English, and Dutch traders arrived in Indonesia in the 16th century, in search of the fabled 'Spice Islands' (the Moluccas). Local Indonesian rulers got caught up in rivalry for economic and political power under the influence of the Dutch East India Co. and at the beginning of the 19th century Indonesia became a Dutch colony. The Dutch set up a plantation economy based on coffee, tea, sugar, and rubber which generated wealth for the Dutch and poverty for the Indonesians up until World War II.

Indonesia was occupied by the Japanese from 1942 to 1945. Sukarno and Mohammad Hatta, on behalf of the Indonesian people, proclaimed national independence on Aug. 17, 1945, but official transfer of sovereignty from the Dutch only came four years later, after a devastating war and negotiations supported by the Dutch.

The president of the new republic was the great nationalist and spell-binding orator Sukarno. For 20 years he provided colorful and vigorous leadership, but the government gradually got bogged down in bureaucratic arbitrariness and corruption. Chaotic economic policies led to disastrous inflation (more than 600% in 1964-65). On Sept. 30, 1965 an intra-army coup, later alleged to have been led by the Indonesian Communist Party, failed; it eventually resulted in Sukarno's political demise. The coup attempt was followed by mass killings of Communists; student movements in major cities denounced Sukarno's 'Guided Democracy' and supported an army group led by General Suharto. In 1967, Suharto was named president and Sukarno was forced into retirement until his death in 1970.

Pres. Suharto's 'New Order' government has had a very mixed record; opposition to it (with repression to match) has been rising for several years. Early 1978 was marked by vocal student objections to Pres. Suharto's scheduled re-election to another five-year term by the 'People's Consultative Assembly' (60% government appointees). In early 1980, 50 prominent Indonesian leaders sent a letter to Suharto, accusing him of using his power for personal aggrandizement. Several of them were later placed under house arrest. Worldwide criticism of Indonesia's invasion and occupation of East Timor since 1975 has had little effect on the flow of massive amounts of foreign investment and aid into the country, which have deeply penetrated the economy.

Culture and Customs

With more than 200 ethnic groups, each with its own cultural-linguistic tradition, Indonesia defies generalization about culture and courtesy. What is perfectly appropriate in Central Java may be out of place in West Sumatra and vice-versa. However, a few customs and attitudes are widespread enough to deserve mention.

The idea of privacy, or of traveling alone, seems more unsettling than desirable to most Indonesians. Thus, people may invite you to their homes (though you've only just met) or to share their meals (even in restaurants). Such invitations are sometimes sincere, sometimes formalities. An invitation to someone's house should be accepted vaguely—"Ya, kapan-kapan, kalau ada waktu" ("Sure, sometime, if there's time"); an invitation to eat should at first be refused—"Mari, silakan, saya baru habis makan" ("Please, go ahead, I've just finished eating"). If the person is serious, s/he will get specific about a time or repeat the offer.

A guest is always served something to drink in Indonesian homes. No matter how parched your throat is, let it sit (sometimes 20 min.) until your host says "Mari, silakan," and gestures that you should drink. Also, don't empty your glass, unless you want more.

Expression of emotion in public is quite restrained, especially in strongly Moslem areas (e.g. Aceh). Physical contact between the sexes other than shaking hands is frowned on, though contact between members of the same sex is quite common. Dress standards are also conservative: gross neglect of personal cleanliness, torn clothing, shirtless men, and bra-less women in low-cut or tight-fitting tops will not be well-received. Also, shorts are best worn only at the beach.

Punctuality is not highly valued; life goes on at a relaxed pace with little of the urgency that propels so many westerners. Indonesian ideas about time are reflected in the term 'jam karet' ('rubber time'). Don't fight it; roll with it.

Body language is perhaps as important a mode of communication as spoken language in Indonesia. The feet, for example, are considered the lowliest part of the body and, especially in Java, it is a serious insult to point your feet at someone or expose the soles of your feet (e.g. by propping them up on a table). Placing your hands on your hips is a sign of anger and is quite rude if done while speaking to an older person. If you need to beckon someone (e.g. a passing becak driver), don't use a crooked finger—extend your right hand, palm down, and wave downwards. Pointing is done with the thumb (in Java) or the hand, not the forefinger. Never use your left hand to touch someone, or to give or receive things. The left hand is unclean according to Moslem tradition; also, Indonesian toilet practices call for water instead of paper, applied with the left hand only.

Indonesians generally don't like to articulate strong differences of opinion and confrontations are avoided. (In other words, aggressive bahavior in the immigration office will get you nowhere.) A negative response is often communicated by tone more than by words ("thank you," less than enthusiastically), by implication ("perhaps another time," meaning not now) or by vagueness ("yes, that would be nice sometime" but neglecting to say specifically when).

People may express an apology or embarassment with a short laugh; this is an effort to maintain smooth and friendly relations rather than to belittle the importance of the matter.

When asked for directions, Indonesians often answer whether they have the information or not (a problem encountered by Indonesian as well as foreign travelers). This is intended as a hospitable gesture, not a deception (the same is true in the Philippines; see p.226).

In many areas offices close and transportation stops at 11 am on Fridays so Moslems can go to the mosque to pray. Moslems

56 INDONESIA

don't eat pork, and during the fasting month (bulan puasa) they don't drink, eat, or smoke during daylight hours. When visiting mosques, men should wear long pants and a shirt, women should wear modest dresses and cover their head with a scarf. In Hindu Bali, women are prohibited from entering temples during their menstrual periods. (Note: if asked what your religion is, don't say thay you're an atheist—make up something if you have to.)

Bargaining, a highly-developed art in Indonesia, isn't limited to markets and small shops; always ask for a 'discount' when buying domestic air tickets at travel agencies. Prices at restaurants and most Chinese stores are fixed. See bargaining tips in the **Before You Go** chapter.

Some customs considered impolite in western countries are not rude in Indonesia. For example, it is common for strangers who meet on trains, etc. to ask each other quite personal questions: whether the other person is married, how many children s/he has, etc. (women traveling alone should be aware that such questions from men are not necessarily part of a 'hustle,' as they might be in other countries). Also, Indonesians are not big on standing in line (e.g. in the post office).

Note to American travelers: be prepared for a lot of preconceived ideas about the U.S. anywhere that TV and movies reach, thanks to Mannix, Kojak, and Charles Bronson. It is assumed that all Americans are very rich and the proverb 'time is money' summarizes the most prevalent impression of American culture.

Travelers planning to spend any time in Java and/or Bali are strongly urged to become familiar with the **Ramayana** and the **Mahabharata**, two Indian epics which have been inexhaustible sources of inspiration for all forms of Javanese and Balinese art—from the stone reliefs on ancient temples and traditional shadow plays to newly-created dances and contemporary short stories. The Ramayana recounts the adventures of Rama, an exiled prince, the abduction and rescue of his wife Sita, and his eventual triumphant return to his kingdom; popular characters, besides Rama and Sita, include the white monkey Hanuman and Kumbakarna, the noble giant. The Mahabharata is based on the tragic conflict between two related families—the Pandawa and the Korawa; favorite characters include the heroes Arjuna and Bima and the punakawan (clowns) Semar, Petruk, Gareng, and Bagong. If you can't read up before you arrive, pick up short English-language synopses of both epics in the bookstores of major cities.

Of Indonesia's diverse arts, those of Java and Bali are best-known outside the country and are the ones most likely to be seen by travelers. They include:

• **Wayang kulit**, an all-night shadow puppet play, is controlled by one person, the dalang, who manipulates the carved leather puppets, weaves the dialogue (speaking the part of each character), chants narration, sings, and directs the gamelan ensemble. A performance is a sacred event, commissioned in honor of a marriage, circumcision, etc. Different versions in Bali and Java.

- **Wayang golek**, another version of puppet theater, uses costumed wooden puppets. Most popular in West Java.
- **Wayang orang** is a form of dance-drama which originated in the Javanese courts; it takes stories, music, and even some movement techniques from wayang kulit.
- **Wayang topeng** is a dance-pantomime by masked actors.
- **Ketoprak** is popular theatre based largely on East Javanese tales; acting style is realistic.
- **Sandiwara** are historical and contemporary plays, usually staged in West Java.
- **Ludruk** is the closest thing in Java to modern western theater, though female roles are played by men and young boys. Most popular in Surabaya.

Two major types of orchestra are the **gamelan** and **angklung**. A gamelan may consist of as many as 70 (mostly percussion) instruments, divided into two sets with different tuning scales; different versions in Bali, Central Java, and West Java. Angklung are instruments made from various lengths of bamboo tube; popular in West Java.

Festivals

Most festivals spring from religious tradition and, because religious calendars don't match our 365-day reckoning (the Balinese 'year,' for instance, has 210 days), the dates vary. The greatest Islamic celebration—Idul Fitri (or 'Lebaran'), the feast day ending the month-long fast of Ramadan—moves up 10 days each year on our calendar (early August in 1981). Balinese (Hindu) holidays are frequent and colorful, and Christmas is merrily celebrated among many of the Batak in North Sumatra and the Minahasa in North Sulawesi. August 17, Independence Day, is celebrated in most cities with special performances and festivities; this can be a good opportunity to see some of the traditional dances of the area you happen to be in. Check with tourist information centers for details.

Language

Indonesian (Bahasa Indonesia), the national language, is based on Malay and influenced by Javanese, Dutch, Arabic, and English. It's used for all official purposes (education after the 4th grade, radio, TV, government) and serves as a lingua franca

58 INDONESIA

throughout the country. For most people Indonesian is a second language (in fact, many older people in rural areas don't speak it at all); well over 250 different languages and dialects are used for day-to-day conversation in the country's various regions.

Some familiarity with Indonesian will come in handy because English is not widely spoken. You can pick up the basics fairly easily, since the language has no articles, verb tenses or conjugations, or complicated plural forms. Pronunciation is straightforward, and syllable stress (not as heavy as in English) generally follows a basic rule: the second to the last syllable is stressed unless that syllable contains an "e," in which case the last syllable is stressed.

Family terms are used for almost everyone in Indonesian. Address an older man as bapak (father), or pak for short; an older woman as ibu (mother) or bu; a woman or man your age as saudari or saudara (sister, brother), a child as anak or adik (child or younger sister/brother). As a foreigner, you will often be addressed more formally as Tuan (for men, roughly equivalent to 'Sir'), Nona (for single women), or Nyonya (for married women)—terms held over from colonial times. Foreigners of both sexes will also frequently be greeted with "Hello Mister!"

Note: Indonesians often use a name and/or title or nothing at all in contexts where English-speakers would use 'you.' For example, "Where do you live?" addressed to an older woman would be "Ibu tinggal dimana?" (literally, "Mother lives where?").

If you study nothing else, at least master **numbers**. You'll get along much better if you can bargain in Indonesian and understand prices quoted to you.

For more information: John Barker's **Practical Indonesian and Malay**, a concise 'communication guide,' on sale for Rp700 all over Kuta (Bali) and in popular travelers' stops in many cities.

Consonants
- **c** like the **ch** in **ch**urch (old spelling(**tj**)
- **g** like the **g** in **g**o
- **h** is always sounded
- **j** like the **j** in **j**oy (old spelling: **dj**)
- **k** like the **k** in **k**iss (but **k** is not fully sounded if it is the last letter of the word—it's a glottal stop)
- **r** is always somewhat trilled
- **ng** like the **ng** in bringing
- **ngg** like the **ng** in longer
- **y** like the **y** in **y**es (old spelling: **j**)

Vowels
- **a** panas (hot) like the **o** in hot
- **a** terima kasih (thank you) like the **u** in sum
- **ay** wayang (puppet play) like the **i** in time
- **e** sate (barbecued meat) like the **a** in date

INDONESIA 59

- **e** losmen (inn) like the **e** in s**e**nt
- **e** k**e** pasar (to the market) like the **u** in s**u**n
- **i** **i**tu (that) like the **ee** in s**ee**
- **o** l**o**smen (inn) like the **o** in h**o**le
- **u** m**u**rah (cheap) like the **oo** in m**oo**n
- **au** m**au** (want) like the **ou** in s**ou**nd
- **ai** pand**ai** (clever) like the **a** in d**a**te or the **i** in t**i**me

Good morning (4-10 am)	**Selamat pagi**
Good afternoon (10 am-3:30 pm)	**Selamat siang**
Good evening (3:30 pm-sunset)	**Selamat sore**
Good night	**Selamat malam**
Goodbye (to someone leaving)	**Selamat jalan**
Goodbye (to someone staying)	**Selamat tinggal**
Welcome	**Selamat datang**
Where are you going? (a common greeting)	**Mau kemana?**
(I'm) taking a walk. (a common answer)	**Jalan-jalan.**
Please (offering something)	**Silakan**
Please (asking for something)	**Tolong**
Excuse me	**Maaf**
Thankyou	**Terima kasih**
You're welcome	**Kembali**
Yes/No	**Ya/Tidak**
City/Village	**Kota/Desa**
Street/Alley	**Jalan/Gang**
Bus/Bus station	**Bis/Stasiun bis**
Train/Train station	**Kereta api/Stasiun kereta api**
Airplane/Airport	**Kapal terbang/Lapangan terbang**
Boat	**Kapal laut**
Hotel/Inn	**Hotel/Losmen**
Room	**Kamar**
Toilet/Bath	**Kamar kecil/Kamar mandi**
Male/Female	**Laki-laki/Perempuan**
Restaurant	**Rumah makan**
Market	**Pasar**
Post Office	**Kantor Pos**
Island/Mountain	**Pulau/Gunung**
North/South	**Utara/Selatan**
East/West	**Timor/Barat**
Turn right/Turn left	**Belok kanan/Belok kiri**
When?	**Kapan?**

INDONESIA

Today	**Hari ini**
Tomorrow/Yesterday	**Besok/Kemarin**
Where is the bus station?	**Dimana stasiun bis?**
I want to go to the market.	**Saya mau ke pasar.**
Is this train going to Yogya?	**Apakah kereta api ini mau ke Yogya?**
Do you have a room?	**Apakah ada kamar?**
I don't understand.	**Saya tidak mengerti.**
Inexpensive/Expensive	**Murah/Mahal**
How much is this?	**Ini berapa harganya?**
Drugstore/Hospital	**Apotik/Rumah sakit**
Near/Far	**Dekat/Jauh**
Here/There	**Disini/Disana**
Good/Fine	**Baik/Bagus**
Bad	**Tidak baik**

1	**Satu**	11	**Sebelas**
2	**Dua**	12	**Duabelas**
3	**Tiga**	14	**Empatbelas**
4	**Empat**	20	**Duapuluh**
5	**Lima**	25	**Duapuluh-lima**
6	**Enam**	47	**Empatpuluh-tujuh**
7	**Tujuh**	100	**Seratus**
8	**Delapan**	300	**Tiga ratus**
9	**Sembilan**	670	**Enam ratus tujuhpuluh**
10	**Sepuluh**	1000	**Seribu**

Here are some useful terms for people who rent bicycles while in Indonesia:

titipan sepeda — place to store your bicycle for a small fee

ban kempes — flat tire

bocor — leak

tambal ban — roadside stands; they'll patch your tire quite cheaply

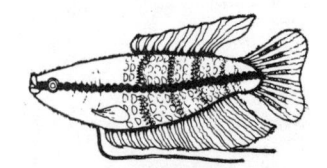

Food

Rice is the indispensable staple, but the dishes served with it vary greatly in style of preparation and ingredients from region to region. Javanese food is sweet, Padang food is hot, some Batak dishes use lots of pork, and Ujung Pandang is famous for its seafood.

INDONESIA 61

In restaurants, write down your order on the slip of paper provided; if there isn't a menu (daftar makanan), a list of the dishes available is probably posted on the wall. In warungs (roadside stands), just say what you want. In many small eating places snacks (shrimp chips, cookies, etc.) are put out in glass jars; help yourself and tell the owner how many you ate at the end of the meal (prices are fixed, usually around Rp25).

Padang restaurants serving delicious, highly-spiced food can be found in cities all over Indonesia. An array of dishes is put on the table, but you pay only for what you eat. Meat, chicken, fish, and eggs are priced by portion (take full advantage of the sauces, they're a meal in themselves), vegetables by the bowl (these are the cheapest), small shrimp by the bowl, and a second serving of rice is always cheaper than the first.

RICE AND NOODLE DISHES

nasi goreng (istimewa) — Fried rice w/meat and vegetables (w/a fried egg on top)
nasi rames — rice w/vegetables and meat or fish
nasi campur — rice w/a little bit of everything
nasi Padang — rice w/many side dishes, most of them quite spicy (native to West Sumatra, but available everywhere)
mie, bihun, bakmie — dishes featuring noodles which are thick, thin, fried (goreng), boiled (rebus), or served in soup

MEAT, FISH, AND EGGS

sate — pieces of meat skewered on bamboo sticks and grilled; served w/a spicy peanut sauce. Made w/pork, beef, chicken, or goat.
daging (babi/sapi/kambing) — meat (pork/beef/goat)
ayam — chicken
ikan/udang — fish/shrimp
gulai — various meats smothered in a thick, spicy sauce
rendang — beef cooked w/coconut and spices (native to West Sumatra)
telor — egg
martabak telor — fried pancake filled with egg and vegetables

SOUPS AND VEGETABLES

sayur — vegetables
cap cai — mixed vegetables, stir-fried (Chinese)
gado-gado — a salad of bean sprouts, green beans, cabbage, potatoes, etc. served w/a spicy peanut sauce
gudeg — young jackfruit cooked in a coconut and palm sugar sauce, usually w/egg.
lumpia — spring rolls (Chinese)
soto — a spicy meat soup
tahu — soybean meal cake, usually fried
tempe — pressed soybean cake, usually fried

SNACKS

ketan hitam — sweet, fermented sticky rice (black)
krupuk — shrimp chips
martabak manis — a folded-over pancake with peanuts, chocolate and/or sugar, and condensed milk inside
pisang goreng — fried bananas
rujak — pieces of not fully ripe fruit served with a sauce ranging from sweet to very spicy
kue/roti — cake/bread

FRUIT

durian — large, w/brown, spiny skin; pungent, foul-smelling odor, but tastes delicious
jeruk — any citrus fruit
kelapa — coconut
rambutan — small, red, hairy fruit; juicy and sweet
salak — small, snake-skinned fruit; tart
mangga — mango
manggis — mangosteen
markisa — passionfruit
nanas — pineapple
nangka — jackfruit
pisang — banana (at least a dozen varieties)

DRINKS

teh (manis) — tea (w/sugar)
kopi (manis) — coffee (w/sugar)
susu — milk
air putih — boiled water
air jeruk — lemonade
es stroop — ice water mixed w/sweet syrup
es jus — a blend of crushed ice, fruit, and sweetened condensed milk; a great treat on a hot afternoon (try es jus apokat susu, made w/avocados)
bir — beer; try Bir Bintang (brewed under the supervision of Heineken brewery)
tuak (brem) — rice wine (Balinese version)

Accommodations

In most towns and cities, **losmen** (inns) offer the least expensive accommodations (Rp1000-2500); they're often clustered near train and bus stations. Losmen generally provide a central bath in which you dip a small bucket into a tub and pour water over yourself to 'shower.' (Don't get into the tub.) Some small **hotels** offer rooms at rates close to those of losmen. In rural areas, you may be able to stay in **penginapan** (guest houses).

INDONESIA 63

Cities vary greatly in the availability of low-cost accommodations; Yogyakarta has many losmen, for example, while Surabaya and Bogor have few.

Transportation

INTERNATIONAL: Jakarta and Denpasar (Bali) are linked by **air** with Australia and Asia's major capitals. Medan (North Sumatra) is accessible by air from Penang and Singapore; several flights a week connect Manado (North Sulawesi) and the Philippines.

It's possible to get to Jakarta (or Medan) cheaply if not comfortably by **ship** from Singapore. The trip involves taking a ferry from Singapore to the island of Tanjung Pinang (4 hr., Rp7500), then boarding the Pelni Lines' 'K.M. Tampomas' for the 36-hr. Rp14,250 journey to Jakarta (or the 33-hr. journey to Medan). The 'K.M. Tampomas' leaves Tanjung Pinang Saturday afternoon, arrives in Jakarta Monday morning, leaves again that same evening for the return trip to Tanjung Pinang, then leaves Tanjung Pinang Wednesday morning for the loop up to Medan. For more details, see the Transportation (International) section in the Singapore chapter. If you're embarking from Jakarta, check with the Pelni office (Jl. Patrice Lumumba) for more information.

INTER-ISLAND: Garuda, Merpati, Bouraq, Mandala, Sempati, and Zamrud provide domestic **air** service. Only Garuda, Indonesia's flag carrier, is allowed to use jets for in-country flights; the rest use prop planes. Garuda is more expensive than the others, and supposedly more reliable. Sample plane fares: Jakarta-Ujung Pandang Rp74,300 (Garuda), Rp64,200 (non-Garuda). Students can get a 25% discount on fares from Garuda and Merpati with a student I.D. and a letter from the school's rector or registrar.

Traveling from island to island by **ship** can be rugged (the ships are often crowded and dirty), but it's a good way to meet people, practice your Indonesian, and learn to play Indonesian dominoes. The cheapest and least claustrophobic way to go is 'dek' class, which means you get on the boat and claim a space with your tikar (a woven mat, easy to find in any market). This mat serves as a carpet by day, a mattress by night. **Bring your own water and food**, also plates and spoons if you want to take

64 INDONESIA

advantage of the simple meals (rice with a few vegetables and/or a chunk of fish) served from the ship's galley. To find out which boats are going where and when, ask around at the harbor (try to master a few phrases in Indonesian beforehand) or go to the local Pelni office. Pelni, the national shipping line, serves all major provincial harbors; unfortunately, printed Pelni schedules are rare (and sometimes fictitious) documents. Pelni fares are generally higher than those of private shipping lines (use them for reference when bargaining with ship captains): Surabaya-Ujung Pandang Rp10,748 (2 days, 2 nights), Surabaya-Ambon Rp18,838 (5 days, 5 nights), Jakarta-Padang Rp11,830 (2 days, 2 nights). 'K.M. Tampomas II' makes the Jakarta-Padang trip in only 36 hr. (deck class Rp14,750).

Ferries link Merak (West Java) & Panjang (South Sumatra), Surabaya (East Java) & Kamal (Madura), Banyuwangi (East Java) & Gilimanuk (Bali), and Padang Bai (Bali) & Lembar (Lombok).

INTER-CITY: There is an extensive network of **railways** throughout Java. In Sumatra, trains connect Medan and Banda Aceh in the north and Teluk Betung and Palembang in the south. Fares vary by train as well as by class. (An 'economy-class' seat on the air-conditioned Bima from Yogya to Surabaya costs Rp12,000; a 2nd-class seat on the Mutiara Selatan for the same trip costs Rp4700.) For economy and reasonable comfort take the night express Mutiara Selatan or the day express Ekspres Siang (which link Bandung and Surabaya via Yogya). The Bima and the Mutiara Utara, which link Jakarta and Surabaya (the former via Yogya, the latter via Semarang), are the luxury trains. The Gaya Baru Malam, Cepat, and Senja trains are slow and crowded. Schedules and fares are now posted in most train stations. If your ticket costs Rp25-100 more than the fare you see listed, it's because a 'station fee' (bea stasiun) has been added; the size of the fee depends on which class ticket you buy. Students can get discounts of up to 25% on 'economy class' (3rd class) tickets. Note that Jakarta and Surabaya have several different stations serving west-, south-, and east-bound trains (more details in relevant transportation sections).

Buying train tickets can be a confusing and frustrating experience; you must often wait in long lines for several hours before getting a ticket (that is, if they haven't run out before it's your turn). Make sure you get in the right line for your train. When all else fails (i.e. tickets have run out, it's too late to buy tickets for your train), see the stationmaster ('kepala stasiun') and plead your case. Stationmasters, especially in Jakarta and Yogyakarta, often save a few tickets for dignitaries and confused foreigners. In Gambir Station (Jakarta) there's a special ticket window for foreigners. Tickets cannot be bought before the day of your departure. However, tickets can be bought and reservations made 1 to 3 days beforehand at Carnation Travel Service, located a block south of the U.S. embassy on the corner of Jl. Kebon Sirih and Jl. Merdeka Timur (just across the street from a huge statue). The service charge (about Rp400) levied by Carnation is definitely worth it; time and sanity are saved for not having to fight the crowds at the station.

Major cities are often connected by **night bus** (bis malam) lines, the largest cities by many. The buses leave in the early evening and arrive the next morning or afternoon, depending on distance traveled. They provide fairly fast service (only one or two stops for light meals) and are reasonably safe. They'll usually drop you off wherever you want when you arrive at your destination, so have a hotel or losmen in mind (exception: Jakarta, where passengers are dropped off at the Pulo Gadung Bus Station). Some companies have newer or more comfortable buses than others—ask around to find out which are currently the best. Get your ticket the morning of the day you want to leave, or better yet, the day before, if you want to choose your seat (long-legged foreigners, take note). Tickets are sometimes sold out by 1 pm. If you buy tickets in advance you can stash your belongings in the night bus company office until departure time. A meal and/or snack is included in the price of the ticket. Sample fares: Bandung-Yogya Rp2650 (Jogja Express), Yogya-Surabaya Rp2500 (OBL), Surabaya-Denpasar Rp3500 (Bali Indah).

Local buses offer slow but frequent service between most towns and cities, and low fares. Sometimes standing room only.

Colts (minibuses) generally link neighboring cities (Yogya-Solo, Surabaya-Malang). They're more expensive and much faster than buses, also much more accident-prone. ('Colt' is pronounced more like 'coll.')

Oplets—small vehicles which open from the back and seat 6-10 people—generally run on fixed routes between cities and nearby towns, and can be flagged down anywhere along the way. Fares start at around Rp50.

INTRA-CITY: Jakarta, Bandung, and Surabaya have **city buses** (with fares of Rp50, Rp30, and Rp30, respectively). Bus maps are not available, so ask for directions. There is a list of bus routes available in Jakarta from the Tourist Office.

Bemos—small, open-backed vehicles—come in several sizes. The smaller, three-wheeled ones (which look like a cross between a pick-up truck and a golf cart) usually pack in 6-8 passengers, while the larger, four-wheeled version can carry a dozen or more. Hail them anywhere along their (usually) fixed routes; again, no maps, so ask for directions. Fares are generally Rp50-75.

66 INDONESIA

Becaks (pedicabs) are easy to find in most towns and cities. Fares vary greatly according to distance and your bargaining skill, also according to the weather (higher if it's raining) and the time of day (higher late at night). Try to find out the approximate fare from an Indonesian friend first; the general range is Rp150-300 (same for one passenger or two). When possible, negotiate with a single becak driver out of earshot of other drivers—he'll be more likely to agree to a 'biasa' (normal) fare. If you've made what you know is a reasonable offer, start to walk away—in most cases he'll call you back. Whatever you do, keep your sense of humor and don't get impatient; haggling for a while is part of the game. Pay with the exact amount since drivers often won't give you (sometimes really don't have) change.

Bicycles and **motorcycles** can be rented in Yogyakarta and in Kuta and Denpasar (Bali). Check the motorcycle (oil, brakes, clutch, cables, battery) before you agree to anything, and then ride **carefully**; serious motorcycle accidents are disturbingly common.

Dokars (horse carts; also called bendi or andong) offer pleasant transportation in many towns and villages. Fares are set by bargaining (an average fare would be Rp200-300).

Jakarta

Originally founded as a trading post in the 15th century, this city on the northwestern coast of Java had already been shaped by Hindu, Moslem and Portuguese influences when the Dutch took over and named the city Batavia in 1619. The northern Kota district reflects the severe character of Dutch architecture. The series of canals and buildings in Kota give an impression of the vision the Dutch had of Jakarta: a tropical Amsterdam. When the Dutch were kicked out, the Sukarno government had its own vision of what the new republic should represent. They built a series of monstrous statues casted in socialist realism. In recent years, the Suharto government also had its own idea for Jakarta: a cosmopolitan city complete with glass and steel Hilton and Hyatt hotels.

None of these visions truly reflects the Jakarta experienced by the vast majority of its inhabitants. The highrises and heroic statues only vaguely camouflage the otherwise sprawling rows of red-tiled housing and open sewers. Jakarta is a vast area mixing up its crowded neighborhoods and noisy traffic with occasional, and unexpected, bursts of green foliage. The distance between the docks at the city's northern edge and the end of Kebayoran suburbs to the south is about 25 km, and thus is a difficult place for a traveler to get around.

Get a city map from the Tourist Development Board (on Jl. Wahid Hasyim) or, if you plan to stay a long time and are willing to invest Rp6000 in a very detailed map, buy the **Falk City Map of Jakarta** at any of the large hotels.

The city basically lies on a north-south axis. The main street is Jalan Thamrin, along which are most of the largest and most modern office buildings, hotels, banks, etc. Be careful: most streets have a different name every four of five blocks. So, in the north Jl. Thamrin turns into Jl. Merdeka Barat and in the south, it becomes Jl. Sudirman. Same street though. The 350 ft. white National Monument (commonly known as Monas) stands in the center of town and is a good landmark to keep your bearings. Lapangan Banteng, the main bus station, is located two blocks northeast of Monas. From Lapangan Banteng, you can take a to any of Jakarta's neighborhoods: Menteng (foreign and local politicians' residences), Kebayoran Baru (nest of the nouveau riche), Kota (Chinatown), etc.

Check out the bizarre array of available transportation in Jakarta. **Buses** reach most parts of the city (Rp50); the central terminal is Lapangan Banteng. The provincial government has been trying to upgrade the quality of Jakartan buses, but as yet they remain for the most part in sad shape. **Metro-minis** are orange Tonka toy-sized buses that follow most of the regular bus routes. **Bajajs** are a recent addition to the Jakartan collection; they are three-wheeled cabs from India that have, seemingly, lawn mower engines. Bajajs are easy to spot sputtering around as they are painted bright orange and sometimes green. Bargaining determines fare (about Rp400 for a 3 km hop) and drivers generally can't speak English. **Helicaks** are maniacal motorcycles with a covered cab in front. The plastic windshields are so blurry and scratched you'll be lucky to see any of the passing traffic. Bargain with exuberance. **Bemos** buzz around on regular routes but no one as yet has really figured out the routes (Rp50). **Becaks** have been prohibited in the center of the city, but thrive in the outlying neighborhoods. Finally, there are **taxis**. The meter will register Rp250 when the flag falls; thereafter it's Rp75 for every kilometer.

Exploring Jakarta

The **National Museum**, housed in the Gedung Gajah (Elephant Building) on Jl. Merdeka Barat across from the Square, has the best archeological displays in the country. Since opening in 1947 it has acquired impressive collections of Hindu and Buddhist statues, stone carvings, ancient weapons, ceramics and models of traditional houses. The museum is somewhat unorganized as things tend to be clumped next to each other without any apparent order. Hours are 9-2 Tuesday to Thurs-

68 INDONESIA

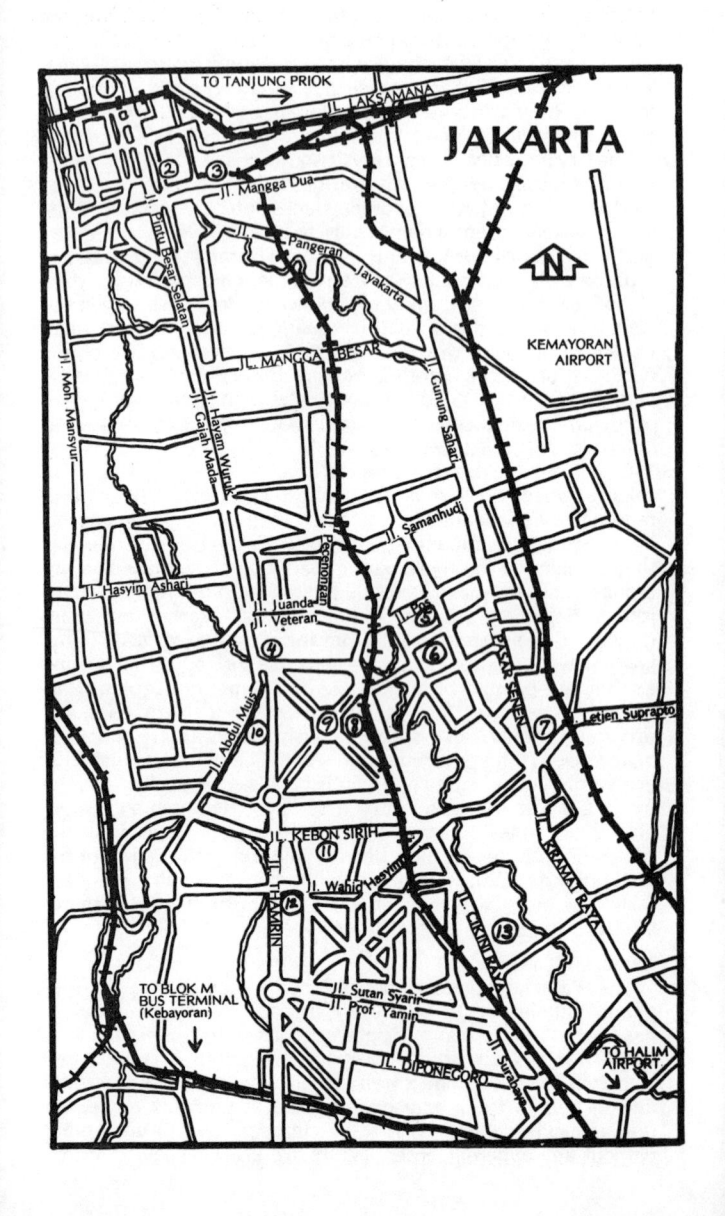

INDONESIA 69

day, 9-11 Friday, 9-1 Saturday and 9-3 Sunday. English tours are given Tuesday and Wednesday at 9:30. On Sunday mornings Javanese or Sundanese gamelan performances are held between 9:30-10:30. Twice monthly, on the 2nd and 4th Sundays all-night performances of wayang golek and wayang kulit are held starting at 9 pm. Reach the museum by taking any northbound bus on Jl. Thamrin; when Monas is due east, you get off and the museum will be right in front of you.

The **Jakarta Fair**, an annual commercial and 'county fair'-type event, runs from early June till mid-July on the southern side of Merdeka Square. It features displays from all over the country and lots of music. Saturday nights are packed.

Taman Ismail Marzuki (TIM), the cultural showcase of the nation, sponsors an incredible variety of events: Sundanese plays, poetry readings, jazz concerts, Balinese dancing, Javanese batik exhibits, etc. There is also a movie theater and planetarium. Most hotels and embassies have a free monthly schedule of TIM's events. Reach TIM, Jl. Cikini Raya 73, by taking the #804 red bus heading for Manggarai from Lapangan Banteng.

Wayang orang is performed every Saturday night, 8:15-midnight, in the **Bharata Theater**, Jl.Kalilio 15, near Pasar Senen. Ketoprak (popular operas) performances are given on Mondays and Thursdays. Tickets cost Rp750, Rp500 & Rp400. (Note: Pasar Senen is a rough area; women shouldn't go alone.)

A trip to Kota in northern Jakarta will take you to the heart of old **Batavia**. Walking through the streets gives you a sense of a transplanted Amsterdam. The Dutch built a series of canals which now criss-cross the area; tropical Jakarta is not Amsterdam and as a result the canals are polluted and mosquito-laden. Taking a SMS blue bus from Banteng to the Kota stop will put you near the **Jakarta Museum** (or Taman Fatihillah). This building was originally built in 1626 and served as the center of the Dutch colonial government. The collections in this fine

---

1 Kota Bus Terminal
2 Jakarta Museum
3 Kota Train Station
4 Istana Merdeka (Presidential Palace)
5 Kantor Pos (Post Office)
6 Banteng Bus Terminal
7 Pasar Senen Market and Train Station
8 Gambir Train Station
9 Monas (National Monument)
10 Museum Nasional
11 Jl. Jaksa
12 Sarinah Department Store
13 TIM (Cultural Center)

museum depicts the development of Jakarta since the 18th century. There are displays of old maps, furniture, porcelain, old weapons, etc. Many of the rooms have enormous oil paintings of stern governor-generals who had ruled the Dutch East Indies. Open 9-2 Tuesday to Thursday, 9-11 Friday, 9-1 Saturday and 9-3 Sunday.

Across the street on Jl. Pintu Besar Utara is the **Wayang Museum** which has puppet collections from Indonesia, China, Malaysia and Cambodia. Walk less than a kilometer north along Jl. Pintu Besar Utara to come to the **Sunda Kelapa Harbor**. The harbor was once a strategic port in the spice trade of centuries past. Sunda Kelapa remains the meeting point of traditional ships, known as prahus. Prahus still make continual trips throughout the archipelago. On the west side of the harbor is **Pasar Ikan**, where fishermen bring in their catches in the early morning. The government has restored a number of old Dutch warehouses and turned them into the **Bahari Museum** (Marine Museum). While the exhibits inside are meager, climb up the tower and up onto the roof to have a look around Batavia and modern central Jakarta.

In the large **Taman Mini Indonesia Indah**, 10 km south of Jakarta, 26 traditional houses are on display, representing the country's 26 provinces. Many serve as showrooms for handicrafts, clothing, etc., and in some of the smaller ones craft-making demonstrations are given. In the middle of the park is a large lagoon with a relief map of the Indonesian archipelago; you can rent a boat and row around the islands. Taman Mini is roughly a ho hum Indonesian version of Disneyland. It's open 9-5 daily. From Banteng take the #40 bus to Cililitan Bus Station, and change to a bus marked 'Mini Indonesia' (the whole trip takes nearly an hour).

Shopping

If you're looking for antiques, many booths along **Jalan Surabaya** in Menteng sell old Dutch lamps, glassware, porcelain, silver, woodcarvings, etc. Most of them are open 9-5 daily. Take a #804 red bus from Banteng bound for Manggarai and get off at Jl. Yamin. Then walk ¼ km east to Jl. Surabaya.

One of the best places in Jakarta to see (but not buy) handicrafts is the **Sarinah Department Store** on Jl. Thamrin, across from the Visitor Information Center. The top floor has an excellent selection of batiks from all over Java. The **Indonesian Bazaar** in the Jakarta Hilton complex at the intersection of Jl. Subroto and Jl. Sudirman also has dozens of expensive shops full of batik, silverware and assorted antiques. Open every day except Monday. Take any bus marked 'Blok M' from either Banteng or Jl. Thamrin.

There are many bookstores in Blok M in southern Jakarta, but the best one for English-language books is **Toko Buku Gramedia**. There are larger bookstores scattered throughout the city but most have only limited supplies of English paperbacks. Though books tend to be expensive, good-quality pirated cassettes can be purchased cheaply (Rp800). The best selection is at **Duta Suara** on Jl. Sabang.

Eating in Jakarta

Jakarta is full of good eating spots, many of them appearing at twilight and others rolling by your door with their characteristic hawkers' cries. With a little caution and an open eye, you're never more than a few hundred meters from a delicious, though sometimes expensive, meal.

Clusters of eating houses serving a wide variety of food can be found on:

- **Jl. Sabang**, the brightly-lit road behind the Sarinah Dept. Store (near Jl. Jaksa), featuring a number of Chinese and Padang restaurants.

- **Jl. Kendal**, which runs parallel to the flood canal and the railroad tracks near Jl. Thamrin in Menteng. Get there by taking any bus going south on Jl. Thamrin and get off after the Hotel Mandarin. Walk south past the massage parlors (on Jl. Blora), then turn left (where the transvestites hang out), and walk for about a hundred meters to a long string of stalls. The first ten or so serve the famous goat's foot soup, yielding to Makassarese broiled fish places and a highly recommended Korean barbecue stall at the far eastern end.

- **Jl. Pecenongan** runs north-to-south between Jl. Juanda and Jl. Batutulis directly north of Monas. At night a humble row of motorcycle shops becomes a busy, lantern-lit night market with many foodstalls serving Chinese food. After dinner, you might retreat southward and make a left (east) turn on Jl. Juanda. Instead of crossing the railroad tracks where the National Mosque is, turn right (south) on Jl. Veteran I and walk until you come across the Italian Ice Cream Parlor.

- **Jl. Mangga Besar**, off Jl. Hayam Wuruk in northern Jakarta, becomes alive after dark. The food stalls offer Chinese, Indian and Padang food. Transvestites might just serenade you during your meal. Further east is Taman Sari where there are plenty more Chinese-run outdoor restaurants along with five movie theaters and a rowdy night market. Take a Kota bus from Banteng and get off at the Hayam Wuruk Plaza.

- **Glodok** is the Chinatown of Jakarta on Jl. Pintu Besar Selatan (the extension of Jl. Hayam Wuruk) and there are a

72 INDONESIA

score of Chinese restaurants and theaters. From Glodok Building Shopping Center walk south a couple of blocks to the best ice cream parlor in Jakarta: New Zealand Ice Cream. Take a bus bound for Kota from Banteng and get off at the shopping center.

• **Pasar Senin**, a kilometer east of Monas, is a shopping center. While there are many restaurants and stalls, the best is on the ground floor in the middle. It has one of the largest selections of food: Javanese, Padang, Medan and Chinese. Pasar Senin shuts down though at night.

• **Meals on Wheels**. Anywhere in Jakarta there are the weird night calls. If you hear someone screech 'Tay, tay, sahhh-tay', it's the sate call of the guys who roam the streets with food carts. 'Wooo-deeee' translates as Woody Woodpecker ice cream. Also available are martabak telor (a sort of Indian omelette), bakso (meat ball & noodle soup), bowls of fresh fruit, etc.

Jakarta also offers a number of fancier eating establishments, most of them expensive, some quite good and a few relatively cheap. **Omar Khayam**, located on Jl. Pintu Besar almost across from the central post office, has excellent Indian food at reasonable prices. **Art'n'Curios**, off Jl. Gondangdia Lama on a side street that runs parallel to the railroad tracks near TIM in Menteng, serves very good Western meals. At Jl. Gondangdia Lama 29, on the other side of the railroad tracks, is **Trio** which serves large portions of Chinese food. You can walk there from the Jl. Jaksa area; then take a #804 bus back. The **Satay House** on Jl. Kebon Sirih 30 (within walking distance of Jl. Jaksa) serves good sate; the better place however is **Sate Blora** on Jl. Sudirman. Take a bus bound for Blok M on Jl. Thamrin. There are many restaurants in **Blok M** with European and Asian cuisines. Late-nighters will appreciate the number of food stalls in Blok M that stay open all night.

Night Life

Jakarta after dark tends to be beyond the pocketbook of a budget traveler. The cheapest entertainment is to walk to **Merdeka Square** and listen to the live rock music at **Taman Ria Monas** every night or go to one of the movie theaters in the Square. Later, you can take a stroll towards Monas, then veer due west and watch the dancing fountain—water jumps and dances to music and colored lights every night at 10:30. Then walk north to see the lit-up Presidential Palace. Turn around and gaze at the flame on top of Monas; you'll see an image of a naked woman that was supposedly built to please Sukarno. You can see her only at night and only from the northern side.

Miss your mum? She's not at the **George and Dragon Pub** but there's plenty of beer instead. It's located on a side road off Jl. Thamrin south of the Hotel Indonesia. **The Green Room**, behind

INDONESIA 73

the Visitor Information Center, usually has jazz-rock music nightly with little or no cover charge. Every Sunday night there is a Dixieland band at the **Pendopo Bar** at the Hotel Borobudur.

Check with the Visitor Information Center for sporting events that occur from time to time at the Senayan Sports Complex on Jl. Sudirman. Another possibility is to ask the Center about the English sub-titled French and German movies that are shown weekly at their respective cultural centers.

Note: Some of the fancier places mentioned above frown on rubber sandals, tank tops, shorts, etc.

ACCOMMODATIONS IN JAKARTA

Wisma Delima, Jl. Jaksa 5 (near Jl. Sabang).

Dorm rooms Rp750, Rp650 for IYH members. Single Rp1500, double Rp2500-3000. Rooms for 4, Rp4000. All rooms w/fan. Well-known travelers' ghetto; unfriendly staff.

Wisma Esther, Jl. Jaksa 40; tel. 344560.

Dorm rooms Rp750, single Rp1500, double Rp1500-2500. Cheap but dingy.

Borneo International Youth Hostel, Jl. Kebon Sirih Barat Dalam no. 35

Dorm rooms w/fan Rp1500. Double rooms w/fan & private bath Rp4500-5500. 10% discount with IYH card. Built in Feb. 1980—very clean. Sign on front desk: 'For your visa extension: Don't go abroad! We can arrange it here.' Cold beer and Coke on hand.

Fru Brouwer's House, Jl. Jaksa 27.

Only two double rooms at Rp2500 & Rp2000. Run by elderly Dutch couple. A touch of home.

Nick's Cafe and Hostel, Jl. Jaksa 16; tel. 353183.

Only 4 rooms. Triple Rp7500 w/ac, double Rp5000 w/ac, 2 doubles w/fan Rp3500. Clean, friendly, expensive.

Hotel Sriwijaya, Jl. Veteran 1; tel. 370409 ext. 4.

Double Rp7000 w/shared bath with next room; double Rp10,000 w/private bath. Centrally located modern hotel. A 5-min. walk west of Banteng.

Bali International Hotel, Jl. Wahid Hasyim no. 116; tel. 345057.

Dorm rooms Rp650-750, single Rp9000, double Rp11,300. Run-down. A last resort when other places are full.

West Java

The name Sunda comes from the original Sanskrit and means pure or white. This refers to the white ashes which spewed forth from the many volcanoes surrounding the core area of Sunda and made it rich and fertile. The language of Sunda is called Sundanese, and, like Javanese, has many levels born out of the feudal Hindu kingdoms of the 8th-12th centuries. Unlike the kingdoms of central Java and Sumatra, Sundanese God-kings never succeeded in consolidating their power in one center.

74 INDONESIA

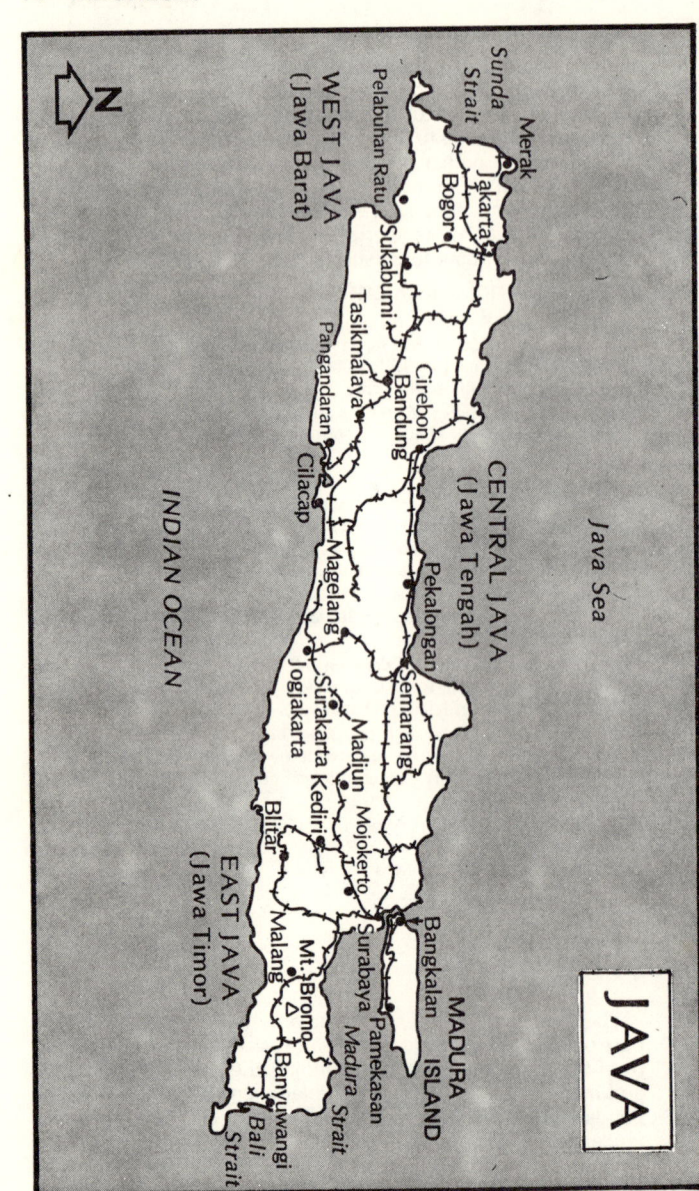

INDONESIA 75

Traditional centers of power were Banten, Sumedang, Bandung, and the trading communities on the northern coast (Sunda Kelapa and Cirebon). Sunda is known for its fertile rice fields, diverse regional performing arts, its majic men from Banten, and its capital and cultural center, Bandung. Sunda is famous for its wayang golek (wooden puppets), its angklung (bamboo instrument) orchestras, and its beautiful flute music (kecapi suling). The region is also set off from the rest of Java by stronger ties to Islam.

Bogor, in the mountains an hour south of Jakarta, is the site of one of the world's most beautiful botanical gardens. The Kebun Raya, established in 1817, is a vast tract of land containing more than 15,000 species of plants and trees. It lies in the center of town; open 8-5 daily (the Orchid House inside is open 8-noon, Monday through Saturday). The Kebun Raya is packed with picnickers on Sundays, when admission is only Rp100; if you go on a weekday (admission: Rp300) you'll have the place almost to yourself.

The Visitor Information Center, Jl. Ir. H. Juanda #38 (southwest of the Kebun Raya), can provide maps as well as information about nearby places of interest.

On the west side of the Kebun Raya, amid lawns with herds of grazing deer, lies the Presidential Palace; built in 1870, it was once the home of Dutch governors-general, and a favorite residence of former President Sukarno.

Just to the left of the Kebun Raya as you face the entrance gate at Jl. Ir. H. Juanda #9 is the national headquarters of the Directorate of Conservation and Preservation of Natural Resources (Perlindungan dan Pengawetan Alam, or PPA); you can get information about visiting Indonesia's wildlife preserves here. Ujung Kulon, a peninsula at the extreme southwest end of Java, is one of these preserves. Only accessible by chartered boat from Labuhan on the coast of West Java, Ujung Kulon is a sprawling wilderness of virgin rainforest and swamps, where tigers, miniature deer, pythons, and the rare one-horned Javanese rhinoceros live. You can camp out in the many bungalows provided by the forestry service there; go in a group to save on the chartered boat fare, because it's quite expensive. Write for permission at least a month in advance to Kantor Perlindungan dan Pengawetan Alam, Jl. Caringin #2, Labuhan.

Good restaurants in Bogor: "Singosari" and "Rumah Makan Cairo," Jl. Ir. H. Juanda, near the Ramayana Theater, "Delima," Jl. Suryakencana #56, and "Asinan Segar," Jl. Veteran, next to the barbershops (asinan=pieces of fruit, vegetables, and peanuts in a hot sauce). Pasar Bogor (Bogor Market), a 2-min. walk southeast of the botanical gardens, is the place to go for fresh fruit; it also has some inexpensive food stalls. For the best and cheapest es apokat (avocados, ice, and

76 INDONESIA

syrup put in a blender) in town, go behind the fruit sellers on the road leading to the train station (Rp100).

Sukabumi, south of Bogor, is a sleepy little town which produces wayang golek (wooden puppets).

Pelabuhan Ratu, on the coast west of Sukabumi, is a resort area offering swimming, hiking, and great seafood. Much more crowded on weekends than on weekdays. Bring your money; accommodations here are not cheap.

West of Bogor the road climbs and winds through tea plantations and small resort towns up to **Puncak**, a mountain pass; this is a popular weekend vacation spot for rich Jakartans. It gets misty at high altitudes, but the views in the early mornings are spectacular. The hiking is excellent, especially near the towns of Cibodas, Tugu, Cisarua, and, on the other side of the pass, at Cipanas. From Cipanas it's a short distance to the turnoff for the Cibodas Botanical Gardens (4 km from the main road). Near the parking area at the gardens is the start of a hiking trail up to Gunung Gede, a volcanic peak overlooking the entire area to the east. Get permission first at the Forestry Office, Conservation division (PPA) in the building next to the Kebun Raya entrance in Bogor (entry fee: Rp500). The hike to the peak takes 6-12 hours. An hour on the trail brings you to a fork; one trail goes to the top and the other descends to a waterfall. Following the trail to the mountaintop, you'll come to some hot springs, with a waterfall cascading down a rock face and steam rising from the gorge below. This hike should be started early in the morning (before dawn if the moon is full) and is not recommended during the rainy season (Nov.-April).

There are two interesting stops on the way up Gunung Gede. Stroll through the fields of Gunung Mas, a huge tea plantation on the slopes of the mountain. Free tours of the tea factory are offered. About 2 km further up the hill, stop at Telaga Warna, a beautiful lake with a path around it.

The provincial capital, **Bandung,** lies in the cool highlands 175 km southeast of Jakarta, located on the bed of a prehistoric lake. When the twin volcano Burangrang erupted it punched a hole in the lake's effluvial base, the water ran out, the lake dried up, and a rich farming community grew up on the rich and level soil. This third largest city in Indonesia (population: over 2 million) is a center of industry (textiles and food processing), education and fine arts. Some 15 universities are located in Bandung, as well as many smaller academies and institutes. Culturally Bandung is very rich, attracting dancers, musicians and artists from throughout Indonesia to study there.

The Tourist Information Center, at the northeast corner of the central square (alun-alun) on Jl. Asia-Afrika, is open 8-2 Mon.-Sat. (except Friday when it's open 8-11). Get around town on hondas or daihatsus (mini-pickups), bemos, and city buses.

Hondas and bemos leave from Kebun Kelapa Station, four blocks south of the central square; new city buses provide regular service on an east-west route along Jl. Asia-Afrika and Jl. A. Yani. In-town rides generally cost Rp75 for bemos, daihatsus or oplets, and Rp30 for the city bus, regardless of distance. Bandung also has numerous becaks; the cost of a ride is strongly influenced by whether your destination is uphill or not.

Set on a bluff overlooking the city, on a satellite campus of Universitas Pajajaran, is the **Dago Tea House**. A fine place to sit, talk, and relax. Take a Dago honda north from the train station to the end of the line, then walk left up the hill (5 min.). The entrance fee is Rp150 after 7 pm. There's also a good Sundanese restaurant nearby, Babakan Siliwangi. Take the Dago honda and get off at Jl. Siliwangi.

ITB (ee-tay-bay), the Institute of Technology at Bandung, is one of Indonesia's most prestigious universities. Meet students (many of them speak English fairly well) in the canteen-type restaurant across from the main gate in the 'Asrama Mahasiswa.' To get to ITB, located on the north of the city, take a Dago honda and get off at Jl. Ganesha.

The **Musium Geologi** (Geological Museum), Jl. Diponegoro 57, near the central post office, has interesting fossils, relief maps, and models of volcanoes. **Gedung Merdeka** (Freedom Building) was the site of the 1955 Asia-Africa Conference; 29 leaders of 3rd World nations—including Sukarno, Nasser, Ho Chi Minh, and Chou En Lai—attended, hammering out the framework for the non-aligned movement of the third world bloc. A fine new museum in this building chronicles the conference. Gedung Merdeka also holds wayang and pop music performances, and exhibitions of painting and sculpture. It's located just south of the alun-alun on Jl. Asia-Afrika.

Wayang golek performances are held every Saturday night at the **Yayasan Pusat Kebudayaan** (YPK), Jl. Naripan 7, just off Jl. Braga. They last from 9 pm till morning; tickets are usually Rp400. YPK also teaches classes in Sundanese dance and music, gamelan, and pencak silat (Indonesian martial arts). At **Rumintang Siang** on Jl. Baranag Siang in the Kosambi district, music of all kinds and plays are performed almost every night. To get there, take a city bus east towards Cicaheum. The **ASTI-Bandung** (Indonesian Institute of Fine Arts) on Jl. Buah Batu often holds performances by its students. Take a bemo from the Kebun Kelapa bus station.

78 INDONESIA

For good food, try the Padang-style **restaurant located right next to the mosque at the alun-alun**. It's on the second story and affords a great view of the square (go at night for a cool breeze and a glance at the lights of Bandung). Also try baso tahu (tofu & fish meatball soup) at one of the dozens of street vendors located on Jl. Dalam Kaum right near the alun-alun. Find great-tasting Chinese food in the same area. Then go see a Western B movie or an Indonesian movie at one of the 10 or so theatres around the square. After the flick, eat durian ice cream with fermented black rice pudding in the alleyway next to the Dian theatre, or try the noodle houses right up that same alleyway. Savor the sate on Jl. Pasir Kaliki (Restoran Klaten, near the railroad tracks overpass) or at the restaurants in front of the train station. A close approximation of French pastries can be found at the three bakeries on Jl. Braga.

The **Bandung Zoo** (Jl. Taman Sari, across from ITB), with many unusual birds from throughout Indonesia and southeast Asia, Komodo dragons, and lots of open park space to spend a quiet weekday or a crowded Sunday, is well worth a visit.

Lembang, 16 km north of Bandung and about 500 meters above it, is justly renowned for its vegetable market, open every day. Freshly boiled corn-on-the-cob costs Rp25. Take an oplet from in front of the Bandung train station (Rp150; 45 min.).

Also north of Bandung are two hot springs resorts, **Maribaya** and **Ciater**, and a volcano, **Tangkuban Prahu** ('overturned boat'). Maribaya (4 km east of Lembang) and Ciater (15 km northeast of Lembang) have baths and swimming pools, generally with moderate entrance fees; both are accessible by oplet or bus from Lembang on Sundays. You can also hike to Maribaya from the top of Dago (3 hr.); great panoramas of rice terraces and the city below. Tangkuban Prahu has impressive craters. Hike to the top from Lembang (take Jl. Jayagiri north out of town)—if you go on Sunday you'll have lots of company (3 hr.). You can also get to Tangkuban Prahu by oplet.

The town of **Sumedang** (2 hr. north of Bandung on the road to Cirebon) was once the center of culture and power in West Java. Visit the museum in the municipal center complex, displaying ancient gamelans and memorabilia from the heyday of Sumedang. Young girls practice traditional dance here every Sunday morning at 9. Sumedang is famous for its tahu goreng (fried tofu); available at any restaurant.

The north coast city of **Cirebon** is the only surviving sultanate in West Java. An extraordinary multi-ethnic city, Cirebon has its own language (a mixture of Javanese, Sundanese, Chinese, Malay, and local dialects). The two old kratons (palaces), **Kanoman** and **Kesepuhan**, are a bit run down but interesting. Kraton Kanoman, the younger of the two, shows signs of Dutch influence in its construction; the Dutch Reformist scenes from

INDONESIA 79

the Bible on the inner walls seem curiously out of place in a Muslim sultan's palace.

Visit Cirebon's harbor during the daytime and see Buginese prahus (sailing ships) and Japanese freighters unload their wares. A number of good Chinese restaurants line the street bordering the harbor; the shrimp is especially good here. Go to the amusement park at the beach (right near the post office) and walk way out into the sea in the very shallow water, or sit on one of the many jetties which the fisherfolk use to cast nets from. Shop for distinctive Cirebon batiks at Batik Permana on Jl. Karanggetas (one of the main streets in town). Note the similarities in batik design with the architecture at the kratons and with the weather patterns in the sky (the famous 'rocks and clouds' motif is in evidence wherever one goes in Cirebon).

Pangandaran, on Java's south coast near the boundary between West and Central Java, has one of the island's few safe beaches. A coral reef helps protect the shoreline from the rough, dangerous surf. The area caters mainly to wealthy Indonesian tourists, but foreigners are welcome. At the tip of the peninsula lies a wildlife preserve teeming with monkeys and cool, shady banyan trees. Watch the wild buffalo (banteng) come out to feed on the grass in the late afternoon, or explore the coral reef at Taman Laut (the southernmost tip of the preserve) when the tide is low.

ACCOMMODATIONS IN WEST JAVA

Bogor:
This town doesn't have any accommodations that are both pleasant and cheap. There are two rather seedy losmen and two hotels:

Losmen Pasundan, Jl. Mantarena 19 (behind Jl. Veteran 19). Doubles w/private bath Rp3000, w/out bath Rp2500; triples (both w/bath) Rp3500-4000. Located about 2 blocks west of the town's main bemo terminal.

Losmen Damai, Jl. Mayor Oking 29, also on the west side of town. Doubles Rp.2000; triples Rp3600; four-bed rooms Rp4000--all w/out private bath.

Hotel Salak, Jl. Ir.H. Juanda 8, opposite the Bogor Palace. Singles w/private bath Rp4500; doubles w/private bath Rp6000 or Rp7500; doubles w/shared bath Rp4500. A little run-down, but the staff is friendly.

Elsana Transit Hotel, Jl. Sawojajar 36. Doubles Rp7500-9000; triples Rp11,000--all w/private bath. Not as nice as Hotel Salak but breakfast is included. Located just off Jl. Gunung Gede, one of the main roads into town (north side).

Puncak:
Hotel Cibulan, in the small town of Cibulan, directly across from a large swimming pool. It's a '40s-vintage, Dutch-style, genteely run-down place with a friendly staff. Doubles, triples, quadruples about Rp4000-6000 on weekdays. Take a colt from Pasar Bogor to Cibulan.

80 INDONESIA

Pelabuhan Ratu:
Rent seaside bungalows on the 4-km stretch between the Pelabuhan Ratu fish market and the luxurious Samudra Beach Hotel. Singles Rp8750-11,250; doubles Rp12,500-15,000. More crowded on weekends.

Bandung:
Penginapan Sakardarna, behind Jl. Kebun Jati. Singles Rp1500; doubles Rp2000. Simple and clean. From the terminal in front of the train station, turn right on Jl. Kebun Jati; find the 'gang' (alley) just after Hotel Melati; the penginapan is behind and beside Hotel Melati.

Wisma Remaja, Gelanggang Remaja Bldg., Jl. Merdeka 64. Dorm beds (6 people to a room) Rp750; doubles Rp750/person. Has a cafe serving reasonably-priced food 8 am-9 pm. Located downtown, on the Kebun Kelapa and Dago colt routes.

Hotel Bandung, Jl. Pecinan Lama 32. Doubles Rp2500. Congenial staff, bustling neighborhood. Walk east from the exit of the train station until you get to the pedestrian overpass over the railroad tracks; go across the overpass, turn right on Jl. Oto Iskandardinata and walk 3 more blocks south to Jl. Pecinan Lama; the hotel is near a large market.

Hotel Lugina, Jl. Jendral Sudirman 526. A fairly stylish hotel and bar offering rooms w/private bath at Rp1500/person to YHAcardholders; rooms for non-cardholders Rp6000 and up. Located on the west side of town, on the main road by buses coming from Jakarta and Bogor. Also on city bus route.

Pangandaran:
Numerous losmen line the main street; most are about the same. Prices range from Rp750 to Rp3000; some include breakfast. Buy fresh fish at the daily fish auction and have the proprietors cook it for you.

TRANSPORTATION FOR WEST JAVA

Buses from Jakarta to towns in West Java leave from Cililitan Bus Station at the southeast edge of the city (get to Cililitan from Banteng Station by city bus). Trains for Bogor, Bandung, etc. leave from the Kota and Gambir Stations.

Bogor: Buses run frequently from Cililitan Station in Jakarta. Take the bus that goes via Jl. Jagorawi, the only superhighway in Indonesia, for a smooth 35-40 min. ride (Rp275). The other route, via Cibinong, takes much longer (1 hr.) but is only Rp250. Trains make 22 runs daily from Jakarta (Rp175, 1½ hr.).

Sukabumi: By train from Bogor, Rp175. There are also frequent buses.

Pelabuhan Ratu: Take a bus or train from Bogor to Cibadak (on the route to Sukabumi), and change there for a colt to Pelabuhan Ratu.

Puncak: From Bogor take a bus bound for Bandung and tell the ticket seller where you want to get off (30-45 min).

Bandung: By bus from Bogor (Rp530, 3½hr.). By bus from Jakarta (Rp900, 5 hr.). By train from Jakarta: the Parahiyangan (2nd class only, Rp2500, 3½ hr.) or the Pattas Ekonomi (3rd class, Rp900, 3½ hr.). Three trains connect Bandung and Yogya daily; the Ekspres Siang costs Rp2550 (2nd class) /Rp1750 (3rd class), 8 hr. By night bus from Yogya Rp1900-2050 (11hr.).

(Night bus companies in Bandung for trips to Yogya: Bandung Express, Jl. Riau 7. Take a Ledang colt to Jl. Wastukencana, get off at Jl. Laksamana Laut and walk one block east. Yogya Express, Jl. Sunda

INDONESIA 81

54, not far from the intersection with Jl. Asia-Afrika.)

Pangandaran: Buses leave almost every hour from Cililitan Station for Banjar (via Bogor, Bandung, Tasikmalaya, Ciamis); from Banjar take a colt to Pangandaran (rp300-400). Or, from Bandung take an early train to Banjar; then change to a colt. The whole trip takes 10-12 hr. The colts let you off at the pasar (market); you must walk the 2 km (or take a becak) to the 'tourist area' of Pangandaran where the hotels are.

Central Java

The greatest of Java's early civilizations, including the Budhist Shailendra and the Hindu Mataram dynasties, flourished on the plains of south central Java. In the palace-cities of Yogyakarta and Surakarta (Solo), the courts of the Sultan and the Susuhunan have actively cultivated Java's rich variety of arts and crafts for centuries. Indonesia's finest batik is made in this region, and wayang kulit (shadow puppet), wayang orang (dance drama), and gamelan performances abound.

Yogyakarta (or Yogya, also spelled Jogjakarta), long a royal city and major trade center, since 1950 has become a university town as well (Universitas Gajah Mada and other schools attract students from throughout the country). It was a major center of nationalist resistance during Indonesia's War of Independence against the Dutch and was capital of the infant Republic 1946-49. Today it is the capital of the Special Territory of Yogyakarta (administratively autonomous from the province of Central Java), with the status of a sultanate. The present Sultan, Sri Sultan Hamengkubuwono IX, was Indonesia's vice-president until he stepped down in March 1978. Once a city of bicycles and pedestrians, Yogya has grown drastically in the last few years; traffic jams, flashing neon signs, and tourists are everywhere.

Stop first at the Tourist Information Center, 16 Jl. Malioboro (Yogya's main street). Open Monday through Saturday, 7 am-10 pm; tel. 2811, ext. 11.

The Sultan's palace, the **Kraton**, is the hub around which the city turns. It's open 8:30-12:30 Sun.-Thurs., and 8-11:30 Fri. & Sat.; tours are offered for Rp200. Gamelan rehearsals are held Mondays and Wednesdays, 10:30-noon, and classical dance rehearsals take place on Sundays, 10-noon.

Southwest of the Kraton are the ruins of the **Taman Sari** (Water Castle), built in 1765. It was once an elaborate complex of bathing pools, underground passages, and galleries, to be used by the Sultan and his entourage. Now most of it is dilapidated and people have built houses around and on top of it. Several sections were restored recently and can be visited for a small fee, but the 'living ruins' are much more interesting. There's also a great bird market nearby.

82 INDONESIA

The **Museum Sonobudoyo**, on the Alun-alun Utara (the square north of the Kraton), has excellent exhibits of batik, musical instruments, palace furnishings, and all kinds of puppets. Open Monday through Saturday, 8 am-noon.

Yogya's famous batik is everywhere. The government-run Batik & Handicraft Research Institute (Balai Penelitian Batik & Kerajinan), at 2 Jl. Kusumanegara, 3 km east of the center of town, offers tours in English and reasonable prices. It's open 8-2 weekdays and 8-1 Saturday. From the post office take a bemo (Rp50, via a circuitous route), a becak (Rp200), or ride a bike. For inexpensive batik paintings (of varying quality) wander through the maze of shops just behind the Water Castle; bargain vigorously. The Terang Bulan batik shop, on the left as you walk south on Jl. Malioboro, has a wide selection of batik goods—set prices (very fair) and reliable quality. Or shop around in the area south of the Kraton, especially on Jl. Tirtodipuran, where there are dozens of small batik factories. Intensive batik courses are offered for Rp5000-7000/wk. (materials included); ask around to find out which are the best.

For silverwork, visit the workshops of the **Kota Gede** area, 5 km southeast of the city's center. Leather goods (bags, sandals) are popular buys. The best place in town to buy wayang puppets is Pak Ledjar's on Jl. Mataram, next to the Mini-Padang Restaurant. (From Helen's on Jl. Malioboro walk east down the alley to Jl. Mataram, then turn left.) Other handicrafts are sold on the sidewalks along Jl. Malioboro at night.

Wayang orang and Ramayana Ballet performances are given nightly (9-11 pm and 7:30-9 pm respectively) at the Sasono Suko **THR** (tay-hah-air) or 'People's Amusement Park,' behind the bus station on Jl. Brigjen Katamso.

To get around in Yogya: 1) Walk. 2) Ride a bicycle; rent one from Hotel Aziatic (Rp300/day) or Hotel Kartika (Rp200/day), both on Jl. Sosrowijayan, near the train station. 3) Take the city bus (orange) or a colt (both Rp50); their routes reach almost every corner of the city. 4) Take a becak; short rides cost Rp100, longer ones up to Rp30. 5) Rent a motorcycle at Yogya Rental (Rp4000/day) on Jl. Pasar Kembang.

Popular places to eat include: Cafe Malioboro and Helen's (opposite each other on Jl. Malioboro), Superman (on an alley between Jl. Sosrowijayan and Jl. Pasar Kembang), and Mama's (on Jl. Pasar Kembang). Very few Indonesians eat in these places, though. Try some of the small warungs off the side streets down towards the post office or near the THR. Pak Amat's on the square north of the Kraton serves excellent sate. The local specialty, gudeg (young jackfruit cooked in coconut milk for several days in a special pot, with chicken and spices), is sold at night by little old ladies on the sidewalks of Yogya. Sit on a tikar (woven reed mat), while the woman serves up a bowlful from her

INDONESIA 83

huge cauldron; top off this splendid meal with a glass of air jeruk panas (hot lemonade).

A visit to **Kaliurang**, 25 km north of Yogya on the southern slopes of the volcano Gunung Merapi, is highly recommended. During the day you can often see smoke and steam billowing out; at night rivulets of fiery red lava sometimes roll down the sides of the mountain while sparks fly high in the air. From Kaliurang you can hike in several hours to a lookout with a magnificent view of the volcano; take along a picnic lunch. Kaliurang also has a spring-fed swimming pool and a waterfall.

The royal cemetery of **Imogiri**, 20 km south of Yogya, sits on a steep hillside at the top of several hundred stone stairs. Only open twice a week—Monday, 10-1 and Friday, 1:30-4—when people come to pay their respects at this sacred place. The graves of the sultans of Yogya are on one side, the sultans of Solo on the other. You must check in with the 'Registration Committee Desk,' pay Rp200, and rent traditional dress for abour Rp150 before you can visit a tomb. Tag along with some of the Javanese pilgrims so you'll know what to do. As they drop flower petals on the graves, many people ask the spirits of the sultans a favor—a good rice harvest, a new bicycle or transistor radio, etc.

Borobudur, 42 km northwest of Yogya, ranks as one of the world's greatest Buddhist monuments. It was built between 750 and 850 A.D. during the reign of the Shailendra kings, then was buried for centuries under lava and ash. In the 1800s it was rediscovered and unearthed. The huge, looming stupa has been in danger of collapse; a restoration project is now underway. Some two million cubic feet of stone had to be hewn, transported, piled, and carved during its construction; there are more than 2500 pictorial and decorative panels and 504 Buddha images. The ten stages of the Bodhisattva (The Buddhist Way of Salvation) are symbolized by the terraces of the monument—six square ones and three round ones, with the large, closed stupa on top as the tenth phase. The carved panels depict, among other things, the hundreds of previous lives of Buddha, as well as many everyday scenes from ancient Javanese court and rural life. Borobudur is a huge mandala, a massive meditational device; by reflecting on it, pilgrims were able to achieve perfect wisdom and nirvana.

Prambanan (Candi Loro Jonggrang) is a stunningly beautiful Hindu temple 17 km east of Yogya on the road to Solo. It was built by the early Mataram kings in the ninth century as part of a huge temple complex. It's dedicated to Shiva and contains statues of Shiva, Ganesha (Shiva's elephant-headed son), Durga (Shiva's consort in her destructive form, shown killing a bull demon), and Mahaguru (Shiva's ascetic manifestation). The first part of the Ramayana story is carved in bas relief on the panels around the outer balustrade. Panels on the temple of Brahma to the south and the temple of Vishnu to the north complete the tale. On the four evenings (7-9 pm) around the full moons from May to October, the 'Ramayana Ballet' is performed in the amphitheater next to the temple (a different segment of the story each night); tickets cost Rp700-2500, depending on the seat. Buy tickets at travel agencies in Yogya or Solo, buy them yourself outside the amphitheater (get there a good two hours early if you buy tickets there). A good synopsis of the Ramayana story, by Chakravarti Rajagopalachari, is available in most large bookstores. Look for the characteristic 'Prambanan motif' on some of the panels: lions surrounded by two trees of life.

Candi Prambanan is the largest of at least a dozen temples lying within a 5 km radius of Prambanan village. If you follow the road off the northeast corner of Candi Prambanan, for example, you'll soon arrive at **Candi Sewu** (or 'Thousand Temples'), passing several small, tumbled-down temples en route. This Buddhist temple complex dates from the mid-9th century, during the Shailendra dynasty. The main shrine is encircled by four rings of 'guard' temples, 240 of them, all but one (restored in 1927-28) in various stages of disarray due to an earthquake early in this century. A fascinating jumble to poke around in. Several kilometers east of Candi Sewu is **Candi Plaosan**, built during the same period.

The beach at **Parang Tritis**, 28 km south of Yogya, is nice for hiking and splashing around (the surf is dangerous for swimming). This area is known as the home of Loro Kidul, Queen of the Indonesian Ocean. Local residents occasionally bring gifts of food and flowers to the goddess in a procession to the beach; the men are very careful not to wear green clothing, as this angers the queen.

INDONESIA 85

The **Dieng Plateau**, 137 km northwest of Yogya, has spectacular scenery, many ancient Hindu temples, volcanic craters, boiling mud pits, lakes, hot springs, and a refreshingly cool climate. There are inexpensive losmen in Dieng and the nearby town of Wonosobo. Warning: it's **cold** at night. Best to go during the dry season (April-November).

Although **Surakarta** (or **Solo**, also spelled Sala) reached the peak of its political importance in the 18th century when it was the capital of the Mataram Kingdom, it is still a major cultural center and source of high-quality batik. Fortunately, Solo has not suffered the inundation of tourists that Yogya has; it remains a slow-paced city where becaks, not cars, fill the streets.

The Solo Tourist Information Center is at 235 Jl. Brigjen Slamet Riyadi, tel. 6508, between the Sriwedari Amusement Park and the Radya Pustaka Museum. Open 8-1 Mon.-Thurs., 8-11:30 Fri., & 8-12:30 Sat. There is a branch office on the same street at #86 (tel. 2009); same hours as #235 except that it closes half an hour earlier on Fri. & Sat.

Kraton Kasunanan, in the southeast corner of town, is the palace complex of Susuhunan Pakubuwono; it has an excellent museum. **Puri Mangkunegaran**, at the northern end of Jl. Diponegoro, is the palace of a lesser royal family. Both are open to visitors every morning except Sunday (Rp400). Gamelan and dance rehearsals are held several times a week in both palaces; ask for more details at the TIC. Dance and music performances are also presented regularly at the Sasono Mulyo (or PKJT) City Center, next to the Kraton Kasunanan.

Wayang orang performances are offered nightly except Sundays at the **Sriwedari Recreation Park**, in the middle of town on Jl. Slamet Riyadi (8 pm-midnight; Rp75-300, depending on the class). Saturday night the best artists perform so those shows are the most popular (buy your ticket in advance). If you just want to wander around the park (and eat at the small restaurants), the entrance fee is only Rp65. You can watch part of the wayang orang performance through the windows along the sides of the theater. Srimulat performances are given regularly at the **Balekambang Recreation Park** (Rp50 entrance fee). Ask at the TIC for details.

The small **Musium Radya Pustaka**, next to Sriwedari on Jl. Slamet Riyadi, has good displays of masks, gamelan instruments, wayang puppets, kerises (daggers), etc.; unfortunately exhibits are not labelled in English.

Solo has at least 300 **batik factories** of various sizes; most are scattered around the southern part of the city. The biggest batik and textile market in Indonesia is **Pasar Klewer**, on Jl. Secoyudan, next to the Kraton Kasunanan. The Danar Hadi Batik

86 INDONESIA

Shop, Jl. Dr. Rajiman 8, is one of several places selling batik goods at fixed prices.

Pasar Triwindu, off Jl. Diponegoro just north of Jl. Slamet Riyadi, is a marvelous flea market.

Sangiran, 15 km north of Solo, is where the 'Java Man' skull was discovered. A small museum exhibits fossils of prehistoric mammals and human beings more than a million years old.

Candi Sukuh, 35 km east of Solo, is a 14th century Hindu temple shaped like a stepped pyramid. It's known as the 'amorous temple' due to numerous erotic reliefs and sculptures.

The port town of **Semarang**, on Java's north coast, is the administrative capital of Central Java. The Central Java Provincial Tourist Office (Kantor Dinas Pariwisata) is on Jl. Mar. Sugiyopranoto No. 1 (the street is also called Jl. Pasar Bulu). The Semarang tourist office, in Wisma Pancasila at Simpang Lima (the town square), has information in English and a helpful staff (hours: 8-2 mon.-Thurs., 8-1:30 Fri., 8-1 Sat.). Not much in this town for tourists, but while you're here visit **Gedong Batu**, an unusual Chinese temple in a huge stone cave on the west side of town. It's a memorial to Sam Poo Tway Jin, a 15th century Chinese Moslem eunuch who served as the Middle Kingdom's emissary to Java. Get around town by city bus (Rp25) or Daihatsu (small orange vans, Rp50).

On your way to Semarang from Yogya or Solo, stop off at **Gedung Songo** (Javanese for 'nine buildings') in the mountains near Bandungan. This series of 9 small Shiva-Hindu temples among the hills and ravines of Gunung Ungaran enjoys the most beautiful location of Java's major temples. Built in the 9th century and devoted to Shiva and Vishnu, most of the temples are still in good condition, and others are being restored. When the mist clears, look out across the plain where Mt. Merapi smolders in the distance, nearly obscured by Mt. Merbabu; below them lie Lake Rawapening and shimmering green rice fields. Spend some time hiking around the ravines and sulphur springs; it's quite steep in parts. Stop at Bandungan's cheap vegetable market on your way down.

ACCOMMODATIONS IN CENTRAL JAVA

Yogyakarta:
Head for Jl. Pasar Kembang and Jl. Sosrowijayan, just south of and parallel to the train tracks. (If you go out the front of the station, turn right, then right again at the first or second street beyond the tracks.) Along these two streets and on the alleys between them are literally dozens of small losmen and hotels offering rooms for Rp500-1500. The most popular include Losmen Beta, Hotel Kota, and Losmen 'Bu Purwo.' Some are cleaner or more congenial than others, so shop around. The following four hotels are slightly more expensive (and thus more comfortable):

Hotel Aziatic. Double Rp2250, triple Rp3300, both w/shared bath.

Serves food, rents bikes; has trips to Dieng (7 am to 6 pm).

Indonesia Hotel. 5 different classes of room (all doubles), **ranging** from Rp1000 'ordinary double' to Rp3500 for double w/bath, shower, fan. Drinks and breakfast available. Rp3750 tour to Dieng.

Hotel Ratna. Double w/bath Rp3000-4500, depending on the size. Triple w/bath Rp4100-6300.

Hotel Asia-Afrika. Double w/private bath Rp3000-3500; double w/shared bath Rp2000-2500; single Rp1250-1750.

For slightly nicer accommodations in a less bustling location, try the following 3 hotels on Jl. Sosrokusuman. Walk south from the train station down Jl. Malioboro about 7 min. and turn left down the alley next to Helen's Restaurant.

Hotel Intan, #1/16. Single Rp2000, w/fan Rp2250; double Rp2750, w/fan Rp3000.

Hotel Puri, #22. Single Rp2000, double Rp2500.

Prambanan Guest House, #18-20; tel. 3033. Double w/o bath Rp2500, w/bath Rp3000; single w/o bath Rp2000.

Kaliurang:

There are numerous guesthouses in town.

Solo:

Two key areas to look for inexpensive hotels: 1) There are at least a dozen within one block's walk of the intersection of Jl. Brigjen Slamet Riyadi (Solo's main drag) & Jl. Achmad Dahlan (old name: Keprabon), on the east side of the city; also lots of small restaurants nearby. 2) There are several dozen within a 5-min. walk east or south of the train station, which in turn is not far from the bus station. The first three hotels below are in the first area, the last three are in the second.

Hotel Timur, Keprabon Timur Gang I/5. Rooms w/double beds Rp750 (1 person)/Rp1000 (2). This small hotel is about 50 m. down a narrow alley which runs off the east side of Jl. Achmad Dahlan next to Hotel Central.

Hotel Wigati, Jl. Slamet Riyadi, Gang II/4 (Keprabon Wetan). Double Rp1000-1250. Walk east from the intersection w/Jl. Achmad Dahlan and turn left.

Hotel Keprabon, Jl. Achmad Dahlan 12/14; tel. 2811. Single Rp1500, double Rp2000, triple Rp3000, quad Rp4000. Spacious.

Hotel Soeboer, Jl. Gajah Mada 172B; tel. 3809. Double w/private bath Rp2450. This hotel doesn't look like much from the outside, but there's a pleasant courtyard inside. A 3-min. walk southwest of the train station.

Hotel San Francisco, Jl. Balapan Solo, Gang II. Single Rp1250-1500, double (w/double bed) Rp1750-2000, double (2 beds) Rp3000. A 3-min. walk east of the train station; walk down Jl. Balapan Solo, and turn left down the alley opposite Hotel Trihadhi. At **Hotel Sinardadi**, across the alley from Hotel San Francisco, doubles are only Rp1500.

Hotel Jayakarta, Jl. Balapan Solo 122; tel. 2813. Four classes of doubles, Rp2057-3630. More expensive rooms have attached bath. Just east of the train station.

Semarang:

There are lots of small hotels and losmen in Semarang, but they must have special permission to admit foreigners; some have this permission, some don't. The following three do:

Hotel Poncol, Jl. Imam Bonjol 60. Single Rp1500, double Rp1800, triple Rp2100. Not very clean, and noisy, but the people are nice. Centrally located, near Pasar Johar.

88 INDONESIA

Hotel Singapore, Jl. Imam Bonjol 12. Single Rp2250, double Rp3500, triple Rp4500. Includes breakfast.

Losmen Oewa-Asia, Jl. Imam Bonjol (across the street from Hotel Singapore). Single Rp2000; double Rp3000; double w/bath Rp4400; triple Rp4500. Includes breakfast.

TRANSPORTATION FOR CENTRAL JAVA

Yogyakarta: Yogya's train station is in the middle of town on Jl Malioboro. The bus station is on Jl. (Brigjen) Katamso on the south side of town, next to the THR amusement park. Many night bus company offices are clustered in the Gedung Serba Guna building—better known as 'Shopping' from the days when it had an English name—on Jl. Senopati, just east of the post office; others line Jl. Mangkubumi (same street as Jl. Malioboro, but north of the train station). Look for travel colt offices on Jl. Diponegoro, just west of the intersection with Jl. Mangkubumi.

Getting to Yogya: Five trains a day from Jakarta, Rp1650-2600 (3rd class), depending on the train (except for the Bima, which has 1st & 2nd class only). More than a dozen night bus companies offer service between Jakarta and Yogya (Rp3500-4300); 14 hr. Three trains daily from Bandung; the Ekspres Siang leaves at 5:30 am, Rp2250 (2nd class)/Rp1750 (3rd class), 8 hr. By night bus from Bandung, Rp2500-2700, 11 hr. Three trains daily from Surabaya; the Ekspres Siang, which leaves in the early morning, costs Rp1750 (3rd class), 6½ + hr. From Surabaya by night bus, Rp2500, 8½ hr.

Kaliurang: From Yogya take one of the four buses which leave daily—at 7, 11, 2, and 5 (Rp175, 1½ hr.); catch them at the bus station or on Jl. Mataram, behind the Garuda Hotel. Or take a colt (Rp275, 1 hr.); they leave roughly every half hour from Jl. Suryotomo, just next to 'Shopping'/Gedung Serba Guna. You can also catch them on Jl. Mataram (same street, further north).

Parang Tritis: Take a colt to Kretek from the intersection of Jl. Parangtritis and Jl. Sugiono, ferry across the river, then walk the remaining 5 km or take a dokar.

Imogiri: Take a colt from behind the Pertamina gas station on Jl. Senopati (Rp150, 30 min.), east of the post office. Or ride a bike.

Borobudur: From Yogya take a bus (Rp125, 45 min.) or a colt (Rp175, 35 min.) to Muntilan, and from there take a bus directly to the temple (Rp75, 30 min.). The colts start from the corner of Jl. Diponegoro and Jl. Magelang, on the northwest side of the city; buses can be caught there or at the station.

Prambanan: Take a bus (Rp100) or a colt (Rp150). Colts start from Jl. Suryotomo next to the shopping center; you can also catch them behind the Garuda Hotel or on Jl. Cik Ditiro, just north of Jl. Sudirman, on the north side of town. A 30 min. trip.

Dieng Plateau: Colts leave for Wonosobo from Jl. Diponegoro in Yogya at 9 am and 2 pm (Rp1050, 2 hr.); switch there to another colt to Dieng. There is no direct bus service to Wonosobo; you have to take a bus to Magelang (Rp225), then another to Wonosobo (Rp275). Note: the Tourist Information Center and some of the hotels near the train station, e.g. Hotel Indonesia, offer moderately-priced one-day tours to Dieng.)

Surakarta (Solo): Solo's train station, Balapan, is on Jl. Balapan Solo on the north side of town. The main bus station, Tirtonadi/Gilingan, is just north of the train station. Most travel colt offices are clustered on Jl. Yos Sudarso, just south of the intersection with Jl. Slamet Riyadi. Travel colts offer non-stop service, and you'll be taken directly to your destination.

Getting to Solo: From Yogya take a bus (Rp350, 2 hr.) or a colt (Rp450, 1½ hr.); colts leave frequently from Jl. Suryotomo, next to 'Shopping,' or catch them behind the Garuda Hotel or on Jl. Cik Ditiro. Several trains also connect Yogya and Surakarta daily (Rp175, 2 hr.). Surakarta can be reached from Surabaya by bus or train (about 6 hr.), and from Semarang by bus (Rp450, 2½ hr.) or a colt (Rp550, 2 hr.).

Sangiran: From Solo take a bus going toward Kalioso, and get off at Kalijambe (past Kalioso); from Kalijambe turn right and walk about 5 km or take a dokar.

Candi Sukuh: From Solo take a bus going to Tawangmangu and get off at Karangpandan (Rp150, 1 hr.); then catch a colt bound for Kemuning (Rp100) and tell them you want to get off near Sukuh. The temple is a short hike off the main road.

Semarang: From Yogya by bus (around Rp350, 3 hr.) or travel colt (Rp1200, 2½ hr.); from Solo by bus (Rp450, 2½ hr.) or travel colt (Rp1000, 2 hr.). Also reached by train from Jakarta (Rp2250-7000, 7½-10 hr., depending on the train and class) and Surabaya (Rp1150-7000, 6½-7 hr., depending on the train and class).

Gedung Songo: From Yogya or Solo, take a bus or colt to Ambarawa; from Ambarawa you can take a colt to Bandungan. At the market intersection, take another colt to Gedung Songo.

East Java

East Java (Jawa Timur) is often just an overnight stop for travelers hurrying on to Bali or Yogya, but it has much to offer those willing to spend some time exploring. While there are no monuments that approach the awe-inspiring scale of Borobudur or Prambanan, numerous smaller structures—candi (funerary temples), hermitages, gates and walls of palaces, etc.—date back to the six centuries (10th to 15th centuries) of East Java's political and cultural ascendancy. The most famous of the many kingdoms which struggled for power were Kediri, Singosari, and the great Majapahit Empire. Due to religious syncretism temples built during this period often show both Shivaite and Buddhist influence; in the monuments and temples of ancient East Java you can see the connecting link between the Hinduistic art of Central Java and the living art of Bali today.

Surabaya, on East Java's northern coast, is a bustling commercial center and major port. Since this city—Indonesia's second largest—is always hot and sticky, the city of Malang to the south is a more pleasant base for day and weekend trips. But

90 INDONESIA

stop in first at Surabaya's East Java Regional Tourist Development Board office, Jl. Yos Sudarso 3 (around the corner from the Bamboe Denn), for maps, a calendar of events, and information on places to visit throughout the province. The office is open 7-2 Mon.-Thurs., 7-11 Fri., and 7-1 Sat. Get around Surabaya by bemo (Rp75), city bus (Rp30), or becak (Rp150-300). The city's becaks are now color-coded: blue for daytime (becak siang), white for night (becak malam). Bus routes run basically north-south. Two main routes are from Tanjung Perak (north) to Joyoboyo bus station (via Jl. Panglima Sudirman) and from Jembatan Merah bus/bemo station to Wonokromo (the market area near Joyoboyo).

Tanjung Perak, Surabaya's harbor, is an interesting place to poke around. Take the city bus going to 'T. Perak' or a bemo from the Jembatan Merah bemo station. To see traditional wooden trading ships ('prahu'), many sailed by the tough Buginese people from Sulawesi, walk to the prahu harbor, just west of T. Perak. For shopping and bookstores, take an evening walk down Jl. Tunjungan, close to the center of the city.

The **Surabaya Zoo** (Kebun Binatang)—on Jl. Raya Darmo, just north of the Joyoboyo Bus Terminal—is one of the best in Indonesia; look for the Komodo dragons and the superb aviary. The museum north of the zoo on the same street is also worth a visit. Sometimes in the late afternoon men practice kuda kepang in the mall in front of the museum (kuda kepang is a type of trance dance performed by men riding plaited bamboo horses).

The **THR** (tay-hah-air), on the east side of town, due north of Gubeng Train Station, is Surabaya's amusement center after dark. The center contains shops selling everything from toothpaste to sarongs; it also has small restaurants, carnival rides, theaters for wayang orang and other kinds of performances, and an amphitheater for concerts of dangdut music (a musical style popular with Indonesian young people, blending Indian and Malay rhythms). On side streets near the THR vendors sell great snacks. Don't miss the terang bulan ('full moon')—pancakes with chocolate and peanuts in the center (ask for hot ones, 'minta yang masih panas').

Eating in Surabaya: local specialties include soto Madura (Madura soup), bakwan campur (soup w/pork balls and wonton), and ayam goreng (fried chicken). Several inexpensive places are clustered around the intersection of Jl. Pemuda and Jl. Panglima Sudirman (check out the ice cream parlor on Jl. Yos Sudarso). Cafeteria Michiko, Jl. Panglima Sudirman 10, features 'turkey' (i.e., Turkish) yoghurt, Rp250 for a large bowl w/fresh fruit. For especially good es jus, go to Ice Juice Purnama Ria: from the intersection next to the Bamboe Denn, take a bus south on Jl. Panglima Sudirman, get off at the Olympic Hotel, and turn left onto Jl. Pandegiling. Walk through the pasar, turn right and cross the river, then left; it's next to the Purnama Theatre. Es jus Rp200-275, bakwan campur Rp450, nasi goreng Rp500. Or try the ayam goreng stalls on the same street.

A dance festival is held on the nights of the weekends bracketing the full moon every month during the dry season (May-Oct.) at **Candra Wilwatikta**. This large, open-air theater sits at the foot of Mt. Penanggungan in the resort town of Pandaan, an hour south of Surabaya. Ask for details at the tourist office. To get there, take a colt from Joyoboyo Station to Pandaan (Rp300); it's another short hop (Rp100) to Candra Wilwatikta.

Madura is a large, rugged island off the coast near Surabaya; the Madurese are known far and wide for their aggressiveness and tenacity. From June to August visitors flock to the island to see the colorful kerapan sapi (bull races); these contests, in which bulls sprint with sled and driver, are held first between villages, then districts and regencies, climaxing in a grand championship in Pamekasan, the island's capital. For locals the races are not just entertainment: since Madura's dry, rocky soil doesn't lend itself to agriculture, stud bull breeding plays a major role in the island's economy. Bulls must meet certain standards to enter the races, and big money prizes go to the winners. For visitors who miss the contests, races are staged in a stadium in Bangkalan throughout the year (ask for details at the tourist information office in Surabaya). In Arosbaya, a fishing village north of Bangkalan, visit Aermata, where the royalty of the Cakraningrat and Cakraadiningrat Kingdoms are buried; great scenery, but watch out for the groups of rambunctious kids.

Head for **Malang**, in the mountains 90 km south of Surabaya, when the coastal heat gets to you. This city is famous for its apples (all the leaves are picked by hand from the apple trees to simulate winter), tobacco (Bentoel clove cigarettes are manufactured here), and cool climate. The Tourist Development Board, Jl. Jend. Basuki Rakmat 72074 (YMCA Bldg.) sells good maps of the city and surrounding area; get around town on foot or by bemo (Rp75). A pleasant place to browse for a few hours: Pasar Besar, the central market a few blocks southeast of the main square. Good food at moderate prices can be found at Cafeteria Aneka Rasa, next to the famous Toko Oen Restaurant and ice cream shop (an anachonism left over from colonial days), just off the square.

Candi Singosari, 12 km north of Malang in the village of Singosari, is a partially restored Shivaite-Buddhist temple dating from the 13th century. Though smaller than Prambanan, the temple has a similar lay-out: four chambers facing the cardinal directions in which different manifestations of the god

Shiva were once enshrined (only one statue is left now; the rest were stolen or sent to museums long ago). The decoration of Candi Singosari was never completed, so it's interesting to compare the detailed carving on the upper part of the temple with the unfinished, roughly formed 'kala' heads (representing celestial deities) below. About 200 m. beyond the temple look for two massive stone guardians, one partly buried, where a gate may once have stood. A short walk past the guardians is Candi Kendedes, a swimming pool filled with cold spring water (Rp100 to swim).

Candi Jago, 18 km east of Malang, and nearby **Candi Kidal** are memorials to Singosari kings. Episodes from the Mahabharata are beautifully carved on Candi Jago's side panels; climb the steps to the top for a superb view of the surrounding village. Candi Kidal, though tiny, is said to be one of the most perfect examples of Singosari temple art.

Probably the most imposing of East Java's monuments is **Candi Panataran**, 80 km southwest of Malang near the town of Blitar. Work on Panataran, the state temple of the Majapahit Empire, went on continuously from late in the 12th century until well into the 15th. Notice the different ornamentation on the three terraces that make up the substructure of what was once the main sanctuary. On the first terrace scenes from the Ramayana are carved in wayang style (characterized by a flat, almost two-dimensional treatment of human figures). The reliefs, according to Claire Holt, are "permeated with supernaturalism"; if you look closely you can find "shapes of animals or spooky beings camouflaged in intricate motifs, so that the atmosphere seems charged with a life of its own." On the second terrace, in a much more naturalistic style, are scenes from the Krishnayana—the adventures of Krishna as he abducts the princess Rukmini just before she is betrothed to another suitor. Caryatids (a sort of winged monster) gaze out from the third terrace.

On the road to Panataran, a short distance from Blitar, is the grave of former President Sukarno, who died in 1970. After being out of governmental favor for over a decade, Sukarno was reinstated as a national hero in 1978, and a lavish US $864,000 monument built over his grave was opened to the public in 1979 (over the protests of Sukarno's family, who wanted him buried in a simple grave under a leafy tree in the hills of West Java, as Sukarno had wished). The monument (Makam Bung Karno) attracts thousands of Indonesian visitors every weekend.

Trowulan, 60 km southwest of Surabaya near Mojokerto, was once a major trade center and the capital city of the Majapahit Empire. On display at the small Trowulan Museum are terra cotta figurines, jars, and household objects, the fragments of which were found in the surrounding area and carefully reassembled (admission: Rp25). A map in front of the museum will show you how to get to the numerous small temples in the area; hire a becak to take you around (2-3 hrs. if you see all the major temples). These include Siti Inggil, a recently renovated temple where people still come to meditate (three days without food, water, or sleep); Candi Bajang Ratu, the ancient gateway of which is said to be cursed—if you walk through it you will never marry; and Candi Tikus (Mouse Temple), so called because it was found when farmers were trying to get rid of some fieldmice. You can rest for a while out of the hot sun at the Pendopo Agung, midway between the museum and Candi Bajang Ratu. This pendopo (an open-air pillared pavilion traditionally found in front of the residences of Javanese nobility) is not a restoration; it was built quite recently by the Indonesian army.

Gunung Bromo, an active volcano south of Surabaya, deserves a visit because the scenery is so stunning, especially at sunrise. The crater, which can be filled with fog in the early morning, looks like a scene from "Star Wars," and has an unearthly, end-of-the-world bearing to it; lately Gunung Bromo has been exhaling frequent clouds of smoke and ash. Start hiking at 3:30 am from the village of Ngadisari (spend the night there) to the outer rim of the crater, cross the Sand Sea, then climb the stone steps to the rim of the active cone, one of the three peaks within the larger crater. You can also hire horses, w/guide, for Rp2000-3000 to the rim and back (6 km one-way). Dress warmly—it's **very** cold (can get down to 10-15°C, or 50-59°F, at night). If you're a slow hiker, start earlier—the sunrise is at 5:30.

The **Tengger** people, whose religion is similar to Balinese Hinduism, live in the mountains around Mt. Bromo. Their ancestors fled to the highlands centuries ago when Islam spread through Java after the fall of Majapahit. The Tengger vegetable gardens, terraced up almost vertical slopes, are a spectacular sight. Once a year, in February, the Tengger trek by torchlight to the top of Mt. Bromo for a ceremony called Kesodo; after various rituals and prayers, offerings of rice, fruit, vegetables, and flowers are thrown into the crater for the god who dwells in the volcano.

At **Pasir Putih** ('White Sand'), a beach about 75 km east of Surabaya on the road to Bali, you can swim, sunbathe, or bargain for a prahu to go out and look at the coral gardens. Go mid-week if you want the beach to yourself; on weekends it will be full of Surabayans. Medium-priced accommodations available.

The **Baluran Game Preserve**, 37 km north of Banyuwangi, is home to large numbers of deer, buffalo, boars, peacocks, monkeys, and other wildlife. It doesn't look like the rest of Java at all: dry, rocky grasslands and forest. Check in with the guards at the main gate, just off the highway at Wonorejo. You can leave bags locked up there. Then walk in 12 km (2½-3 hr.) to the penginapan (guest house) at Mt. Bekol; someone from the preserve will probably accompany you. Best to hike it early in the day. Jeeps can be rented at the gate for Rp4000; the guards may quote an inflated price. The entrance fee, paid at Mt. Bekol, is Rp500. Bring your own food and a flashlight for watching the animals at night. Camping is allowed, but tell the guides where you'll be. There's a watchtower on top of Mt. Bekol; most animals are seen at dawn or dusk. Best to visit during the dry season, June-November, when they have to come to the water holes. A guide will also take you to the beach, 2½ km away, where there's another guest house and monkeys often search for crabs. Swimming is good at high tide; at low tide local people gather shells. Because Baluran has recently been made a national forest, improvements in the road and accommodations are expected in the next two years.

ACCOMMODATIONS IN EAST JAVA

Surabaya:

Bamboe Denn, Jl. Pemuda 19/21. Dorm beds Rp500, doubles Rp1250-2000. A very popular stop, clean, and you can't beat the price. A 10-min. walk west of Gubeng Train Station. (From Joyoboyo Terminal, take a city bus, Rp30, get off at Bank Bumi Daya on Jl. Basuki Rachmat and walk east on Jl. Pemuda).

Hotel Santoso, Jl. Embong Kenongo 40. Large, quiet rooms Rp1825/person; breakfast included. From Gubeng Station walk west down Jl. Pemuda a short distance, left on Jl. Kayun, then right on Jl. Embong Kenongo.

Wisma Ganesha, Jl. Sumatera 34A. Singles Rp3000, doubles Rp3800, triples Rp4800; for 4 people, Rp5800; includes breakfast. Expensive for what you get. It's a 3-min. walk from Gubeng—just turn left as you come out of the station.

Losmen Sono Kembang, Jl. Sono Kembang 2, just off Jl. Sudirman. Rp1000/person plus 10% service charge. Centrally located, clean, has a courtyard w/garden. Travel service next door. Take a city bus from Joyoboyo and get off at Bioskop Bayu (Bayu Theater); the losmen is close by.

Malang:

Losmen Simpang tiga, Jl. Arief Margono (old name: Kasinkidul) 56. A litle noisy, but the rooms are quite clean and comfortable. Singles Rp1000-1500, doubles Rp2000, triples Rp3000. Located on the southwest edge of town, a Rp75 bemo ride from the town square.

Losmen Semarang, Jl. Achmad Dahlan 34. Singles Rp750, doubles Rp2000, triples Rp3000. Spacious rooms. Located on the bus route, near the town square. If this hotel is full, try Losmen Slamet, nearby.

INDONESIA 95

Mt. Bromo:

Stay in Ngadisari at a penginapan (private home which takes overnight guests) for about Rp1500 for two, Rp2500 for four. You must register with the Hansip (local police) there, and they can help you find a room. The new **Wisma Utji** guesthouse rents rooms for Rp7500 (four people). You could also stay at **Hotel Bromo Permai**, up on the crater's outer rim. Rooms are Rp1800-2400 for doubles, Rp4200 for 4. Or camp on the crater rim with a tent and warm sleeping bag.

Baluran:

The two guest houses (one at Mt. Bekol, one at the beach) cost Rp750/room. Rooms have twin beds and up to five people are allowed in a room.

Pasir Putih:

There are four or five hotels in a row along the highway. **Pasir Putih Inn**, at the west end, is most expensive (singles Rp3000, doubles Rp4000-6000, plus 10% service charge, w/breakfast) and **Sidho Muntjul**, at the east end, is the cheapest (Rp3300-4400, 1-3 persons). The beach has several restaurants and fruit stands.

TRANSPORTATION FOR EAST JAVA

Surabaya has three main train stations. Pasar Turi serves trains which run along Java's north coast, while Gubeng and Kota serve trains which travel south (e.g. Malang, Yogya) and east (e.g. Banyuwangi).

Surabaya's main bus station is Joyoboyo, on the city's southern edge. There are dozens of night bus companies, with offices scattered throughout the city. For comparison shopping, check the many companies on Jl. Basuki Rachmat, 36-72. Other offices: Kembang Express, Jl. Tidar 58; Bali Indah, Jl. Akhmaid Jais 102; Jawa Indah, Jl. Samudra.

From Tanjung Priok, Surabaya's harbor, ships set out for cities on almost every major island in Indonesia. For fares and departure dates, ask around in the shipping company offices in the harbor; you can also check with the Pelni office on Jl. Pahlawan, 50 m. south of the Surabaya Theater.

Surabaya: From Jakarta by train: Gaya Baru Malam Utara, Rp2250 (3rd class), 16 + hr., or Mutiara Utara, Rp9600 (1st class only), 15 hr. From Jakarta by night bus: Rp5500-6500 (w/ac), 15 hr. From Yogya by train: Ekspres Siang, Rp1750 (3rd class), 6+ hr.; Mutiara Selatan, Rp7000 (2nd class)/Rp4700 (3rd class), 6½ + hr. From Yogya by night bus: Rp2500. From Denpasar by night bus: Rp3250, 10 hr.

Madura: Buses go directly (via ferry) from Joyoboyo to various towns on Madura (e.g. Bangkalan, Pamekasan). Or, take a city bus to the ferry landing at the harbor (the bus signboard will read: W. Kromo-T. Perak). The ferry leaves every 10-15 min. until 10 pm (then the small Navy ferry runs all night); it will dock in Kamal. From Kamal you can catch colts or oplets to other towns.

Malang: Buses leave from Joyoboyo all the time (Rp350, 2 hr.). Tumapel trains leave at least 5 times a day (Rp350, 2 hr.). Colts also connect the two cities, but they're recommended only for those who like to live dangerously.

[Onward from Malang: Pemudi Express night bus company, on Jl. Sutan Syahrir, offers service to Denpasar (Rp3400, 10 hr.), Semarang (Rp2600, 9 hr.), Yogya (Rp2600, 9 hr.). Or try the Agung Ekspres and Anugerah bus companies at Jl. Gereja 1-3. All three offices are near the town square. Jawa Indah, on Jl. Kauman Merdeka, offers buses to

96 INDONESIA

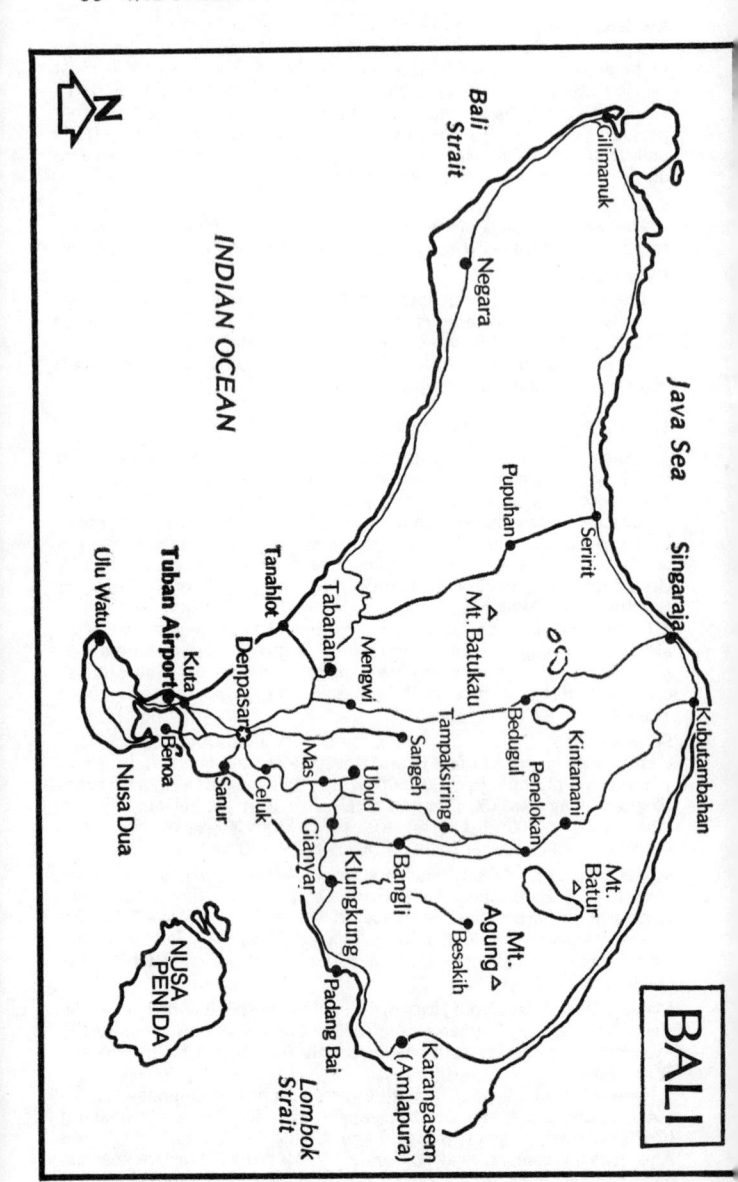

Jakarta (Rp7200, 18 hr.) and Bandung (Rp5500, 15½ hr.).]

Candi Singosari: Take a bemo from Malang to Blimbing (Rp75), then another bemo to Singosari (about Rp75). At the intersection near where the bemo stops turn west down Jl. Kartanegara; the temple is about 500 m. down the road on the right.

Candi Jago/Candi Kidal: Take a bemo from Malang to Blimbing (Rp75), then a colt to Tumpang (about Rp250). Candi Jago is in Tumpang; Candi Kidal is about 4 km southwest of town (take a dokar or walk).

Candi Panataran/Blitar: Get to Blitar from Surabaya by train (Rp525, 4 hr.) or by bus (Rp700, 4½ hr., change in Malang), or from Malang bu bus (Rp350). From Blitar take a bemo or colt to Nglegok (Rp200 by colt). The temple is 2 km further northeast along the main road. It's probably simplest to walk; dokars are also a possibility. Colts will go from Blitar to Panataran (Rp400) but don't make the return trip very regularly.

Trowulan: Take a bus from Joyoboyo heading for Jombang and ask to get off at the Trowulan Museum (the bus passes right in front of it), Rp300. To get back to Surabaya just flag down a returning bus.

Mt. Bromo: Take a bus from Joyoboyo to Probolinggo (Rp375, 2½ + hr.), then change to a colt for Ngadisari (Rp500). Colts run till late afternoon or early evening.

Pasir Putih: Take a bus from Joyoboyo (Rp700, 4 hr.). To go on to Bali: flag down a bus en route to Banyuwangi. Ask people at your hotel about times when the bus passes by. To Ketapang (ferry landing for Bali): Rp600, 2½ hr.

Baluran Game Reserve: Take a bus from Joyoboyo going to Banyuwangi and get off at Wonorejo (Rp1100, 6 hr.). If you're coming from Bali, it's a Rp150-200 colt ride from Ketapang, where the ferry stops, to Wonorejo.

Bali

To the Balinese, heaven is just like Bali. The crew of a 16th century vessel apparently shared this view; they immediately jumped ship in Bali and could not be convinced to leave for nearly two years.

The mountainous island of Bali is marked by steep-sided ravines where rivers have cut deep into the soft volcanic rock. In river valleys and on hillsides, ricefields have been exquisitely sculpted out of the fertile earth, making a patchwork of vivid green or soft gold. When the fields are flooded they look like glimmering mirrors of the sky. Along with rice, other crops grown in the south are tea, tropical fruit, nuts and cocoa. The northern landscape changes from terraced ricefields to flat fields of cabbages, onions, and clove tree forests. In the central highlands mountain lakes are surrounded by dense tropical forests of pine trees, moss, ferns, and wildflowers.

98 INDONESIA

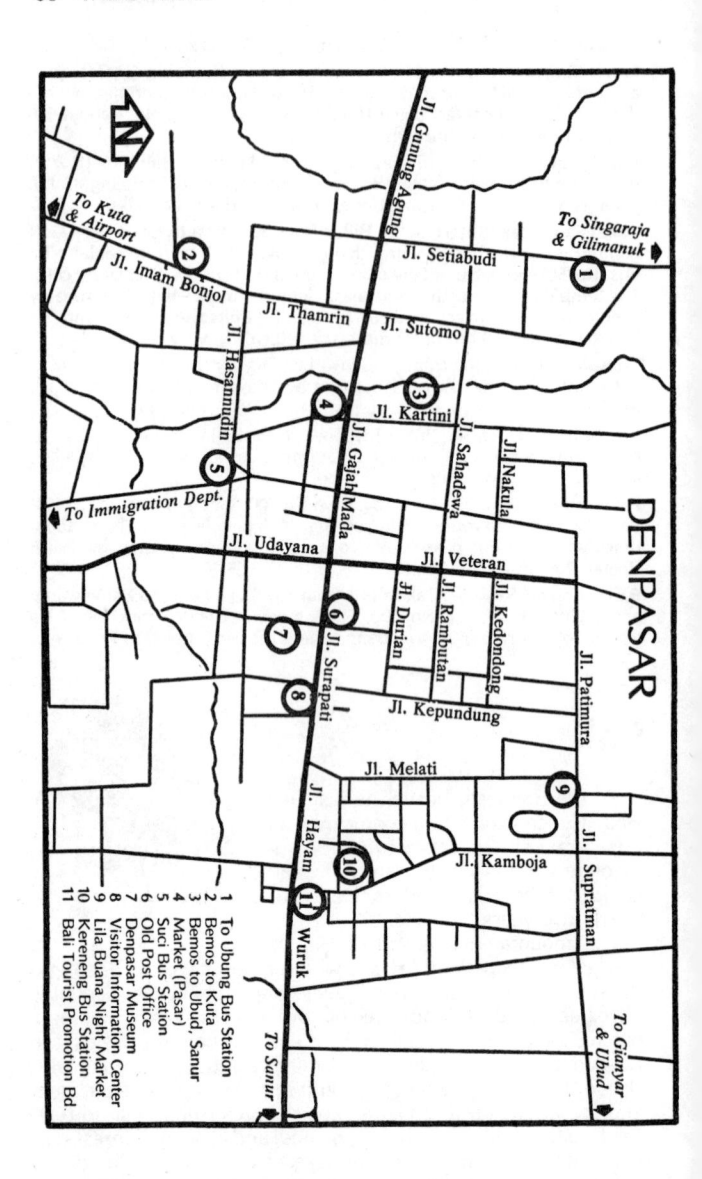

DENPASAR

1. To Ubung Bus Station
2. Bemos to Kuta
3. Bemos to Ubud, Sanur
4. Market (Pasar)
5. Suci Bus Station
6. Old Post Office
7. Denpasar Museum
8. Visitor Information Center
9. Lila Buana Night Market
10. Kereneng Bus Station
11. Bali Tourist Promotion Bd.

There are small temples everywhere, in the verdant forests and even in the most arid scrub land. Worship and giving offerings are daily activities for the Balinese who find no day complete without praising God in some way or placating other deities.

The secret to Bali's appeal lies in "the rare harmony between Bali's lush tropical nature and equally lush art," says Claire Holt in **Art in Indonesia**. The vitality expressed in festivals carries over into the plastic arts of sculpture, painting, and temple ornamentation. The Balinese sculpt from wood, stone, or horn and take their themes from nature. Dances and music are dynamic in their fast-paced movements and electrifying rhythms. Almost everyone can create something since artistic expression has never been confined to an intellectual class.

The Indonesian government is aware of Bali's appeal and has been promoting and developing the island for the tourist trade. The Nusa Dua resort on the island's southernmost peninsula, currently under construction, will help accommodate an estimated 1 million tourists a year by 1984.

Bali began absorbing cultural influences from Java before the 14th century. One of these was the caste system which Bali observes today in a less strict manner than India. The bulk of the population are Sudras, or non-aristocratic Balinese. The other three castes are Brahmanas (priests), Satrias (princes) and Wesias (merchants).

In the 16th century, during the decline of the great Hindu-Javanese Majapahit Dynasty, Bali became the refuge for Javanese nobility, priests, scholars, and artists who were fleeing Moslem invaders. This Hindu-Javanese culture and religion was superimposed on Balinese animism to create the artistic, Hindu-Balinese culture which flourishes today.

Balinese religion is monotheistic. The supreme deity, Ida Sanghyang Widi Wasa, manifests itself in three main forms: Brahma the creator, Wisnu the preserver, and Shiva the destroyer. The Balinese also believe that a host of other deities and spirits inhabit their island. At the core of Balinese religion is the belief in the eternal struggle between good and evil. In the interest of maintaining harmony between two powerful forces, Balinese religion requires that much time be devoted to performing rituals, ceremonies, and making offerings. Bali is alive with exuberant festivals of exorcism, purification, or celebration. Each family and village temple has a birthday celebration; entire villages may march to the sea for ritual cleansing accompanied by a traveling gamelan orchestra. There are festivals dedicated to learning, percussion instruments, metal objects, and the return of anecestral spirits. Each major festival is accompanied by sumptuous offerings of fruit and flowers and by dance-dramas and gamelan music. Equally common are dances and activities of a purely secular nature such as the Joged dance, kite-flying, or cockfighting.

100 INDONESIA

To view a ceremony, first be sure you are welcome. Sometimes a fee will be required and visitors should follow the Balinese custom of wearing a sash around the waist when entering temple grounds (often available on loan near the temple entrance for a small fee). Note that women are not allowed inside temples during their menstrual periods.

Balinese and Javanese dance have many stylistic similarities, but Javanese dance is more restrained, while Balinese dance is much more 'charged.' Performances of the dances described below are frequently given in and around Denpasar, Sanur, Kuta, and Ubud.

- **Barong**—a ritual enactment of the conflict between 'black' destructive power and 'white magic.' Rangda, the queen of evil spirits with her lolling tongue and pendulous breasts, battles Barong, a marvelous mythical beast in the role of protector of humanity. Kris (dagger) dancers rush to aid Barong when he is threatened. They wave their krises at Rangda but she turns their fury against them, and in a trance state they try to plunge their krises into their own chests. Barong makes them invulnerable so the krises have no effect; a priest then brings the dancers out of the trance.
- **Legong**—a delicate and very difficult courting dance performed by a pair of young girls (with a prelude by a female attendant). The classical dance par excellence of Balinese girls.
- **Kecak**—the 'monkey dance,' a creation of the 1930s. Usually performed at night, in the flickering light of an oil lamp; 100-150 men, seated on the ground in concentric circles, chant 'cak, cak, cak' contrapunctually and weave their arms and bodies in unison. In the middle of the circle dancers re-enact a small segment of the Ramayana, usually the abduction of Sita by the wicked Rawana.
- **Pendet**—the presentation of an offering in dance form; very short.
- **Baris**—a traditional war dance.
- **Oleg Tambulilingan**—the dance of the flirting bumblebees; a recently created dance.
- **Kebyar**—a male solo dance, executed entirely in a sitting position. A relatively new dance.
- **Wayang Topeng**—masked dance-plays, based on stories about the Javanese Prince Panji.

Stodgy government buildings and a touristy main street, Jl. Gajah Mada, shape most travelers' first impressions of **Denpasar**, which is the capital both of Bali and of Badung regency. But away from downtown Denpasar's residential areas are still divided into traditional neighborhoods (banjar), each with its own meeting hall. For maps and information on ceremonies and dances, stop by the Badung Tourist Office, 2 Jl. Surapati (east of downtown, Jl. Gajah Mada becomes Jl. Surapati); open 7:30-

INDONESIA 101

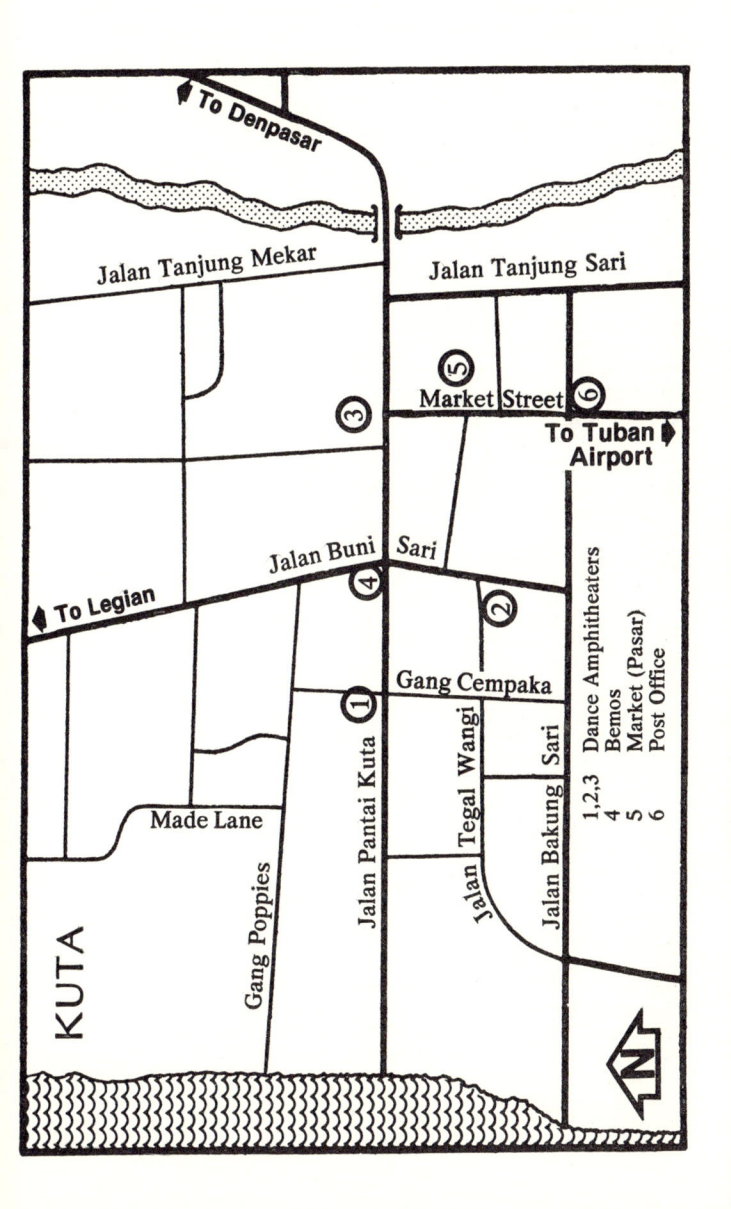

102 INDONESIA

1:30 Monday through Thursday, 7:30-11:30 Friday, and 7:30-12:30 Saturday. The Bali Museum, open every morning but Monday, is nearby, on the town square. Also on the square is the old post office, where in summer 1980 you could still buy stamps. The new central post office is very inconveniently located in the middle of the rice paddies 2 km southeast of town, in an area called Renon. There's also a branch post office on Jl. Diponegoro, on the bemo route. The Immigration Office is near the end of the bemo line in Sanglah, on the south edge of town; dress neatly to minimize hassles. Bemos provide in-town transportation (there are no becaks in Bali). The basic routes are circular and the fare is Rp50. Eating in Denpasar: the Chinese restaurants on Jl. Gajah Mada are good if not quite cheap, and outdoor food stalls appear nightly in the downtown area. The Lila Buana night market, at the corner of Jl. Supratman and Jl. Melati, has tasty martabak and coconut pastries.

Word of the attractions of **Kuta Beach**, 9 km south of Denpasar, spread long ago on the travelers' grapevine; today it's spilling over with restaurants, losmen, tie-dye T-shirt shops, and unmuffered motorcycles. But the beach is still one of Bali's best and the sunsets are spectacular. Bicycles (Rp400/day), motorcycles (Rp4000/day), and surfboards are widely available for rent. You can see dance performances almost every night at one or another of several locations (see map of Kuta); tickets are Rp900. The variety of food available defies description (but be aware that mushroom omelets may alter your consciousness for a while). Note: swimming and nude sunbathing at Kuta are risky—the former due to a treacherous undertow and strong currents, the latter due to periodic government crackdowns. The local police also frown strongly on conspicuous drug use/dealing. **Legian**, 2 km north of Kuta (Rp50 by bemo), gives you an idea of what Kuta was like about six years ago: less rowdy, the foreigners not quite outnumbering the locals. Legian also has nightly dance performances.

Luxury hotels and bungalows lie patio to swimming pool along Bali's other famous beach, **Sanur**, 7 km. east of Denpasar. The surf is much more tame here. Visit on the night of the full moon when lots of Balinese, especially young couples, walk or ride bikes out to the beach.

Balinese art and craftwork are internationally famous, though many feel that standards have fallen drastically to match tourists' tastes. You can watch artisans at work in the many craft villages, each with its own specialties, clustered 10-20 km northeast of Denpasar on the roads to Gianyar and Ubud. **Batubulan** is the center of stone carving, **Celuk** is known for its gold and silver jewelry, **Batuan** villagers weave, paint and carve, and **Mas** produces the island's best woodcarvings.

Ubud, 25 km north of Denpasar, is the center of Balinese painting and a popular tourist stop, though a much more relaxed one than Denpasar or Kuta. Two basic artistic styles are evident: the more traditional paintings use softer, muted colors and usually depict characters from Hindu epics, while paintings in the more 'modern' style feature brightly-colored scenes of rice farming and village life. Much of the work displayed on the roadsides is that of young artists. Visit Ubud's museum, Puri Lukisan (open 8-5), to get a better idea of the variety of painting styles and subjects.

In the village of **Tampaksiring**, near the center of the island, is Pura Tirta Empul, a temple built around a holy spring. The spring water is said to have curative powers and is used in purification rituals. Nearby, along the Pakerisan River, there are nine rock-hewn candi, dating back many centuries. In Tampaksiring you can also see the presidential palace where Sukarno stayed during his frequent trips to the island.

When the weather's clear you can get a spectacular view of the smoking cones and huge lake inside Gunung Batur's vast volcanic crater from the villages of **Penelokan** and **Kintamani**, perched near each other on the crater's rim. Lake Batur is close enough for a morning hike (or take the bemo from Penelokan, Rp100 going down, sometimes more going up). The hike up Batur's main cone is highly recommended (the trail is well marked); get an early start. You can also go by boat to **Trunyan**, a village on the far side of the lake with customs akin to those of pre-Hindu Bali, but we suggest that you pass it up because in recent years it's become an expensive tourist trap. (Note: the people in the Penelokan area are the pushiest and roughest in Bali, notorious for harassing and even threatening visitors. Avoid dealing with them as much as possible. If you come by motorcycle, don't leave it at the lake, because parts may be missing when you get back.)

Besakih, 60 km northeast of Denpasar, is Bali's 'Mother Temple'; it sits on the slopes of Gunung Agung, the highest volcano on the island and the center of Balinese cosmology. During Galungan, the greatest of Balinese festivals, Besakih becomes a hive of activity. The 10-day long festival occurs once every 210 days (in 1981 it falls in August).

The port town of **Padang Bai**, 56 km east of Denpasar, is the jumping-off point for trips to Lombok and Nusa Tenggara (the chain of islands to the east).

Sangeh, 21 km north of Denpasar, is a small forest of pala trees—a species not native to Bali and found nowhere else on the island. The forest is considered holy, as are the hordes of

104 INDONESIA

mischievous monkeys who live in it. They hang around Sangeh's two temples and wait (some less patiently than others) for visitors to feed them peanuts.

The temple at **Tanah Lot**, 31 km northwest of Denpasar, was built several hundred years ago on a tiny rocky island which becomes a peninsula at low tide. Sea snakes live in large nearby caves. (In summer 1980 this temple was hard to get to because the road between Kediri and Tanah Lot was in bad shape.)

Singaraja, 78 km from Denpasar on Bali's north coast, served for a while as an administrative center under the Dutch. The culture of this area is quite distinct from that of south Bali—more subdued, more relaxed. There are several beautiful beaches nearby, especially along the coast to the west, where small losmen have been proliferating for the last few years.

ACCOMMODATIONS IN BALI

Denpasar:

Puri Oka, Jl. Kaliasem I/4. Single Rp750, double Rp1500. Small but comfortable; food available. From the square in the middle of town walk 150 m. down Jl. Kaliasem, then turn down the narrow alley on the right when you see the losmen's tiny sign.

Hotel Adi Yasa, Jl. Nakula 11. Doubles w/shared bath Rp1500 (Rp1000 single occupancy), doubles w/private bath Rp2000. Once a famous/cheap stopover on the traveler's trail, now much more subdued in atmosphere.

Two Brothers Inn, Jl. Banjar Tegal. Single Rp750, double Rp1500. Clean and quiet; breakfast available. A 2-min. walk from Jl. Imam Bonjol (the road to Kuta).

Kuta/Legian:

Inexpensive losmen are impossible to miss, since there are over 100 of them. Most rooms are in the Rp1000-1500 range. Shop around in order to compare amenities (e.g. bananas and tea, black rice pudding, etc.). Legian is a little less rowdy than Kuta.

Peliatan/Ubud:

Lots of pleasant homestays in Ubud and nearby Peliatan, Rp1000-1500. Many have semi-permanent residents—dance students, etc. Poke around some of the side roads; you'll have no trouble finding a place.

Puri Agung Peliatan Homestay, off the main road in Peliatan. Rp1000-1500/person, depending on the room. The proprietress is a former dancer who once traveled to the U.S. with the Peliatan dance troupe.

Mandala Homestay, down the road roughly opposite Puri Agung. Single Rp1000, double Rp1500. Lovely setting.

Chandry's, in the middle of Ubud. Single Rp600-750, double Rp1200-1500. A popular gathering place.

Losmen Mustika, on the right side of the road as you come into Ubud. Doubles only, Rp1000.

Hotel Menara, on Ubud's main road, opposite the Puri Lukisan Museum. Doubles only, Rp2500/3000/3500, all with private bath. By 1981 a new addition will be completed with even more plush accommodations. (Lovely view of rice paddies out back.)

INDONESIA 105

Kintamani/Penelokan:

There are inexpensive accommodations in both villages. Penelokan is closer to Lake Batur and offers a more spectacular view, but the people in this area are incredibly obnoxious. We recommend staying in Kintamani, only a 10-min./Rp75 bemo ride further along the crater rim, for the much more peaceful atmosphere. Be sure to bring warm clothes—it's bitter cold at night. (Note: Room prices can sometimes be negotiated if business is slow.) All the places listed below serve food.

Hotel exLosmen Puri Astina, a 5-min. walk past the market/bemo stop in Kintamani. Doubles only, Rp1500. Has a fireplace.

Losmen Kencana, next door to Hotel Puri Astina. Single Rp1500, double Rp3000. Has a fireplace.

Losmen Lingga Giri, a 1-min. walk past the market in Kintamani. Single Rp750, double Rp1000-1500, depending on the season. Rooms are plain but the food is good; very friendly management. Also has a fireplace.

Losmen Supermen, lower end of Kintamani. Single Rp750-1000, double Rp1000-1500, depending on season. All rooms w/private bath. No fireplace, but nice view from the glassed-in 'dining room.'

Lakeview Homestay, on the right side of the road in Penelokan, just as you come around the corner and catch your first breath-taking view. Double Rp1000 and Rp1500, w/private bath Rp2500. Rooms w/5 beds and attached bath, Rp5000.

Losmen Gunawan, ¼ km past Lakeview Homestay, also w/a fantastic view. Doubles only, Rp1500.

Singaraja:

Singaraja has lots of hotels, but there's no need to stay in town. Head west instead, to Lovina Beach and other places along the coast where cheap, congenial inns have been profilerating for the last several years. Most of these places are small—some with only 5 or 6 rooms—and offer a 'family' atmosphere as well as snorkeling equipment, dugout canoes (jukung), and food/drinks. To get to them take a bemo (Rp50-100) from the Banyuasri bus station going towards the town of Seririt and watch for the signs along the road. (Note: these places are havens of tranquility compared to the chaos of Kuta; with some care by both travelers and inn-keepers, maybe they can stay that way.)

Krisna Beach Inn, 13 km west of Singaraja. 'Chalet' rooms, Rp1000-1200; 'bungalow' rooms, Rp1500-2000; 'cottage' rooms, Rp2000.

Tasik Madu, Lovina Beach (11 km west of Singaraja). '3rd class' doubles, Rp2000, and singles, Rp1000; '2nd class' doubles, Rp4000; '1st class' doubles, Rp8000. Breakfast included.

Manggala, next to Tasik Madu. Singes Rp600-800, doubles Rp1200-1500; bungalows (2 beds) w/private bath Rp3000.

Ayodya Accommodation, Kalibukbuk (10 km west of Singaraja). Singles Rp1000, doubles Rp1200-1500.

Lila Cita Beach Homestay, Anturan (7 km west of Singaraja). Doubles Rp1500, w/private bath Rp3000. Brand new.

Simon's Seaside Cottages, Anturan (6 km west of Singaraja). Doubles only: losmen-style Rp1500, nice pavilions Rp3000. Simon provides useful information sheets on Singaraja and north Bali.

Agung Homestay, next to Simon's. Singles Rp1000; doubles Rp1500; one dorm-style bungalow, about Rp500/person, depending on how many people share it.

TRANSPORTATION FOR BALI:

Denpasar has two main bus/colt stations: Ubung, on the northwest edge of town, and Kereneng, on the east side of town between Jl. Melati and Jl. Kamboja. Ubung serves destinations to the west and north; most night buses from Surabaya will let you off here. It's a Rp50 bemo ride to the middle of town. (To get to Ubung Station from downtown catch a bemo on Jl. Kartini.) Kereneng, which serves destinations to the northeast, is on a main in-town bemo route. There are at least a dozen night bus company offices in Denpasar, most of them clustered near the small Suci Bus Station at the intersection of Jl. Diponegoro and Jl. Hasanuddin. A few companies, like Gita Bali, offer pick-up service from Kuta.

Note: with a few exceptions, public transportation is non-existent in Bali after nightfall. Plan ahead and avoid getting stranded.

Denpasar: From Surabaya by train & bus combination: the Mutiara Malam Timur leaves in the late evening from Kota (and Gubeng) Station, Rp2400 (3rd class), 10+ hr. (ticket fare includes ferry and bus connections from Banyuwangi). The Mutiara Siang Timur, a slightly cheaper train, leaves in the late morning. Fares for the night bus trip from Surabaya range from Rp3000 to Rp3500 for the 10+ hr. trip. From Yogya a night bus costs Rp4500-5000.

Kuta: Take a bemo from Jl. Imam Bonjol, at the southwest corner of Denpasar (Rp100, 15 min.). Sometimes you can also catch a bemo off Jl. Gajah Mada. Transportation is scarce after 8:30 pm.

Tuban Airport: Tuban is near Kuta, and southwest of Denpasar. By bemo to Kuta, Rp75; by bemo to Denpasar, Rp175.

Sanur: Take a bemo from Kereneng Station or catch a Sanur-bound bemo on its loop through town (Rp100, 15 min.).

Kintamani/Penelokan: Take a bus (Rp175) or a colt (Rp300) from Denpasar to 'Pertigaan Bangli,' a three-way intersection between Gianyar and Klungkung. From there take a bemo to Penelokan or Kintamani, Rp300.

Ubud: Take a bemo from Kereneng, Rp150.

Other destinations to the northeast: Take a bus or colt from Kereneng.

Tanah Lot: Take a bus or colt from Ubung to Kediri, then change to a bemo to Tanah Lot. In summer 1980 the road from Tabanan was in very bad condition, so leave early to allow plenty of time.

Sangeh: Take a bemo from Jl. Kartini in downtown Denpasar, Rp200.

Singaraja: Take a colt (no buses go) from Ubung (Rp600, 2 hr.).

Singaraja has two main bus/bemo stations: Banyuasri on the west side and Kampung Tinggi on the east side. The former serves destinations to the west, including Seririt and Gilimanuk, and Denpasar to the south; the latter serves destinations to the east, including Amlapura (Karangasem) and Kintamani. You can take night buses to Surabaya from Singaraja as well as from Denpasar. Singaraja-Gilimanuk: 1½-2 hr., Rp600.

Other destinations to the northwest: Take a bus or colt from Ubung.

Sulawesi and the Moluccas

Sulawesi, the seventh largest island in the world, lies between massive Kalimantan and the smaller Molucca Islands to the east (once known as the Spice Islands). the island has an incredible topographic variety, ranging from low-lying savannah and deep inland jungle to some of the most awe-inspiring mountain scenery in Indonesia. The island's people are equally diverse—nearly 50 languages are spoken and customs vary greatly.

Sulawesi Selatan (South Sulawesi) is dominated by three main ethnic groups: the Bugis, the Makassarese and the Torajas. The first two groups populate the more level southern region, while the Torajas inhabit the mountainous region to the north.

Formerly Makassar, **Ujung Pandang** was a Portuguese stronghold in the early days of colonization and later came under the control of the Dutch. In spite of foreign control, the Bugis and the Makassarese continued a smuggling trade with competitors of the Dutch, who were trying to monopolize all trading in the area. Port Makassar is the main harbor for the famous Bugis prahus, the extremely sturdy cargo vessels that sail throughout Indonesian waters carrying everything from copra to cattle.

The tourist information office (Kantor Pariwisata Sulawesi Selatan) is in the huge, new governor's office at Jl. Yani 2, just off Jl. Sulawesi. The Immigration Office (Kantor Imigrasi) can be found at Jl. Seram 8-12. Get around town by becak (Rp100-200).

Benteng Makassar, an old fort on the waterfront, is worth a visit; inside there is a museum. Across the street from the fort you can catch one of the boats leaving hourly for Pulau Kayangan (Kayangan Island), not the most attractive place to swim but there's lots going on there in the evenings. A kilometer down the road is a fish market, an interesting place to wander at dawn and in the early afternoon when the fish are brought in. At Samalona Island, 40 min. away, swim and snorkle among the coral gardens; to get there take a prahu from the fish market (early in the morning before the sea gets rough).

Good places to eat in Ujung Pandang: Rumah Makan Malabar, Jl. Sulawesi 216 (near Hotel Nusantara) serves good Chinese food; Empang, Jl. Riau, has delicious seafood.

108 INDONESIA

Malino, a small weekend resort town in the mountains 75 km east of Ujung Pandang, is a pleasant place to escape the heat. A large waterfall can be found a short hike (4 km) south of town. **Bantimurung**, 41 km northeast of Ujung Pandang, is famous for its waterfalls and amazing butterflies.

Tana Toraja, rapidly becoming a popular stop on the traveler's circuit, is located on a high mountain-bounded fertile plateau 10-12 jaw-rattling hours by bus from Ujung Pandang. **Rantepao**, the market town of the region, is a good base from which to go exploring. Most visitors go in August and September (good weather and many festivals).

To get around in Tana Toraja, be prepared to do some hiking. Public transport is scarce and the roads are few—the Torajas are walkers. The whole region is laced with beautiful, though often rugged paths.

On market day in Rantepao villagers flow into town carrying bundles of bamboo lengths filled with frothing tuak (palm wine), squealing hogs are tied up by their feet to sturdy bamboo poles, and woven baskets filled to the top with rice. The livestock section of the market is located on the northern edge of town down a side road. A kerbau (water buffalo) can be the most valuable thing a Toraja owns costing as much as a hectare of land or a car.

Fifty percent of the Torajas are Christians, at least according to the census-takers, but the traditional culture is still very strong. The local religion, Aluk Todolo, centers around the worship of Puang Matua (the Creator), Deatas (the caretaker of dieties), and the souls of ancestors. The Toraja bury their dead in caves or in wooden coffins suspended from cliff faces. Many gravesites are near Rantepao—the closest ones, **Londa** (6 km from Rantepao) and **Lemo** (12 km), near the road to Makale, are crowded in peak tourist season, but do give visitors a sense of Toraja culture. The caves at Londa are interesting to crawl through.

Walk north out of Rantepao along Pangli Road. After crossing the stone bridge on the northern side of town, turn left (west) on the road that leads across the valley floor to Tikala, and then climbs up to **Pana**, a burial site nestled in a bamboo forest. It could be as much as a 3½ hr climb to Pana; the path is easy to follow and generally is in good condition. Though it isn't too steep, it can be slippery and muddy in the rainy season. When you reach Pana, stop to see the graves—they are among the oldest in the valley. From Pana continue your climb another 20-30 minutes and you'll reach the unpaven road, it is 3 level kilometers to **Lo'Ko'Mata**, a large stone outcropping that has many graves carved into it. From there you can go on to **Pangala'**, a small market village, or you can return to Batutu-monga, a village just beyond the intersection (to the east) with the trail you came up on. The schoolmaster in Batutumonga speaks English and can give you a place to stay overnight. Alternatively, you can catch a colt back to Rantepao (Rp750). There are 2 or 3 colts running down the mountain in the afternoon, so you may have to wait awhile. You could possibly catch an early colt from Rantepao to Pangala' (Rp800, 7am). The views along this ridge are inspiring.

Ceremonies play a large part in the lives of the Torajas; the funeral feast held when members of noble families are buried is probably the most elaborate. A few hints about attending ceremonies: bring cigarettes, don't sit in front of anybody, try to find out who the host and village dignitaries are and shake their hands, and be discreet with your camera. The most interesting parts of the festivals (dancing, chanting, etc.) take place at night.

The two or three restaurants in Rantepao serve tasteless and expensive food. Eat in warungs (food stalls) instead. Simple Torajanese food is available at Warung Pada Kita in the market; it has good fried fish and the best coffee in town. Warung Roma, on Jl. Pasar across from the south side of the market, is also recommended. Tuak can be purchased in the west end of the market.

Sulawesi Utara (North Sulawesi) is the land of the Minahasas, the six tribes of Proto-Malays who migrated to the island in megalithic times. With a large Christian population and showing strong Dutch influence, **Manado**, the capital of Sulawesi Utara, presents a decided contrast in culture and life-style with other areas of Indonesia.

Manado now has an international airport receiving occasional flights from Manila and Zamboanga as well as regular domestic flights.

Most of the sights that would interest travelers lie outside the city. South of the city there are a series of sandy beaches and quiet sea coves—excellent snorkeling and scuba diving. Lake Tondano sits high on a mountain plateau; it's a cool retreat for Manado residents. The new port town of Blitung, overshadowed by volcanoes, is at the easternmost tip of the island, 45 km from Manado.

Manado has a tough immigration policy, in part because of its proximity to the Philippines. As soon as you arrive, you must report to the Kantor Imigrasi and perhaps to the police as well. Like Palu to the south, Manado is expensive. Look for penginapan rather than hotels.

The **Moluccas**, or Spice Islands, contain over 1000 islands. These were the prize of world commerce during the early days of European exploration and were fought over by the Spanish, Portuguese, British, and Dutch merchant armies. Cloves are

110 INDONESIA

still a valuable crop here, but foreign investors are now extracting timber, tin, and asbestos as well.

Ambon is the name of both the capital of the province and the tiny, hoof-shaped island the city sits on. Get around town by bus (Rp30) or becak (Rp100-150). Southwest of Ambon at Batu Capeo (5 km) are beautiful coral gardens and a rocky shoreline; further along the coast at Eri and Latihalat there are nice beaches. On the other side of the island visit Natsepa or cross the mountains towards Hitu and Hila to see the sites of old Portuguese forts.

ACCOMMODATIONS IN SULAWESI AND THE MOLUCCAS

Ujung Pandang:
Pleasant, inexpensive accommodations are hard to find in this town.

Ramayana Hotel, Jl. Bakawaraeng 121; tel. 22165. On the eastern edge of town town on the road to the airport. No singles, cheapest doubles Rp4000. Bemos, buses, and taxis pass in front of it regularly. Its location makes becak fare to anywhere in town at least Rp350, but it's clean, cool, and friendly.

Nusantara Hotel, Jl. Sarappo 103, near the port at the northern end of the downtown commercial area. Singles Rp1500; doubles Rp2750. The rooms are tiny but clean. The ride by becak from the bus/bemo station should cost Rp100-150; don't try to negotiate with the becak drivers at the station, however—walk at least a block away, then look for one.

Alaska Hotel, Jl. Sungai Saddang. Hot and dirty; not recommended.

Rantepao:
The cheapest (and quite comfortable) accommodations are provided by two losmen: **Flora** (near the Liman Station, across from the mosque) at Rp1000/person and **Wisma Pola** (near the Damri Station, facing the soccer field south of the market) at Rp3000/person.

Manado:
Hotels are expensive; try the few penginapan in town (Rp600-800).

Ambon:
The **Kampung Markida Hotel** is the most reasonable of the several hotels in town.

TRANSPORTATION FOR SULAWESI AND THE MOLUCCAS

Ujung Pandang: Pelni ships from Surabaya cost Rp10,728, deck class (2 days, 2 nights). Leaves every 2 weeks; buy tickets 3 days in advance. Expect a rough trip and bring your own food. Unless you're fairly hardy, a plane is the better bet. A flight from Surabaya costs Rp40,875 (Mandala Airlines). Take a bemo from the airport into town (16 km); if the drivers at the airport ask for an outrageously high fare, walk to the main road (½ km) and flag down one of the regularly passing bemos.

There is a new bus station on the edge of town where all incoming buses from the north must stop; take a bemo into town.

Malino: Mini-buses leave Ujung Pandang daily, usually in the morning. About Rp700 for the 75 km trip.

Tana Toraja: About Rp1500 by bus from Ujung Pandang; 10 + hr. There are several bus companies to choose from: Liman (located near the

INDONESIA 111

central bus station) has old buses but they're best at handling tourists; Fa. Litha (Jl. Gn. Merapi near the Alaska Hotel) has newer buses and is the company the Torajas prefer; Sabar (Jl. Veteran) is the fastest and fairly comfortable; Damri (Jl. Gn. Latimojong) is hopeless. Buy your ticket in advance; the good seats are gone the day before the bus leaves.

Ambon: Pelni boats leave Surabaya every 2 weeks; Rp18,838 deck class (5 days, 5 nights). There is also frequent plane service (Rp80,775 on Mandala from Surabaya).

Sumatra

Sumatra, the world's fifth largest island, makes up 25% of Indonesia's total land area and contains 17% of the country's population. Of the ten ethnic groups which live on the island, probably the best known are the Acehnese (in the far north), the Batak (in the Lake Toba area), and the Minangkabau (in the central area). Sumatra produces many income-generating natural resources—oil, tin, natural gas, rubber—and thus plays a significant role in the national and international economy. The Bukit Barisan (Parade of Mountains), which is like a spine that stretches almost the full length of the island, contains 93 volcanoes—Krakatau (Krakatoa) is easily the most famous. Sumatra's history has been much influenced by its strategic location on the trade route between India and China; the kingdom of Srivijaya, centered near present-day Palembang, once attained great power through control of the lucrative trade passing through the Straits of Malacca.

A huge white mosque dominates the center of town in **Banda Aceh**, capital of the special province of Aceh in north Sumatra. The Acehnese are known for their devout belief (Aceh is the only province specifically ruled under Islamic law), also for their fierce resistence to Dutch (or any other 'outsider's') control. They're a friendly people, very proud of their culture. For pleasant day trips from the city visit Lhok-nga Beach, 12 km west of town (take a bemo from the station near the big mosque) or take a ferry to the small island of Sabang, just off the coast.

The provincial capital of North Sumatra and third largest city in Indonesia, **Medan** is mostly a business town, not a cultural center. The city's population is well above 2 million and includes a mixture of Bataks, Javanese, Chinese, Acehnese, Minangkabau, Sikhs, Tamil and Malays—many of which prefer not to mingle with each other.

Maps and information are available at the Medan Tourist Office (Kantor wilayah Pariwisata Sumatera Utara), Jl. Palang Merah 66; tel. 22099.

In a half-day walking tour, you can visit the **Mesjid Raya** (Great Mosque) on Jl. Sisingamangaraja and the **Istana Mai-**

moon (Maimoon Palace) on Jl. Katamso which are near each other in southeast Medan. Both were built by the Sultan of Deli in the 1800's; both are magnificent structures but due to lack of maintenance are a bit rundown. The Medan Fair—held May-June each year in the city's amusement park (Taman Ria) on Jl. Binjai—features industrial exhibits, sports tournaments, etc. Other than that there isn't much in Medan for travelers to see.

Eating in Medan: Chinese food is delicious, abundant and a little expensive. The place to splurge is Jl. Silat Panjang, an entire street of Chinese food stalls; it looks like a miniature Hong Kong. It's located between Jl. Pandu and Jl. Nusantara, parallel to and two blocks from Jl. Yani (Medan's main strip). Any movie theaters in the area. There is a good pasar malam (night market) in front of Taman Ria serving Chinese and Indonesian food. For a good Javanese meal, try Jenar Restaurant on Jl. Gatot Subroto across from Taman Ria.

A bemo ride south along Jl. Sisingamangaraja will take you to Taman Margasawata (Medan's zoo), but if you really want to see Sumatran wildlife, spend two days visiting the **Pusat Rehabilitasi Mawas** (Orangutan Rehabilitation Center) in Bukit Lawang, a 5-hr ride from Medan. You can spend the night at the guest house there; bring your own food, though, or plan on walking to the nearby village to eat (1½ km). Visitors can go into the reserve in the mornings and evenings to watch feedings; the hike through the jungle is fascinating.

The **Batak**, an ethno-linguistic group including both Christians and Moslems, live in the area around Danau Toba (Lake Toba) in the north Sumatran highlands. There are actually six different tribes, each with a distinctive culture and dialect; the Karo and Toba Bataks are the best known. If you're going to this area from Java, prepare for minor culture shock; the Bataks are much more frank and aggressive than the Javanese or the Sundanese.

The Bataks are also distinguished by their unique kinship system; everyone belongs to a clan (marga), and marrying within one's clan is forbidden. Genealogy is very important to the Bataks; people can trace their roots 15 or more generations. Intricate records are kept in the Batak written language. Education is highly valued within the Batak community; whole clans will scrimp and save in order to put the best and brightest youths through college. The strategy seems to have paid off; Bataks hold many of the highest positions in government, military, and academic circles. Weddings are an unforgettable affair; thousands of people sit down to a feast of slaughtered pig and water buffalo. The Batak bridegroom traditionally gives the bride's parents a huge dowry (of land, money or livestock) in 'payment' for the bride. A cornerstone of the Batak value system is the concept 'hagabeon,' which essentially means 'have as many children as possible.'

Brastagi is a popular resort town 70 km south of Medan in the Karo highlands. Great hiking and swimming, and while you're there try the fruits and vegetables for which this town is famous. Walk to the nearby villages of Lingga or Barusjahe to see traditional Karo Batak houses.

The bus from Medan climbs through lush pine forests to the crest of an old volcanic crater before dropping down to the small, but growing resort town of Prapat on the shore of **Danau Toba** (Lake Toba). Prapat caters more to the high-budget traveler, so catch a ferry that leaves irregularly to Samosir Island (Rp200). Samosir Island is the home of the (Toba) Batak people who over the centuries dispersed to outlying highlands and formed new tribes known as Karo, Simalungan, etc. The ferry stops at several villages on the island (Tomok and Tuk Tuk are the largest), where you can stay with Batak families for Rp200/night. A road connects the villages but the coastal path is more beautiful; the villages are about 3 km apart. You can get a sense of a traditional Batak village at Ambarita, but it's better to hike to the highland villages.

From Prapat you can easily take a bus to **Sibolga** on the western coast. Sibolga has an incredible natural harbor with beautiful sunsets and sandy beaches. The real treasure lies 125 km west of Sibolga, the island of **Nias**. The megalithic culture of Nias flourished up into this century—obelisks, tables, benches and all sorts of things carved from stone can be found in south Nias villages. the people of Nias, the Niha, are Christians.

The unique **Minangkabau** culture blends Islam with a matrilineal social system. Though the matriarchy is breaking down somewhat in Padang, in the highlands the women still control the land and local economy. Traditionally the men are treated as 'house guests' and have no permanent residence. For this and other reasons (primarily economic) they go on a 'merantau' (voluntary migration) to other parts of Indonesia for varying periods of time. In recent years, many men have brought their families along as well so now half of the Minangkabau population live outside their native homeland.

Along with the rest of the Malay race, the Minangkabau people originated in Yunnan and arrived in central Sumatra a few centuries A.D. after the Batak people. The Minangkabau have no actual knowledge of where their ancestors came from but folk legend has it that in ancient times a ship belonging to the son of Alexander the Great landed on a small island. The water then receded, enlarging the small island into the whole island of Sumatra. The small island where the ship landed is now the top of Mt. Merapi, near Bukittinggi. People then descended from Mt. Merapi and set up villages.

The Minangkabau are also known for their carabao-shaped

roof of their traditional houses (rumah gadang). It is said that the roofs are supposed to remind them of their great past when hypothetically they were a seafaring nation; the pointed rooftop signifies the two masts of a boat covered by a bamboo roof in the form of a bow. Since scholars have acknowledged that in prehistoric times Madagascar was colonized by the Malays, there may be some thread of truth to the unique design of the rumah gadang. In any case, the stylized roof only reinforces the characteristics of the modern Minangkabau with their passion for learning, teaching, travel and return to their homeland.

Padang, the capital of West Sumatra, is a small international port and administrative center. The Tourist Information Office (Bapparda) is located at Jl. Koto Tinggi 5. To get around take bemos (Rp40), oplets (Rp40-60), bendis--horse-drawn carts-- (bargaining determines fare), and two city buses (Rp50).

For excellent Padang food, try the Pagi-Sore on Jl. Pondok, the Simpang Raya on Jl. Pasar Baru, Bopet Buya on Jl. Aziz Chan (near the post office), and Bopet Kubang on Jl. Yamin; all these restaurants are within walking distance of the central market. (See the Food section for a description of how Padang restaurants operate.) The city is not long on night life. Several moviehouses (most are located in Padang's Chinatown in the south of town) show films for Rp800-1000; for a real bargain go to the Imam Bonjol Stadium across the central market, where different films play nightly for Rp250.

Pasir Putih, 7 km from Padang, is a fine beach—beautiful sunsets and sometimes the waves are body-surfable. Best to go in the late afternoon when it's cooler. Take either an oplet or a bus (Rp50) from the central market and get off at the university campus at Air Tawar. Walk along the path which borders the southern edge of the campus until you come to the beach. There are some interesting fishing villages a few kilometers north along the beach. Another beautiful beach is **Teluk Bungus**, beyond Padang's harbor (12 km from the city). Sheer cliffs, coconut trees, sandy beaches, emerald green water and occasional sharks (Rp200 by oplet from the Padang oplet station).

For a spectacular hike along the coast near Padang:take a bemo to Muaro, the estuary just south of the city (Rp45); a canope will ferry you to the other side of the river (Rp25). Then walk up through the Chinese cemetery that overlooks the town, and follow the dirt path that continues on over the hills covered with clove and banyan trees. Above you there may be a swinging gibbon and below you the waves will be crashing against the shore. After a kilometer the path will descend to a white sand beach, **Air Manis**. In the morning (low tide) you can wade out to Pulau Pisang Ketek (Small Banana Island), but be sure to return before high tide. Pulau Pisang Gadang (Big Banana Island) can be reached by boat (bargain first). Continue along the beach until you come to the river, then cross it and climb the steps up the hill and then descend into **Teluk Bayur**, Padang's harbor. From here, you can take an oplet (Rp50) back to Padang.

Bukittinggi, 90 km north of Padang, is in the Minangkabau heartland. On a small hill up the street from the market you'll find a zoo and a good museum on Minang culture. Though the zoo specializes in Sumatran wildlife, the animals themselves are in poor shape; you have to go through it get to the museum housed in a rumah gadang (admission: Rp100). **Ngarai Sianok**, a park which sits on the rim of a steep canyon at the town's edge, contains caves dug by the Japanese during WWII. Pasar Atas—a market with a wide variety of merchandise—is also worth a visit. For good food, try the Simpang Raya on Jl. Minangkabau.

Several villages offering a variety of craftwork lie within an hour's bus ride of Bukittinggi. Sungai Puar is best known for blacksmithing, Koto Gadang for silversmithing, Guguk Tabek-Sarojo for goldsmithing and Pandai Sikat for woodcarving and weaving. Ngalau Kamang (also known as Gua Kamang) is a large cave stretching a few kilometers; bring a lamp or hire a local guide to see the limestone stalactites and stalagmites.

For good hiking and beautiful scenery visit **Danau Maninjau** (Lake Maninjau), 36 km west of Bukittinggi; take a bus (Rp350) from near the Hotel Yogya. There is an expensive hotel and a rundown losmen at lakeside.

ACCOMMODATIONS IN SUMATRA

Banda Aceh:
Hotel rooms and food are expensive in Banda Aceh. **Hotel International** and **Hotel Parapat**, Rp3000. Clean, pleasant w/fans in each room.

Medan:
Hotel Irama, located on a small alley 50 m. off Jl. Palang Merah, between Jl. Imam Bonjol and Jl. Listrik. Dorm beds Rp500; singles Rp1000. Hotel is in the process of being expanded. Surly proprietors, but you can't beat the price.

Si Gura Gura, Jl. Suprapto near the Garuda office. Dorm beds Rp500.
Bukit Lawang:
D. Bangun's Guesthouse, Rp1000/night. (Warning: they kick out unmarrieds who try to share a room).

Brastagi:
Stay at **Wisma Sibayak**, Rp1000. A lovely place, nice hosts.
Samosir Island:
In Tomok, stay at **Mongoloy's** or **Edison's**—only Rp125-150/night and the food is inexpensive. In Tuk Tuk (more crowded and touristy) stay at **Bernard's, Murni's**, or any of 25 other places. All charge about Rp150/

116 INDONESIA

night. **Carolina's** is nicer—more privacy, better view—for Rp800-1000.
Nias:
Stay at one of the losmen in Teluk Dalam (about Rp300/night).
Padang:
Hotel Tiga-Tiga, Jl. Pemuda 31, near the bus station. Doubles Rp1200. Nice hotel, but a little noisy since it's on a major street.

Machudum's, Jl. Hiligoo 45, near the bemo station. Rooms start at Rp1200 but the area is much more interesting; such night life as there is in Padang is close by. (From the bus station take a bemo to the bemo station and walk.)
Bukittinggi:
Stay at **Hotel Jogja** (Rp1000) or in one of the many hotels along Jl. A. Yani (Rp1000-1200).

TRANSPORTATION FOR SUMATRA

The Trans-Sumatran Highway is still in poor condition, but if you're the hardy type and don't mind long bus rides through winding jungle roads, you can reach any town in Sumatra by bus from Jakarta. Sumatra-bound buses depart from Grogol Bus Station (bus companies are located nearby) for Merak, a town on the northwest tip of Java. From there a ferry crosses to Pelabuhan Panjang on Sumatra, 15 min. from Tanjung Karang Bus Station, from which buses leave for cities throughout the island. The ticket you buy in Jakarta covers all the necessary connections; you can even get a free 'pick-up' service from wherever you're staying in Jakarta to the bus station.

You can also take a train to Merak, ferry across to Sumatra, and catch a bus on your own at the Tanjung Karang Bus Station. Trains leave twice daily (5:45 am/pm) from Jakarta's Tanah Abang Station (Rp1250, 3rd class; 4 hr.).

Two suggestions on Sumatran bus-riding: sit towards the front for a less bouncy ride, and try to get on a bus that has a winch (buses with winches can pull themselves out of the mud more easily).

Banda Aceh: From Medan by bus (Rp4500, 12-14 hr. in the dry season). Try Kurnia Buses—fast, punctual. Road narrows to a chicken path at times, but is in solid condition for most of the journey.

Medan: From Jakarta you can take the Pelni ship, KM Tampomas, which leaves Jakarta's Tanjung Priok every Monday at 6 pm on a route that passes through Muntok, Tanjung Pinang, and finnaly Belawan, Medan's port. It arrives on Thursday; departs from Belawan on Friday. Fares: Rp34,250 (1st class); Rp33,500 (2nd class); Rp18,000 (deck class). From Belawan, take a bus into the city (26 km). From Padang, take an ANS bus from Jl. Sisingamangaraja, Medan, Rp3800, 24-26 hr. There is no longer boat service between Medan and Penang, Malaysia, due to smuggling; fly MAS, Rp28,000. Garuda is more expensive.

Bukit Lawang: Take a bus from Sungei Wampu Bus Station, Medan (leaves 2 pm, arrives 6:30 pm; Rp1200). Buses return to Medan from Bukit Lawang at 6 am daily.

Brastagi: Can be reached most quickly by the smaller buses running along Jl. Iskandar Mudah across from Pasar Pringgan (market), Medan, Rp400.

Prapat: Rp1500 by colt/bus from Medan. The bus company is right across from the Mesjid Raja on Jl. Sisingamangaraja. From Padang, the trip costs about Rp3200.

Samosir: Catch the ferry from the harbor (Tiga Raja) in Prapat—Rp250 (Rp100 on market day). Or take the ferry owned by the Tuk Tuk Hotel; it's free for their guests but others can pay the regular fare. The ferry makes about 4 runs a day; no fixed hours.

Nias: Take a bus from Medan or Bukittinggi to Sibolga. From there take a boat to Teluk Dalam, on Nias' southern tip, for about Rp2300 (17-24 hr.); don't go to Gunung Sitoli (northeast side of the island) because all the interesting things to see are on the southern coast. Note: boat service is irregular—usually several times a week.

Padang: By ANS bus from Medan, Rp3800, 24-26 hr. From Prapat, Rp3200, 16-20 hr. By bus from Jakarta, Rp13,000. A bone-jarring 3-day trek. Better to take the KM Tampomas which leaves Jakarta on Saturday at noon for a 34 hr. voyage. Fares: Rp27,250 (1st class); Rp20,250 (2nd class); Rp14,750 (deck class). Or, the slower Pelni ship, KM Bogowonto, which leaves Wednesday at noon for a 54-hr. trip. Fares: Rp19,750 (1st class); Rp16,500 (2nd class); Rp11,250 (deck class). Bring your own mat, eating utensils, etc.

Bukittinggi: 2 hr. by bus from Padang (Rp425).

Bibliography

Art in Indonesia: Continuities and Change, by Claire Holt. You won't find a better book on the subject. Beautifully written and illustrated.

Island of Bali, by Miguel Covarrubias. Old, but still an excellent source.

The Religion of Java, by Clifford Geertz. Scholarly, but readable.

Indonesia Handbook, by Bill Dalton. Very detailed, lots of helpful maps.

The 10,000 Things, by Maria Dermout. This fictionalized autobiography by a Dutch woman gives a fascinating account of life in Java in the 1920s and 30s.

Guide to Java and **Bali**, two Apa Photo Guides, ed. by Peter Hutton and Hans Hoefer, and Star Black and David Stuart-Fox, respectively. The pictures are wonderful; enjoyable reading.

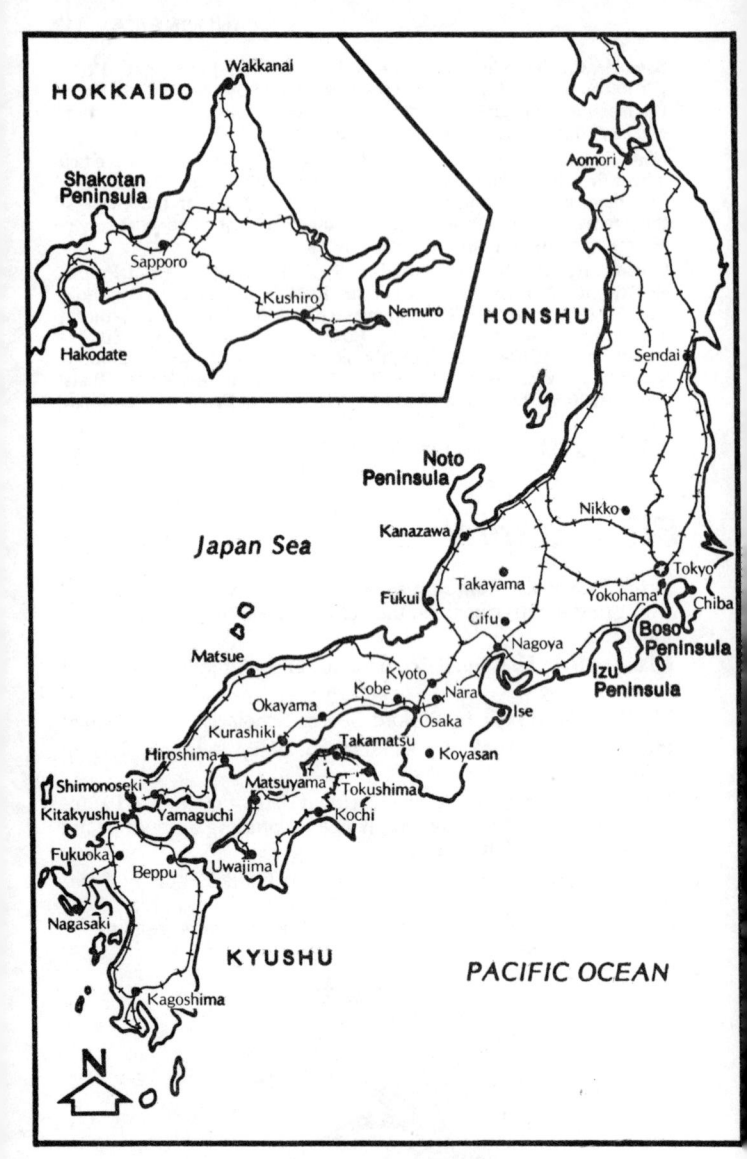

JAPAN

JAPAN 119

General Information

Arrival: Most travelers will arrive at the controversial new Tokyo International Airport in Narita, 65 km east of Tokyo. Though most of the airport facilities were completed eight years ago, a coalition of displaced farmers and students was able to prevent the airport from opening until May 1978. Security remains tight with watch towers, barbed-wire fences, and riot police constantly in sight, but there is no danger to the traveler. At times only passengers are allowed into the airport; at other times passengers and people seeing them off or meeting them; and sometimes anyone can get in.

Disgruntled travelers may want to join the ranks of the protesters, given the inconvenience of getting back and forth between Narita and Tokyo. There are five basic routes (plus a sixth via Haneda Airport, which formerly was Tokyo's international airport and now primarily serves domestic traffic), some involving several transfers and all of them time-consuming. Options include the airport limousine bus, the Toei Ichigo-sen Subway Line, Japan National Railways (JNR) trains, Keisei Line (private) trains, and taxis; all are described in great detail in the weekly tabloid "Tour Companion," available at Tourist Information Centers. The route we recommend (as of November 1980) is the Keisei limited express, which takes 73 min. to get from Narita airport Station to Keisei Ueno Station in Tokyo. (Keisei Ueno Station is ½ block southwest of Ueno Station, where you can catch a subway or get on the Yamanote Train Line.) The fare is Y640, plus Y100 for the 1-km shuttle bus trip from the airport terminal to the train station; buy your ticket at the Keisei ticket counter just outside the arrival lobby. The Keisei Line also operates an express train (90 min.) for the same fare as the limited express, and a 'Skyliner' non-stop, reserved-seat express (Y1240, plus Y100 bus fare: 60 min.); the 'Skyliner' may be the best way to go during rush hours because it's not a local service train and so won't be crowded. For more details on transportation to Tokyo, ask at the TIC desk just outside the arrival lobby.

As of this writing, passengers on China Air Lines were still flying into Haneda airport, located just outside Tokyo. The easiest way to get into the city from Haneda is by monorail. Trains leave every 7 min., 6:40 am-11:33 pm, from an underground station near the terminal; they arrive 15 min. later at Hamamatsucho Station, where you can connect with JNR local lines. The fare is Y230, and as with all trains in Japan, your ticket is punched when you board but not collected until you get off (so keep it in a safe place). To get to the monorail station, turn right as you leave the arrival building and walk about 250

120 JAPAN

meters, then go down the staircase behind pillar #5 of the building in front of you.

Whichever airport you arrive at, be sure to change some money, especially around New Year's and the first week of May, when banks are closed for several days in a row due to holidays. Those arriving at Narita should also stop at the Tourist Information Center.

Departure from Narita: Again we recommend the Keisei limited express (except during rush hours, when the 'Skyliner' would be much more comfortable); it runs roughly 6:30 am-9 pm. If you take a limited express or express train, be sure to get off at Narita Airport Station, the next (and final) stop **after** Narita Station. At Keisei Ueno Station buy a Y740 ticket which includes the station-airport shuttle bus fare (keep your ticket; it will be collected on the bus). Board the shuttle bus going to the departure area on the terminal's 4th floor, not the arrival lobby on the 1st floor.

Plan to arrive at the airport terminal at least 1¾ hr, preferably 2 hrs, before departure. Three security checks, in addition to check-in and immigration formalities, will use up the time.

The airport departure tax is Y1500.

Currency: The yen is a floating currency; the exchange rate in November 1980 was 208 yen (Y208) to the US dollar. (The Japanese pronunciation of 'yen' sounds more like 'en.').

Visas: 43 countries, including France, West Germany, Canada, the Netherlands, and the United Kingdom, do not need a visa to enter Japan as a tourist. Check with a Japanese embassy or consulate for complete information. United States citizens **must** obtain a visa. Tourist visas are good for 60 days; transit visas are good for 15 days; both are valid for four years.

Climate: Temperate zone weather. Four clearly defined seasons; hot summers, cold winters. A short rainy season usually starts in June and ends in July (except in Hokkaido, which has no rainy season and is quite cold in the winter).

Sources of Information

The **Japan National Tourist Organization** (JNTO) operates three Tourist Information Centers (TIC):

Tokyo International Airport TIC: 1st floor of the airport terminal. Open 9-8 weekdays and 9-noon Saturdays.

Tokyo TIC: Kotani Bldg., 6-6, Yurakucho 1-chome, Chiyoda-ku, Tokyo; tel. (03)502-1461 and 1462 and 1463. Located near the Yurakucho JNR Station. Walk out of the station on the Hibiya side (it's marked) and go left until you reach a stoplight (one block); the TIC is directly across the street. Open 9-noon and 1-5 weekdays, 9-noon Saturdays.

Kyoto TIC: 1st floor, Kyoto Tower Bldg., Higashi-Shiokoji-cho, Shimogyo-ku, Kyoto; tel (075)371-5649. Open 9-noon and 1-5 weekdays, 9-noon Saturdays.

The Tokyo TIC is the best source of English-language travel information for the entire country. The friendly TIC personnel seem to have a photocopied sheet of information to answer any question, as well as an impressive collection of free brochures and maps; the "Traveler's Companion" and "Budget Travel in Japan" pamphlets are especially useful. Ask for a copy of the weekly newspaper "Tour Companion" (also available at major hotels), which carries a complete calendar of events, maps, and details on Tokyo-Narita transportation. The JNTO **Official Guide to Japan** is excellent and comprehensive, but you'll want to use the copy at the TIC as a reference book because it costs around Y5000.

The **Japan Travel Bureau** (JTB) has offices all over Japan, usually near the train station in each major city. They can be helpful in recommending low-cost accommodations, but sometimes it's difficult to find JTB staff who can speak English well, especially in outlying areas.

Most cities also offer some kind of **tourist information service** at the main train station. Again, the staff may not speak English, but they can often give you English-language maps of the area.

This chapter does not include admission prices to specific temples, museums, shrines, gardens, etc. Be prepared to pay between Y50 and Y400 to enter these attractions; most of them are cheap, and all of them are worth seeing.

Background

Japan's traditions, like the clop-clop of geta (wooden sandals) on Tokyo's paved streets, echo within modern Japanese lifestyles. Especially in Tokyo, a visitor's first impressions are formed by the city's modern appearance; but those travelers who explore more of Japan than downtown Tokyo, Kyoto, and Osaka will appreciate the extent to which Japan's culture has been insulated from foreign influences.

Japan's contact with the outside world was largely limited to China and Korea until the 19th century. Written language made extensive use of Chinese characters originally, and Confucian concepts of order, self-control, loyalty, and etiquette were introduced along with Buddhism as early as the 6th century (though they didn't gain widespread influence until the Edo Period).

The power of the early imperial rulers was often contested by rich landowning families. The Heian Period, 794-1185, ended in

JAPAN

clan rivalry which led to rule by a series of shoguns during the Kamakura Period (1185-1333), the Muromachi (Ashikaga) Period (1336-1573), and the Tokugawa (Edo) Period (1600-1867). The shoguns ruled by force of arms, and it was during this era that the samurai class—warriors who served the shoguns with a tremendous spirit of loyalty and sacrifice—had a strong influence on Japanese culture.

During the Edo Period (when the Tokugawa were shoguns), a national isolation policy was enforced, prohibiting Japanese from visiting foreign countries and limiting all contact with the outside world to the 'peephole' at Nagasaki (on Kyushu). This policy effectively controlled the power of the rising merchant class and prevented other rival groups from aligning with foreign powers against the oligarchy of Japan's feudal system. This 200-year period of isolation ended when a sizeable American naval force headed by Commodore Perry arrived at Uraga to demand the inauguration of trade relations. Faced with guns, the Tokugawa signed a treaty, and Japan gradually opened its door to other foreign nations as well. The 15th Tokugawa Shogun was forced to resign in 1868 and the new government, under Emperor Meiji, began dismantling the feudal system and embarking on the task of 'modernization.' During the latter part of the 19th century, Japan began a series of international conquests which included victories in Korea, Taiwan, Manchuria, China, and finally Southeast Asia. Though Japan was defeated at the end of World War II, neighboring Asian countries still harbor resentment against it for its imperialist policies during this quest for world power (and more recently for some of its economic/trade policies).

Japan was occupied by the U.S. from September 1945 to April 1952. The most outstanding feature of Japanese history since that time has been its spectacular economic growth. Today Japan is the most industrialized country in Asia and one of the world's major economic powers. A new trade and friendship treaty with China, growing fear of Soviet aggression in the area, and calls for a military buildup of Japan's Self-Defense Forces ensure a continuing active role for Japan in Asia.

The Japanese archipelago consists of the four principal islands of Hokkaido, Honshu, Shikoku, and Kyushu, plus thousands of smaller islands. More than 80% of the country is mountainous; arable land per farmer is about 1/50 of that available in the U.S. Farming is therefore very intensive, and the yield per acre in Japan is among the highest in the world. Except for coal, Japan has few mineral resources in significant quantities; plentiful water is the country's one great natural resource.

Japan's population—at 116 million—is the sixth largest in the world. Approximately 80% of the people live in cities (about the same percentage as in the U.S.). Of this urban population, 58% is crowded into the 'Big Four' metropolitan areas around the cities of Tokyo, Osaka, Nagoya, and Kitakyushu.

Culture and Customs

In general, Japanese are quite receptive to foreigners; the traveler who stands in downtown Tokyo and opens up a map will find that within minutes a passerby will offer assistance. But at the same time, foreigners ('gaijin,' literally, 'person from the outside') who have lived in Japan for years state that a gaijin can never become fully integrated into Japanese society. Even second and third generation Chinese and Korean families remain 'outsiders' and rarely become naturalized citizens.

Many of Japan's cultural traditions have their roots in ancient Chinese civilization. Buddhism, for example—one of Japan's two principal religions—became a court religion after it was introduced from China during the 6th century. It never completely replaced the native, animist religion of Shintoism, however. Shintoism could be described as a combination of nature worship and ancestor worship; there are numerous gods and goddesses, the most important of which is the Sun Goddess. Festive ceremonies honor particular deities at specified times each year. **Shrines** are Shintoist and are easily distinguished by their torii (toh-ree)—a sort of gate consisting of two tall pillars with one or more crossbars at the top. Shinto priests always wear white robes. While shrines are usually fairly small, Buddhist **temples** are often large and lavishly decorated buildings. Buddhist priests wear black robes. Many Japanese are both Buddhists and Shintoists; the religions play different roles in their lives. Weddings, for example, are frequently Shintoist, while burials follow Buddhist rites.

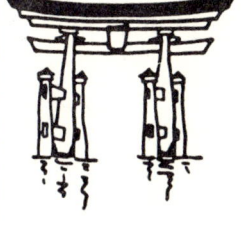

During the **Heian Period** (794-1185) Japanese culture developed many of its most attractive elements. The ancient capital city of Kyoto remains the cultural center of Japan today, featuring beautiful imperial palaces, landscaped gardens, and Buddhist temples. The samurai, or warrior class, became a strong force in Japan's feudalistic society during the rule of the powerful shoguns (1185-1867). These warriors adopted the Zen sect of Buddhism as a means of self-discipline and also became masters of the tea ceremony. Other Japanese arts developed at this time as a means of spiritual stimulation—the Noh form of drama, flower arranging (ikebana), Kabuki theater, and the many Japanese martial arts. These traditions, whether defined as forms of art, sport, or religious practice, are still studied by Japanese as a means of self-discipline and strengthening one's 'inner being.'

124 JAPAN

Japan has a group-oriented rather than an individualistic society. People often travel in groups and join clubs or organizations which dominate their social lives. Within businesses, an office worker ('salaryman') usually stays with the same company his entire life, receiving life-long benefits and becoming part of the company's 'family.'

The concept of face underlies many aspects of Japanese social relations; people control their emotions and pay careful attention to the social status of those around them. It is important never to discredit, dishonor, or contradict a person (especially someone older) in front of other people.

Japanese reluctance to express negative feelings can sometimes be perplexing to the traveler. For example, a Japanese will try not to let on if s/he doesn't completely understand what is said (whether the speaker is a foreigner or another Japanese)—out of concern for the speaker's feelings and also for fear of losing face. Japanese friends may not express their feelings even if quite upset by something you do. Though Japanese are very tolerant of the unintentional mistakes foreigners make, it will help to be familiar with the more important social customs.

Gift giving is one of the more complex aspects of Japanese social relationships. You should bring a small gift whenever visiting a home, and small gifts are also the most appropriate way to show appreciation for kindnesses. Gifts which are too large and expensive may cause embarrassment; mementoes from your home country are ideal—small pictures, T-shirts (for students), candy, little dolls (which are not 'made in Japan'), etc. If you need to buy something locally, a box of candy is a good idea, or stop by one of the shops that can be found in every train station selling items for just this purpose. (Gifts, which should be wrapped, are usually not opened immediately.)

If you ever study Japanese you will discover the myriad honorific terms indicative of politeness and formality in social relations. First names are seldom used, except within families and among schoolmates. Unless they indicate otherwise, address Japanese friends by their last names with the suffix '-san' (a sort of all-purpose title for both women and men). Bowing, not expected of the traveler but much appreciated, is the traditional form of greeting. (You show deference to the other person by bowing lower and longer.)

For information on etiquette in homes and ryokan (inns), see the **Accommodations** section.

Attempts to express gratitude or apology in Japanese will be well received, regardless of poor pronunciation. Unfortunately for the traveler, some of the more commonly used words of courtesy have subtle differences in meaning which are difficult to translate. But in moments of utter confusion a smile and 'Wakarimasen' ('I don't understand') will help smooth things out.

Some final hints: since you must remove your shoes every time you enter temples, ryokan, etc., wear shoes or sandals that you can slip in and out of easily; public washrooms and bathhouses are sometimes mixed—just ignore everyone else, because they'll ignore you; carry a small stash of toilet paper, because public toilets often run out; never bargain in Japan; tipping is not necessary; try to avoid eating on the street.

Festivals

Japan has a variety of public holidays celebrated according to the Gregorian calendar, as well as local festivals at Shinto shrines throughout the country.

Offices and stores close down for nearly three days around New Year's; public transportation tends to be very crowded at this time. The 'Golden Week,' which includes April 29 (the Emperor's Birthday), May 3 (Constitutional Memorial Day), and May 5 (Children's Day), is another time when offices and stores close for several days. The JNTO pamphlet "Annual Events in Japan" describes the major festivals and holidays throughout the country. Japanese often take vacations during the cherry blossom season (late March to early May, depending on the climate of the area).

Most Japanese work a 5½- or 6-day week and Sunday is the only full day they can spend with their families. For this reason, parks, museums, and other well-known attractions tend to be crowded on Sundays.

Language

Most Japanese have studied some English, but the traveler who can use Japanese to ask a few simple questions, greet people, and return courtesies will be able to open doors which might otherwise remain closed. Ryokan and minshuku (see **Accommodations**) sometimes turn foreigners away due to language problems. The traveler will rarely find people outside of Tokyo who can speak fluent English.

The list of words and phrases below may come in handy. The romanized version of each Japanese term (called 'romaji') is given, followed by its phonetic pronunciation. Keep in mind that Japanese is not a stressed language, like English; in general, every syllable should receive an equal amount of stress, in metronomic fashion. Also, Japanese has only five vowel sounds: **a** as in father, **e** as in pen, **i** as in street, **o** as in smoke, and **u** as in tune.

Good morning	**Ohayo gozaimasu** (oh-hah-yoh goh-zai-mas')
Good afternoon	**Konnichiwa** (kohn-ni-chi-wah)
Good evening	**Konbanwa** (kohn-bahn-wah)

126 JAPAN

Good night	**Oyasuminasai** (oh-yah-su-mi-nah-sai)
Goodbye	**Sayonara** (sai-yoh-nah-rah)
How are you?	**Ogenki desu ka?** (oh-gehn-ki des' kah?)

Please (when offering something)	**Do-o-zo** (doh-zoh)
Please (when requesting something)	**Kudasai** (ku-dah-sai)
Thank you (politely)	**Arigato (gozaimasu)** (ah-ri-gah-toh...)
You're welcome	**Do itashi mashite** (doh-ee-tah-shi mah-shi-teh)
Excuse me	**Gomen nasai** (goh-men nah-sai) or **Sumi masen** (su-mi mah-sehn)
Yes	**Hai** (hai)
No	**Iie** (ee-yeh)

City/Town	**Shi/Machi** (shi/mah-chi)
Street	**Michi, Dori** (mi-chi, doh-ri)
Train/Train station	**Kisha/Eki** (ki-shah/eh-ki)
Bus/Bus stop	**Basu/Basu tei** (bah-su/bah-su tei)
Subway	**Chikatetsu** (chi-kah-tet-su)
Ferry	**Feri** (feh-ri)
Hotel/Inn	**Hoteru/Ryokan** (hoh-teh-ru/ri-oh-kahn)
Restaurant	**Resutoran** (res-toh-rahn)
Temple/Shrine	**Otera/Jinja** (oh-teh-rah/jin-jah)
Post office	**Yubinkyoku** (yu-bin-kyoh-ku)
Toilet	**Toire** (toh-ee-rei)
Bath	**Ofuro** (oh-fu-roh)
Female/Male	**Josei/Dansei** (joh-sei/dahn-sei)
Island/Mountain	**Shima/Yama** (shi-mah/yah-mah)
North/South	**Kita/Minami** (ki-tah/mi-nah-mi)
East/West	**Higashi/Nishi** (hi-gah-shi/ni-shi)

When?	**Itsu?** (eet-su?)
Today/tomorrow	**Kyo/Ashita** (kyoh/ah-shi-tah)
Yesterday	**Kino** (ki-noh)

Where is —?	**— wa doko desu ka?** (— wah doh-koh des' kah?)
I want to go to —.	**— ni ikitai desu.** (— ni ee-ki-tai des')
Is it far?	**Toi desu ka?** (toh-ee des' kah?)
Is this (the one) to —?	**— yuki desu ka?** (— yu-ki des' kah?)
Stop (please)	**Tomete (kudasai)** (toh-mei-tei...)
Do you have a room?	**Heya wa arimasu ka?** (hei-yah wah ah-ri-mas' kah?)
How much is it?	**Ikura desu ka?** (ee-ku-rah des' kah?)
I don't understand.	**Wakarimasen.** (wah-kah-ri-mah-sehn)

Inexpensive	**Yasui** (yah-su-ee)
A little expensive	**Chotto takai desu kedo.** (choht-toh tah-kai des' keh-doh)
Good/Bad	**Ii desu** (ee des')/**Dame desu** (dah-mei des')

There are two different numbering systems in Japan, but you can use the system below to count anything—though you'll occasionally be using it inappropriately you will still be understood.

1	**Ichi**	20	**Ni-ju**
2	**Ni**	30	**San-ju**
3	**San**	100	**Hyaku**
4	**Shi**	400	**Yon-hyaku***
5	**Go**	1000	**Sen**
6	**Roku**	7000	**Nana-sen***
7	**Shichi**	10,000	**Ichi-man**
8	**Hachi**	90,000	**Kyu-man***
9	**Ku**		
10	**Ju**		

***Yon** (4), **nana** (7), and **kyu** (9) are more common in compound numbers.

When you're speaking English with Japanese acquaintances, it may be helpful to know that since Japanese words usually end with vowels, Japanese sometimes add vowel sounds (usually **o** or **u**) to English words that end with consonants. For example, "beer" becomes "beeru." Also, since there is no **l** sound in Japanese, an **r** sound is often substituted. Thus, "hotel" becomes "hoteru." You may even find that sometimes, if you're having trouble communicating, it helps to adjust your pronunciation accordingly to make yourself more easily understood. Another thing to be aware of is that if you ask a question in the negative ("Isn't this the right bus?"), a Japanese will answer "yes" (meaning, "yes, this isn't the right bus") where an American would answer "no." A final note: sometimes it helps to write down what you want to say—many Japanese can read English far better than they can speak it.

Food

For the gourmand on a low budget, Japan is no paradise. Restaurant food is generally more expensive than in the U.S. and some dishes—especially steak and other forms of beef—cost much more. But if you're looking for a simple meal, you won't have to wander very far to find restaurants offering reasonably-priced noodle or rice dishes and filling soups. Many inexpensive restaurants have plastic replicas of their most popular meals displayed in the front window; a cooperative waitress or waiter will step outside with you so you can point out what you want. Even expensive restaurants often have lunch dishes (sometimes called 'business lunch' or 'quick lunch') that are reasonably inexpensive.

Hungry foreigners will discover a bonanza in large department stores, which maintain low-cost restaurants as a convenience to their shoppers rather than as profit-making operations in and of themselves. The top floor will often have a sit-down establishment (or two) where the procedure is something like this: Choose your meal from a numbered array of plastic models, then write down the number of the dish and pay a cashier, who hands you a receipt with a number on it. Enter the dining area and sit down, giving your receipt to the waitress. After a few minutes your meal should appear.

Rock-bottom prices can also be found in the basements of the big stores, reserved for 'supermarkets'—though most of the food is already prepared and ready to eat. It's often as good as, or better than, restaurant food, and the basements offer the pick-and-choose convenience of a cafeteria. (They are also frequently jammed with elbow-to-elbow crowds.) Both the basement markets and the top-floor restaurants are open only during shopping hours, roughly 10 am-6 pm.

Most every coffee shop offers a quickie breakfast that's cheap, called 'morning service.' You'll get coffee or tea, an egg, and toast for Y400-500. For a great and filling meal of sushi for only Y700 or so, go to one of the fast-food sushi shops (genroku) that are scattered throughout Tokyo. You sit around an oval-shaped conveyor belt, while workers make the sushi in the back of the shop, place it on the belt, and you take the plates of sushi as they move past. Y100 per plate of two sushi.

Eating Cheap in Japan (see Bibliography) is a good guide for those who want to eat off the beaten track.

RICE DISHES
KARE RAISU カレーライス Curry stew over rice.
OCHAZUKE お茶漬 Rice w/ fish broth or tea over it.
OYAKO DONBURI 親子丼 Rice topped w/ chicken and onion cooked in egg.
TAMAGO DONBURI たま丼 Rice topped w/ sliced onions cooked in egg and dried seaweed.
TEMPURA てんぷら Vegetables or seafood dipped in batter and deep-fried, eaten w/ a sauce.
TEN DON 天丼，てんどん Rice w/ shrimp tempura and pickles.
YAKIMESHI (CHAHAN) やきめし Fried rice.

NOODLE DISHES
RAMEN ラーメン Chinese noodles.
SOBA そ ば Japanese buckwheat noodles.
UDON うどん Japanese wheat or barley noodles.
(The above are usually served in broth or dipped in a sauce.)
YAKI SOBA 焼そば Chinese noodles fried w/ vegetables, pork and sometimes squid or shrimp.

A LA CARTE DISHES
ODEN おでん Stewed vegetables, tofu (bean curd), fish cake and sometimes octopus.
SASHIMI さしみ，刺身 Raw fish (choice of many kinds), served w/ soy sauce and horseradish.

YAKI TORI 焼 鳥, やきとり Chicken meat or liver, and sometimes vegetables, skewered on bamboo sticks and grilled.

DISHES PREPARED AT THE TABLE

MIZUTAKI 水炊(き) Chicken, vegetables, tofu and vermicelli boiled in broth, eaten w/ a spicy sauce.

OKONOMI YAKI お好焼 Thick, spicy pancake containing vegetables w/ meat, seafood, or egg, served w/ a sauce.

SHABU SHABU しゃぶしゃぶ Sliced beef or chicken, vegetables and tofu boiled in broth, eaten w/ spicy sauces.

SUKIYAKI すき焼 Beef, vegetables, tofu and vermicelli cooked in sake (rice wine), sugar, and soy sauce, eaten w/ rice and raw egg for a dip.

MISCELLANEOUS

AN あ ん Sweet red bean paste.

GOHAN (RAISU) ごはん Rice.

O-BENTO お弁当 Box lunches sold at train stations, etc.

SHOYU しょう油 Soy sauce.

SUSHI 寿 司, すし Rice balls covered w/ raw fish; there are many varieties.

TAMAGO 卵, 玉子 Egg.

TEISHOKU 定 食 "Today's special"—usually a good buy, w/ rice, misoshiru, and the main course included.

KOCHA 紅 茶 Black (Western-style) tea.

O-CHA お茶 Japanese green tea.

Accommodations

Japan Youth Hostels, Inc. (JYH), a private company, operates 483 **hostels**, while the government subsidizes another 75 public youth hostels. Rates vary from Y950 up to Y1150 for a bed, and from Y300 to Y700 for a meal; the public hostels are cheapest. Sleeping sheets are required; if you don't have one, you can rent one for Y150. JYH hostels require international membership cards; if you don't already have one they're available at the main office of the JYH in the Hoken Kaikan Bldg. (2nd floor), Sadohara-cho, Ichigaya, Shinjuku-ku, Tokyo, 162 (tel. 03-269-5831)—only a 5 min. walk from Ichigaya Station (JNR Sobu Line). They can also be purchased in a corner of the 2nd basement of the Sogo Department Store on the west side of the Yurakucho Train Station (one block from the Tokyo TIC). An International Guest Card for foreigners—good from Jan. 1-Dec. 31, is Y2000. Youth Hostel Handbooks (in Japanese) are also available for Y380. The TIC puts out a free "Youth Hostels in Japan" pamphlet with the address, phone number, number of beds, and one line of directions for each hostel, but for more extensive travel outside major cities it's worth buying the Japanese handbook because it includes small maps. The JYH International Service Club offers an information service for foreign hostellers Tuesday and Saturday evenings at Yoyogi Youth Hostel, Tokyo. Ask at the JYH office for details.

Most youth hostels offer dormitory accommodations, with a central bath and kitchen facilities for those who cook for themselves rather than buy the meals offered by the hostel. (We recommend that you skip the hostel meals—the food is usually uninteresting at best. You can sample a much wider variety of tasty Japanese dishes at outside restaurants for very little more than what you would pay if you ate in the hostel.) Hostel regulations require all members to check in between 3 pm and 8 pm (arrive by 6:30 pm if you're eating dinner at the hostel), retire at 10 pm, and leave the hostel by 10 am. Between 10 and 3 the hostels are closed. The front door is locked at 9 pm, lights out at 10 pm. The 10 pm curfew may cramp one's style in the larger cities like Tokyo and Kyoto.

It's a good idea to make reservations in advance when possible, especially during August when students are on vacation. You can write ahead (ideally at least a week in advance), but an easier way is to have the personnel at the hostel you're currently staying in call ahead for you. If you're not in a hostel, any JTB office will make the call for you. Or try the computerized YH reservation centers at: Keio Department Store in Shinjuku, Seibu Department Store in Ikebukuro, or Sogo Department Store in Yurakucho (all in Tokyo). Reservations are good for up to three days only, but if there is a vacancy you can stay longer.

Re: youth hostel listings in the **Accommodations** sections of this chapter. Since addresses are not very useful, they will not be included. If you need them in order to write ahead for reservations, refer to the youth hostel handbook. Phone numbers are included so they'll be easily available in case you want to ask someone to call ahead for you. For each hostel listing two prices will be given (e.g. Y1100/Y2100)—the first is the cost of a single night's lodging, and the second includes the cost of two meals.

Kokumin Shukusha ('People's Lodges') and **Kokumin Kyuka Mura** ('National Vacation Villages') are two types of facilities designed for vacationing Japanese, but open to foreigners as well. Most Lodges are built and maintained by local governments, mostly in parks and hot-spring areas. Some of the 300 lodges provide Western-style bunk beds, as well as traditional Japanese rooms. The average tariff is Y3900 per night, including two meals. The Villages, located in some national and quasi-national parks, are more complete resort communities, with various facilities for recreation. The cost of these accommodations is usually Y5500 (two meals included). Both the Lodges and Vacation Villages are heavily used during vacation periods. The JTB can help make reservations at these places; reservations for the Villages can also be made at the National Vacation Village Corporation's Tokyo Service Center on the first floor of the Tokyo Kotsu Kaikan Bldg., near Yurakucho Station (JNR Yamanote

Line). Their hours are 10 am-6 pm.

Minshuku ('family inns') offer lodging in a private home. There are thousands of minshuku in Japan; they vary from small private hostels where you share a room with several other travelers to homes where you can enjoy delicious meals, sake, and conversation with your hosts. The cost is usually Y3800 (two meals included). The Tokyo Minshuku Center, in the basement of the Tokyo Kotsu Kaikan Bldg., Yurakucho (tel. 216-6556), has information about members of the Japanese Minshuku assn. willing to accept foreign guests. In Osaka, check with the Osaka Minshuku Center, Dojima-Chikagai (near Nishi-Umeda Subway Station); tel. 345-2101. Reservations should be made in advance because unprepared hosts don't expect gaijin and are not sure what to do when they arrive; the inability to communicate may make for a tedious evening. We recommend that you try a minshuku, but only after you've stayed in a ryokan and are familiar with the customs. Be prepared to pay Y1000 in advance and around Y300 for the 'handling charge.'

Those travelers who can occasionally afford more expensive accommodations might enjoy the quiet atmosphere of a traditional Japanese inn, called a **ryokan**. Prices for these range anywhere from Y3500 without meals to Y7500 (and up) per person, including two meals and a private bath. To find an inexpensive ryokan, ask at a JTB office or explore the side streets near the railway stations. Some ryokan politely refuse to accept foreigners, feeling that they likely won't know the customs of Japanese home life and will thus make countless blunders. If you speak a little Japanese your chances of being accepted are much better.

As for important manners in ryokan: First accustom yourself to taking off your shoes in the entry hall, where you change to soft slippers provided by the ryokan. Wooden clogs are sometimes left around the doorway for short trips outside the inn. Change to a second set of slippers for the toilet area, and take off your slippers altogether before entering any room with tatami (straw) mats on the floor. Only stockings or bare feet are allowed on tatami. In the ryokan, meals will usually be served in your room, which makes for a very comfortable, private dinner atmosphere. Shortly before bedtime, the futon, which consists of several quilts, sheets, and a pillow, will be laid out on the tatami. The proper way to wear the yukata (cotton bathrobe) provided by the ryokan is to fold the left side over the right, tying the bow at the back or side. The opposite (right over left) is only used to dress dead bodies.

The Japanese toilet (obenjo), which you will undoubtedly find in a ryokan (if not sooner) can be disconcerting to foreigners. The rules for its use are simple—just squat, facing the small hood. If it is any consolation to you as you teeter and totter, remember that doctors say this method is much more natural for our internal plumbing. A word of caution for those who carry wallets, maps, passports, etc. in their back pockets: be careful that they don't drop out of your pants into the toilet and disappear forever. Also, you may have to supply your own toilet paper.

The Japanese bath (ofuro) may prove to be your most pleasurable discovery in Japan. Be sure to soap yourself and rinse well **outside** the tub, using the faucets and small buckets in the bathroom (use the water from the tub if there aren't any faucets). The bath will be filled only once each night, so you must not dirty the water in the tub, since people after you will use the same tubful. Likewise, do not add too much cold water or the bath will be too cool for those following. The Japanese prefer scalding hot baths. The trick is to lower yourself into the water gradually up to your neck and remain very still once you are immersed. This way your body cools the water touching your skin. Above all, exercise good judgment. Often a freshly-drawn bath will be too hot for anyone. In that case, rather than stoically parboiling your skin, judiciously add some cold water, keeping in mind the conditions mentioned above. You'll find these baths an exquisite joy after a busy day. Beats California hot tubs any day.

Ryokan do not have 'single' and 'double' rooms; bedding can be provided for one person or several in the same room. Ryokan rates are on a per person per night basis, and a 10-15% service charge is routinely added to the bill. At some ryokan you are expected to pay in advance.

Business hotels, a recent phenomenon, serve people who must travel often for their work. They provide rooms with air-conditioning and private bath for Y4000-5000, and most offer a buffet breakfast (both Japanese and Western food) for about Y600. They often also have small restaurants next to them, and the individual rooms and lack of a curfew allow you more privacy and freedom to come and go than youth hostels.

Transportation

INTERNATIONAL: Tokyo's new international airport at Narita finally opened in May 1978 (in spite of fierce local resistance), replacing the more conveniently located but cramped facilities at Haneda (see **General Information** for details).

Taiwan and South Korea are the two most likely destinations for those leaving Japan by ship. The Tokyo TIC has excellent information sheets with all the latest details on those routes, but the following information was accurate as of June 1980.

Shimonoseki is the port of embarkation for ferry service to Pusan in the **Republic of Korea**. There are departures on

Monday, Wednesday, and Friday at 5 pm for the 14-15 hour crossing. Fares range from Y12,000 for first class rooms to Y8000 for second class—which entitles the passenger to a spot on the floor of a carpeted room, shared intimately with 30 other travelers. Tickets can be booked at the office of the Kampu Ferry Co. on the fourth floor of the Ginza Asahi Bldg. (behind Matsuya Dept. Store), 3-8-10, Ginza, Chuo-ku, Tokyo; tel. (03) 567-0971. Sleeping car trains make the 15-hr. trip directly from Tokyo to Shimonoseki, leaving in the late afternoon (Y15,100 to Y21,600, depending on the train). Another option is to take the Shinkansen train from Tokyo to Shin-shimonoseki leaving in the late afternoon (Y15,200, 7 hr.). From that station it is only 10-min. ride on a local train to Shimonoseki. Visas for South Korea are available at the Korean Embassy, 2-5, Minami-Azabu 1-chome, Minato-ku, Tokyo (near Hiroo Subway Station on the Hibiya Line); tel. (03) 452-7611.

To reach **Taiwan** by ship, you must first sail to Naha, Okinawa, and then change to another boat bound for Keelung, Taiwan. Ships to Naha leave from Tokyo, Osaka, Kagoshima, and Fukuoka, usually once every 4-6 days. An Arimura Sangyo Co. ship leaves Naha at 5:30 pm every Friday, arriving in Keelung at 7 am Sunday (with stops en route at Miyako and Ishigaki); 2nd class fare is Y13,600. Booking in advance is required. Ask at the TIC for more information and for the shipping company addresses (offices in Tokyo, Osaka, and Naha). Since Japan no longer maintains diplomatic relations with Taiwan, you must get a visa through the Association of East Asian Relations, 2nd floor, Heiwado-Boeki Bldg., 1-8 Higashi Azabu, Minato-ku, Tokyo; tel. (03) 583-8030.

Nakhoda, USSR, is also a popular destination from Japan since it is the end point of the Trans-Siberian Railway. Ask at the Tokyo TIC for details.

INTER-CITY: The **Japan National Railway** (JNR) operates three basic kinds of trains: local (futsu), which stop at every station; express (kyuko), which stop at major stations only; and limited express (tokkyu), which seldom stop. The famous 'Bullet Train' (Shinkansen), which runs between Tokyo Station and Hakata (Fukuoka) in Kyushu, is considered a limited express. (In late 1981 the new Shinkansen line running from Tokyo's Ueno Station to northern Honshu will be ready.) Passengers pay a basic fare calculated upon the distance of their travel. This fare alone entitles them to a trip on the slow local train. For 'extra' service, such as passage on an express or limited express, a reserved seat, a seat in first class ('green car'), or a berth, there is an additional charge and usually a separate ticket. Since passengers pay extra for fast service, any significant delay entitles them to a refund on arrival at the Fare Adjustment window. In most cases, reserved seat (shiteiseki) tickets are only slightly more expensive than the basic unreserved (jiyuseki) ticket. They are often necessary during the holidays and summer vacation season. Reservations may be purchased up to one week in advance at train stations or at JTB offices. All the seats on limited express trains are reserved, except for certain cars on the Shinkansen and on some of the main lines. Passengers must be careful to keep their train tickets, since they may be checked by conductors during the trip and must be given up at the destination.

There are two types of Shinkansen—the **Hikari** ('Light') stops only at major stations, and the slightly less expensive **Kodama** ('Echo') stops at every station but is still quite fast. On the Hikari all seats are reserved except for the first four cars, which as a result are often crowded. On the Kodama, **only** the first four cars have reserved seats, and car #16 is for non-smokers (suits against JNR may lead to expansion of non-smoking areas in the future, but don't hold your breath). Non-reserved seats on a limited express (including Shinkansen) are valid for two days, including the day of purchase. A non-reserved ticket on an ordinary express can be used anytime. Because the Shinkansen is quite expensive, check out other trains as well. The JNTO can provide you with a "Condensed Railway Timetable" containing schedules for most limited expresses, including Shinkansen, and general information on the JNR system (check the section on discounts).

There are also various **private railways** which operate in and around large cities and resort areas. They often offer cheaper and/or more convenient service than the JNR.

It is possible to purchase railroad **excursion tickets** (shuyuken) which are good for a limited length of time—usually one or two weeks—for travel to, from, and within a specified region of Japan (e.g. Hokkaido, Kyushu, etc.) for the same price as a reserved round-trip ticket to that area. Traveling of this sort is best planned through the JTB, which has offices at most train stations.

In addition to trains, **highway buses** run between most cities and in more remote areas. Travelers will be especially interested in the buses between Tokyo, Nagoya, Kyoto, and Osaka— mostly overnight runs. They are not comfortable and are usually slower than trains, but are relatively cheap. Traveling overnight also saves the cost of a night's lodging, though you may be so tired and sore that the next day could be a total loss. Ask at the TIC where you can get up-to-date information on routes and fares.

Hitchhiking is rarely attempted by Japanese travelers, but Westerners who try usually have good luck, especially in areas away from the big cities. People who are hitching should be prepared for two things: first, being picked up by drivers who are interested in practicing their English, which may be next to non-existent, and second, receiving hospitality and kindness to an extent that is almost embarassing. You might want to carry a supply of small souvenirs from home to give to people who offer you rides. Hitchhiking alone seems to bring better results.

INTRA-CITY: Most of Japan's cities are served by excellent systems of public transportation. The largest centers have subways and local trains, in addition to the buses that run in most towns. Streetcars are very rare now—only found in a few cities in western Japan (mainly Shikoku and Kyushu). Old maps and guidebooks that show streetcars in Kyoto, for example, can confuse travelers.

The **subway and train systems** in Tokyo and Osaka are bound to be confusing at first. However, with a little patience and practice, any traveler can use them. English-language maps are available at the TIC, as well as in many of the free weekly tourist information publications. Subway and train cars are painted the same color as that used to indicate their route on the map. By comparing your map with the one on the station wall, it should be possible to calculate the correct fare, even though the wall map is in Japanese. If this is too confusing, then the simplest solution is to buy the cheapest ticket, then go to the fare adjustment window at your destination. Vending machines dispense tickets and correct change. Most subway and train platforms have English signs giving the name of the station as well as the ones before and after it. So, if it is possible to find a seat where you can see the platform out the window, there shouldn't be much problem getting off at the right stop.

Entrances to subway stations can be identified by one of the two marks shown at the right. The mark on the far right indicates a Tokyo Government-operated line (To-ei), and the nearer one indicates a private line. Don't get stranded by staying out too late since all subways stop running at midnight, or slightly earlier.

Buses are somewhat more difficult to use due to the lack of English signs at the stops. But once a visitor learns a few basic routes, this form of transportation can be easy and convenient. In Tokyo the bus fare is Y110.

Given the overseas news coverage it receives, it seems almost trite to remind travelers that Japan's public transportation is incredibly overcrowded during rush hours (7-9 am and 5-7 pm). For the visitor who forgets the obvious, a single trip at that time of the day will serve as a permanent reminder.

Taxis are expensive, but at times indispensable. Since few taxi drivers speak English, have your destination written down in Japanese. Even with this information, the driver may have to stop several times to ask directions—Japanese addresses are notoriously hard to find. In Tokyo fares start at Y380 for the first two kilometers, plus Y70 for each additional 415 meters; they go up another 20% after the subway stops running (11 pm-5 am). Because many foreigners are unaware of this higher late-night rate and get angry when they think they have been overcharged, taxi drivers are often reluctant to pick up foreigners; it may be almost impossible to get a taxi to stop for you during this time. When getting in and out of taxis, be prepared for a door opening/closing device which the driver operates by remote control—unsuspecting passengers occasionally receive a door in the shins courtesy of these mechanical marvels.

NOTE: The transportation prices quoted in this chapter were current as of mid-1980, but all fares—train, subway, bus, taxi—were scheduled to rise as much as 15% by the end of the year.

Tokyo

Tokyo was founded in 1457 (originally it was named Edo), and has been growing ever since. Today it's probably the largest city in the world, with more than 11 million people living in the greater metropolitan area. Since it covers more than 800 square miles, don't be surprised if you have trouble getting oriented.

Think of Tokyo as a collection of districts, each with its own name and personality—with the Imperial Palace in the center of everything. East of the Palace is Marunouchi, the city's main commercial district; Tokyo Station is located here. Southeast from the Palace is the Ginza, the colorful, crowded shopping district packed with huge department stores and little specialty shops. Asakusa and Ueno Park are northeast, and Roppongi and Akasaka are southwest of the Palace (see below for more information on these districts). Indispensable to any traveler is the clear, highly detailed "Tourist Map of Tokyo," put out by the TIC. While you're there, pick up the small English-language guide to Tokyo's subway system.

Before setting out on a sightseeing expedition, visitors should be aware of the difficulties involved in locating addresses in Japan, especially in Tokyo. There are virtually no street addresses. Street names are recently given and seldom used, and buildings are assigned numbers according to the order in which they're constructed rather than in a linear progression from one end of the street to the other. Most places are located by reference to the nearest street intersection, the name of which often applies to a whole district, for example Roppongi. If this sounds a bit confusing, it may be reassuring to know that the locals sometimes have trouble finding their way around as well. For that reason there are police boxes ('koban') every few blocks in major cities for policemen and policewomen whose main job is giving people directions.

Some hints for getting around with minimal difficulty: First, have your destination written down in Japanese; Tokyoites are helpful almost to a fault and will do their best to guide you if they understand where you're going. Second, get directions that are as explicit as possible, including a description of nearby shops and landmarks; if someone can draw you a map, so much the better. Third, give yourself plenty of time to get places.

Exploring Tokyo

Start by calling the TIC's 'Teletourist Services' at (03) 503-2911 for tape-recorded information on major events in and around Tokyo (updated weekly).

An oasis of tranquility in the center of Tokyo, the **Imperial Palace**, built in the 15th century, remains as fine an example of castle architecture as can be found. To visit the palace and its extensive gardens, apply a day or two in advance with the Imperial Household Agency, located at the main gate on the east side of the grounds. On Sunday the Japan Bicycle Industry Association supplies 500 free bicycles for people to ride the 5.5 km course around the Palace gardens. The bikes are available at the Palace police station from 10:30 am to 4 pm.

The spacious parks in the downtown areas also offer pleasant retreats from the nearby noise and confusion. **Hibiya Park**, near the Imperial Palace, becomes a lunch-hour haven for city workers when the weather is fine. **Ueno Park**, near Ueno Station (JNR Yamanote Line, or Ginza or Hibiya subway lines), features several museums, the famous Toshogu Shrine, and a zoo, all in a lovely setting dotted with cherry trees. The **Ueno Zoo** is open every day except Monday. **Korakuen Garden**, built in the 17th century, is beautiful and serene, boasting a lake, a lotus pond, an island shaped like a turtle (symbolizing longevity), and cherry trees four centuries old.

The **Meiji Shrine**, another of the striking attractions in Tokyo, stands in the middle of a large park of pine forests, beautiful gardens, and huge torii gates. Visitors should remember that all shrines are built to honor the memory of a respected person—in this case, the emperor who brought Japan into the 'modern world'—and act accordingly. The shrine itself stands within the Inner Garden, which is separated from the larger Outer Garden by several city blocks. These two parks also contain most of the facilities used to stage the Tokyo Olympics in 1964. The shrine is open from sunrise to sunset.

For a Y950 view of the city and environs, take a trip to the top of the **Tokyo Tower**, standing at the edge of Shiba Park. If the day is clear, the view of the sunset over Mt. Fuji is stunning. To get there ride the subway (Toei Line no. 6) to the Onarimon stop. You can also find some fairly high perches for picture-taking or sightseeing on the upper floors of the skyscrapers in the Ginza, notably the Sony and San Ai buildings, as well as in Shinjuku and one (the tallest, at 60 stories) in Ikebukuro.

The JNTO brochure, "Museums and Art Galleries in Japan" (available at the TIC)—lists some 30 **museums** in Tokyo. Four of

138 JAPAN

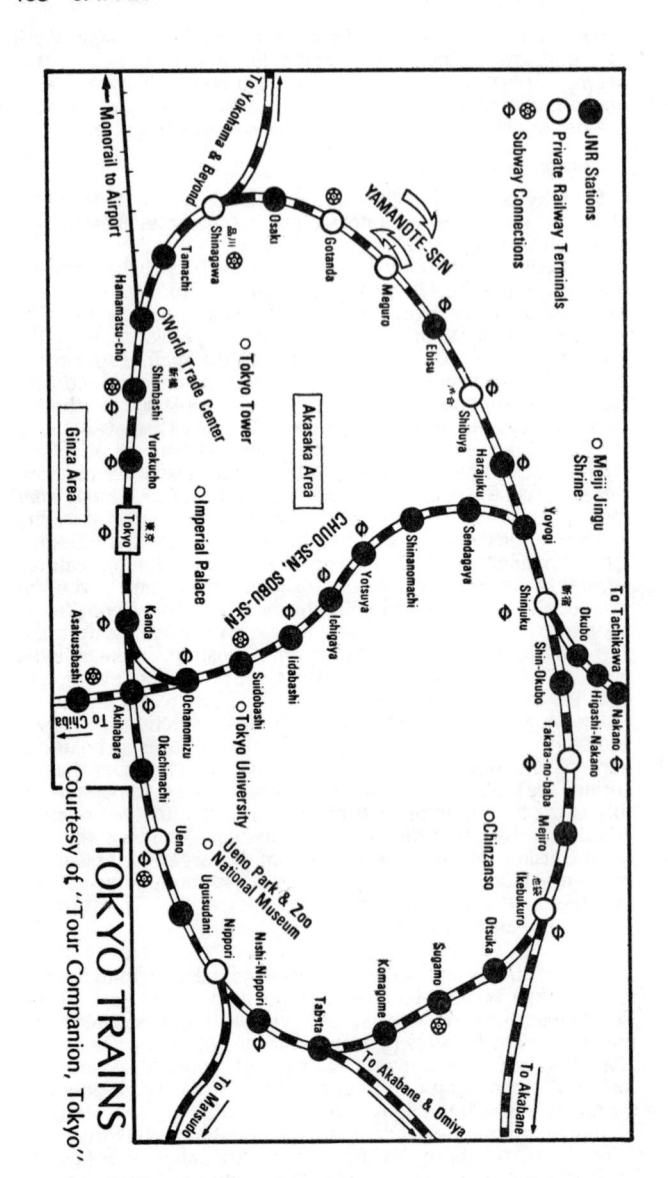

JAPAN 139

them—the National Museum (traditional art), the Tokyo Metropolitan Fine Art Gallery (contemporary Japanese artists), the National Science Museum (natural sciences), and the National Museum of Western Art—are located amid the pleasant surroundings of Ueno Park. The National Museum of Modern Art (Japanese arts and crafts since 1907) and the Science Museum (not to be confused with the National Science Museum) can be found in Kitanomaru Park, north of the Imperial Palace. Although the explanations are written in Japanese, the Science Museum is interesting for its working models of everyday mechanical devices. It's also worth the price of admission just to watch the rosy-cheeked, uniformed schoolchildren staring wide-eyed at the displays. Other unique exhibits can be seen at the Paper Museum, the Museum of Sumo, the Japanese Sword Museum, and the Japan Folkcraft Museum. The brochure gives the location and hours of all these and more; note that most museums are closed Mondays.

For those interested in Japanese drama, both the Kabuki-za and the National Theatre of Japan stage regular performances of **kabuki** plays. The plots of kabuki drama are based on Japan's medieval history, though the plays are written by modern playwrights. An all-male cast gives a performance featuring lots of action, colorful costumes, elaborate sets, and unique music, guaranteeing that foreign theatergoers will be entertained even if they don't understand the sing-song dialogue. Both theaters put out English-language leaflets which give the details on their current performances, along with a synopsis of each (available at the TIC). Ticket prices are Kabuki-za are Y1000-7000, at the National Theatre of Japan Y2800-4000. Summer is the off season for kabuki.

The small hall of the National Theatre also provides occasional programs of **classical music and dance, bunraku** (puppet plays), and other **traditional arts**. Tokyo has several theaters presenting **Noh** drama, but most foreigners find this form difficult to appreciate. Noh, heavily influenced by Zen Buddhist thought and philosophy, is highly esoteric, and the ritualized acting and bare stage lack the interest of kabuki for the uninitiated.

If you watch television in Japan you might see one of the six annual **sumo wrestling** tournaments. Sumo rules are simple—the contest is decided when one of the heavyweight wrestlers throws the other to the ground (or out of the ring). Individual matches rarely last more than a minute, but are preceded by various rituals. **Judo** enthusiasts may observe experts in action at the headquarters of judo in Tokyo, the Kodokan Judo Hall, near the Korakuen Station (Marunouchi subway line). There are free spectator seats on the third floor balcony. Other martial arts, such as karate, aikido, and kendo also have headquarters in Tokyo. The **Nippon Budokan Hall**, in the northern corner of Kitanomaru Park, is a good place to observe all types of martial artists practice, as well as being an interesting piece of architecture. Check at the TIC for further information.

Just outside the entrance of Shibuya station is a small plaza with a statue of a dog named Hachiko. This is **the** rendezvous point for young couples who want to get out from under mama-san's watchful eye. Go there any afternoon and see literally thousands of youths anxiously awaiting their boyfriends or girlfriends.

Those who like kinky entertainment should cruise over to Yoyogi Park on Sundays when the roads are closed off to cars, to watch one of Japan's newest and most bizarre phenomena, the 'bamboo shoot kids' (takenoko-zoku). Defying a society that gives them few outlets for free self-expression, these groups of young people (most aged 14 to 16) have taken to wearing wild and colorful clothes and makeup that would make a punkrocker blush, while dancing in the streets of the park to the blare of music from cassette tape recorders.

Nightlife

Tokyo's nightlife is characterized by two features—it can easily be very expensive and (perhaps because of that) it ends early. Even on the Ginza, where expensive clubs do their best to whittle down businessmens' fat expense accounts, most shows end by 11 and bars and restaurants close by midnight.

As in anything else, Tokyo offers an abundance of nighttime entertainment of all types. The most economical activity is always **walking** and **watching**. Japan has almost no violent crime, so aside from an occasional pickpocket, there's no reason to worry about your safety any time or any place. Each of the districts discussed below has all the necessary qualifications for a lengthy session of people-watching.

For young people, **coffee shops** (kissaten) are probably the most common source of low-cost entertainment. These cozy establishments are often equipped with an impressive stereo system that fills the shop with a particular type of music—classical, jazz (either 'hot' or 'cool'), disco, hard rock, even country-western. For the price of a cup of coffee ('koh-hee') you are entitled to sit and enjoy the music, read, write, talk, or just rest, for as long as you like. Coffee shops create a good atmosphere for talking informally with Japanese students. A cup of coffee will cost Y250-500, depending on the place. Most shops offer several different blends, as well as snacks, if you can figure out how to order them. Since coffee shops open around noon, they also provide an air-conditioned spot to enjoy some iced coffee ('ah-ee-soo koh-hee') on a hot afternoon. There are many 'jazz bars' that operate in a similar vein, except that they serve liquor. Many customers buy a full bottle of Japanese whisky, put their name on the bottle, and store it in a cabinet at the bar, to be quaffed from whenever they come in.

For a place to have a drink after work, Japanese working people can't afford a luxurious nightclub any more than a

JAPAN 141

budget traveler can. So it's only appropriate that you follow their lead and patronize the **beer halls**, or, in the summer, roof-top **beer gardens**. A regular mug of beer (Asahi, Kirin, Sapporo, and Suntory are popular brands) will cost around Y500, with large mugs at Y700. This type of night spot allows patrons to relax in a rowdier way than would be suitable in quiet coffee houses or bars. A further note: There is not such a stigma attached to drunkenness in Japan as there is in many other societies, so don't be surprised if you see working men in expensive three-piece suits staggering toward the subway station on their way home from a little after-work socialization with their buddies from the office. Women, however, rarely get drunk in public.

For dancing, to either live or recorded music, **discotheques** are numerous. Cover charges vary greatly; many now include food, and some discos give cheaper rates for foreigners. Also, there are often higher rates for men than women. Ask about the cover charge price before you enter so you aren't unpleasantly surprised later. The Japanese discotheque set is very quick to pick up the latest disco steps from abroad, so travelers may find themselves outclassed on the dance floor.

Of Tokyo's nightlife districts, **Shinjuku** is the favorite of Japanese college students and young people. The area to the east of Shinjuku station is a maze of streets and alleys, mostly closed to traffic, which are lined with every type of coffee shop, bar, discotheque, and strip show imaginable. Specific shops and bars come and go quickly and would be impossible to locate among hundreds of similar places, so we won't make any particular suggestions. But discotheques here are cheaper than in other neighborhoods, there are lots of students in the coffee shops, and the summertime beer gardens atop the Kinokuniya Bldg. and the Mitsukoshi Dept. Store are lots of fun.

Go to Harajuku district (get off at Harajuku Station), and visit one of the wild and trend-setting coffee shops and boutiques. People in this area are at the cutting edge of new fads and lifestyles in Tokyo. One traveler reports entering a coffee shop where every single person was wearing black. Japan's cleaner version of Telegraph Ave. in Berkeley.

The **Asakusa** (ah-sahk'-sah) district, centered on the 1300-yr.-old Asakusa Kannon Temple (east of Ueno Park), is known as 'Old Tokyo.' The area around the temple contains narrow streets, stalls selling religious articles, occasional processions, and the homes of the Edokko (native Tokyoites). Walking through this dimly-lit area at night is a distinctly different experience from a stroll through the neon jungles of Ginza and Shinjuku. Things close up early here, so this might be the place to start an evening.

Roppongi is the area where chic young couples and 'swinging singles' make the scene. Discotheques and bars are very trendy and more expensive than Shinjuku, and there are a considerable number of excellent but expensive restaurants representing various world cuisines. One thing to recommend Roppongi is that the aspiring jet-setters keep things going after midnight, when most other parts of the city are quiet. But remember that there are no subways after midnight.

Most of the entertainment offered in **Akasaka** and **Ginza** is beyond the realm of 'low budget.' Akasaka does have some discotheques and there are several beer halls and gardens in Ginza. Walking in these areas is interesting and free.

Shopping

Tokyo is not the place for great bargains, but window shopping can be fun. The major stores are open 10 am-6 pm and usually are closed on either Wednesdays or Thursdays (a few are closed on Mondays).

Foreign visitors can purchase many items tax-free, including cameras and electrical appliances. This discount can be 15-20%, so it is worth investigating. If you purchase any tax-free items, a form will be attached to your passport. As you leave the country you must present both the form and the item for inspection at Customs.

For **pottery, pearls,** and other **handicraft products**, the best price is at the point of manufacture, not in the department stores. For example, Mashiko, a notable pottery village, and Ise, the center of pearl culture, are not far from the regular tourist routes.

Maruzen department stores have good English bookstores, usually located on the third floor, where they sell books on almost all facets of Japanese life. Kinokuniya bookstores also offer a wide range of books in English. Two of their easier-to-reach locations: one block east of the Shinjuku JNR station, and on the second floor of the Toho Twin Tower Bldg., one block west of the Tokyo TIC. Jena, two blocks east of the TIC, stocks many English publications.

Meeting Students

Most major universities have student associations called ESS (English Speaking Society). Try visiting a university in the afternoon and asking at the gate where the ESS clubhouse is. Many ESS members are eager to meet foreign students and exchange ideas.

Three of the largest universities in Tokyo are: Keio University, one block east of Sendagaya JNR station, on the Chuo or Sobu Lines; Waseda U., a 10 min. walk northeast from Waseda Station on the Tozai Subway Line; and Tokyo U., just west of Ueno Park on Hongo-dori Ave.

JAPAN 143

ACCOMMODATIONS IN TOKYO

Lodgings in Tokyo are not cheap. The TIC offers a list of reasonable accommodations; the places listed here are the cheapest and therefore the most popular. Especially during the summer, reservations are practically a must. Making reservations by phone is tricky—so ask someone at the TIC office to call for you, or write ahead.

Ichigaya Youth Hostel, 1-6, Gobancho, Chiyoda-ku; tel. 262-5950 or 261-6839. JNR: Ichigaya Station.

Y850/person; Y150 for a sleeping sheet and Y100 for heating in winter. A large hostel with 128 beds, Japanese bath, and a self-service kitchen which lodgers can use for a small fee; also a cafeteria serving meals of average quality. Guests must be in by 9:30 pm, lights out at 10.

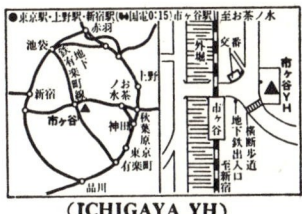

(ICHIGAYA YH)
市ヶ谷ユース・ホステル

Asia Center of Japan, 10-38 8-chome, Akasaka, Minato-ku; tel. (03) 402-6111. Subway: Aoyama-Itchome Station on the Ginza line.

Single w/o bath Y3200, w/bath Y4100-4800; twin w/o bath Y4400-5400, w/bath Y7200. Has 176 Western-style rooms, a snack bar, and a restaurant with reasonably-priced meals. Many international travelers stay here.

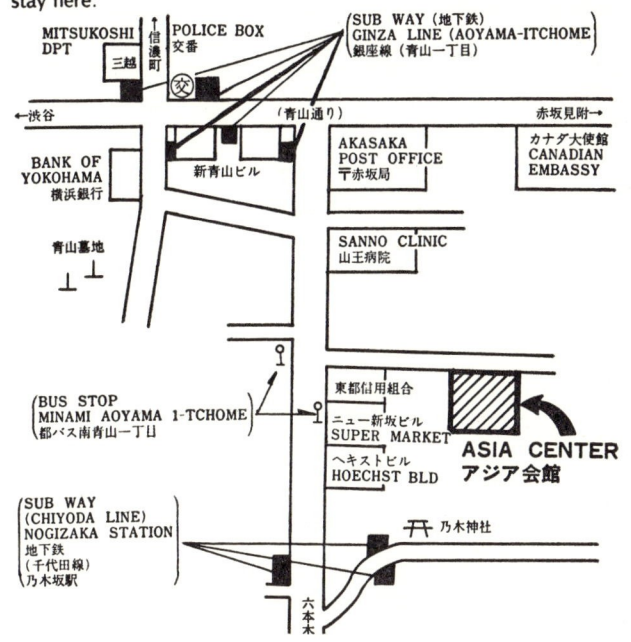

144 JAPAN

Gotanda Chisan Hotel, 1-1, Nishi-Oi 6-chome, Shinagawa-ku, tel. (03) 785-3211. Subway: Nakanobu Station on the Toei-Ichigo Line.
  Singles w/private bath Y3800-4000, twins w/private bath Y7000-8000. Only a 3 min. walk from Nakanobu Station.

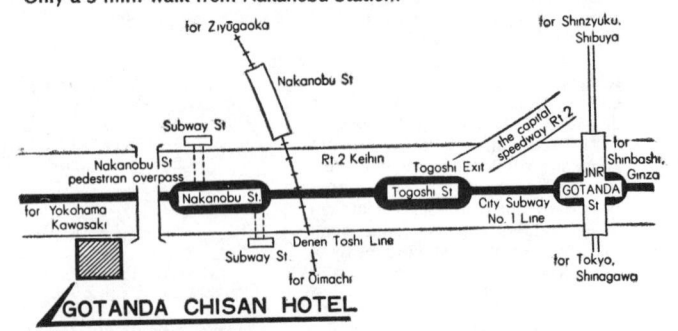

Japan YWCA Hostel, 8-8, Kudan Minami 4-chome, Chiyoda-ku; tel. (03) 264-0661. JNR: Ichigaya Station.
  Women only. Single w/o bath Y   , twin w/o bath Y   ; Japanese-style rooms Y4000/person. Convenient location; only a 5-min. walk from Ichigaya Station.

Tokyo YMCA Hotel, 7, Kanda Mitoshirocho, Chiyoda-ku; tel (03) 293-1911. Subway: Kanda Station on the Ginza line or Awajicho on the Marunouchi Line.
  Men only. Single w/o bath Y4200, w/bath Y4840; twin w/o bath Y7400, w/bath Y8200; triple w/o bath Y11,100.

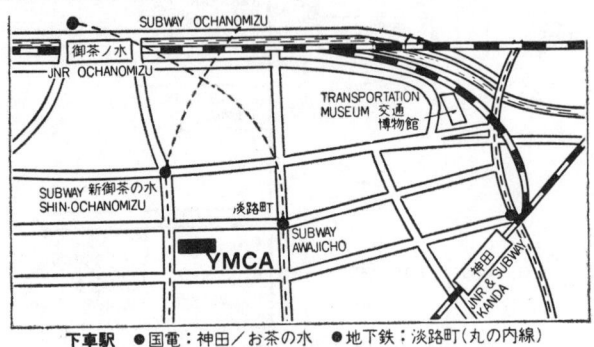

Tokyo Station Hotel, 9-1, Marunouchi 1-chome, Chiyoda-ku; tel. (03) 231-2511, JNR: Tokyo Station.
  Single w/o bath Y6280; twin w/o bath Y8800-9800, w/bath Y14,600. Located next to Tokyo Station; a more central hotel can't be found.

Akasaka Shanpia Hotel, 6-13, Akasaka 7-chome, Minato-ku; tel. (03) 583-1001. Subway: Akasaka Station.
Single w/bath Y5200-5600, twin w/bath Y8800.

Tokyo Marunouchi Hotel, 1-6, Marunouchi, Chiyoda-ku; tel. 215-2151. Near Tokyo Central Station and the Imperial Palace grounds.
A well-kept, modern business hotel. Singles Y6500-9000, twins Y11,000-13,000. All rooms w/ac, private bath, television. Its sister hotel, **Ginza Marunouchi Hotel**, 4-1-12, Tsukuji, Chuo-ku (tel. 543-5431), has singles at Y5500-9000, twins at Y9500-12,000. Reservations for both hotels can be made in the U.S.; the San Francisco number is (800) 227-4320; the New York number is (212) 697-3694.

Ryokan are generally expensive in Tokyo and few innkeepers can speak English. The prices quoted below do not include meals. Try to have a Japanese speaker call for you to make sure there is a vacancy and to make your reservation.

Sagamiya Bekkan, 2-5, 4-chome, Shinjuku, Shinjuku-ku; tel. (03) 354-7662. Subway or JNR to Shinjuku Station.
Y2900 per person w/o bath. To get there go out the south exit of Shinjuku Station.

Fujikan, 36-1, 4-chome, Hongo, Bunkyo-ku; tel. (03) 813-4441. Subway: Hongo-Sanchome Station on the Marunouchi Line.
Y3000 per person w/o bath.

Kimi Ryokan, 1034, 2-chome, Ikebukuro, Toshima-ku; tel. (03) 971-3766. JNR or subway to Ikebukuro station, west exit. Get a map from TIC.
Single w/o bath Y2200, double w/o bath Y3500. The 'businessman's hotel' located next door is Y2000 a night; there are discounts for longer stays.

Hotel Tokiwa, 328 Nishi-Okubo 2-chome, Shinjuku-ku; tel. (03) 202-4321. JNR: Shin-Okubo Station on the Yamanote Line.
Single w/o bath Y4400, w/bath Y5000-6880; twin w/o bath Y7800, w/bath Y9000-12,760. English is spoken at this ryokan; it also accepts reservations from abroad.

Kanto

Kanto is the name for the area around Tokyo.

The Japanese saying goes, "You can't use the word 'kekko' (magnificent) until you've seen **Nikko**." The air is refreshing; the mountains, Lake Chuzenji and the numerous shrines are fascinating. Start walking around Nikko early in the morning; otherwise you'll be accompanied by large tour groups. You can walk from two youth hostels (Nikko YH and Nikko Daiyagawa YH) up to Toshogu Shrine, where it is worth it to pay the full entrance fee and spend a couple of hours exploring all the buildings and inner sanctuaries. Inside the shrine are exquisitely carved tombs and mausolea of Ieyasu Tokugawa, founder of the Tokugawa Shogunate (and inspiration for the fictional character Toranaga in the novel **Shogun**), and his grandson. 2½ million gum wrapper-sized sheets of gold leaf were used to adorn the mausolea during its construction in 1636.

Below the shrine, catch the public bus which runs up the main road, winding through the 28 turns of the steep highway, to Chuzenji. Here you should visit Kegon Waterfall, to the right as you enter the village on the bus, and Lake Chuzenji, a short walk off to the left. An avid hiker might consider climbing Mt. Nantai. For those who enjoy spectacular views but are too lazy to hike, a cable car runs to the peak, which overlooks Chuzenji. The trip to Nikko from Tokyo can be done in a day, but the best plan would be to stay in one of the youth hostels overnight and see Nikko early in the morning before all the tourists arrive.

Mashiko, one of Japan's most famous pottery-making villages, lies 120 km northeast of Tokyo. There are some 150 kilns scattered around the small village, a few dating back to 1852. Some shops allow visitors to watch pots being made, and even try their own hand at it. The trip to Mashiko takes several hours, but those who intend to buy pottery will find much better bargains here than in any of Tokyo's department stores. Ask at the Tokyo TIC for travel information on getting to Mashiko.

The **Nippon Minkaen Park** brings together 16 homes, farmhouses, and inns 150-300 years old from all parts of Japan. Fully furnished with the tools and utensils of its particular period, each of these fascinating buildings has its own niche in the park's hilly landscape. A walk through this park will give you a good glimpse of life in feudal Japan. Open every day except Monday, Nippon Minkaen is only a 40-min. ride on the Odakyu-sen ('sen' means line) from Shinjuku Station; get off at Mukogaoka Yuen Station.

Despite its proximity to Tokyo, the **Boso Peninsula**, on the southwestern side of Tokyo Bay, has remained relatively unexplored by tourists. The coastline, vegetable farmlands, and fields of flowers are especially beautiful during the spring.

Take a day trip to explore **Yokohama** and **Kamakura**, both about an hour by train from Tokyo. The port city of Yokohama is the home of a U.S. Navy base, and of Sankeien Garden, one of the finest in Japan, though off the major international tourist paths. Sankeien is a purely Japanese landscape garden; it contains an ancient tea ceremony house, samurai villa, pagoda, and farmhouse, all three to five centuries old. To get there, take the JNR Yokosuka Train or the Tokaido Main Line to Yokohama Station. Inquire at the train station JTB office for the bus number to Sankeien.

Get back on the Yokosuka Line or the Keihin-Tohoku Line for **Kamakura**, ancient capital of Japan from 1192-1333 during the

Minamoto Shogunate, and location of hundreds of temples and shrines. The highlight of the area is a 700-year-old statue of Buddha that is 11.4 meters tall. The statue (known as the Daibutsu) can be reached in 10 min. from the Hase Station on the Enoden Railway Line, or in 8 min. by bus from Kamakura Station. In the same area is the Hase Kannon Temple, which houses an 11-faced Goddess of Mercy said to have been carved in 721 from a single camphor log. The temple is open 8 am-5 pm. Only a 10-min. walk from Kamakura Station is the Tsurugaoka Hachimangu Shrine, where every Sept. 16 a festival is held; archers in samurai costume come screaming down a narrow crowd-filled lane on horses, shooting arrows over the heads of the crowd into very small targets. Within the shrine compound there are three museums.

ACCOMMODATIONS IN KANTO

Nikko: There are several youth hostels in Nikko; consult the Handbook. Or stay at the more expensive **Nikko Kanaya Hotel**, Kami-Hatsuishi-cho, Nikko; tel. (03) 271-5215 (Tokyo) or (0288) 4-0001 (Nikko). Twin w/o bath Y5500 for single occupancy (Y2000 extra in peak seasons); twin w/shower Y8000 for single occupancy (Y3000 extra in peak seasons); twin w/bath Y8500 for single occupancy (Y3000 extra in peak seasons). Located 5 min. by car from Nikko Station.

Mashiko: Accommodations in this town are all Japanese-style and tend to be full on weekends, so make reservations in advance if possible. the **Okadaya**, a 10-min. walk from Mashiko Station, offers rooms at 4200 per person, including two meals (2800/person w/o meals). Closer to the station, the **Tozanso** charges Y2800 per person w/o meals and Y3800-Y5000 per person w/two meals.

Boso Peninsula: Ryokan in the area average Y5000-6000 (w/two meals), and hotels usually cost Y8000-Y15,000. An inexpensive hotel in Chiba is the **Chiba Keisei Hotel**, 14-1, Honchiba-cho; tel. 22-2111. Single w/bath Y3800, double w/bath Y5000-6500. Located near Chiba Station. Many minshuku are springing up as surfing becomes popular on the Pacific side of the peninsula.

148 JAPAN

TRANSPORTATION IN KANTO

Nikko: Nikko is served by the private Tobu Railway's Nikko Line from its station in Asakusa and by the JNR from Ueno Station. For up-to-date fare and schedule information, see the TIC sheets on Nikko.

Mashiko: From the Ueno Station in Tokyo to Utsunomiya Station is an 80-min., Y2600 ride by special express (express train is 86 min., Y1900; local is 2 hrs. 6 min., Y1200). Walk 5 min. to the Miyanohashi bus stop of the Toya Bus Co. to catch a bus for Mashiko (Y500, 1 hr.).

Boso Peninsula: Trains leave every half hour, 7 am-7 pm, from platform #4 (underground) near the Marunouchi-guchi exit of Tokyo Central Station. Tickets are Y1700 for local, Y2400 for express, and Y3100 for special express (non-reserved seats), and the trip takes 1-2 hr.

Kamakura: Take one of the trains on the Yokosuka Line leaving from Tokyo Station tracks 9 and 10. One-way fare is Y550.

Chubu

Central Honshu is generally known as Chubu. Within this region there are six quasi-national and seven national parks, including the Fuji-Hakone-Izu National Park, possibly the most popular recreation area in all Japan. In the highlands of Chubu along the coast of the Sea of Japan the peaks are high and there is heavy snowfall in winter. Chubu's main city is Nagoya, a prosperous industrial city.

Although climbing **Mt. Fuji** may sound like an attractive adventure, you should be warned that many travelers who make the ascent come away somewhat disappointed. Throughout most of the year Mt. Fuji is too cold for comfortable climbing, so during the few weeks of ideal weather, large crowds of people stream up and down the mountain, leaving the trails littered behind them. This tends to destroy the romance of the climb for nature-lovers. Mt. Fuji is officially open to climbers July 1-August 31, but the peak season is from mid-July to mid-August, when all the stone-hut shelters on the main climbing trails are open. It's very dangerous to climb during other times. Several youth hostels dot the area and even if you don't climb Fuji, it might be enjoyable to tour the neighboring five lakes by bus or to hike in the surrounding countryside where there are fewer people. Mt. Fuji, the lakes at its base, and the surrounding forests are all part of the Fuji-Hakone-Izu National Park.

The TIC publishes an information sheet for a two-day trip to the **Izu Peninsula** which gives all the necessary details regarding transportation, as well as the addresses of two Kokumin Shukusha ('People's Lodges'—see **Accommodations**). The peninsula is a scenic area with many well laid-out 'hiking courses' ('haikingu kosu'). Ito, on the east coast of the peninsula, offers beaches, hot springs, and hiking on nearby trails. Try the 'hiking course' from Ito to a small fishing village called Izu Kogen—it follows a gorgeous coastline and passes a waterfall cascading into the sea. Youth hostel accommodations are available. Secret Beach, no longer a secret, lies several kilometers west of Shimoda at the southern tip of the peninsula. A road now tunnels through the mountains which once hid this small cove, but it is still possible to camp here in relative solitude during the week. Kokumin Shukusha are available near Shimoda and Secret Beach for about Y3400. From Shimoda you might make the 2-hr. trip through Amagi Pass to Shuzenji, where you can enjoy bathing in hot springs and hiking. The trail from Shuzenji Spa to Mt. Daruma, over Hida Pass, is one of the best hiking paths on the peninsula; there is a campsite near the pass, about 8 km from the spa (50 min. by bus).

Gifu, north of Nagoya, is most famous for the night cormorant fishing (ukai) which takes place on the Nagara River from May to October. Ukai, once the traditional method of catching a fish called ayu, has become a popular spectator sport. The tame cormorants have collars strapped to their necks, which the fishermen control with a long cord in order to prevent the birds from swallowing the catch. A large fire in an iron grate at the bow of each boat attracts the fish. The boats go out each night after the moon sets or before it rises (moonlight distracts the fish from the decoy fires). A flotilla of five or six boats works to corner the fish for the cormorants. You can pay to see the ukai from a spectator boat, but the view is just as good from the banks of the river.

Further into the mountains past Gifu lies the calm old castle town of **Takayama**, often called 'Little Kyoto.' The city offers the Hida Folklore Museum (2 km west of the station) with its restored thatched-roof clan dwellings, a morning farmers' market on the river, and fine lacquerware.

Those intrepid travelers who have the time and energy to travel beyond Takayama should head for **Noto Peninsula**, via Toyama. The peninsula features beautiful coastal beaches and islands. Those going on to Osaka or Kyoto along the coast of the Japan Sea can stop at the Zen Buddhist **Eiheiji** Temple, located in the small village of Shibidani (about 16 km east of Fukui). There's a youth hostel near Eiheiji, and if you stay overnight, see the sunrise service at the temple before continuing. The route around the Noto Peninsula and along the coast of the Japan Sea to Fukui is remote and would be easiest for travelers who have picked up some ability in Japanese.

South of Nagoya are the **Ise Jingu Shrines**, or Ise Grand Shrines, the most venerated shrines in Japan which together are the seat of Shintoism. There are two complexes, 6.2 km apart, set in a 200-acre park. The Geku (Outer Shrine) is dedicated to Amaterasu-Omikami, the sun goddess. The shrines, built with unpainted cypress, are excellent examples of indigenous Japanese architecture, a style predating the introduction of Chinese architecture in the 6th century. The Emperor comes here once a year to report to the sun goddess on the state of the nation. More than 8 million Japanese visit the shrines annually.

Just beyond Ise is **Toba**, where you can see demonstrations of pearl diving and the process of culturing pearls.

ACCOMMODATIONS IN CHUBU

Mt. Fuji: There are several youth hostels in the area; see the Handbook. There are also two Kokumin Shukusha, both charging Y2200 (w/o meals) and Y3900 (w/two meals). To get to **Kawaguchi** Lodge (tel. 6-7611), take a bus from Kawaguchiko Station to Ohishi; get off at 'Lodge-mae' and walk 5 min. **Motosu** Lodge (tel. 2022) can be reached directly by bus from the Kawaguchiko Station.

Gifu: Gifu Youth Hostel tel. 0582-63-6631; Y750/Y1750.

Takayama: Tenshoji Youth Hostel, tel. 0577-32-6345. A 15-min. walk from Takayama Station. Y1000/Y2000.

Noto Peninsula: There are several youth hostels. See Handbook.

Ise: Ise-Shima Youth Hostel, tel. 05995-5-0226; Y1150/Y2100.

TRANSPORTATION IN CHUBU

Mt. Fuji: There are three options: by private Odakyu Railway train from Shinjuku Station (Y1650, 1½ hr.); by bus from Hamamatsucho JNR Station in Tokyo to the 5th stage on Fujisan (Y1800, 3 hrs.); and by JNR express train from Tokyo's Shinjuku Station to Kawaguchiko (Y1790, 2 hrs.), then by bus from Kawaguchiko to the 5th stage (Y1000, 55 min.).

Gifu: A local train from Tokyo to Gifu costs Y4200 (7 hrs.). Or, from Tokyo you can ride the Shinkansen to Nagoya (Y7100, 2 hrs.), and change there for a 30-min. trip by local train to Gifu (Y380). If you're coming from Osaka, the trip to Gifu takes 2¾ hrs. by local, 2½ hrs. by express train on the Tokaido Main Line.

Takayama: From Gifu take a train on the Takayama Line (Y1500).

Noto Peninsula: The easiest way to explore the peninsula is by JTB Tour Bus, because the connections for local transportation is irregular. However, you can travel on the JNR Nanao Line, which runs from Kanazawa to Wajima.

Ise: Take an express train from Nagoya to Toba (1½ hr.), then switch to local train or bus for the short trip to Ise. If you're coming from Namba (in Osaka), the trip is 2½ hrs. long by express train (Y2260).

Kansai

Kansai is the name of the area around Osaka and Kyoto; sometimes it is also referred to as Kinki.

Kyoto

For roughly five centuries, 794-1180 and 1338-1467, Kyoto was Japan's undisputed political and cultural capital. After the Meiji Restoration Kyoto lost its pre-eminent status to Tokyo, but it is still the historical center of Japan. Supposedly American sympathy for Kyoto's cultural treasures allowed it to escape the fire bombings that devastated much of urban Japan at the end of World War II. As a result, unlike most big cities, Kyoto is a city of wood and has a low profile. It stretches out across a broad, flat valley about 480 km south of Tokyo. Castles, shrines, imperial villas, and 1,500 Buddhist temples are scattered throughout the city.

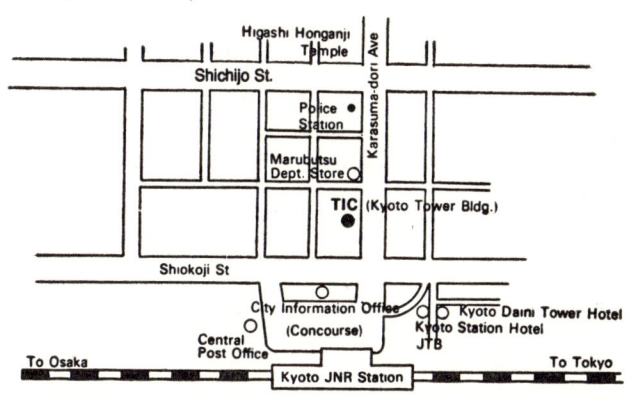

Since Kyoto is Japan's premier tourist city, it's easy to get assistance here. On your right as you leave Kyoto Station is the JTB office, right in front of you is the City Information Office, and just across the big street in front of the station is the TIC office. The TIC is the best equipped to help English-speaking travelers. Stop here to get the excellent "Tourist Map of Kyoto-Nara" and brochures for walking tours in the two cities, and to get help in finding a place to stay. The TIC can also arrange for a Japanese student to act as your guide in Kyoto. There is no charge for such a service, as the students are eager to practice their English, but you are expected to cover their

152 JAPAN

expenses (bus fares, meals, etc.) while they're with you. If you'd be interested in a 'home visit' with a Japanese family, it can be arranged through the City Information Office in the Kyoto Kaikan Hall near Heian Shrine (apply at least a day in advance). The families that you would meet through this program are wealthier than most.

A wealth of material has already been published describing the various sights in and around Kyoto: Heian Shrine, Kinkakuji (Temple of the Golden Pavilion), Ginkakuji (Temple of the Silver Pavilion), Sanjusangendo Hall, Nijo Castle, etc. But there are countless lesser-known cultural treasures to be discovered by the visitor with a few days to spend exploring. Kyoto has had over 1000 years to build up an accumulation of temples and shrines and it shows on every street; just pick a small area on the map and then take a leisurely walk through it. Sections of town particularly interesting to tour on foot include: the **Higashiyama Area** (near Heian Shrine); **Arashiyama Park**, once the retreat of Heian emperors (walk along the river and watch the fishermen bring in fish after fish using trained cormorants); **Gion**, the oldest section of Kyoto; and the central shopping district, located near the intersection of Shijo and Kawaramachi St. (Maruzen, with its English-language bookstore, is one of the largest department stores in this area).

Daitokuji Temple, on the northern side of the city, is actually a collection of five temples, abbots' living quarters, and several of the finest dry gardens in Japan. Regarded as a 'National Treasure,' the garden of the subordinate Daisen-in Temple is a slight 100 square meters and perhaps the most intense expression of nature ever created using only rocks, raked pebbles, and a few small plants. The whole complex dates from the Muromachi Period (1338-1573). To get there take bus #12, 61, 76, 204, or 205 to 'Daitokuji-mae,' then look for the small 'Daitokuji' sign pointing down a side street.

The dry garden of **Ryoanji Temple**, although also composed of rocks and raked pebbles, is meant to be an abstraction of nature rather than a realistic reflection. As the most famous Zen garden in the nation it draws visitors from afar to contemplate its beauty and significance. Take bus #59 on the Sanjo Keihan route.

The oldest building in Kyoto is an ancient 'lecture hall' dating from the Nara Period (7th century) at **Koryuji Temple**. Several 'National Treasures' are housed in the lecture hall and adjacent museum, including an image of Miroku-Bosatsu, the Buddha of the future who will someday come to save the world. The wooden statue dates from the Asuka Period (552-645) and is one

JAPAN 153

of the best examples of Korean influence on ancient Japanese art. To reach Koryuji take a westbound bus #11 or the Arashiyama Train Line to Uzumasa Station, walk 150 meters west from the station, and then one block to the north.

To visit the **Old Imperial Palace**, the **Katsura Imperial Villa**, or the **Shugakuin Imperial Villa** (all highly recommended), you must get permission from the Imperial Household Agency office on the grounds of the Old Imperial Palace (open 9-12 and 1-4; tel. 211-1211). The Palace, a sprawling complex of gardens and buildings, is open for escorted tours at 10 am and 2 pm on weekdays, and 10 am on Saturdays; register at the Imperial Household Agency office 15 min. before one of the scheduled tours. The Imperial Villa at Katsura has tours every day at 10 am and 2 pm, and reservations must be made at least a day in advance. The Katsura Villa is considered one of the finest examples of the Japanese aesthetic of simplicity. The Shugakuin Imperial Villa, known for its beautifully laid-out gardens, has tours at 9, 10, & 11 am and 1:30 & 3 pm; reservations must be made a day in advance.

On the 1st and 25th of each month, **Toji Temple** and **Kitano Shrine**, respectively, hold flea markets where you can buy all kinds of antiques, sometimes at bargain prices. Toji Temple is a short walk southwest of Kyoto Station and Kitano Shrine is easily reached by bus (#204, #50).

Three unique places to see off the beaten track are the **Ohara area**, **Sanzen-in Temple**, and **Mampukuji Temple**. Ohara is a quiet, remarkably rural area that can be reached by taking bus #18 from Kyoto Station (55 min., Y330), or bus #12, #14, or #16 from Sanjo Keihan Station. The women wear distinctive narrow sashes (obi) here, cover their arms and legs with white cotton, and carry enormous loads on their heads. From Ohara bus station it's a 10-15 min. walk to the Sanzen-in Temple of the Tendai Buddhist sect, built a thousand years ago. The main hall's ceiling is shaped like the bottom of a boat, and the walls are covered with mandala paintings.

Mampukuji Temple, almost undiscovered by tourists, is the headquarters of the Obaku sect of Zen. Built by a famous Chinese priest from the Ming Dynasty, the temple is very Chinese in style. The walls of the main hall are teak from Thailand. A large, interesting religious service is held daily at 4 pm. Take the Keihan Electric Railway Uji Line to Keihan Uji Station (Y140, 30 min.), and walk north at the bridge. Before heading back to Kyoto, stop at **Byodo-in Temple**, 5 min. south by foot across the bridge from Keihan Uji Station. The main hall is a registered 'National Treasure,' and is shaped like a mythological phoenix descending to earth.

154 JAPAN

Nara

If you have come as far as Kyoto it would be a big mistake not to go the extra kilometers to the more ancient city of Nara. From 710 to 784 Nara served as Japan's first cultural and political capital. It was here that Buddhism first put down roots in Japan. At one time the city was more vast, but repeated fires have pared the former capital considerably down in size. Today Nara is, for the most part, a modern-looking city, with only the large area occupied by Nara Park retaining the buildings of earlier times.

From Nara Station, walk out to the street in front, take a jog 40 meters to the left, and then turn right on Sanjo Dori. One kilometer up the street you'll enter Nara Park, with its several square kilometers of grass, trees (cedars, oaks, and cypress), hills, and temples. Of particular interest are Kofukuji Temple, Todaiji Temple (with its giant statue of Buddha), and the Nara National Museum, featuring Buddhist art. Todaiji Temple's Daibutsuden (Hall of the Great Buddha) is the largest wooden structure on earth. However, the most pleasant attraction may be the hundreds of tame deer which wander about and eat from the hands of visitors, but not before bowing politely.

Osaka

Osaka is Japan's second largest city, with a population of 5 million. It prides itself on being the country's main commercial center. The thriving business atmosphere is readily apparent— and perhaps the prevalence of business activity accounts for the lack of sightseeing spots. The main attractions in this city, in fact, are the shopping malls and department stores. They are opulent, well-stocked, and the big ones often have free art exhibits inside that are quite interesting.

You will arrive in Osaka at Osaka Station or Shin-Osaka Station, depending on which train you take. They are connected to each other and all other points of interest in the city by an efficient subway system. Both have TIC booths; the one in Shin-Osaka Station is located on the lower level, near the entrance to the subway. The TIC staff may not speak English, but they can give you street and subway maps in English.

From Shin-Osaka Station (if you came by Shinkansen) take the Midosuji Subway Line to Umeda Station, the stop directly beneath Osaka Station. Below Osaka Station, in what is called the **Umeda Area**, is a huge underground shopping arcade. While you're here try an Osakan specialty called 'okonomiyaki,' a sort of Japanese pizza made with buckwheat flour and filled with whatever filling you select. It costs about Y500.

From Umeda get back on the Midosuji Line and head for **Shinsaibashi**, a dazzling mall of shops and restaurants. It is possibly the most famous shopping district in Japan. Here you can find the Takashimaya, Daimaru, and Sony department stores. This is a good place to try sushi, the Japanese snack that consists of a piece of raw fish on a ball of rice.

The one well-known tourist spot in Osaka is massive **Osaka Castle**, originally built in the late 16th century, but now disturbingly modern (it has elevators!); its current incarnation dates from 1931. From Umeda Station take the Midosuji Subway Line to Honmachi (Y100), then change to the Chuo Line and get off at Morino Miya. From there it's a short walk to the castle. It has acres of grounds on which to stroll and a small museum.

A nice place to visit just outside of Osaka is **Hattori Park**, and there's a youth hostel there for those who want to spend the night. Just a moment's walk from the hostel is a compound of eight traditional Japanese farmhouses where you can get a sense of pre-modern farm life. The park also includes three large ponds, tennis courts, a baseball field, a large public swimming pool, and a beautiful garden. To reach Hattori Park, take the Hankyu Line from Umeda Station to Sone Station (the sixth stop). From Sone, you can walk to the park, or take a short taxi ride.

Koyasan

Nestled in the mountains south of Osaka, Koyasan, the center of the Shingon Buddhist sect, has been a temple city for over 1000 years. Today there are 120 temples, but at one time there were hundreds. Koyasan also has a unique and unusually beautiful cemetery, containing the graves of Kobo Daishi (Kukai), founder of Shingon Buddhism, and many other famous figures of Japanese history. An avenue 2½ km long winds among the tombs and monuments, shaded by huge cryptomeria and pine trees. 'Serene' is the only way to describe this place. Stay at least a night so you can join in the early morning services at many of the temples.

ACCOMMODATIONS IN KANSAI

Kyoto:
Maps for all of the following accommodations are given out at the Kyoto TIC.

Tani's House (tel. 492-5489). Y1000 (plus Y50 for heat in winter) for space in a tatami room; no meals. Tani's is particularly popular with European and American travelers (but not with Japanese). To get there, take bus #204 or #214.

Uno's (tel. 231-7763). Y1000 (plus Y50 for heat in winter) for space in a tatami room; no meals. You're more likely to meet Japanese students here. Take bus #4, 14, 54, 200, or 215.

156 JAPAN

Kyoto Traveller's Inn, 91 Enshoji-cho, Okazaki, Sakyo-ku (tel. 771-0225/6). Single w/o bath Y3000, w/bath Y3800. Breakfast costs Y300, dinner Y700-1000. Opens daily at 4 pm. Take Municipal Bus #5, or #300 from Kyoto Station. The hotel is located in front of the Heian shrine and also near the Kyoto Municipal Museum.

Kyoto Business Hotel (tel. 222-1220). Single w/o bath Y4000, twin w/o bath Y5500.

Fukiage Arms Chrysanthemum (tel. 462-1540). Room w/shower Y2800. For women only.

Youth Inn Kyoto Shijo (tel. 255-4617). Rooms Y4000-4500 with breakfast included at this modern hotel. 1 min. walk from Karasuma/Shijo in the heart of Kyoto.

Ryokan in Kyoto:

Shichijo-so (tel. 541-7803). Y3200 for a large room and two good meals. One of the most interesting (and least inexpensive) ryokan in Japan. The owners of this inn are amateur art collectors and confirmed pack rats—the place is crammed with pottery, woodblock prints, silk scrolls, and knickknacks.

Sanyu (tel. 371-1968). Y1500 per night; no meals.

Ichiume (tel. 351-9385). Y1600/night; no meals.

Yuhara (tel. 371-9583). Y2300 per night; meals not included.

Nashinoki Inn, Teramachi-Nishiiru, Imadegawa, Kamikyo-ku (tel. 241-1543). Y3800 w/o meals or Y7000 per person with 2 meals. Located just across the street from the Imperial Palace.

Aoi-so Inn, 16-8 Nakamizocho, Koyama, Kita-ku (tel. 431-0788). Y1800 w/o meals or Y2300 with 2 meals. Take bus #36 or #206 to Karusuma-Shimofusacho stop; follow instructions on the map given out at the TIC.

The TIC can also make arrangements for you to stay in a Buddhist temple—for example, **Myorenji** (tel. 451-3527), Y3000/night.

Nara:

Nara Youth Hostel (tel. 22-1334), Y1150/Y2050. Located near the park.

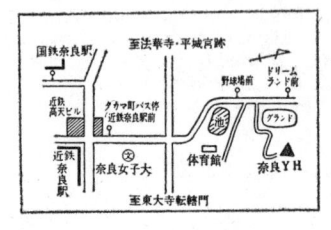

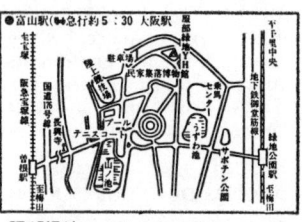

奈良ユース・ホステル (NARA YH)　　服部緑地ユース・ホステル (HATTORI RYOKUCHI YH)

Osaka:

Osaka-Shiritsu-Nagai Youth Hostel (tel. 06-699-5631), Y400/Y1150. Take the Midosuji Subway Line from Umeda Station to Nagai Station. The hostel is a 7-min. walk from the station.

YMCA Hotel. Y4200 for a room. From Umeda Station take the Yotsubashi Subway Line to Higobashi. Emerging from the subway go 200 meters to the right and you'll see the YMCA sign on the right.

Hotel Luther (tel. 06-942-2281). Singles Y4000, twins Y5500 and up. Y600 for breakfast (Japanese or Western food). This hotel is often full; call ahead to make a reservation. Located near the north exit of Tanimachi 4-chome subway stop. Also close to Keihan-Temmabashi Train Station.

Hattori Ryokuchi Youth Hostel (tel. 06-862-0600), Y850/Y1500. Ask at the TIC in Osaka for directions to the hostel.

Osaka Tokyu Inn (tel. 06-315-0109). Tokyo reservations no.: (03) 462-0109. Single Y5600. Breakfast costs about Y800. A very nice business hotel. Advance reservations recommended. A short walk from the Hankyu Umeda Station or JNR Osaka Station. Near Sonezaki Police Station.

Koyasan:

To stay in one of the numerous temples in town, go to the information center (in town or at the cablecar station); they will book you into a temple (Y3500 and up—includes sharing in the priests' meals), and sell you a coupon for it.

Henjoson-in Youth Hostel (tel. 07365(6)2434), Y1000/Y2000. This is by far your best and cheapest bet for accommodations; it also is located in a temple. Near the museum. The place is packed with Japanese students in the summer, so call ahead for reservations.

TRANSPORTATION IN KANSAI

Kyoto: 2 hr. 53 min. from Tokyo by Shinkansen (Y9500), or 9½ hr. by express train (Y7500). Going back to Tokyo, one option is the sleeper train (Shindaiken), Y10,200; leaves Kyoto 10:51 pm and arrives at Tokyo 9:36 am.

Nara: Trains leave for Nara from Kyoto Station every 40 min. (Y490, 70 min., or Y600, 33 min. for the private line).

Osaka: The trip by Shinkansen from Tokyo to Shin-Osaka Station in Osaka takes 3 hrs. 10 min. (Y9900). There are many options for the short trip between Kyoto and Osaka: The Shinkaisoku JNR train (Y440, 35 min.) leaves frequently and arrives at Kyoto Station in Kyoto and Osaka Station in Osaka. The limited express ('tokyu') train on both the Hankyu and Keihan lines is cheaper (Y250, 45 min. The Hankyu arrives at Umeda in Osaka (close to the JNR Osaka Station) in Kyoto; the Keihan stops at Temmabashi in Osaka (a 5-min. walk from Hotel Luther) and at San-jo, Shijo, and Shichijo in Kyoto.

Koyasan: From Umeda Station in Osaka take the Midosuji Subway Line to Namba Station. Change here to the Nankai Railway Line to Koyasan. The last part of the journey is by cog train up the mountainside. A Y810 ticket (buy it at Namba Station) covers both train rides. From Koyasan take the bus into town (Y190).

158 JAPAN

Chugoku

To the west of Osaka and Kyoto lies the less-traveled Chugoku district, encompassing five prefectures. Geographically it is split into two smaller regions, one facing the Inland Sea ('San-yo'), and the other facing the Japan Sea ('San-in').

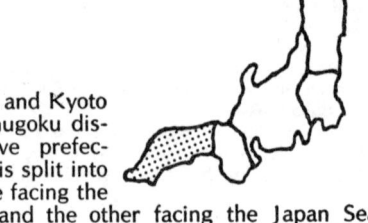

Okayama and Kurashiki

Okayama is just a few hours west of Osaka by express train. Though it's mainly an industrial center, the city does offer two interesting places for a morning of sightseeing: **Okayama Castle & Museum** and **Korakuen Park**.

When you arrive in Okayama, walk down the huge street in front of Okayama Station for 300 meters. From there you can see the castle and easily find your way. The castle has a small museum of samurai weapons and a good view of the city from the top. Okayama Museum, next to the castle, has a fine collection of local pottery called 'biyenzaki,' famous for its fire-burned patterns. Across the river from the castle is Korakuen Park, a massive expanse of lawns, flowers, and teahouses.

More interesting than Okayama is the nearby town of **Kurashiki**. Kurashiki has one of the most interesting and varied collections of museums, ranging from modern art to folk crafts, in all of Japan. Most of the museums are converted old rice granaries strung along a canal lined with willow trees in the Old Quarter of Kurashiki, a 10-min. walk from the train station. Get a good information sheet on Kurashiki from the Tokyo TIC before you leave Tokyo.

Ivy Square (a 10-min. walk from Kurashiki Station) is a good starting point for a walking tour of the museums. Walk out the back of Ivy Square Plaza, turn left, and walk 100 meters down the cobbled street. You are now standing in the Old Quarter, an area that dates from the Tokugawa period some 200 years ago.

Cross the willow-shaded river and enter the museum on your left. This is the **Kurashiki Kokokan** (Archaeological Museum), which displays many objects from the vicinity of Kurashiki, plus a few relics from China. Next door is the **Kurashiki Mingeikan**, a folkcraft museum with a good collection of pottery. Next to it is the **Japan Rural Toy Museum**, which exhibits homemade toys from all over Japan. Further down the same street is the one odd building in the Old Quarter, a Greek-style building containing the **Ohara Museum of Western Art**. Next door is a ring of six buildings that comprise the **Ohara Museum of Eastern Art**, where you can see an array of pottery (Chinese and Japanese), paintings, weaving, woodblocks, and wood carvings.

Setoda and Omishima

West of Okayama the train travels along the coast of the **Inland Sea**. Though once known for its beauty it has in recent years become increasingly polluted by industrial wastes. The Inland Sea is dotted by thousands of tiny islands, some only large rocks with a pine tree or two clinging to them. The two most famous are **Setoda** and **Omishima**. Setoda is best known for the brightly colored shrine, Kosanji, which closely resembles the grand shrine at Nikko. There are numerous temples and hiking trails to explore; if you want to spend a night or two on the island there is a youth hostel here. The nearby island of Omishima also has good hiking trails.

Hiroshima

Three hours west of Okayama by express train is the city of **Hiroshima**, where the U.S. exploded the world's first atomic bomb on Aug. 6, 1945. The city was demolished; it has been completely rebuilt since the war, and this is the most modern-looking city in Japan. The memory of the bomb lingers, however; at the Red Cross Hospital cases of radiation poisoning are still being treated. Each year on Aug. 6 a memorial service is held in **Peace Park**, which, along with an adjoining museum, is the focal point of interest for most visitors to Hiroshima.

Peace Park is located on the tip of a triangular island between the Honkawa and Motoyasu Rivers. From Hiroshima Station there is a constant stream of buses and streetcars heading there. Get off in front of the **Atomic Dome** (you'll be able to see its steel skeleton long before you reach it). From the dome you can wander through the park reading the signs (in English) posted by each monument. At the far end of the park is the **Peace Memorial Museum**. English tape recorder guides are available for Y120 but aren't really necessary. The captions under the pictures and the pictures themselves can tell the story. Across from the Peace Memorial Museum, to the right as you face the Atomic Dome, is the **Peace Auditorium**. 5 times a day they show a 25-min. film in English about the bomb and its effects; it's brutally honest, but worth seeing.

Get back on the streetcar in front of the Atomic Dome and head back toward Hiroshima Station, but this time get off at the intersection where the Tenmaya and Fukuya department stores are located. Walk about 400 meters up the broad street to the left to the **Prefectural Art Museum**. Behind it is lovely **Shukkeien Park**. The clever arrangement of hills, paths, and ponds creates an impression of spaciousness far greater than the park's actual boundaries would suggest. A stop at one of the teahouses in the recesses of the park is highly recommended.

From Shukkeien Park it's only a 5-min. walk to **Hiroshima Castle**, surrounded by a moat and low stone walls. In the donjon there is a museum of old paintings, clothing, and weapons.

Miyajima

From Hiroshima a side trip that shouldn't be missed is a visit to **Miyajima** ('Shrine Island'). The **Itsukushima Shrine** on Miyajima, with its large torii built over the water, is considered by most Japanese to be one of the country's finest sights. Rising behind Itsukushima are the forested slopes of **Mt. Mizen**. Hike to the top (a 1¼-hr. climb); the path begins just behind the shrine. Along the way you'll pass waterfalls and several small shrines, and catch occasional glimpses of the Inland Sea. You'll also see other hikers—many Japanese climb the mountain to pray at one of the shrines at the peak. Once you reach the top you can take a cable car back down for Y600. (Of course, you could also take the cable car up and walk down...)

From Hiroshima you can take the train on west to Shimonoseki and then travel south to Kyushu, or you can loop around through northwestern Chugoku and return to Kyoto. Northwestern Chugoku is far from the main thoroughfares; a visit to this area will give you a good idea of rural life in contemporary Japan.

Yamaguchi

Yamaguchi is an old wooden town with many temples. The **Fukuya Ryokan** is a nice place to stay, and you can borrow bicycles from the inn to explore the city. Places to visit include the five-story pagoda in **Rurikoji Park** and **Sesshu's Garden**, named after its famous designer.

Several interesting side trips can be made from Yamaguchi. One hour away by bus is the **Akiyoshidai National Park**, famous for its high plateau of weird rock formations and the gigantic limestone **Shuhodo Cave**, third largest cave in the world after Carlsbad and Mammoth. If you want to spend several days hiking in the park there is a youth hostel.

Also little more than an hour from Yamaguchi is the ancient city of **Hagi**, best known for its pottery, 'hagiyaki.' (Hagiyaki is said to be born in the kiln, not made by the potter. It gets better the more you use it; age adds lustre and interesting patterns to the pottery's surface.) Scores of temples and shrines are tucked among the town's traditional buildings. A good way to tour Hagi is by bicycle (Y800/day)—rent one from one of the shops just in front of Higashi Hagi Station, the last stop of the bus from Yamaguchi. These same shops will deliver luggage to and pick it up from your minshuku or youth hostel if you rent a bike from them.

Yamaguchi to Matsue via Izumo

Get off the train in **Izumo** (35 min. before Matsue) and transfer to the small railway that goes from Izumo out to the town of Taisha where the **Izumo-Taisha Shrine** is located (Y120, 15 min.). From Taisha go straight for 50 meters after leaving the station and then turn right. Down this big street you can see the enormous stone torii, the largest in Japan, that marks the entrance to the shrine. This shrine is often visited by worshippers seeking a marriage blessing.

From Izumo you can take a bus out to the peninsula of **Hinomisaki**. Buses leave from the station near Izumo Shrine every half hour (Y350). A 40-min. ride puts you out on a jagged coast of precipitous cliffs with pine trees clinging to them—spectacular on a windy day.

Since there are no inexpensive places to stay in the area you should return to Izumo and continue on to Matsue.

Matsue, located on one side of the large saltwater Lake Shinji, is a well-known tourist spot among the Japanese. Though it's an important commercial center for the surrounding farmlands, the town itself has changed little with the passage of the years. One of the first Americans to live in Japan, Lafcadio Hearn, settled in Matsue for a year in the latter part of the 19th century, and the Matsue he wrote about, the town with the clop-clop of geta and the black eaves of Matsue Castle, still exists.

The Matsue travel office, where you can get maps of the city in English, is just across the street from the train station. They can also call and make reservations for you at the youth hostel or one of the inns in town.

Sights to see include Matsue Castle, Matsue Museum, and the Lafcadio Hearn Home and Museum.

Matsue Castle, built in 1611 and recently reconstructed, is unusual because of the dark color of its roof and walls. Lafcadio Hearn's house lies just behind it. Hearn, who lived in Japan for many years, was the first American to write about the Japanese with any sensitivity or perception; his many books are still good reading today. Also near the castle is the modern-looking **Matsue Museum.**

A good side trip from Matsue is one to nearby **Daisen-Oki National Park**. The park consists of ten peaks and the adjacent seacoast. There are lots of hiking trails in the area, but a particularly good one is the trail to the top of Mt. Daisen (1575 meters high). To get to the park take the train to Yonago (30 min.). From just outside the station buses run up to the mountain town of Daisenji (Y450, 1 hr.). From Daisenji trails

162 JAPAN

branch off up into the mountains. The park office, located on the town's main (and only) street, can give you trail maps.

Matsue to Kyoto

On your way back to Kyoto there's one more stop you should try to make. Get off the train in Miyazu and take a ferry across the bay to Ichinomiya. From there you can see **Amanohashidate** ('bridge to heaven'). The 'bridge' is a long, sandy causeway lined with trees that runs out into the bay; it has long been considered one of the three most beautiful landscapes in Japan.

You have to return to the town just before Miyazu, called Amanohashidate, to catch a train for Kyoto.

ACCOMMODATIONS IN CHUGOKU

Kurashiki:
Kurashiki Youth Hostel (tel. 0864-22-7355), Y1150/Y2100. 15 min. by foot beyond Ivy Square.

Kamoi Minshuku (tel. 0864-22-4898), Y3400; includes two meals. A 10-min. walk from Kurashiki Station.

Setoda: Shin-Setoda Youth Hostel (tel. 08542-7-0224), Y1100/Y2100.

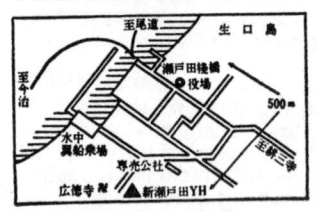

新瀬戸田ユース・ホステル
(SHIN-SETODA YH)

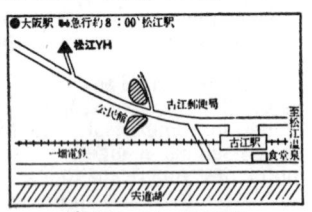

松江ユース・ホステル
(MATSUE YH)

Hiroshima: Hiroshima Youth Hostel (tel. 0822-21-5343), Y1100/Y2100. Take a 10-min. bus ride to Ushida-Shinmachi; from there the hostel is an 8-min. walk. This popular hostel often has students from all over the world.

Miyajima: Makoto Kaikan Youth Hostel (tel. 08294-4-03828). Y1100/Y2050. Only a 7-min. walk from the ferry landing.

Yamaguchi: Fukuya Ryokan, Eki-doori 2-1-3, Yamaguchi (tel. 08392-4-0941). Inexpensive, traditional ryokan—staff speak English; two meals included. There is also a youth hostel in town but it's far from the center of town and hard to find.

Akiyoshidai National Park: Akiyoshidai Youth Hostel (tel. 08376-2-0341), Y1150/Y2050.

Matsue: Matsue Youth Hostel (tel. 0852-36-8620), Y1150/Y2100. Located on the outskirts of town; get directions at the Matsue travel office.

Miyazu: Amanohashidate Kanko Kaikan Youth Hostel (tel. 07722-7-0121), Y1000/Y2000. A 10-min. walk from Ichinomiya.

TRANSPORTATION IN CHUGOKU

Okayama: From Shin-Osaka Station in Osaka, Okayama is 1¼ hr. away by Shinkansen, or 2½ hr. by express train.

Kurashiki: 18-21 min. by train from Okayama (Y210).

Setoda/Omishima: From Okayama, take an express train to Mihara City (1½ hr.). From Mihara harbor ferries leave regularly for Setoda, then on to Omishima. From Omishima you could also go to Imabari on Shikoku Island.

Hiroshima: 3 hr. from Okayama by express train.

Miyajima: Take a local train from Hiroshima to Miyajima-guchi (Y270, 25 min.). The ferry landing is only 100 meters from the train station. Boats leave frequently until 11 pm and take 10 min. to make the crossing (Y120).

Yamaguchi: Take an express train from Hiroshima to Ogori (3 hr.), and switch there to a train bound for Yamaguchi (Y140, 25 min.).

Izumo: Accessible by train from Yamaguchi via Masuda.

Matsue: 35 min. by express train from Izumo.

Shikoku

The smallest and most rural of Japan's four principal islands, Shikoku is usually bypassed by foreign visitors. A fair number of Japanese come here, however—many of them devout Buddhists on a pilgrimage to the 88 holy temples of the Shingon sect scattered around the island. Shikoku also boasts some of the best preserved castles in Japan. It has fine scenery; a trip along the southern coast is particularly recommended, though not during the typhoon season of late August to mid-October. Brush up on your Japanese phrases before coming here because little English is spoken.

Accessible only by ferry or plane, Shikoku will soon be joined with Honshu by 3 bridges. This will surely spur development of Shikoku's Inland Sea coast, where factores are already beginning to spring up, making this part of the island look more like urban Honshu every day.

The city of Takamatsu in northern Shikoku is the main gateway to the island. From here you can loop through the eastern half of the island (continue on to Tokushima) or the southern half (go directly to Kochi), or, if you have 4-5 days, completely circle Shikoku. The following description assumes the longest route. To leave Shikoku you can return to Takamatsu, or you can take a ferry from Matsuyama in northwestern Shikoku to Hiroshima (see **Transportion in Shikoku**).

The best-known attraction in **Takamatsu** is **Ritsurin Park**, with its beautiful landscaped gardens. It covers 134 acres of pine forest and took more than a century to complete. Be sure to visit the handicraft exhibition hall. A short trip away by bus or train is the **Yashima Plateau**, which offers a panoramic view of the Inland Sea. An hour west of Takamatsu by train is **Kotohira**; there you can visit the **Kompira Shrines**, which rank in fame next to the Grand Shrines of Ise.

In **Tokushima**, on Shikoku's east coast, you can climb Mt. Bizan and visit the gardens of Tokushima Castle (famous for its 'blue stones,' which are unique to the area). Both are within walking distance of the train station. If you travel through Tokushima in mid-August, you can see the summer dance festival 'Awa Odori,' during which the streets of the city are filled with musicians and dancers.

The whirlpools in the **Naruto Straits** (40 min. north of Tokushima by train or bus) are an amazing sight. The turbulence of the water as the tide sweeps in and out through the mile-wide channel is due to the abrupt change in depth between the Inland Sea and the Pacific Ocean.

The train to the small town of **Hiwasa** runs along the beautiful Anan coastline. In Hiwasa you can visit Yakuoji Temple, known for its power to dispel misfortune; the temple is a 10-min. walk from the train station. The Senba Kaigai, cliffs reaching up to 250 meters in height, stretch for two kilometers along the coast—walk to the harbor and take a sightseeing boat for Y450. If you're passing through between late May and late July, you can see the giant sea turtles which come to lay their eggs at Ohama Beach.

Cape Muroto, west of Hiwasa, offers an excellent view of the Pacific Ocean and well laid-out hiking trails.

A visit to Kochi Castle in the seaport of **Kochi** is a must—it's a fascinating, genuine old castle, not a reconstructed one like Osaka Castle and many others (5 min. by bus from the train station). Godaisan Park, 20 min. from Kochi by bus, has excellent scenery. Nearby Chikurinji Temple and the Makino Botanical Garden are also well worth a visit. While in Kochi you might try renting a bicycle from the Japan Bicycle Assn. (Y800/day) to tour around the city.

The scenery at **Cape Ashizuri**, west of Kochi, is not the best in Shikoku, but there are many hiking trails there. **Kashiwajima**, northwest of Cape Ashizuri, is a small fishing village, near which are the scenic Odo Cliffs.

Uwajima is famous for its bullfights, which take place six times a year. Visit the Warei Shrine, a quiet and cozy spot. The Nametoko Canyon, 1½ hours by bus from Uwajima, is particularly beautiful during spring and fall.

Ozu, a small, quiet town with many old streets and houses, is sometimes called Little Kyoto. In Ozu you should go out in an ukai boat (see description of cormorant fishing, p. 152). The nice thing is that you can get on the boat (about 10 people/boat) and spend a pleasant evening on the river before the fishing actually starts. Bring a box dinner and a bottle of sake; the boat ride costs Y1000 and lasts from 7 to 9.

Matsuyama is Shikoku's largest city. The three-story Matsuyama Castle and Dogo Spa (20 min. from the city by train) are two of its attractions. From Matsuyama you can return to Takamatsu or take a ferry to Hiroshima.

ACCOMMODATIONS IN SHIKOKU

The cheapest places to stay are the youth hostels, which can be found in many cities, including Takamatsu, Kotohira, Tokushima, Naruto, Hiwasa, Kochi, Kashiwajima, Uwajima, Ozu, and Matsuyama. They charge Y500-1150 for lodging only, and Y1200-2150 for lodging and two meals. Consult the Youth Hostel Handbook for phone numbers and maps. In Konowa, camp at the beach campground for Y300; dinner and breakfast are available for a small fee. Adventuresome people with a little more cash might try minshuku (family inns), which cost around Y3400/night (two meals included). There are also numerous ryokan.

TRANSPORTATION IN SHIKOKU

Takamatsu: Accessible by ferry from Uno (1 hr.), a convenient connection, or by ship from Kobe (3½ hr.) or Osaka (5½ hr.); 2nd class fare from Kobe or Osaka is Y2300. Hydrofoils are available but expensive.

Tokushima: 2½ hr. by train from Takamatsu. Also accessible by ferry from Tokyo.

Hiwasa: 2 hr. by train from Tokushima.

Cape Muroto: Take the Mugi Line from Hiwasa to Kaifu (30 min.). From there take a bus to Konowa, and transfer to a Cape Muroto bus.

Kochi: From Cape Muroto take an express bus (2½ hr.). From Takamatsu, take the regular train (5 hr. 40 min.) or the express train (2 hr. 40 min.).

Cape Ashizuri: Take the Dosan Line from Kochi to Nakamura (3 hr.). From Nakamura take a bus to Cape Ashizuri (2 hr. by express bus).

Kashiwajima: Take a bus from Cape Ashizuri to Tosa-Shimizu (30 min.), and change there for a bus to Kashiwajima (2 hr. 50 min.).

Uwajima: Take a bus from Kashiwajima to Sukumo (Y820, 80 min.). From Sukumo, take a bus to Uwajima (2 hr.).

Ozu: Take the Yosa Line from Uwajima to Ozu (1 hr. 40 min.).

Matsuyama: 2 hr. from Ozu by train; 3 hr. from Takamatsu by express train.

Hiroshima: From Matsuyama, take a bus to the harbor (30 min.), then a ferry to Hiroshima harbor (Y1260) on the mainland. From the harbor it's only 25 min. by bus or tram to Hiroshima Station.

Kyushu

There are several ways you could go about seeing Kyushu, depending on the amount of time (and daring) you have.

The most common and shortest route takes 2½-3 days to cover. From Fukuoka go directly to Nagasaki by super-express train. From Nagasaki take a Ken-ei bus to Unzen, changing there to another bus for Shimabara. From Shimabara ferry across to Misumi and take the bus to Uto. From Uto take the train to Kumamoto and from there return by train to Fukuoka.

A slightly longer route would include the island of Hirado, the city of Beppu, and add at least two days. Again starting from Fukuoka, take a super-express train to Arita. From there Imari is just a short hop by train or bus. From Imari take a bus to Hirado. Take the ferry from Hirado to Kashimae, then go by bus along the Yamanami Highway between Kumamoto and Beppu. From Beppu you can return to Fukuoka by train or take the ferry to Osaka.

For an extended trip (requiring at least 8 days) you might want to try the route described in detail below, which more or less circles the island. The starting point is Kumamoto, accessible from Fukuoka by train.

Kumamoto

Kumamoto, the commercial center of central Kyushu, has a population of 500,000. The best way to get around this attractive city is by streetcar. The fare starts at Y80.

When you get off the train at Kumamoto Station, turn left as you exit to find the JTB office. The JTB staff can supply you with English maps of the city and help you with inn reservations.

Just in front of Kumamoto Station there is a stop for the #2 streetcar, which goes past **Kumamoto Castle** (10 min.). You can easily see the castle from the streetcar and so know when to get off. The castle was originally built in the 16th century but was destroyed in the Satsuma Rebellion. The new version, built in 1960, commands a view of the downtown area. The central donjon (keep) has a museum filled with old maps, pictures, samurai armor, and weapons.

From the large shopping center near the castle, you can take the #3 streetcar out to **Hommyoji**, an attractive Buddhist temple, or take the #2 streetcar again (for 10 more minutes) on to **Suizenji** Park. This park was created in 1632 under the direction of a Buddhist monk. Its beautifully sculptured grounds are dominated by a hill shaped Like Mt. Fuji.

JAPAN 167

To return to Kumamoto Station just catch the #2 streetcar in the opposite direction.

Kumamoto to Beppu Via Mt. Aso

From Kumamoto a trip well worth taking is the Kyushu Sanko Bus Company tour to Beppu. The trans-Kyushu highway which the bus takes is aptly named the Yamanami Highway ('mountain-wave highway') since it glides up and down grassy hills the whole way.

There are several interesting places along this route where you may want to stop and sightsee. The first is **Mt. Aso**, 50 km. (2 hr.) east of Kumamoto. The base of the original volcano now forms a huge crater, some 40 km. across, inside of which are towns, rice fields, and the more recently formed cone of Mt. Aso. Buses from Kumamoto, including those which continue on to Beppu, go to the lip of the crater. From there you can take a combination of cable car and bus along the 'Aso High Line' and peer into the steaming caldera. If you want to break up your trip or hike some of the many foot trails in Mt. Aso National Park, you can spend the night at one of two inexpensive places (see **Accommodations in Kyushu**).

Beppu

In Beppu, famous throughout Japan for its hot springs, the second to the last stop the bus makes is right in front of the JTB office (several hundred meters from Beppu Train Station, the last stop). Ask the JTB people for help in arranging accommodations.

Things to do in Beppu include riding the cable car up Mt. Tsurumi, visiting a park full of monkeys at Mt. Takayaki, and touring the bubbling hot springs, called 'jigoku' ('hell'). Tours of the hot springs are conducted by the Kamenoi Bus Company for about Y850. The JTB can help make arrangements.

Miyazaki and Aoshima

From Beppu take the train down to Miyazaki on Kyushu's Pacific coast. There you can visit the Miyazaki Shrine, dedicated to the Emperor Jimmu, Japan's legendary first ruler. It is said that he first established himself at Miyazaki and only later conquered all of Japan.

From Miyazaki it's a 35-min. hop to the resort of Aoshima. From Miyazaki Station just exit, cross the street, and walk to your left 50 meters to get to the bus depot. The #2 bus leaves every 15 min. for Aoshima (Y340). Get off at Kodomo-no-kuni (a children's park). Both a youth hostel and a camping ground are quite close by (see **Accommodations**). The campground's greatest asset is its location, right next to Nichinan Beach, Aoshima's prime attraction.

Aoshima is sometimes referred to as Kyushu's Acapulco, but basically it's just a small fishing town with a few big hotels and a nice beach. Very low-key—the perfect spot to relax and enjoy the Pacific Ocean for a day or two. Sights to see include the town of Aoshima itself; tiny Aoshima Island, covered with tropical trees and birds; Saboten Park, a garden of cacti; and Horikiri Pass, a combination of rocky seacoast and tropical vegetation. These last two places can be visited by bus for only Y300.

Kagoshima

This pleasant city at the southern end of Kyushu is dominated by the smoking but dormant volcano Sakurajima. At one time Sakurajima was actually an island in Kagoshima Bay, but the 1914 eruption sent forth streams of lava that joined the island to the mainland. The volcano continues to produce an impressive amount of smoke and ash.

When you reach Kagoshima, get off the train at Nishi-Kagoshima Station rather than Kagoshima Station. If you're planning to stay at the Sakurajima Youth Hostel (see **Accommodations**) you may want to check your luggage and do some sightseeing before taking the ferry across the bay. There is an information window in the station where you can get an English map and advice about buses and streetcars.

On the big street in front of the station catch the #2 bus to **Mt. Shiroyama** (Y90). At the foot of the mountain are statues of leading figures from the Kagoshima area who have been influential in Japanese politics and industrial development in the last 150 years (there are explanatory signs in English). From the statues you can walk to the top of Mt. Shiroyama for a panoramic view of the city and Sakurajima.

From Shiroyama take the #2 bus back to Nishi-Kagoshima Station; this time board bus #1 and head for **Iso Garden and Beach** (Y90, 35 min.)—bringing along your luggage if you had checked it. There's a nice view of Sakurajima from the pond in the garden, and you can swim at the nearby beach. Then get back on the #1 bus and return to the ferry landing, which the bus passed en route to Iso Garden. Boats leave every 10-30 min. for Sakurajima from 5:30 am to 10:00 pm. (Y60, 20 min.).

Side Trips from Kagoshima

About 40 km. north of Kagoshima is **Kirishima-Yaku National Park**. The park, which contains 23 dormant volcanoes and 10 crater lakes, is famous in Japanese mythology; it is said that the grandson of the sun goddess descended to earth from heaven at Takachibo Peak, located in park.

Tucked into a flat valley about halfway between Kumamoto and Kagoshima is the city of **Hitoyoshi**, famous for its whiskey, its turtles, and its white water rapids. The whiskey, called kumajochu, is made from old sweet potatoes and rice and is extremely strong. The freshwater turtles are eaten by the local residents in a kind of soup. The rapids take up a lengthy stretch of the Kuma River: for Y2200 you can take a 2½-hr. (18 km.)

trip down them in an ancient-looking but apparently safe canoe, accompanied by two oarsmen and a woman guide who will sing folksongs for you. The boats leave from just opposite the ruins of Hitoyoshi Castle, and the boat company is called Kumagawa Kudari. (Since there is no youth hostel in Hitoyoshi, you may want to shoot the rapids of the Kuma River during a day trip from Kagoshima or Kumamoto.)

Shimabara and Unzen

From Kagoshima take the 3-hr. train trip north along the scenic Ariake coast to the town of **Uto**. From there take a bus to the fishing village of **Misumi** and ferry across the Ariake Sea to Shimabara.

Shimabara is now a quiet and peaceful town, but 300 years ago it was the center of a Christian revolt against the government. In the early 17th century the Tokugawa Shogunate banned Christianity; for a mixture of political, economic, and religious reasons the people of the Shimabara area revolted against the Shogun's ruling. In the end they were overwhelmed by the sheer numbers of the government forces. At Hara Castle in Shimabara, 30,000 people were killed in the final battle that crushed the rebellion. (Hara Castle was completely destroyed; in 1963 it was rebuilt and given the name Shimabara Castle.)

Shimabara Castle has an excellent museum inside with exhibits (in English) about the Christian revolt. Particularly interesting are the statues and the figurines of Mary and Jesus carved by Japanese craftsmen. The differences in rendering from Western versions is startling. (Admission: Y200).

From Shimabara the resort town of Unzen in the middle of Unzen National Park is only an hour away by bus.

Unzen was Japan's first National park, established in 1934. It is a region of rugged volcanoes, lakes, and thick forests, and its cool climate makes it especially attractive in the summer. It also has an abundance of bubbling hot springs (jigoku) which have been tapped as a source of soothing water for the many luxury hotels and spas in the area. In the town of Unzen you can stroll through the steamy jigoku area and see numerous small lakes and gardens; if you are more adventurous, there are hiking trails to the top of the nearby peaks like **Mt. Kinugasa** and **Mt. Fugen**. Maps and information can be obtained at the Unzen Park Office in the center of the resort.

Nagasaki

From Unzen, take the 2½-hr. bus ride to Nagasaki and get off in front of Nagasaki Station. Next to the station is a JTB office with helpful English-speaking personnel. Reasonably-priced accommodations are also located nearby.

Before World War II, Nagasaki was probably one of the better-known Japanese cities outside the country. For almost 200 years, from the mid-1600s to the mid-1800s, it was Japan's single link with the outside world—after 1637 only Chinese and Dutch were allowed to trade there. (The Dutch, during all their years in Nagasaki, were confined to a tiny island in Nagasaki Bay to prevent contamination of Japan by Western ideas. The island, called Dejima, is no longer an island due to extensive bay fill, but the buildings of the Dutch community still stand and can be visited. Take the #1 streetcar from Nagasaki Station going south.) Later, after the Meiji Restoration in the late 1800s, Nagasaki was the gateway for the introduction of foreign goods and technology. Nagasaki was also the target of the world's second atomic bomb, dropped by the U.S. on Aug. 9, 1945.

Outside of Nagasaki's modern business district, traditional styles still prevail. On the steep hills on either side of the long, narrow bay, small wooden houses are stacked up one on top of another, and streets not more than 2½ meters wide meander among them—great for exploring.

If you have 5-6 hours, a do-it-yourself tour of Nagasaki can be done as follows: From Nagasaki station take the #1 or #3 streetcar heading north. (The fare is always Y70.) Get off about 10 min. later at the Hamaguchi stop. Walk up the hill on your right for 5 min. and you'll come to the **International Culture Hall** (admission: Y50). Inside are relics and reminders of the destruction the atomic bomb brought to Nagasaki.

A 5-min. walk back down the hill (at an angle from the way you came up) will bring you to **Peace Park**, dominated by a large bronze statue symbolizing peace. From the park walk back to the streetcar stop and board the #3 in the opposite direction, riding it past Nagasaki Station and all the way to the end of the line. Exit to your right and head up the hill. This area is called 'Oteramachi' or 'Temple Town.' After going up the hill several hundred meters turn right and follow the winding streets along the curve of the hill. There is no danger of getting lost because you can always see the downtown buildings to keep your bearings. Before your path is blocked by a tennis court a half-hour walk later, you will pass through a fascinating array of tiny wooden houses, graveyards, and temples.

From the tennis court descend until you reach the first big street. You are now near **Kofukuji Temple**, which you can enter for Y100. From here, turn left and follow the street until you reach the Hamamachi Shopping Arcade. The stores specialize in pearls and tortoise-shell jewelry. In front of the shopping center you can catch the #5 streetcar out to Benten Bashi (7 min.).

From the streetcar stop it is only a 5-min. walk to Glover House and Oura Cathedral, and the YH.

Glover House, built by Thomas Glover in the late 1800s, sits on a hilltop that commands a view of the Pacific Ocean, Nagasaki Bay, and Nagasaki City. (For a detailed history of the house and its occupants, see the JTB pamphlets.) Descending from Glover's House you will pass **Oura Cathedral**, built in 1864. Though the architecture is European—flying buttresses, stained glass windows, etc.—the church has distinctly Japanese touches like bamboo mats and inscriptions in Japanese (admission:Y200).

Nagasaki to Hirado

Take the 2-hr: bus trip north along the coast of the Nagasaki peninsula to **Sasebo**. Just before you reach Sasebo you will cross **Saikai Bridge**. At this point in and outgoing tides mix, creating a tremendous maelstrom. This is a popular spot for eating lunch; restaurants line the hills on both sides of the bridge.

In Sasebo catch another bus to make the short trip to the ferry landing in Kashimae. There are three ferry companies operating out of Kashimae; two of them run roundtrips to the south through the famous **99 Islands** that take about one hour. The third, the Hirado-Guchi Transportation Co., runs a ferry north to **Hirado Island** (see **Transportation**). The scenery on the trip north to Hirado is as nice as that in the more southern 99 Islands.

As the ferry pulls into the tiny harbor, Hirado's two main sights are visible: Hirado Castle and St. Xavier's Cathedral.

Hirado Castle, perched on a hill overlooking the harbor entrance, is the classic Japanese castle. It is small in comparison to other castles, but that only adds to its special qualities. There is a museum inside (admission: Y200) which has a complete and original collection of Hokusai's "36 Views of Mt. Fuji." This is an extremely rare set of woodblock prints depicting Mt. Fuji from many different angles in different seasons.

From the castle you can walk, following the curve of the harbor, to **St. Xavier's Cathedral**. At this site, in the 18th century, Christians prayed secretly in order to avoid notice by the Tokugawa authorities. Now a gothic-spired cathedral commemorates their faith.

Perhaps Hirado's greatest virtue is that it is simply a quiet, sleepy little fishing village—a different side of Japan from that represented by the bustle of downtown Nagasaki.

Hirado to Fukuoka Via Arita and Imari

From Hirado you can travel to the two adjacent towns of Arita and Imari in half a day's time; both are famous for their fine ceramics (though most of the pottery is now produced in Arita). There are three kinds: Kakiemon (characterized by a milky white background and subtle use of blue and red), Nabeshima (originally made only for samurai; pastel colors), and Ko Imari (usually has gaudier patterns of greens, blues, reds, and golds). In Arita there are several kilns near the train station, and also a ceramics museum. You can get maps to these places at the station, though they'll be written in Japanese. In Imari catch a bus from the terminal in the middle of town to the hill where most of the kilns are located.

From either of these towns you can return to Fukuoka by train.

ACCOMMODATIONS IN KYUSHU

Kumamoto:

Two good inns are the **Fukisaki** (tel. 43-7166) and the **Setenkaku** (tel. 54-1304); medium prices. The JTB can call to make a reservation and give you directions to either of these inns.

The best deal in town, however, is the **Ryokan Shokaku** (tel. 52-1468), a member of Japan Youth Hostels, Inc. It's only an 8-min. walk from Kumamoto Station. Just walk down the wide street directly in front of the station; after passing a supermarket you will cross a small river. Before you cross the large steel bridge that spans the second river, turn right. You then walk down a street lined with old wooden buildings for 250 meters, keeping to your right at the one fork. The Ryokan Shokaku is on your left. It is a splendid example of traditional architecture, not at all like the typical youth hostel. Y2000/Y2500.

Aso:

At the Aso-High Line office, where the bus from Kumamoto stops, you can get a map and directions to the two places listed below (you'll have to take a local bus down the hill).

Aso Youth Hostel (tel. 4-0804), Y1150/Y2100. Located 15 min. by foot from Aso Train Station.

O-Aso Kokuminshukusha (tel. 2-0721). One night's lodging w/two meals, Y3400. 15 min. by foot from Miyagi Station.

Beppu:

The cheapest hotels are about an 8-min. walk up the street from the JTB office and right next to Beppu Train Station. At the business hotel **New Hayashi Hotel** (tel. 24-5252), for example, you get a room and a Western-style breakfast of bread and coffee for Y3600.

A good ryokan is the **Hotel Shimizuso** (tel. 22-1434); it charges Y4500 for one night w/two meals, but the food is great.

Beppu Youth Hostel (tel. 23-4116), Y1150/Y2100. Take a 20-min. bus ride to Kankajii; from there it's a 4-min. walk to the hostel.

Beppu Campground is about 15 min. from Beppu Station. Get maps and directions at Beppu Station or at the JTB office. There is a small fee for camping.

Aoshima:

Miyazaki-ken Seinen-Kaikan Youth Hostel (tel. 5-0961), Y1150/Y2100. A 5-min. walk from Kodomo-no-kuni, the children's park.

A better place to stay in the summertime is **Aoshima Campground**. For Y100 you get a camping space, and access to charcoal grills, showers, and toilets. For an extra Y800 you can rent a 5-person tent. The camping ground is right next to Kodomo-no-kuni on one side, and borders the beach on the other.

You could also stay at the **Hama-so Youth Hostel** (tel. 24-3019), Y1050/Y2000.

Kagoshima:

There are no cheap hotels in Kagoshima, only youth hostels. Of these the best and cheapest is the **Sakurajima Youth Hostel** (tel. 099293-2150), Y1150/Y2150. It's located at the foot of the volcano of the same name, and overlooks Kagoshima Bay. To get there take bus #1 from Nishi-Kagoshima Station to the ferry landing. Boats leave every 10-15 min. for Sakurajima from 6 am to 8 pm.

Shimabara:

The only inexpensive place is the **Shimabara Youth Hostel** (tel. 2-4451), Y1150/Y2100. Only 5 min. by foot from the ferry landing or a 3-min. walk from the train station.

Unzen:

Seiunso Youth Hostel (tel. 095773-3273), Y1050/Y2050.

There is also a small campground at **Lake Shirakumo**. Tents can be rented for Y450-Y1000; showers and toilets, cooking grills and tent space are free. Get a map and directions at the Unzen Park office.

Nagasaki:

Accommodations in Nagasaki are unfortunately on the expensive side. There's a host of business hotels within a 10-min. walk of the train station. Just walk out of the station up across the bridge and climb the hill. Most of these hotels cost about Y3500 for a single room w/private bath. No food is included. Exact prices are posted in English in the window in front of each hotel.

There are also business hotels along the street parallel to the station. The street is immediately recognizable by the unusually large number of pachinko parlors lining it. If you walk to the right as you leave the station you will find the **Moto Funa** (tel. 21-2400) in 5 min. on your right. Farther along the street is the **Bus Terminal Hotel** (tel. 21-4111). Both charge around Y3500 for a single room w/no food. If these are full, the other hotels in this area are about the same.

The **Nagasaki Oranda-Zaka Youth Hostel** (tel. 22-2730), on Hollander's Hill at the end of the #5 streetcar line, has a great view of the city at night. Y1050/Y2050. There are also two other youth hostels in town.

Hirado:

A fantastic place to stay is the **Higoya Minshuku** (tel. 2467). For Y3500 you can have a single room and two enormous and delicious meals (featuring the seafood for which Hirado is famous). Located less than a 2-min. walk from the ferry landing; just walk up the hill one block, turn left, and you'll find the Higoya 100 meters up the road.

TRANSPORTATION IN KYUSHU

Fukuoka: Accessible from Hiroshima by Shinkansen (Y5800, 2 hr.) or limited express (Y3800). A limited express train from Arita or Imari costs Y2800.

Kumamoto: 2 hr. from Fukuoka by limited express (basic fare + Y1470).

Beppu: From Kumamoto, take the Kyushu Sanko Bus Co. tour to Beppu. The bus company office is just across the street from Kumamoto Station. Buses leave at 8:30, 9:30, & 10:30 am, and arrive in Beppu 7½ hr. later. The fare is Y4620, a bit steep, but it includes a bus guide who will sing folksongs; a box lunch of rice, vegetables, and fish; and the not inconsiderable pleasure of air-conditioning.

If you are entering or leaving Kyushu through Beppu, try the **Kansai Kisen Steamship Co.**, which offers ferry service between Osaka and Beppu via Takamatsu and Matsuyama (on Shikoku). The scenery in the Inland Sea is beautiful on this trip. A second class ticket for the 15-hr. trip costs Y5700 (well below the cost of taking trains from Osaka to Beppu). Every day three ferries leave Osaka (4:30, 9, & 9:40 pm) while three others leave from Beppu (5, 5:30, & 9:30 pm). All arrive at their destinations the following morning.

Mt. Aso: Buses leave from the Kyushu Sanko Bus Co. in Kumamoto every hour from early morning until 1:30 pm, arriving 2 hr. later. The bus stops for 2 hr. at the lip of the large crater; from there for Y850 you can travel by cable car and bus along the 'Aso High Line' (or walk; it takes 20 min.).

Miyazaki: 4 hr. from Beppu by limited express train (Y4400).

Kagoshima: From Miyazaki, 3 hr. by limited express train (Y3100). From Kumamoto, the trip by limited express train costs Y3800 (3½ hr.).

Okinawa: The Oshima Steamship Co. has boats leaving Kagoshima for the city of Naha on Okinawa every other day during the summer at 6 pm (5 pm for the hydrofoil), arriving in Naha at 8 the next evening (1 pm for the hydrofoil). Second class fare is Y10,500 one-way. Order tickets from the company in Tokyo (tel. 273-8911), or at the Kagoshima Shin-ko port, a 15-min. bus ride (bus runs every hour) from JNR Nishi-Kagoshima Station.

Uto: The trip from Kagoshima by limited express train costs Y3600 (3 hr.). Uto is only a 30-min. train ride from Kumamoto.

Shimabara: Take a train from Uto to Misumi. From Misumi, take a 1-hr. ferry ride to Shimabara (Y660, 2nd class); en route the boat passes under a famous bridge and near numerous tiny islands.

Unzen: Take a Ken-ei bus from Shimabara to Unzen (Y390, 1 hr.). If you're coming from Nagasaki, the trip takes 2¾ hr. and costs Y1100.

Nagasaki: From Unzen, the Ken-ei Bus Co. has buses leaving from its terminal, a big round building in the center of Unzen, at 10 min. and 40 min. after each hour (Y1100, 2½ hr.).

Sasebo: Across from Nagasaki Station, under the 'Nagasaki Trade and Tourist Center' sign, is the Kei-en Bus Co. terminal. Buses leave for Sasebo every hour (Y1000, 2 hr.).

Kashimae: Catch a bus in Sasebo to the ferry landing in Kashimae.

Buses leave every half hour from platform #8 and the trip to Kashimae, the end of the line, takes 25 min. (Y150).

Hirado: The Hirado Guchi Transportation Co. has boats leaving almost every hour, 9 am-4 pm, for Hirado. Take one of the slower boats (1½ hr.) since the scenery is beautiful, and the ticket is only Y2200. These slower boats leave Kashimae at 9:05 & 11:05 am and 3:05 pm. The faster boats leave at all the other times. (The name of the Hirado Guchi Transportation Co. boats that run between Kashimae and Hirado is Kobaruto. When at the ticket desk ask for the 'Koburato Line to Hirado.')

Arita/Imari: Starting from Hirado, take a ferry or bus to the city of Hirado-Guchi on Kyushu proper (both leave from the same small terminal on the waterfront). From here you can go to Imari by train. From Imari take the 20-min. trip by train to the town of Arita.

Okinawa and the Ryukyu Islands

The Ryukyus, a 400-mile long chain of 73 islands nearly 1000 miles from Tokyo, are a world apart from the hustle and bustle of the main islands of Japan. Okinawa is the largest and best known of the islands. Inhabitants of the Ryukyus are from Malay, Chinese, Korean, and Japanese stock; their culture and way of life are consequently quite different from the rest of Japan. Here you can spend slow-paced days swimming and diving in the tropical coral waters, or slog your way through jungles to impressive hidden waterfalls; at night listen to the locals play folk songs on their unique string instruments while slowly sipping awamori (a wine made from fermented yams), after a filling meal of peanut tofu and boiled pig ears (two delicacies of the islands).

According to Ryukyuan mythology, Tedoko, the God of the Sun, is the supreme being from whom all inhabitants of the islands are descended. The Ryukyuan kingdom, based in Okinawa, flourished from 600 A.D (when written records began) to 1372, when it became a nominal subject of China, paying tribute for 250 years to the emperors of the Middle Kingdom. The year 1609 marked the beginning of Japanese domination of the islands, which lasted until WWII. During this time much of Okinawa's indigenous culture was lost or played down by the Japanese.

The terrible battle of Okinawa in 1945 lasted 3 months; over 260,000 people lost their lives as the Japanese and Americans fought for control of the island. Okinawa remained under U.S. control until 1972, when it was finally returned to Japan; its lengthy occupation was a sore spot for U.S.-Japan relations for two and a half decades.

The TIC in Tokyo has information on travel and accommodations for Okinawa, Ogasawara, and other islands in the Ryukyu

Tohoku

The six prefectures of Tohoku, or northeastern Honshu, are generally more rugged and less densely populated than the rest of Honshu. In the highland areas the climate is delightfully cool; in fact, if you head for the mountains, take warm clothing. Tohoku is noted for its traditional crafts, especially dolls and lacquerware, as well as its uncluttered countryside; Sendai is the main city. JNR trains criss-cross the region, making travel fairly easy. All trains leaving Tokyo for Tohoku depart from Ueno Station. The 60 youth hostels in the area provide good lodging at relatively low cost. Remember that traveling in the northeast takes extra patience and a willingness to get lost now and then because English speakers are rare.

One excellent excursion into the region: take a morning express train from Ueno to Shiroishi (Y5500), a small town 4½ hr. north of Tokyo. A Y600 bus ride from Shiroishi takes you east to the Minami-Zao Youth Hostel (tel. 02243-7-2124) in **Zao Quasi-National Park**. The panoramic views of the surrounding green mountains during the 80-min. ride are worth twice the price of the ticket. The hostel itself is located several miles from the nearest town, so buy your groceries before you get on the bus if you intend to do your own cooking.

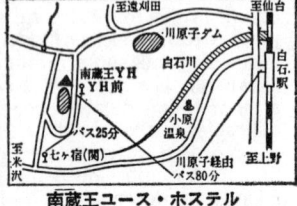

南蔵王ユース・ホステル
(MINAMI-ZAŌ YH)

A couple of minutes' walk from the hostel is Lake Choro, an ideal place for swimming and rowing and the starting point for hiking on Mt. Zao, an extinct volcano. During the summer months, hiking on the mountain attracts the hearty, and from December to April no better skiing can be found.

Matsushima can be reached by train via Sendai (take the Senseki Line to Matsushima Kaigan Station, 40 min. north of Sendai). The bay of this small coastal resort is dotted with hundreds of islands. Some are just pinnacles jutting above the water with pine trees clinging to them; others are much larger, with picturesque caves, tunnels, and archways. Boats tour the bay regularly, charging Y1000-2200 for several hours of sightseeing (you can walk to the boat landing from the train station). A 2-min. walk from the docks is Zuiganji Temple, founded in

828; the current buildings were built in 1609 in the massive, unfinished wood and plaster style of the Momoyama Period. A small museum inside contains the artwork of this old Zen seminary's priests.

The **Matsushima Youth Hostel** (tel. 02258-8-2220) has the area's least expensive accommodations (Y1150/Y2100). It's located a fair distance out of town; take the Senseki Line on to Nobiru Station. From the station cross the small bridge and walk down the street for about 10 min. When you reach a large street bordered by woods turn right and walk 10 min. more. The hostel is on the right, about 50 meters back from the street.

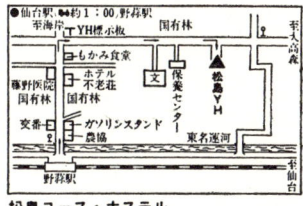

松島ユース・ホステル (MATSUSHIMA YH)

From Matsushima you can continue on to Aomori, the northernmost of Honshu's cities, and from there cross the Tsugaru Straits to Hakodate on Hokkaido.

Hokkaido

Hokkaido can be reached by train from Tokyo in less than 24 hours, so it is not out of reach for the determined traveler, even one with limited time in Japan. **Aomori** is the point of departure for JNR ferries to Hokkaido. Be sure to stop at the Aomori Prefectural Museum, with excellent exhibits on the history and folk traditions of northern Honshu. Aomori was almost completely destroyed in WWII, and has since been rebuilt. The 4-hr. ferry trip from Aomori to Hakodate on Hokkaido is a beautiful trip in good weather. Hokkaido is an island of stunning volcanic and seacoast scenery, with the lowest population density in Japan. The last of the four main islands to be settled, it is something of a frontier for the Japanese, and, because of its distinctive history and climate, it provides many interesting contrasts with the rest of the country.

Sapporo, site of the 1972 Winter Olympics, is the cultural, economic, and political center of Hokkaido, and most visitors to the island will eventually arrive here. For a bit of quiet and greenery in the middle of this large, modern city, visit the Botanical Garden, where you will also find a small museum displaying artifacts from the Ainu, the indigenous inhabitants of this island. Also worth a visit is the excellent Historical Museum of Hokkaido located in Ebetsu, near Sapporo. To keep warm on those cold winter nights, stop in at one of the bars in the lively, student-oriented Sasukino district of Sapporo. Most bars here are inexpensive and crowded at night.

Little of the original Ainu culture remains, but in **Shiraoi**, a coastal town south of Sapporo, one can get a glimpse of what it was like at one time. Near the Shiraoi Youth Hostel is a small village of reed houses where Ainu, dressed in traditional clothing, explain the culture of their ancestors, perform dances, and sell handicrafts. It can be overcrowded and touristy at times, and the presentation is in Japanese, but no better opportunity can be found to see something of this interesting and rapidly disappearing culture.

Southwest of Sapporo lies **Shikotsu-Toya National Park**, where you can enjoy some of Hokkaido's beautiful scenery without traveling too far. This park surrounds two lakes: Lake Toya, over which looms the symmetrical volcanic cone of Mt. Yotei, and Lake Shikotsu. Also in this volcanically active area is Noboribetsu Spa, with its colorful hot springs called Jugokudani ('Valley of Hell').

Northwest of Sapporo lies the **Shakotan Peninsula**, famous for its ruggedly beautiful coastline, particularly between the city of Otaru and Cape Kamui.

The peaks of central Hokkaido are the main attractions in **Daisetsuzan National Park**. Here, and almost throughout Hokkaido, winter visitors will have no difficulty finding skiing facilities, and skiers can compare techniques and equipment with the rapidly-growing number of Japanese enjoying the sport.

ACCOMMODATIONS IN HOKKAIDO

Sapporo: There are several youth hostels. **Sapporo House Youth Hostel** (tel. 721-4236) is located only 7 min. by foot from Sapporo Station. Y1150/Y2100. Other hostels include Sapporo Miyagaoka YH, Nakanoshima YH, Sapporo Shiritsu Lions YH, and Jozankei YH; see the Handbook.

Yaesu Hotel, Kita Shichijo-Nishi 3-chome, Kita-ku, Sapporo; tel. 731-8171. Singles Y2860-3450, twins Y7040. Only a 1-min. walk from Sapporo Station.

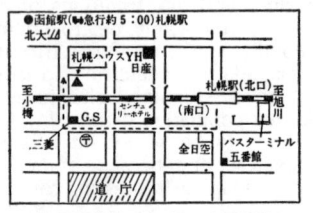

札幌ハウス ユース・ホステル
(SAPPORO HOUSE YH)

Shiraoi: Shiraoi Youth Hostel (tel. 2-2302), Y1150/Y2100. A 10-min. walk from Shiraoi Station.

Shakotan Peninsula: Youth hostels near Cape Kamui include Shakotan YH, Shakotan Kamoi YH, and Nishi-Shakotan YH; consult the Handbook. In the tiny fishing village of Bikuni: **Bikuni Youth Hostel** (tel. 4-2610), Y1150/Y1850.

TRANSPORTATION FOR HOKKAIDO

Hakodate: Take a limited express from Ueno Station in Tokyo to Aomori (Y9600, 8 hr.). The ferry ride from Aomori to Hakodate takes 4 hr.

Sapporo: 4½ hr. by limited express from Hakodate. The entire trip from Tokyo to Sapporo costs Y9500 (basic fare) + Y3800 (limited express charge) = Y13,300. Ask at a JTB office about the special ticket which allows you several stops along the way. The trip by plane from Tokyo is more expensive (Y21,274 on JAL, 1 hr. 25 min.) but much quicker if you're pressed for time. Call the Japan Airlines (JAL) office in Tokyo for bookings (tel. 747-2111), or one of the domestic airlines.

Bibliography

Japanese Society, by Chie Nakane. A perceptive exposition of Japanese life.

The Japanese, by Edwin Reischauer. America's former ambassador and noted authority on Japan gives a readable and insightful discussion of the Japanese and their customs.

Japan: Past and Present, by Edwin Reischauer. A short but complete survey of Japanese history.

In Search of What's Japanese about Japan, by John Condon and Keisuke Kurata.

Japanese Festivals, by Helen Bauer and Shervin Carlquist (Tuttle).

Zen and Japanese Culture, by D. T. Suzuki. The most readable book on Japanese aesthetics and philosophy that is available in English.

Robert's Guide to Japanese Museums, by Laurance P. Roberts.

Eating Cheap in Japan: The Gaijin Gourmet's Guide to Ordering in Non-tourist Restaurants, by Kimiko Nagasawa and Camy Condon. Available in paperback in Japan.

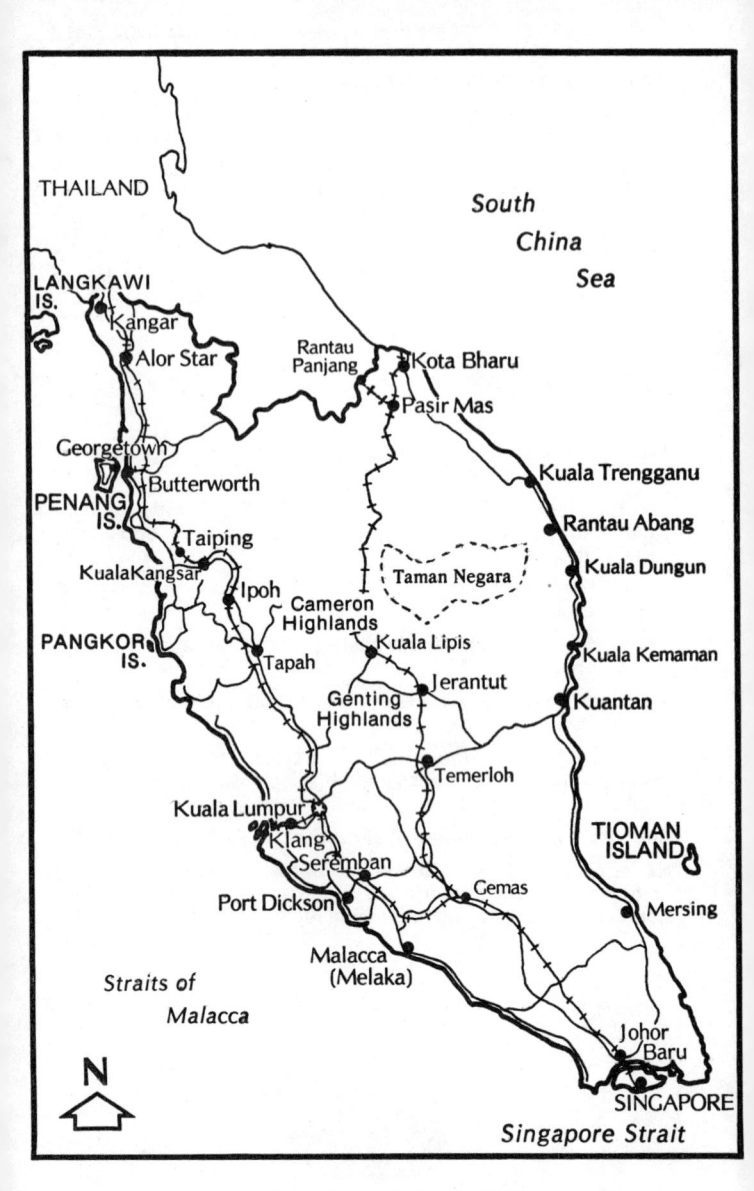

MALAYSIA

General Information

Arrival: Many travelers enter peninsular Malaysia by train from Thailand. Those going to the west coast usually get off in Butterworth, a short ferry ride from Penang, or in Kuala Lumpur. Those arriving on the east coast enter via Sungei Golok (Thai side of border)/Rantau Panjang (Malaysian side), near Kota Bharu. For more details on entry see Penang (p. 191), Kuala Lumpur (p.199), Kota Bharu (p.213), Sabah (p.215) and Sarawak (p.218); for details on entering peninsular Malaysia from Singapore see **Transportation**, p.188.

Departure: The airport departure tax is M$7 on all international flights except those to Singapore for which the tax is M$4. For more details on departure from Kuala Lumpur see p. 199.

Currency: the exchange rate in November 1980 was 2.12 ringgit (M$2.12) to the U.S. dollar.

Visas: Commonwealth citizens do not need a visa. Citizens of most Western European countries and the United States do not need a visa for a stay of three months or less; their passports are stamped with a 14-day visitor's pass on arrival, and free extensions are easily obtained at the Immigration Office in any major city. Nationals of most other countries can visit for 14 days without a visa.

Climate: Hot all year round but not extreme, thanks to sea breezes. Humid along the coasts: cooler in the highlands. No clearly defined wet and dry seasons, but more rain Oct.-Feb. The wet season in Sabah and Sarawak is Nov.-Feb.

Sources of Information

Tourist Development Corporation (TDC) headquarters, Wisma MPI (17th and 18th floors), Jln. Raja Chulan, Kuala Lumpur; tel. 423033. Open 8:30-4:30 weekdays, 8-12:45 Saturday.

Malaysian Tourist Information Centre, Kuala Lumpur International Airport, Subang; tel. 755707. Open 9:15-10:30 daily, including Sundays.

Malaysian Tourist Information Centre, Jln. Tun Perak (near Jln. Raja/Jln. Tuanku Abdul Rahman), KL; tel. 80778. Open weekdays, 8-5, and Saturday, 8-12:45.

Kuala Lumpur Tourist Association, Railway Station, Jln. Sultan Hishamuddin, KL; tel. 81832. Open weekdays 8:30-4:30, and Saturday 8:30- 12:30.

Background

Malaysia is a federation of 13 states, 11 on the Malay peninsula and 2 on the northern side of Borneo. A mountain range which divides the long, narrow peninsula has contributed to the distinctly different atmospheres of its two coasts. Along the west coast are rolling hills which have been developed as large rubber and oil-palm estates and alluvial plains which are suited for rice cultivation. Due to its natural resources and strategic location along the straits of Malacca, the west coast is Malaysia's urban and manufacturing region. Traces of Islamic sultanates and European colonial empires can be seen amid the busy cities which have sprung up. The east coast remains comparatively undeveloped; some coastal rice cultivation intersperses lush rain forest. The population is predominantly Malay, unlike the west coast's racial mix, and more traditional lifestyles continue in the small towns and fishing villages.

The peninsula has always been strategically located at the crossroads of maritime trade between India and China—Hindu and Buddhist influences undoubtedly intersected here. By the 15th century, Malacca became a significant commercial port as Arab traders began to penetrate Malay markets. As a result, Islamic beliefs were diffused throughout the peninsula. The Portuguese, who conquered Malacca in 1511, were interested in trade, not conversion and control. In 1614, the Dutch occupied Malacca and other west coast ports for purposes of trade and strategy. By the late 18th century, the English took over the west coast, including Singapore. The effect of each successive conquest was to disperse the Malays away from the European-controlled ports.

The discovery of tin deposits and the establishment of rubber plantations, both export-oriented, caused dramatic social and economic transformation. As Malays shied away, substantial numbers of Chinese flowed into the west coast to work in the British-owned mines, and when they were eventually displaced by mechanization, they found opportunities in estates, urban commerce and small-scale industry. A similar influx of Indian immigrants came to work on the rubber estates. By the end of the 19th century, the labor force was stratified along ethnic lines, with immigrants providing cheap labor and middlemen for British colonial ventures while the Malays remained in

MALAYSIA 183

traditional agricultural production.

While British colonial policy did not intend to pit one ethnic group against another, it did nevertheless reinforce ethnic isolation except at the level of exchange. Non-Malay middlemen became the highly visible link between the Malay-dominated subsistence sector and the British-controlled capitalist sector--as a result, the Chinese and Indians were targets of antagonism arising out of unequal economic relations.

Japanese occupation during WWII intensified the already strained ethnic relations by adopting separate policies for each ethnic group. While the end of the war did unleash nationalist sentiments, political aspirations were divided along ethnic lines. The returning British instituted the Malayan Union which proposed to grant citizenship to non-Malays. Malays responded by rejecting the Union. Divided by class, ethnic, linguistic and political differences, neither the Chinese nor the Indians could gather enough political strength to demand equal rights in a single nation. To accommodate Malay sentiments, the British established the Federation of Malaya in 1948 to replace the Union. The British, with the support of the Malay aristocracy, retained political authority. Rejecting the legitimacy of the colonial government, the Chinese-dominated Malayan Communist Party went underground in order to foment revolution that would lead to independence and the establishment of a communist state. Because the Malayan Communist Party was mostly Chinese and the counterinsurgency forces were mostly British and Malay, the war of independence contributed further to ethnic hostility.

By 1957, the Federation of Malaya secured its independence from the British. A ruling coalition was formed so that Chinese business interests, aligned with Western capital, were protected while the Malays retained political control. (Meanwhile, Sabah, Sarawak and Singapore joined the Federation in 1963, but within two years Singapore withdrew.)

In 1969, tensions in Malaysian society erupted into violence because of a Malay fear that their economic position had not substantially improved since independence. The riots destroyed the consensus on economic and political specialization along ethnic lines which had been the basis of the Federation. In 1970, the government adopted the New Economic Policy which aimed at creating a viable commercial and industrial Malay business community and ensuring 30% Malay employment and ownership in all sectors of the economy by 1990. The Chinese business community, though resentful of NEP, has adjusted by going into partnership with Malays or bribing their interests through.

The 1969 riots highlighted the dangers of a multiethnic society with substantial economic disparities. The stability of Malaysia will depend on the progress of reducing these disparities.

Culture and Customs

There isn't really any general statement that can be made about 'Malaysian culture'—within the country many distinct cultural traditions live side by side. ('Malaysian' is a political term referring to the country's 13 million citizens.) The population is roughly 45% Malay, 35% Chinese, 10% Indian, Ceylonese or Pakistani, and 10% the indigenous people of Sabah and Sarawak (including Land Dayaks, Sea Dayaks and Ibans, among others).

Travelers should keep a few Moslem customs in mind. Only the right hand is used for eating, touching, giving, receiving and gesturing. (The left hand is regarded as unclean.) Most restaurants now provide a fork and spoon, but Malay Moslems (and Indians) still often eat with their right hand. Take your shoes off before entering a mosque (or temple); long pants and skirts are preferred (robes will sometimes be provided) and women should cover their heads. Smoking, loud talk, etc. are forbidden in mosques. See **Culture and Customs** in Indonesia, p.54 for a brief survey of Malay manners.

Festivals

For the Malay community, **Hari Raya Puasa** is the great Islamic holiday which marks the end of the fasting month and the 10th month of the Muslim calender. Hari Raya is expected to fall on August 2-3, 1981. The **Birthday of Mohammed** is celebrated February 2; **Hari Raya Haji** (when pilgrims visit Mecca) takes place in October.

The most important festival for the Chinese is the **Chinese New Year** which will fall on February 5, 1981—Year of the Rooster. Following the Chinese New Year is the 12-day **Ban Hood Huat Hoay** (the Ten Thousand Buddhist Gathering) which draws thousands to Kek Lok Si Temple on Penang. The **Dragon Boat Festival** celebrated in Penang in July honors the legendary Chinese poet and scholar Chu Yuen, who drowned himself in the 3rd century BC in protest of corrupt government. The

MALAYSIA 185

Hungry Ghosts Festival is celebrated on August 14; the Chinese community offers fruit, meat and prayers for the dead. During the **Festival of the Nine Emperor Gods**, September 28-October 6, firewalkers at Kew Ong Yeah Temple in Kuala Lumpur carry chairs bearing imagesof the nine emperor gods across burning coals.

Deepavali, which means 'Festival of Lights', is celebrated by Hindus. This festival signifies the triumph of righteousness over evil. According to Hindu legend, a demon was once born on earth to terrorize the people. To end the tyranny, Lord Krishna killed him in a fierce battle. Deepavali is celebrated in late November. **Thaipusam** is one of the most important Hindu festivals, celebrating the birth of Lord Subramaniam. Crowds follow penitents with 'kavadis' (decorated frames with skewers that pierce the flesh) in procession. Thaipusam is celebrated in February at the Batu Caves.

Hari Kebangsaan Malaysia (National Day) is celebrated August 31; classical music and dance performances in the Lake Gardens are the main attractions. There is also a month-long festival in December on Penang. The **Pesta Pulau Penang** has a number of cultural performances, a trade fair, kite-flying contests, etc.

Language

The national language of Malaysia is Bahasa Malaysia which is quite similar to Indonesian. English is widely spoken as a second language; it is used in hotels, ships, restaurants and offices throughout the country.

Good morning	**Selamat pagi** (SLAH-maht PAH-gi)
Good afternoon	**Selamat petang** (SLAH-maht peh-TAHNG)
Good night	**Selamat malam** (SLAH-maht MAH-lahm)
Good bye	**Selamat tinggal** (SLAH-maht TING-gahl)
How are you?	**Apa khabar** (AH-pah KHA-bahr)
Please	**Sila** (SI-lah); **Tolong** (TOH-lohng)
Thank you	**Terima Kaseh** (TRI-mah KAH-sei)
You're welcome	**Sama-sama** (SAH-mah SAH-mah)
Excuse me, I'm sorry	**Maafkan saya** (Mah-AHF-kahn SAI-yah)
No	**Tidak** (TI-dah')
Yes	**Ya** (Yah)

186 MALAYSIA

Street	**Jalan** (JAH-lahn), **leboh** (leh-BOH)
Bus/Bus Station	**Bas/Steshen bas** (BAHS)
Train/Train station	**Keretapi/Steshen keretapi** (KREH-tah AH-pi)
Hotel	**Rumah rehat** (ROO-mah REI-haht)
Room	**Bilek tidor** (BI-lehk TI-dor)
Restaurant	**Kedai makan** (Ke-DAI MAH-kahn)
Market	**Pasar** (PAH-sahr)
Post office	**Pejabat pos** (Peh-JAH-baht pohs)
Toilet	**Tandas** (TAHN-dahs)
Bath	**Bilek mandi** (BI-lehk MAHN-di)
How much is it?	**Ini berapa harga?** (EE-ni be-RAH-pah HAR-gah?)
Too expensive	**Mahal sangat** (mah-HAL SAHNG-aht)
Inexpensive	**Murah** (MOOR-ah)
Good	**Baik** (BAI')
Bad	**Tidak baik** (TI-da' BAI')
Where is—?	**Dimana—?** (Di-MAH-nah—?)
I want to go to—.	**Saya nak pergi ke—** (Sai-yah NAH PER-gi keh—)
Is this the bus to—?	**Bas ini pergi ke—kah?** (BAHS EE-ni PER-gi keh—kah?)
I don't understand	**Saya tak faham** (SAI-yah tak FAH-hahm)

(**Numbers:** See Language section in Indonesia chapter.)

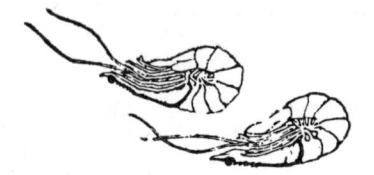

Food

Malaysia offers a great variety of Chinese, Malay, and Indian dishes. Small cafes and food stalls selling inexpensive meals are easy to find in towns and cities throughout the country. In Indian restaurants eat spicy currries served with rice on a banana leaf (eat with your right hand—there's usually a sink where you can wash up before and after). Cities on the west coast specialize in Chinese dishes, while Malay food is more prominent on the east coast. Coastal towns everywhere offer excellent seafood.

There are lots of open-air night markets; portable kitchens with tables and chairs materialize at nightfall in most towns, serving noodles, satay (Malaysia's national dish), sugar cane juice (air tebu), and much more.

Indian roti (bread) shops offer a cheap and filling breakfast—look for the round, pancake-like bread being grilled in small, open-front restaurants. You dip the bread in the spicy side dishes served along with it.

MALAY DISHES

nasi goreng — fried rice
sayor campor goreng — mixed fried vegetables
laksa asam — noodles w/meat and spices
otak otak — white filet of fish
satay — barbecued meat on skewers, served w/ peanut sauce
ayam/daging/kambing/babi — chicken/beef/mutton/pork
ayam perchik — barbecued chicken (East Coast)
rendang — beef cooked with coconut milk and spices
gado gado — vegetables served with rice and peanut sauce
sop kambing — spicy lamb soup

INDIAN DISHES

chapati — wheat pita bread
dalcha — dahl curry
curry ikan — fish curry (a breakfast side dish)
katchandral — corn dip (a breakfast side dish)
mutton mysore — chunks of dry-fried lamb
murtabak — fried pancake filled w/minced meat, egg & onions
mee goreng — fried noodles, Indian style
beriyani — saffron rice, often served with chicken
(Plus numerous **curries**)

CHINESE DISHES

cha kway teow — fried noodles
kway teow — noodles in soup
air tauhu [tau cheong] — soybean milk (served hot for breakfast)
tau sah mee — noodle soup w/pork or shrimp dumplings

DRINKS

teh/kopi — tea/coffee (usually served w/milk and sugar)
air/susu — water/milk
air tebu — sugar cane juice
kelapa muda — coconut milk w/sugar and ice

FRUIT

(See Food section of Indonesia chapter.)

Accommodations

The **Hotel Lists** published by the Tourist Development Corp. include some modestly priced hotels as well as plush ones, but youth hostels and Chinese hotels offer the least expensive accommodations. **Chinese hotels** are often located near railway and bus stations; singles (which usually have double beds) cost M$8-12, doubles M$10-14, except in KL, where everything is expensive. Rates at **youth hostels**, generally located on the outskirts of major towns, are M$2.50 for Youth Assn. members; others pay M$1-2 more. During the summer months it is advisable to phone or write for reservations at hostels.

NOTE: Room rates are subject to a 5% government tax.

Transportation

INTERNATIONAL: The **airports** in Kuala Lumpur, Penang, Johore Baru, Kuching and Kota Kinabalu handle international flights.

The **Ekspres Antarabangsa** (International Express) train leaves Butterworth (Penang) for Bangkok at 7:55 am three days a week (Monday, Wednesday, Friday). It arrives in Bangkok at 6:45 am (Thai time) the following day. From Bangkok, it leaves for Butterworth at 4:10 pm (Thai time) three days a week (Monday, Wednesday and Saturday). It arrives at 5:53 pm the following day. Fares are M$61.40 (1st class) and M$31.00 (2nd class); a berth costs M$5.80 (upper) or M$8.70 (lower).

The **Ekspres Rakyat** (People's Express) train leaves Butterworth (Penang) for Singapore via Kuala Lumpur in slightly over 13 hours. It leaves Butterworth at 8:30 am daily and arrives in Kuala Lumpur at 2:50 pm. From Kuala Lumpur, it leaves at 3:15 pm and arrives in Singapore at 9:40 pm. The return trip leaves Singapore at 8 am and arrives in KL at 2:30 pm. From Kuala Lumpur, it leaves at 3 pm and arrives in Butterworth at 9:15 pm. Fares for Butterworth/Singapore are M$46 (w/ac) and M$27.60 (w/o ac); for KL/Singapore they are M$26 (w/ac) and M$15.50 (w/o ac).

For either of these trains, book a few days in advance to be sure to get a seat.

MALAYSIA 189

From Butterworth there are two trains daily (6:50 and 7:55 am) to Haadyai, arriving there at 11:20 am and 12:32 pm (Thai time) respectively. Fares are M$20.90 (1st class) and M$10.10 (2nd class). The return trips are at 10:43 am and 11:40 am (Thai time) and arrive at 5:53 and 5:39 respectively.

There is no regularly scheduled **boat** service between Penang and Medan, Indonesia due to smuggling problems.

Buses offer inexpensive transit across Malaysia's border with Singapore. From Johore Baru at the southern tip of Malaysia you can catch a bus to downtown Singapore (Rochor Rd.). Comfortable express buses leave frequently (M$.80, 35 min.); local buses which cost even less are also available.

INTERCITY: The main rail line connects the principal cities along the west coast. The **Ekspres Rakyat** line starts in Butterworth (Penang) at 8:30 am and stops in many cities including Ipoh (arrives at 11:27 am), Kuala Lumpur (arrives at 2:50 pm), Seremban (arrives 4:27 pm), Tampin (arrives 5:22 pm), and Johore Baru (arrives 9:12 pm). The return trip begins in Singapore but you can catch it in Johore Baru at 8:30 am with stops in Tampin (at 12:37 pm), Seremban (at 1:18 pm), Kuala Lumpur (at 2:30 pm), Ipoh (at 6:16 pm) and Butterworth (at 9:15 pm). The fares between Butterworth and Johore Baru are M$27.60 (w/o ac) and M$46 (w/ac); Butterworth/KL are M$15.50 (w/o ac) and M$26 (w/ac).

Ekspres KTM trains are slightly quicker for the Butterworth/KL and KL/Johore Baru connection. They leave Butterworth at 1:10 pm and arrive in KL at 5:55 pm. The return trip begins at 3 pm and arrives at 9:15 pm. The Ekspres KTM leaves KL at 7 am and arrives in Johore Baru at 12:20 pm (arrives in Singapore at 12:45 pm). The return trip from Johore Baru to KL begins at 11:41 am and arrives in KL at 7 pm. The fares are the same as the Ekspres Rakyat.

There is also a line running from Tumpat (near Kota Bharu and Pasir Mas) through the central highlands connecting the West Coast Line at Gemas in the southern part of the peninsula. The Ekspres train leaves Tumpat at 10 am (stops in Kuala Lipis at 5:39 pm), and arrives in Gemas at 12:09 am. The return trip starts at 3 am and arrives in Tumpat at 4:40 pm.

For more detailed information, obtain the railway timetable with fare chart ("Jadual Waktu Keretapi Tanah Melayu") at the major train stations.

Rail passes for 10 or 30 days can be obtained at major railway stations for M$70 and M$150 respectively. Prices do not include sleeping berth but allow a choice of any class of passenger coach, including the Ekspres Rakyat.

MAS (Malaysian Airline Service) has a full line of domestic **flights**, including some good economy night flights. In KL you can call their 24 hr./day reservation office; tel. 206633.

Bus service is efficient and comfortable. Many of the well-traveled routes are covered by air-conditioned express buses at quite reasonable prices. The Mara Express Bus Co., one of many, operates the fastest buses between most points. Express bus offices are often (but not always) located at bus terminals. It's best to purchase tickets a day or two in advance. Local buses also operate between all towns and cities, usually leaving every couple hours. They are crowded, slow, and cheap.

Shared taxis offer fast, comfortable and relatively inexpensive service between major cities. They leave from special stands usually located next to bus stations (in KL, from the second floor of the Puduraya Terminal). Taxis are generally available between 6 am and 7 pm, but departures are most frequent mid-day. No fixed schedules—taxis start out as soon as they're full (usually four passengers). Fares are slightly higher than some train and most bus fares. For example, from KL to Butterworth, a shared taxi costs M$23/person (6 hr.). The regular train costs M$19.90, 2nd class & M$12.50, 3rd class (9 hr.). A bus costs M$11.50, M$14-15 w/ac (7½ hr.). Taxis are the way to go if you're in a hurry or prefer a flexible departure time. Other sample fares: KL-Malacca M$9, KL-Kuantan M$15, KL-Kota Bharu M$35.

Hitchhiking is easy due to the large number of private cars and the friendliness of the people. Start early in the morning to catch the longer rides. Rides are easiest along the West Coast, where traffic is heaviest; timber trucks often pick up riders.

NOTE: During the monsoon season, Nov.-Feb., flooding occasionally disrupts bus and ferry service along the East Coast.

Penang and the Northwest

Penang (Pulau Pinang)

Penang (Pulau Pinang or "Island of Betelnut Palms") was ceded by the Sultan of Kedah to the British East India Company in 1786, in return for military protection which was never provided. When Francis Light took possession of the island for the Company in August of that year, there were fewer than 1000 people living on it, mostly fishermen. The new settlement soon became a busy trading post and immigrants flowed in steadily, among them Malays, Chinese, Ceylonese, Siamese and Britons. Today the island has nearly ½ million people.

Entry

Penang's Bayan Lepas International Airport is 17 km south of Georgetown. A yellow bus passes the airport every 20 min. en route to the capital, Georgetown (40 min., M$.60). Walk out to the highway in front of the airport and wait at the bus stop. The bus will stop at Jalan Maxwell, near Jalan Pinang (Penang Road). Walk northward along Jalan Pinang for four or five blocks and you'll come to streets like Leboh Chulia and Leboh Leith where many Chinese hotels are located.

Taxis from the airport to most hotels cost M$7-8; settle on the price before jumping in as taxis refuse to use meters on this run.

If you're traveling by train or bus, get off in the city of Butterworth, a short ferry ride from Penang. The ferry concourse is attached to the train and bus stations; ferries leave regularly around the clock. The trip to Penang is free, and the return trip is only M$.40. From the ferry landing take a rickshaw to a hotel (around M$1.50). See **Transportation**, p. 188.

Exploring Penang

The best way to explore **Georgetown** is on foot. Begin by visiting the Penang Tourist Assn., 10 Jln. Tun Syed Sheh Barakah, a 10-min. walk north of the ferry landing. From the ferry landing walk up Gat Leboh Pasar for two blocks. At Leboh Pantai turn right and walk four blocks towards the clock tower. Behind it is the tourist office. They're open 8:30-4:30 Monday-Friday (closed for lunch, 1-2) and 8:30-1 on Saturday. Pick up a free map and the 'Penang for the Visitor' pamphlet (M$.50).

192 MALAYSIA

From the tourist office, cross the street to **Fort Cornwallis**, built on the site where Francis Light raised the Union Jack to signify British possession in 1786. Originally a wooden stockade, the fort was rebuilt with masonry walls between 1808 and 1810 by convict labor.

Walk out the other side of the fort and across the park to the stately **City Council** building. In the shade of the trees next to the building sit men who for a small fee will type letters and documents people bring to them.

About 100 meters past the City Council, at the corner of Leboh Light and Leboh Pitt, stands the **Supreme Court House**, also dating from colonial days. Turn left onto Leboh Pitt and walk a block to **St. George's Anglican Church**, the first church for Anglican worship in Malaysia.

Further down Leboh Pitt is **Kwan Yin Teng** (Goddess of Mercy Temple). Certainly not Penang's largest temple, it is one of the most patronized. Two blocks south along Leboh Pitt is the Hindu **Sri Mariamman Temple**. Continue another block to the **Kapitan Kling Mosque**, built in 1916. There's a post office (pejabat pos) across the street.

About three blocks past the mosque, between the Yap Temple and Leboh Acheh turn left through a tunnel into a small square dominated by **Khoo Kongsi**, or Dragon Mountain Hall. This intricately decorated clan house, originally built in 1906, was renovated in the '50s. Green stone miniatures on the walls of its central hall depict the 24 forms of filial piety. Kongsis, or Chinese clan houses, originated as associations for people with the same name and have now become benevolent associations for their members. The Khoo Kongsi is open 9-5 Monday-Friday and 9-1 on Saturdays; sign in upstairs in the building on your right as you enter the square.

For places out of Georgetown, make use of Penang's efficient bus system. Fares quoted here (M$.15-.40) are usually from the terminus to their final destination. If you ride for a shorter distance you pay less; just tell the fare collector where you're going.

Kek Lok Si Temple (Temple of Supreme Bliss) is built on a rocky hillside above Ayer Itam which has a good view of the surrounding mountains and the village below. It's especially peaceful in the afternoon when most of the camera-toting visitors have gone. The dominating structure of the temple complex and gardens, which covers 30 acres, is the Pagoda of Ten Thousand Buddhas. Its architecture reflects three cultures: the lower section is Chinese, the middle section is Siamese, and the top section is Burmese. To get there, walk to Jln. Maxwell, near Leboh Carnavoran (Yellow Bus Terminus), and hop on the #1 or green bus to Ayer Itam (30 min., M$.40).

Taking the funicular railway to the top of **Penang Hill** is a

MALAYSIA 193

good way both to enjoy the cool breezes and to glimpse twilight over Georgetown. The railway, which opened in 1923, starts at a station near Ayer Itam village. Trains generally leave every ½ hr., starting at 6:30 am until 8:45 pm (11:45 pm on Wednesday and Saturday). Avoid the school rush hour (12-1) where throngs of schoolkids race through the station leaving you in the wake of their dust. Roundtrip fare is M$3. To get to Penang Hill from Georgetown take either a green bus or a #1 city bus from the Yellow Bus Terminus of Jln. Maxwell to Ayer Itam. From Ayer Itam (close to Kek Lök Si Temple) take a #8 city bus (M$.15) for the short ride to the lower railway station.

The serenely beautiful **Botanical Gardens** (also known as the Waterfall Gardens), located 8 km outside of Georgetown, are inhabited by hundreds of tame monkeys. There's a Hindu temple in the gardens where the colorful Thaipusam Festival takes place in January or early February each year. To get there take a #7 city bus from Leboh Victoria, Leboh Chulia or Penang Rd. (M$.30).

A **round-island trip** by bus is pleasant and inexpensive (about M$3), but you have to be willing to spend time waiting at bus stops. Start early—the trip can easily take a full day.

From the Yellow Bus Terminus on Jln. Maxwell take a yellow bus to the **Tunku Abdul Rahman Aquarium**; #77 goes directly, while #66 drops you off on the main road (15 min., M$.30). The aquarium is open 10-6 daily except Wednesdays; it has an interesting fisheries exhibit. Back on the main road, catch a #66 to the **Snake Temple** (10 min., M$.25) so-named because dozens of Wagler's pit vipers doze on altars and cross-bars under the tables, or loop themselves across the branches of potted plants. Defanged snakes are on display in an adjacent room—for a fee they'll pose with you for a photograph. From the Snake Temple get back on #66 bus and head for Balik Pulau, a small town on the far side of the island (40 min., M$.65). There you have to change to another yellow bus, #76, to continue on to Teluk Bahang; five buses leave daily, the last two at 2:15 and 4 pm (ask a bus conductor in order to doublecheck departure times). En route you'll pass the Titi Kerawan Waterfall. Teluk Bahang has a beach and several batik factories which are open to visitors. To get back to Georgetown catch the #93 blue or silver bus (M$.75). The road follows the coastline, passing Penang's most popular beaches at **Batu Ferringhi**—a fancy resort and fishing village—and **Tanjung Bungah**. At either place you can buy food and cold drinks at small stands overlooking the ocean. The bus route ends at the Blue Bus Terminus on Jln. Maxwell.

194 MALAYSIA

Eating in Penang

Penang long ago established a reputation for the variety of its food. Malay, Chinese and Indian restaurants and food stalls are seldom more than a 3-min. walk away.

For a sampler of Penang cuisine at its cheapest, look for the night market where food stalls compete for space with vendors of everything from pirated cassettes to Chinese buttons. The market changes location every two weeks; check your hotel or the tourist office where it's going to pop up next. Permanent clusters of food stalls include:

• **Gurney Drive**, at the water's edge on the northwest side of town (take either a #2 city bus or a #93 blue bus from the Blue Bus Terminus on Jln. Maxwell). Chinese seafood served.

• **Padang Brown** (formerly known as Dato Keramat Gardens), on Jln. Perak. There's the usual assortment of satay, noodle dishes, ice cream, etc., plus a special treat called **lok lok**, a variation of the 'steamboat.' Sit at one of the tables with a pot of boiling water in the center; the waiter brings numerous plates of seafood and other tidbits on skewers which you cook yourself, then eat with peanut and chili sauces. You are charged at the end by the number of empty skewers (color-coding determines pricing). You can feast on squid, octopus, prawns, clams, mussels and fish for around M$3. Take a #4 bus from Jln. Maxwell to where Jln. Anson intersects Jln. Perak.

• **Oriental Cafe**, on Jln. Macalister near Penang Rd., across from the 8-story Malaysia Borneo Finance Building. From its outside tables, you can watch the street scene while you munch on teow, laksa or seafood. Good fruit juices.

• **Jalan Maxwell**, just west of the bus terminus. Foods sold here include corn-on-the-cob, steamed bao and lots of fresh fruit. There's also clothing, jewelry and cassettes.

There are a series of Indian restaurants along Leboh Campbell but the best seems to be **Tajmahal Restaurant**, 161 Penang Rd.

A few blocks to the north is the **Magnolia's Snack Bar**, 54 Penang Rd., home of some of Malaysia's best ice cream (M$.70 a scoop). They're open until 11 pm.

Night Life

At night, walk along Penang Rd. and mingle with the crowds. The shops and sidewalk stands sell all kinds of handicrafts and other merchandise. On Leboh Chulia and Jln. Macalister you can find second-hand bookstores (books though aren't cheap).

After visiting the night market, walk to the northern end of Penang Rd. to the Merlin Hotel and go up to the **Zodiac**, their 14th floor revolving restaurant and bar. You get a spectacular view of the city lights in all directions. Drink slowly, though—a beer costs M$2.88.

If you feel like seeing a film, Penang has a half dozen ac theaters which show relatively recent movies (including quite a few American films for M$.65-2.00).

ACCOMMODATIONS IN PENANG
Georgetown:

Georgetown has dozens of cheap Chinese hotels (singles and doubles for M$7.50-12), most of them a M$1-1.50 rickshaw ride from the ferry terminal. They're generally clean, centrally located and some are raided by the police periodically for prostitution. Popular places include the **New China Hotel** (Leboh Leith), the **Swiss Hotel** and the **Tye Ann Hotel** (Leboh Chulia), the **Modern Hotel** (Leboh Muntri) and the **Pin Seng Hotel** (Love Lane). Since hotels are clustered in one area, it's easy to shop around.

Penang Youth Hostel, Jln. Farquhar; tel. 60553. For IYH members and students. Dorm beds M$3 for the first night, M$2 after that—usually a 3 night limit. Located on the north edge of town next to the E & O Hotel (within walking distance of downtown). The sign in front is in Malay ('Pusat Belia, Tata Rakyat dan Asrama'). Usually full during Malaysian student holidays.

YMCA, 211 Macalister; te. 362211/362311. Dorm beds M$4; single M$12. w/ac M$14; double M$17, w/ac M$18; triple w/ac M$24. All rooms except dorms have private showers. Located on west edge of town; bus #7 stops right in front.

YWCA, 8A Green Lane; tel. 60876. Dorm beds M$8; single M$12; double M$20. A 10-min. bus ride from downtown. Take a #1 or a green Ayer Itam bus and get off at the intersection of Ayer Itam and Green Lane. The Y is to the left of the State Mosque.

Embassy Hotel, 12 Burma; tel. 65145/6. Single M$18.70, w/ac M$22; double M$20.90, w/ac M$24.20.

Peking Hotel, 50-A Penang Rd.; tel. 22455. Single M$18.70, w/ac M$22-30. Has seafood restaurant and a small bar. Located on the coast on the north edge of town.

Tanjung Bungah:

This village on Penang's northern coast has several Chinese hotels which are both inexpensive and risk-free, in contrast to the accommodations available in Batu Ferringhi and Teluk Bahang (see below). For example, **Hotel Loke Thean**, a 5-min. walk east of the bus stop, offers doubles w/private bath for M$12, or M$16 (3 people), or M$18 (4 people). Or try **Heart's Delight**, where doubles are M$5. nothing fancy—it's more like a camp than a hotel—and the location is pleasantly secluded. Just past the bus stop turn left up the hill; every time the road forks keep to the right. It's about ½ km from the main road. And don't be intimidated by the 'security check' sign on the gate, just go through the door to the left.

To get to Tanjung Bungah take a blue or silver bus from the Blue Bus Terminus on Jln. Maxwell (M$.40).

Batu Ferringhi:

This well-known resort, west of Tanjung Bungah, is packed with luxury hotels, none of which offers rooms which could even be called 'moderate' in price. A cheap but chancey alternative: M$3-5 for a room in or attached to local villagers' houses. Usually clean—some newly built. Just walk into town; little kids will show you where to go. (Note: Immigration officials come through regularly and clear everyone out—they give foreigners 24 hr. to leave the country).

Take a blue bus from the Blue Bus Terminus to Tanjung Bungah (M$.40), then another bus to Batu Ferringhi (M$.25).

Teluk Bahang:

As in Batu Ferringhi, locals will rent rooms to travelers for a few dollars a night. Take bus #93.

Short Trips from Penang

About a stone's throw south of the Thai-Malaysian border and 32 km off the coast is **Langkawi Island**, the largest in a group of 99 heavily jungled, mostly uninhabited islands. Its convoluted coastline was once a refuge for pirates who preyed on the lucrative trade passing through the Malacca Straits. Langkawi's well-known beaches include Tanjong Rhu (northern tip of the island) and Pasir Hitam (Black Sands). Or swim in the pools at the foot of the Telaga Tujoh waterfall. Trips from Langkawi to nearby islands are easy to arrange—negotiate with local fishermen.

If Penang seems a bit crowded, check out **Pangkor Island**, with its long beaches and clear water. The island was an 18-century Dutch stronghold and, like Langkawi, a pirate's hideout in the mid-1800's. You can follow trails from beach to beach, or hike around the island in less than a day; boats can also be rented (best done in a group). Don't count on any nightlife here as most of the village people are out on fishing boats well before sunrise. Lots of solitude (especially mid-week) in beautiful surroundings. Cool sea breezes.

Taiping, 91 km southeast of Butterworth contains the famous Lake Gardens and an interesting museum of Malay artifacts. It also has a 20-acre zoo. **Kuala Kangsar**, 32 km east of Taiping, has one of Malaysia's loveliest mosques, the onion-domed Masjid Ubudiah. **Ipoh**, 175 km southeast of Penang, is the capital of the state of Perak and the tin mining center of Malaysia. It's said to have the best Chinese food in the country. Both north and south of the town deep caves in the limestone cliffs have been converted into Chinese and Hindu temples.

Hikers should head for **Cameron Highlands**. Located 5,000 ft above sea level in the heart of peninsular Malaysia, this hill station is famous for its terraced vegetable gardens, flower

MALAYSIA 197

nurseries and tea plantations as well as for its 'jungle walks.' There are three small towns: the main one, Tanah Rata, is 13 km above Ringlet and 3 km below Brinchang. (Shared taxis connect the towns more frequently and almost as cheaply as local buses.) A tourist information office in Tanah Rata which keeps somewhat erratic hours sells very approximate maps of local jungle walks. Some of these 'walks' are actually rugged hikes — good shoes are recommended. Lots of butterflies.

ACCOMMODATIONS FOR SHORT TRIPS FROM PENANG

Langkawi Island:

Hotel Asia, tel. (04) 749284. Single M$10; double M$15, w/ac M$20.

Government Rest House, Kuah; tel. (04) 749209. Single M$10-12; double M$15-18. Has a bar and restaurant.

Youth Chalet, tel. (04) 749206. A government-run dormitory arrangement w/beds for M$1/day.

Pangkor Island:

Sam Khoo's Mini-camp, Pasir Bogak Single M$3.70; double M$6.30. Rustic thatched huts from single to family-sized. Snacks and simple meals for M$2 or less. Bring a flashlight as there's no electricity after 11 pm. If the camp is full, head for the **Government Rest House**, also at Pasir Bogak. It has inexpensive doubles and several chalets.

Cameron Highlands: There are lots of inexpensive Chinese hotels in all three towns — Ringlet, Tanah Rata and Brichang. Room prices fluctuate with the season; different hotels define 'peak season' differently, but in general April, August and December qualify. You can also negotiate if you're going to stay more than a few days. Almost all hotels have hot water and many provide quilts (it gets chilly up here).

Town House Hotel, no. 41, Tanah Rata (on the main road); tel. (05) 941666.

Single w/common bath M$8; double w/common bath M$10-12, w/private bath M$20-22. Prices go up 33% during the peak season. Immaculate restaurant serves fresh strawberries and ice cream. This hotel is the local agent for the Mara Bus Co.

Seah Meng Hotel, No. 39, Tanah Rata; tel. (05) 941618.

Single w/common bath M$8, w/private bath M$12; double w/private bath M$14 (off-season rates). Clean, comfortable.

Wong's Villa, Brinchang.

Doubles only, M$4. Nice place. It's a 3-min. walk up the hill from the stop on the left.

TRANSPORTATION FOR SHORT TRIPS FROM PENANG

Langkawi Island: Take a bus from Butterworth to Alor Star (frequent departures), then another bus to Kuala Perlis. Ferries leave Kuala Perlis for Langkawi (30 km, 1½-2 hr.) at 10:30 am & 3 pm daily. They leave Langkawi at 8 am & 1 pm. The economy fare is M$4.50.

Pangkor Island: rom Ipoh take a local bus to Lumut (M$2.50) or a shared taxi. Express buses also run from Butterworth to Lumut (via Taiping) for M$7 (3½ hr.). from Lumut, ferries leave every ½ hr. (8 am-7:30 pm) for Pangkor for less than M$1 (30 min.). Get off at Pangkor Village, the

198 MALAYSIA

fishing village to the place you plan to stay at Pasír Bogak (M$2).

Taiping: Trains leave from Butterworth at 8:30 am (Ekspres Rakyat), 9:15 am (Ekspres), 1:10 pm (Ekspres KTM), 8:25 pm (Teren Biasa), and 10:00 pm (Ekspres), and arrive in Taiping at, respectively, 9:55 am, 11:09 am, 2:31 pm, 10:37 pm and 11:56 pm. Fares for Ekspres and Teren Biasa are M$10.40 (1st class), M$4.90 (2nd class) and M$3.10 (3rd class). Fares for Ekspres Rakyat/KTM are M$16.10 (w/o ac) and M$11.00 (w/ac).

Buses are also available from Butterworth that leave frequently for Taiping (M$3, 2½ hr.).

Ipoh: Trains leave Butterworth at the same time as above but arrive in Ipoh at 11:27 am, 1:04 pm, 3:53 pm, 12:30 am and 1:50 am respectively. Fares for Ekspres and Teren Biasa are M$19.60 (2nd class), and M$5.80 (3rd class). Fares for Ekspress Rakyat/KTM are M$8.80 (w/o ac) and M$16.00 (w/ac).

Trains from Ipoh to KL: 11:30 am (Ekspres Rakyat), 1:15 pm (Ekspres), 3:55 pm (Ekspres KTM), 12:45 am (Teren Biasa) and 2:30 am (Ekspres). Trains arrive, respectively, at: 2:50 pm, 5:25 pm, 6:55 pm, 5:15 am, and 6:35 am. Fares for Ekspres and Teren Biasa are M$22.20 (1st class), M$10.50 (2nd class(, and M$6.60 (3rd class). Fares for Ekspres Rakyat/KTM are M$9.60 (w/o ac) and M$17 (w/ac).

Buses are available from Butterworth that leave at 8 am and 1 pm for Taiping (M$4, 3½ hr.). From Ipoh, there are buses (Jasaramai Ekspres) at 8 am and 1 pm for KL (M$6).

Cameron Highlands: From Butterworth take an express bus to Tapah, on the trunk road to KL (M$7, 5hr.(, then switch to a local bus for the ride from Tapah up the windy road to CH (M$1.95, 2 hr.; 4 departures daily, the last two at 2:30 and 4 pm). A Mara Bus goes directly to CH from KL's Puduraya Terminal at 8:30 am daily (M$7.50, 4½ hr.).

Trains from Butterworth to Tapah: 8:30 am (Ekspres Rakyat) and 9:15 am (Ekspres). They arrive respectively at 12:21 pm and 2:17 pm. The Ekspres Rakyat is M$10.50 (w/o ac) and M$18 (w/ac); the Ekspres is M$7.50 (3rd class). There are other trains but you'll end up stranded in Tapah.

By train from KL to Tapah: The Ekspres Rakyat leaves at 9 am and arrives at 11:55 am in time to catch a bus to CH. The fares are M$8 (w/o ac) and M$14 (w/ac).

(Note: The Town House Hotel in Tanah Rata is the local agent in CH for the Mara Bus Co.; a bus leaves from in front of the hotel for KL at 2:30 pm daily. They can also get you to Butterworth by bus for M$9.95, including the change in Tapah.)

Kuala Lumpur and the Southwest

Entry

If you arrive in Kuala Lumpur (KL) by plane, stop by the airport's Tourist Information Centre for a copy of 'Kuala Lumpur This Month,' which includes a map. Buses (#47 and #61) leave the airport regularly for KL's Klang Bus Stand on Jln. Sultan Mohamed (M$.75, 45-60 min.) from 6 am to 11 pm. If you want to make the 23 km trip by taxi instead, buy a coupon from the taxi booth; the fares are set for various destinations in KL (average, M$12).

If you arrive by train, stop by the Kuala Lumpur Tourist Association office in the railway station. Take a taxi to your hotel (M$1-2)—unless you're going to stay at the YMCA or the Lido Hotel, which are within walking distance—because the few buses that stop near the station don't go into town. (See **Transportation**, p. 188, for trains from Bangkok, Butterworth and Singapore.

Departure

The airport departure tax is M$7 on all international flights except those to Singapore, M$4 on all flights to Singapore, and M$2 on domestic flights.

If you're leaving KL by plane, take a bus to the airport (28 km away) because a taxi is nearly 20 times as expensive. Bus #47 (blue) leaves from in front of the Klang Bus Stand every hour on the hour, 6 am-10 pm; the fare is M$.75. At night the trip takes 45 min.; during the day it may take up to an hour due to heavy traffic. Bus #61 (red) also serves the airport—it starts from inside the Klang terminal, leaves less frequently than the #47 bus, and takes a slightly longer route. The problem with taking a taxi is that only certain taxis are licensed to take passengers from the airport to KL, so regular taxis going **to** the airport have to come back empty. They usually won't make the trip for less than M$13-15.

Exploring KL

Kuala Lumpur was founded in 1857 when major tin exploration in the area was getting underway. Today it is a sprawling city of over one million including Malays, Chinese, Indians and Eurasians.

Getting around in KL is a bit tricky, partly thanks to the Gombok and Klang rivers which run through the middle of the

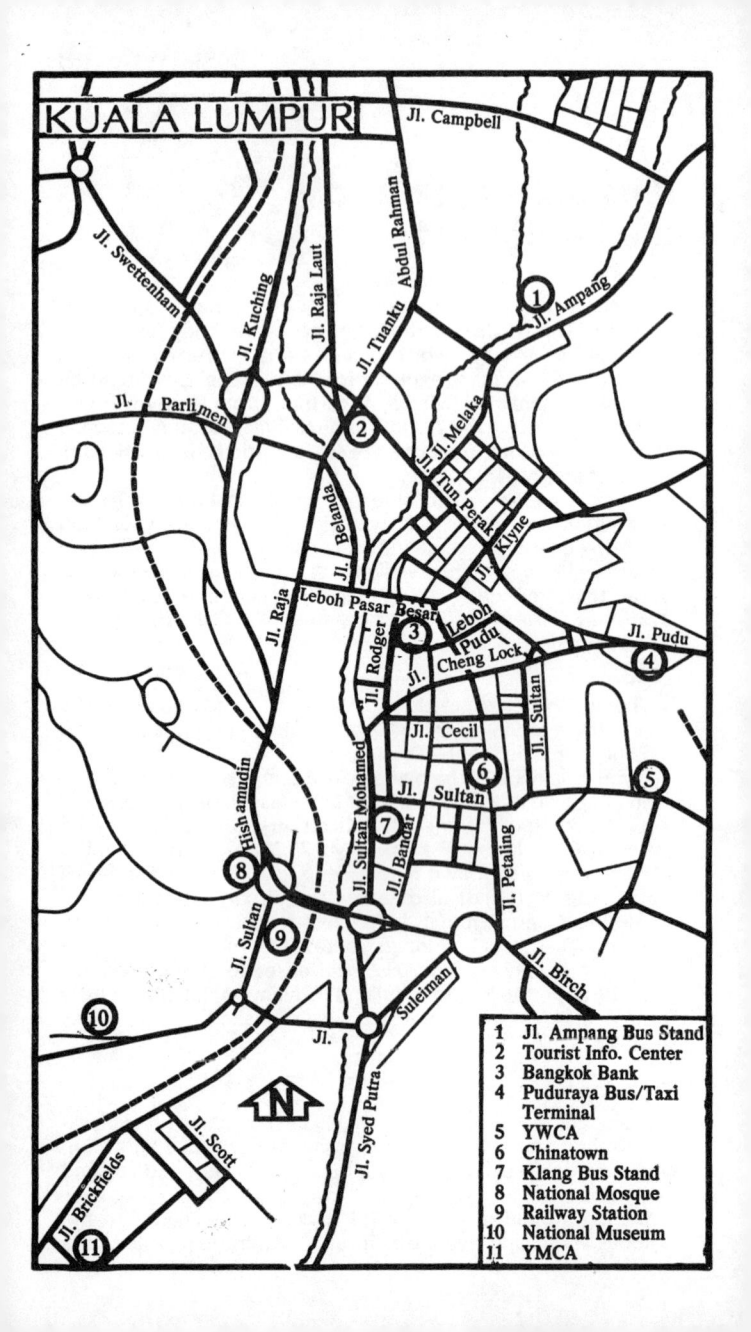

KUALA LUMPUR

1. Jl. Ampang Bus Stand
2. Tourist Info. Center
3. Bangkok Bank
4. Puduraya Bus/Taxi Terminal
5. YWCA
6. Chinatown
7. Klang Bus Stand
8. National Mosque
9. Railway Station
10. National Museum
11. YMCA

MALAYSIA 201

city (joining just below the Jame Mosque).

Buses run frequently and are quite cheap (M$.10-.50), but there are no published route maps or bus guides because so many companies operate within the city. The largest of the half dozen or more are Sri Jaya (blue) and Klang (red and gray). Fares are charged according to the distance traveled, so have a destination in mind, or give the ticket seller M$.30, enough to cover an average ride.

The three major bus stands are:

• **Puduraya Bus/Taxi Terminal**, Jln. Pudu (which becomes Jln. Cheng Lock to the west). This is the largest, the starting point for local and express buses to cities all over peninsular Malaysia as well as for city buses going to northern and southern KL.

• **Klang Bus Stand**, Jln. Sultan Mohamed. Located below a 5-story 'car park' with a large Toshiba sign on top. Some buses start from inside, others pass by in front or just north of it, serving the southern, western and central sections of the city.

• **Jalan Ampang Bus Stand**, Jln. Ampang, across from the AIA building. Serves northern and eastern KL.

Minibuses—which charge a flat fare of M$.40—generally stop at the same places buses do (except Puduraya Terminal). For descriptions of about 15 main routes, see the 'Kuala Lumpur This Month' pamphlet.

The **taxis** which roam all over the city charge M$.60 for the first mile, M$20 for every additional half-mile, and M$.10 for each additional passenger in excess of two; there's also a small charge for luggage. Make sure the meter is on; KL taxi drivers are so wily even the locals complain.

The **National Museum** (Museum Negara), on Jln. Damansara, is built in old Malay style with murals on the front depicting historical events and Malaysian crafts. On the first floor are displays of wayang puppets, clothing, jewelry, handicrafts and exhibits on Malaysia's 'orang asli' (aborigines). The second floor is divided into a natural history section and an economic activities section with displays on tin mining, forestry, rubber, agriculture, etc. Open 9-6 daily except on Fridays when it's closed 12-12:30. Free admission.

A 10-min. walk north of the museum is the Moorish-style railway station and up the street from it, the **National Mosque** (Mesjid Negara). The mosque's central prayer hall is surrounded by marble courtyards, pools, and fountains that give a feeling of cool restfulness. At any time of day you're likely to find people reading, playing, even sleeping. The main roof, shaped like an 18-pointed star, represents the 13 states of Malaysia and the five pillars of Islam; the white latticework enclosing the hall is done in traditional Islamic designs. Black robes (for those too informally dressed) and scarves for women are provided at the gate; take your shoes off before going into the mosque. Open 9-6 Saturdays through Thursdays, 2-6 Fridays.

A short walk west is the **Lake Gardens**, a 160 acre park containing the Parliament House, the National Monument and a large lake, Tasek Perdana. Boats can be rented on weekday afternoons and all day on weekends and holidays. This is a popular area for family picnics, strolling couples and even an occasional jogger.

For local handicrafts and a wide variety of food stalls, try the **Sunday Market** on Jln. Raja Muda Musa in the northeastern part of the city. Open every day, but Saturday nights are the most lively.

Batu Caves, about 13 km north of KL, are interesting both as a natural phenomenon and religious gathering place for the Hindu community. The festival of Thaipusam, which marks the birthday of Lord Subramaniam, is celebrated here in late January or early February. Climb the 272 steps to the coves' entrance and you're rewarded by cool temperatures inside the caverns, complete with bats. Another cave at the foot of the limestone outcropping contains brightly-painted statues of Hindu deities. Take minibus #11 from the Klang Bus Stand or one of the buses marked 'Batu Caves' from the Jln. Ampang Bus Stand (45 min.).

Templer Park, one of the smaller national parks (4,000 acres), is only 19 km north of KL and has trails through lush scenery. Take a #66 or #207 bus from the Puduraya Terminal (M$.75). Cross the highway and follow the sign pointing left to the waterfalls; on the way you'll pass a signboard with a map of the trails. The walk to the first waterfall takes about 10 minutes; if you go higher, some of the pools are good for swimming. This is a popular local spot so don't be surprised if you meet a crowd of teenyboppers with transistor radios.

Eating in KL

The Waspada Restaurant in Wisma Yakin on Jln. Melayu (near the Tourist Information Centre on Jln. Tun Perak) is a local favorite for Malay dishes (M$2-3/meal). Malay food is also served in many outdoor eating stalls (see below). For Chinese food, head for Chinatown, centered at Jln. Petaling. At the night market, between Jln. Sultan and Jln. Cecil, you can buy fruit and snacks of all kinds as well as clothes, jewelry, etc. There are a lot of inexpensive Indian restaurants on Jln. Masjid India, parallel to and one block east of Jln. Tuanku Abdul Rahman; at the Zam Zam Restoran, mutton curry is M$1.80 and a large bowl of rojak costs M$1.

KL is blessed with a number of excellent outdoor eating stalls, most of which appear at nightfall. The largest variety in any one place can be found on Jln. Campbell, a couple of blocks west of Jln. Tuanku Abdul Rahman. Another cluster of stalls materializes after sunset in a parking lot next to the river, just across from the Jame Mosque; they seem to specialize in 'nasi ayam' (chicken rice). Stalls line many of Chinatown's streets and alleys, but ask about prices before you order because some are on the expensive side. On Saturday night, head for the 'Sunday Market,' off Jln. Raja Muda Musa, which has dozens of small restaurants and shops.

If you're looking for live entertainment, check the local paper for current details. One popular night spot is the **Golden Key Restaurant** (at the back on the 2nd floor of the Pertama Complex, across from the Odeon Theater on Jln. Tuanku Abdul Rahman), which has live music nightly 8-12. During happy hour (4-7 pm Monday thru Friday) a beer is M$1.80. While you're there you may want to check out the rest of the Pertama Complex, which is full of coffee shops, snack bars, shops and pool rooms.

Behind the Dashrun Hotel at 285 Jln. Tuanku Abdul Rahman is **The Brass Rail**, a British-style pub. A beer at happy hour (4-7 pm) is M$1.60. Open until midnight.

Meeting Students

KL has two universities: the University of Malaya and the National University (Universiti Kebangsaan). Both are located a short distance from KL, en route to the town of Petaling Jaya.

ACCOMMODATIONS IN KUALA LUMPUR

If you arrive by train it will be easiest to take a taxi to wherever you want to stay because there are no bus stops near the station. If you arrive at Puduraya Bus Terminal, you can take buses (M$.10-.15) or mini-buses (M$.40) to various parts of the city.

All room prices quoted blow are subject to a 5% government tax (except for YW/YMCA and the Youth Hostel).

YMCA, 95 Jln. Kandang Kerbau, off Jln. Brickfields; tel. 441439.

Dorm beds M$5; single, double or triple w/common bath M$12, M$18 and M$24; single and double w/private bath & ac M$20 and M$28. Family room w/private bath & ac M$36. Non-members are charged M$1 for temporary membership. To get there take bus #5,33,40,49,49A or 243

204 MALAYSIA

or minibus #12 from Klang Bus Stand; ask for 'Cinema Lido' (near the Y).

Lido Hotel, 7A-9A Jln. Marsh Brickfields (behind the Cinema Lido); tel. 441258/441753.

Single and double, M$12 and M$14; double w/ac M$20. Good restaurant downstairs. Located just across the street from the YMCA (see directions above).

YWCA, 12 Jln. Davidson; tel. 202510.

Women only. single, M$15; shared room M$12.50/person. Many of the people staying here are Malaysians who work or go to school in KL; when the rooms reserved for transients are full you can sometimes share a room with a resident. The inconvenience of some of the Y's rules (i.e. breakfast served between 7 and 8 only) is made up for by the attractiveness of its location—fairly central yet quiet.

Coliseum Hotel, 100 Jln. Tuanku Abdul Rahman; tel. 926270.

Single M$7, double w/ac M$14 (no doubles w/o ac). A KL landmark, built in 1921—the bar downstairs was a planter's hangout in colonial days and the hotel's restaurant is famous for its sizzling steaks. It's located right in the heart of the city, but the area's busy night life may make this place less attractive to single women travelers.

Wisma Methodist Guest House, 9th floor, Wisma Methodist Bldg., Lorong Davidson, off Jln. Davidson; tel. 202797/202501

Double w/bath & ac M$18-20. Check in at the office on the 8th floor. Located near the YMCA.

Wisma Belia, 40 Jln. Lornie; tel. 290724/26803.

Rooms with one single and one double bed, M$9 (1 person); M$13 (2), M$16 (3). Double w/bath M18, w/bath and ac M$22. Located on south edge of town. From Klang Bus Stand take bus #52 or #65, or minibus #14 or #19.

Shiraz Hotel, 1/3 Jln. Medan Tuanku, off Jln. Tuanku Abdul Rahman (near the Odeon Theatre); tel. 920159/922625.

Single M$14, w/ac M$20; double M$17, w/ac M$23.81. Hotel restaurant specializes in Pakistani and North Indian food. Take bus #1 or #2 from Klang Bus Stand or minibus #29 or #31.

South East Asia Hotel, 69 Jln. Haji Hussein; tel. 926077.

A large, modern hotel offering students w/ISICSs shared rooms for M$16/person (otherwise prices zoom up to M$32-60). Has an Australian Union of Students (AUS) travel office on the 2nd floor. Take bus #1 or #2, or minibus #29 or #31. Located one block east of the north end of Jln. Tuanku Abdul Rahman.

Tai Ichi Hotel, 78 Jln. Bukit Bintang; tel. 427533.

Single w/bath & ac M$24; double w/bath &ac M$28. There are similarly priced hotels nearby. From Puduraya Terminal walk east on Jln. Pudu, then turn left onto Jln. Bukit Bintang.

Youth Hostel, No. 9, Jln. Vethavanam, off Ipoh Rd. (3½ milestone); tel. 660872.

For YH members, M$2.50 for the first night and M$2/night thereafter. For non-members, M$4, then M$3. Way out on the north edge of town. Take bus #66, 146, or 147 from Puduraya or #71 or 143 from Jln. Ampang.

Sidetrips From Kuala Lumpur

Malacca, 158 km southeast of KL, is an historic trading capital which served as the center of Moslem, Portuguese and British empires over the centuries. Begin a walking tour with a visit to the Tourist Information Centre on Jln. Kota in the heart of old Malacca to pick up a city map; it's open Monday to Friday 8:30-4:30 and Saturday 8:30-12:45. History buffs can buy an excellent book detailing the history of the area (M$5). When you leave the Centre you will be facing **Christ Church**, built in 1753 and one of the best examples of Dutch architecture in Malacca, with its heavy carved doors and thick walls. Some of the tombstones in the floor are 200 years old. From the door of the church you can see the salmon-colored **Stadhuys** building on your left. Built in the mid-1600s, it's possibly the oldest Dutch building in Asia. Walk past it and turn left onto Jln. Kota, which leads to the beach. Two blocks down, on the left, is the small **Malacca Museum** in a Dutch house built around 1660. The assortment of exhibits includes old Portuguese maps of the city, photos, weapons, jewelry, furniture, clothing, porcelain and farm tools. One block further along Jln. Kota is **Porta de Santiago** on the left. This is all that remains of a Portuguese fortress built in 1512. When the British took over Malacca in 1807, they began to destroy what was left of the fortress, but Stamford Raffles intervened to spare this last gateway. Behind the gate, climb the stairs to **St. Paul's Church**, first built as a chapel in 1512. It was later used by St. Francis Xavier during his visit to Malacca, and he was briefly buried here before his remains were moved to Goa. Return to the bottom of the hill and continue to follow Jln. Kota inland till you come to Jln. Gereja; here turn right. At the next corner you'll see the **Church of St. Francis**, another old church bearing many signs of early European influence. A short distance away on Jln. Tokon (see city map) is the **Cheng Hoon Teng**, the oldest Chinese temple in Malaysia. Built in the early 1700s, it's exquisitely decorated and meticulously maintained. Walk back to Jln. Temenggong and turn left. The street name shortly changes to Kampong Hulu. Two blocks further on the left is **Masjid Kampong Hulu**, which is over 150 years old and holds the tomb of the Sultan of Johore; the Sultan signed the cession of the island of Singapore to Sir Stamford Raffles in 1819. From the mosque it's a two-block walk to the city bus terminal.

206 MALAYSIA

Restaurants in Malacca serve excellent seafood. In the evenings, dozens of brightly lit food stalls appear along Jln. Taman on the water's edge. Be sure to try satay chelop, a Malacca specialty: various satay sticks (squid, octopus, eggs, cockles, pork, shrimp, vegetables, etc.) dipped in a spicy boiling broth. You do your own dipping and cooking, and pay according to how many sticks you eat. The best satay chelop is served at the Kingtu Satay Cafe, T-182 Jln. Munshi Abdullah (next to the Cathay Theatre). Jln. Tranquera has lots of Chinese restaurants. For ice cream and desserts, try the Tai Chong Hygienic Ice Cafe, 42G Bunga Raya Rd.

Port Dickson, 96 km southeast of KL, is a sleepy town with an 18-km stretch of beach. KL residents descend upon the beach on weekends and holidays so it's bound to be crowded. Deep-sea fishing gear and boats can be rented.

Taman Negara, sprawling across parts of three states to the east of Cameron Highlands, is Malaysia's largest and most spectacular national park. It's a great place for hiking, swimming, river-rafting and watching wildlife. Reservations must be made in advance through the Chief Game Warden's office (see address below), and all visitors must enter via park headquarters at Kuala Tahan. Accommodations available within the park include a hostel (M$3/night), a rest house (single M$10, double M$15), and chalets (expensive). Or rent camping equipment (M$3.50 plus M$1/night for campsite) for longer treks—but you must bring your own food, have suitable clothing, etc. For more information: write to the Chief Game Warden, Bangunan Kerajaan, Block K20, Jln. Duta, KL (tel. 94110); or visit any Tourist Information Centre. The centers in KL and Kuantan can help you make reservations, and explain the costs involved (e.g. for transportation to Kuala Tahan, park entry fee and so forth).

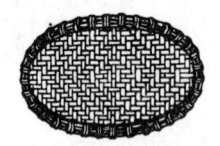

ACCOMMODATIONS FOR SHORT TRIPS FROM KUALA LUMPUR

Malacca: All of these hotels are within a 15-min. walk of the bus station/taxi stand. Walk out of the station to Jln. Hang Tuah, turn left, then left again, across the river onto Jln. M Abdullah. Jln. Burga Raya and Jln. Bendahara branch off of this street.

Valient Hotel, 41-A Jln. Bendahara; tel. 22323/22799.
  Double M$11, w/bath; triple w/bath M$16, w/ac M$25. Clean and comfortable; quiet if you can get a place in back.

MALAYSIA 207

Federal Hotel, 60-B Jln. Bendahara; tel. 2161.
Single M$12; double M$15, w/bath (shared toilet) M$18. Friendly staff.

Cathay Hotel, 100-104 Jln. Munshi Abdullah (Newcome Rd.); tel. 23337/23744.
Single M$9; double M$12, w/ac M$18; triple w/bath M$15.

International Hotel, 144A Jln. Bunga Raya; tel. 23286.
Single w/bath M$9 (1 person), M$10 (2); double w/bath M$14. Usually full.

Hong Kong Hotel, 154-A1 Jln. Bunga Raya; tel. 23392.
Single w/bath M$8 (1 person), M$10 (2) w/shared bath.

Ng Fook Hotel, 154-HI, Jln Bunga Raya; tel. 28055/28206.
Single M$11; double M$13, w/ac M$17. All rooms with private bath.

Malacca Youth hostel, 9th mile Pantai Kundor, Tanjung Kling.
A 50-bed hostel with very basic facilities. M$1/night for members, M$2 for non-members. Located 14½ km north of Malacca; take bus #57, which leaves Malacca's bus terminal hourly. (Note: For about the same price you can also stay in fishermen's huts nearby; try 'SHM's', for example, a 3-min. walk away).

Port Dickson:

Port Dickson Youth Hostel, 3¾ mile, Jln. Pantai.
A 40-bed hostel charging M$2.50-3.50. Located 3¾ (6 km) from town.

New Hai Tian Hotel, 266 AB1 mile Jln. Pantai; tel. 791378.
Double w/bath M$14; triple w/bath and ac M$20.

Pantai Hotel, 9th mile, Jln. Pantai; tel. 795265.
Double M$14; triple w/ac M$20. Has a bar and restaurant. Located on the beach.

TRANSPORTATION FOR SHORT TRIPS FROM KUALA LUMPUR

Malacca: A 2-hr taxi ride (M$8) or 2½-hr bus ride (M$4) southeast of KL. Buses leave from KL's Puduraya Terminal 5 times a day (8, 10, 10:30, 1 & 3); buy tickets a day in advance. From Johore Baru by bus—M$6.50, 4 hr; by shared taxi—M$13, 3½ hr. From Singapore by bus—S$8, 5½ hr.

Port Dickson: A special weekend excursion rail service operates between KL and Port Dickson on Sundays. The train leaves KL for the 2 hr trip at 7:30 am and returns at 5:20 pm (M$4 roundtrip fare); bus service is provided at Port Dickson Station to take passengers to and from the beach. By shared taxi from KL—M$6.50, 2 hr. By bus from Malacca—M$3, 2hr.

Taman Negara: From Kuantan take an express bus to Jerantut, M$6, 4 hr (leaves twice daily at 8:30 and 2); from Jerantut to Kuala Tembeling take a taxi (½ hr, M$15) or bus (infrequent). You must arrive before 2 pm when the boat leaves daily for Park Headquarters at Kuala Tahan (3 hr, M$10/person). Note: You can spend the night in Jerantut at the hotel or in the government rest house (single M$10, double M$15).

From Kuala Lumpur, take a bus to Temerloh (M$5, 3 hr); from Temerloh take a local bus to Jerantut, 1 hr (leaves every hour).

You cannot enter the park on your own—you must take the government boat from Kuala Tembeling to Kuala Tahan. Make reservations first through the Chief Warden's office in KL (see text for address).

The East Coast

Attractions on the east coast (the states of Kelantan, Trengganu, Pahang, and part of Johor) include beaches, fishing villages, batik and handicrafts, and turtle-watching. If you arrive between April and June you may also get to see some traditional Malay festivals, which feature kite flying, giant top spinning (main gasing), shadow puppet plays (wayang kulit), sea sports, dancing, and music. The 'weekend' falls on Thursday and Friday in Kelantan and Trengganu. Since most offices will be closed on these days, the beaches may be more crowded.

The people of **Kelantan state** are deeply religious and have always led the other states in the institutionalization of Islam; note all the hajis in their white caps (showing that they've been to Mecca). Kelantanese handicrafts—including batik, kain songket (handwoven silk with intricately worked motifs in gold or silver thread), silverware, kites and tops—are famous throughout the country.

Kota Bharu, the capital and royal town of Kelantan, is the seat of traditional Malay culture. It's small but lively (at least during the day). In summer 1980 the Tourist Information Centre was on the ground floor of the the Wisma Iktisad on Jln. Maju (next to the Emporium Batek); by 1981 it is supposed to relocate to Jln. Sultan Ibrahim, 2 blocks south of Pasar Besar (Big Market), which in turn is near the bus station. Hours: 8-12:45 & 2-4 Sat.-Wed. and 8-12:45 Thur.

There are lots of places in and around Kota Bharu where you can buy handicrafts and/or see them being made. Silverware factories cluster near the palace (Istana Kota Lama) in Kampong Sireh, by the river. The Samasa Batek Factory is on the south edge of town off Jln. Kuala Krai (turn right at 'Lee Motors' and walk in about ½ km). Pasar Besar (Big Market), in the middle of town, is a good place to buy mats, songket, and brassware, and the Emporium Batek has lots of small shops selling modern and traditional batik. Dozens of handicraft stores also line the road between Kota Bharu and Pantai Chinta Berahi (Beach of Passionate Love), 9 km northeast of the city. Take bus

#10 and watch for the signs; you could also take a becak to visit shops like 'Che Minah's' which are close by. (The area is called Kampong Penambang). Kampong Kijang, about 6 km further out, is famous for its kites (wau). The 'Local Handicraft Centre,' about 1 km before the beach, gives demonstrations of batik and kite making, silverwork, etc.

Istana Balai Besar and Istana Kota Lama are Kota Bharu's two palaces. By 1981 the former is supposed to be part of a 'traditional zone' with a museum and stage for cultural performances; inquire at the tourist office.

Kota Bharu has plenty of good, cheap restaurants. At Taman Sekebun Bunga, on the banks of the Kelantan River off Jln. Tok Hakim, a large cluster of outdoor stalls opens just before sunset. There are also lots of eating stalls next to the stadium on the east side of town.

Popular local beaches: Pantai Irama, south of Kota Bharu near the town of Bachok, has the nicest scenery (take bus #2); Pantai Dasar Sabak is on the way to the airport (take bus #9); and Pantai Chinta Berahi is the most famous (take bus #10). Keep in mind that bus service stops at around 6 pm.

From Kuala Besut, 64 km south of Kota Bharu, you can get to the nearby islands of **Perhentian**, noted for their beaches, clear water, and coral reefs, by fishing boat. (Plenty of market traffic daily; the fishermen usually charge around M$10 one-way.) There are two islands, Kecil and Besar: Kecil has the fishing village, Besar is the one to visit. Day trips or overnight camping are possible, but bring your own food.

Kuala Trengganu, 166 km southeast of Kota Bharu, is the capital and royal town of Trengganu. There are several places you can go for information. The Trengganu Tourist Information Centre is in the Wisma Maju (Maju Building) on Jln. Paya Bunga, near the bus station. For more complete information head for the TDC East Coast Regional Office, Wisma MCIS, Jln. Sultan Zainal Abidin, on the other side of town (tel. 21433). Hours for both offices: 8-4 Sat.-Wed. and 8-12:45 Thur.

The local beach, Batu Burok, runs along the south edge of town. Don't miss the Main Pantai Festival held here if you're in the area in May. Villagers from all around come to the beach to celebrate the end of the rice harvest with boat races, sports, dances and music. This three-day festival is the event of the year in Trengganu.

From the jetty behind the taxi stand at the end of Jln. Paya Bunga you can take a small ferry boat to Duyung Island (Pulau Duyung) in the river mouth for M$.30. At the nearby central market, watch the fishermen unload their catches in the morning. The Malaysian Handicraft Development Corp. (Pusat Kemajuan Kraftangan Malaysia), 339 Jln. Sultan Omar, is a training center where you can watch students at work, while

Wan Ismail's on Jln. Sultan Zainal Abidin near the TDC office—specializing in batik and brassware—is a good example of local cottage industry. Handicrafts as well as beaches can also be found south of Kuala Trengganu in the neighboring villages of Rusila and Marang (frequent bus service).

Some interesting, out-of-the-way places can be reached in day trips from Kuala Trengganu. Sekayu Waterfalls (Air Terjun Sekayu), about 55 km inland, offers swimming, gorgeous scenery and excellent hiking trails. Take a bus from Kuala Trengganu (start early) and get off in Kampong Sekayu; cross the bridge over the river and follow the path through the jungle to the waterfalls, a short walk away. (Last return bus leaves around 4 pm.) Pulau Kapas, an uninhabited island offshore from the fishing village of Marang, is famous for its coral, seashells, and clear water. The Pantai Motel, on Jln. Persinggahan in Kuala Trengganu, offers tours at reasonable cost (as little as M$10/person, if enough people go). Or go to Marang and negotiate with local fishermen.

Turtle-watching is a popular pastime in **Rantau Abang**, 64 km south of Kuala Trengganu. Between late May and early September about 1,500 female Giant Leathery Sea Turtles migrate to the coast near Rantau Abang to lay their eggs. The turtles, some weighing ½ a ton or more, clamber ashore at night to bury clutches of 80-100 eggs in the sand. Unfortunately, the eggs bring such a high price in the market that they're pilfered by collectors almost as soon as they're buried. The government now transplants some eggs to hatcheries to ensure the survival of the species.

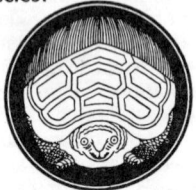

About 160 km south of Rantau Abang, past Dungun, Kemaman, and Cherating (site of Asia's first Club Mediteranee Holiday Village), lies **Kuantan**, capital of Pahang and jumping-off point for Kuala Lumpur. In 1980 the Pahang Tourist Information Office is on the south edge of town, a 1-km walk from the bus station on the same street. By mid-1981 it's supposed to move to the Kompleks Teruntum on Jln. Mahkota (the tallest building in town, can't miss it). Open 8-5 daily; tel. 22422. Besides filling you in on local attractions, the people here can help you make arrangements to go to the National Park (see p.207).

Like most of Malaysia's major towns, Kuantan is next to a

MALAYSIA 211

river. Cross it by boat to visit the fishing village of Paramu or Tanjong Lumpur for only M$.30. The boat for the former starts from the jetty behind the main bus station, for the latter from the jetty about ½ km further north next to the fish/vegetable market. To make a circular trip: take the boat to Paramu, walk out to the main road and turn left to get to Tanjung Lumpur, then take another boat back.

The Telok Chempedak Beach, 4½ km from town, is lovely, and has some nice places to stay (see **Accommodations**). A bus leaves for Telok Chempedak from the small station on Jln. Mahkota every hour (M$.40, 10-15 min.). Note the wooden boat abandoned in the middle of the beach—transportation for refugees from Vietnam.

The Sungai Lembing Tin Mine, the second largest and deepest lode tin mine in the world, is one hour from Kuantan by bus (M$1.75); you can make a small detour en route to visit Cheras Caves (Panching Caves). Or take the bus to Beserah, 8 km north of Kuantan, to see songket weaving, shell crafts, and a batik factory; there's also a beach.

South of Kuantan the east coast changes a great deal. There are fewer people, smaller villages, and less in the way of attractions or accommodations for the traveler. The only sizeable town between Kuantan and Johor Baru is **Mersing**, 208 km south of Kuantan. The action in Mersing centers around the pier and the market, located within sight of each other near the bus station. Watch the fishermen unload their boats and repack the fish in ice for crating and shipping to Singapore.

Off the coast near Mersing is a string of volcanic islands, the largest of which is **Pulau Tioman**. Good swimming and skin-diving. Get there from Mersing by passenger launch for M$15-20 (check with the Mersing Tourist Office to make charter arrangements). Or hitch a ride on a fishing or cargo boat from Mersing's pier—it takes longer but costs less.

ACCOMMODATIONS FOR THE EAST COAST

Kota Bharu:
Bali Hotel, 3655 Jln. Tok Hakim (near the river, a 10-min. walk from the bus station); tel. 22686.

Single M$8, double w/private bath M$10.
Maryland Hotel, 2627 Jln. Tok Hakim (a 5-min. walk from the bus station); tel. 22811.

Single M$10; double M$12, w/ac M$18. Most rooms w/private bath.
Hotel Tokyo, 3945/6 Jln. Tok Hakim (a 3-min. walk from the bus station); tel. 22466.

Doubles M$8-12, w/ac M$13-20. All rooms w/private bath.
Geria Asrama (Geria Hostel), 2002-H Bulatan Wakaf Siku, Jln. Kuala Krai (south side of town, near a traffic circle); tel. 25236.

Dorm beds M$4/night. Accommodates about 40 people in three rooms. Take a becak there for about M$1. (The Asrama Kobenek, in the

212 MALAYSIA

stadium building on the east side of town, offers dorm beds for the same price, but it's grubby.)

Hotel Irama Bharu, 3180-A, Jln. Sultan Ibrahim (south side of town); tel. 22722.

Single M$20.70, w/ac M$34.50; double M$23, w/ac M$36.80. All rooms w/private bath.

Kuala Trengganu: The first three hotels listed below are less than a 5-min. walk from either the bus station or the taxi stand.

Trengganu Hotel, 12 Jln. Paya Bunga; tel. 22900.

Single M$14, w/ac M$22; double M$16, w/ac M$26. All rooms w/private bath.

Hotel Tong Nam, 29 Jln. Paya Bunga.

Single M$10, double M$12. Simple but clean.

Hotel Hoover, 49 Jln. Paya Bunga; tel. 24655.

Single M$14; double M$16; triple M$18, w/ac M$22. All rooms w/private bath. Due to renovation in late 1980, prices will probably go up at least 15%.

Sri Tregganu Hotel, 120A/B Jln. Paya Bunga; tel. 21122.

Single M$14, w/bath & ac M$26; double M$16, w/bath & ac M$28.

Rantau Abang:

Awang's Bungalows, Rantau Abang (sign is visible from the road), 1 km south of Rantau Abang Visitors' Centre.

35 bungalows (all doubles), M$8. Has a restaurant.

Yen/Hakim Cottages, next to Awang's.

Similar accommodations for M$8. Has a restaurant too.

Kuantan: Most of the cheap hotels in Kuantan tend to be a little crusty. (Hotels for women travelers to avoid: Raya, Planet and Meriah.) The ones listed below are on the main street, Jln. Besar/Jln. Telok Sisek. For more congenial accommodations stay at Telok Chempedak Beach every hour from the small bus station on Jln. Mahkota, a 5-min. walk from the main bus station (10-15 min., M$.40).

Asrama Bendahara, near the Hyatt Hotel, Telok Chempedak; tel. 22506.

Single M$8, double M$10, family room M$14. (M$2 for a cot, blanket & pillow in the hall only if all rooms are full.) Restaurant downstairs.

Golden Beach Motel, 18/20 Jln. Sim Lim (to the left from the bus stop), Telok Chempedak; tel. 22646.

Rooms for M$10-22 depending on size, w/ or w/o bath, and w/ or w/o ac. Well kept-up, as is the **Wady Motel** across the road where singles are M$8, doubles M$10. The **Sri Pantai Motel** down the street offers similar-priced rooms.

Kuantan Hotel, behind the Hyatt, Telok Chempedak; tel. 24755.

Doubles M$20.70, w/ac M$24.50; triples M$40.25. All rooms w/private bath. Restaurant downstairs.

Annexe Rest House, Jln. Telok Sisek (about 1½ km out of town on the way to Telok Chempedak); tel. 21043.

Doubles w/private bath, M$12. Only ½ km walk from Telok Sisek Beach.

Embassy Hotel, 58/60 Jln. Telok Sisek, Kuantan; tel. 24844.

Single M$8, double M$10.

Moonlight Hotel, 50/52 Jln. Telok Sisek, Kuantan; tel. 24277.

Single M$9, w/private bath M$11; double M$10, w/private bath M$12.

Hotel Shamrock, 236 Jln. Telok Sisek, Kuantan; tel. 21644.

Single w/o private bath) M$16, double w/private bath M$25. All rooms w/ac.
Hotel Tong Nam Ah, Jln. Besar 98, Kuantan; tel. 21204.
Double M$10, triple M$15. Quite near the main bus station.

TRANSPORTATION FOR THE EAST COAST

Entry to Thailand from Kota Bharu: Take bus #29 to Rantau Panjang, on the Malaysian side of the border (the town of Sungei Golok is on the Thai side)—50 min., M$1.70. It leaves every 45 min. starting between 6:15 and 6:30 am. Or take a shared taxi, M$2.50. A rapid train leaves Sungei Golok daily at 10:40 am. An express train leaves Sungei Golok at 8:30 am on Sun., Tues., Thurs., & Sat. Both arrive in Bangkok the next morning.

Another option is to take an express bus from Kota Bharu to Haadyai. Choose from two companies: Tanjung Express and Dara Express. Buses leave at 8 am daily (M$12, about 4 hr).

The **railway** starts from Tumpat, near Kota Bharu, in the northeast corner of Malaysia and runs south to Pasir Mas. From Pasir Mas one branch loops up to Rantau Panjang/Sungei Golok on the Thai border; the other branch runs south through Kuala Lipis in the central highlands, connecting with the West Coast line at Gemas. See **Transportation**, p.187, for departure times.

Kota Bharu: Several Mara and Ikatan Setia buses make the 12-hr trip daily from KL's Puduraya Terminal. An ac bus leaves at 8 am (M$24); the two non-ac buses leave at 7:30 and 8:30 pm (M$18). From Kuantan, there is an overnight express bus for M$12. A shared taxi from Kuantan will cost M$23; from KL. M$38.

Kuala Trengganu: A Mara bus from KL is M$15. From Kuantan, it's M$6 by bus. A shared taxi is M13 from Kuantan; M$10 from Kota Bharu.

Kuantan: Four Mara bus departures daily from KL—8. 9 (ac), noon, & 2. The 4½-hr trip costs M$7 (ac, M$10). By shared taxi—M$15, 4 hr. From Johor Bharu, a shared taxi costs M$20. From Kota Bharu, a shared taxi will cost M$20.

East Malaysia

Sabah

Nicknamed by sailors 'Land Below the Wind' because it lies south of the typhoon belt, Sabah has much to make a visit worthwhile. Kota Kinabalu, the capital of this state, is small, relaxed, and near perfect for two or three days of lounging. Not far from the capital looms Mt. Kinabalu, the tallest mountain in Southeast Asia. And for those who have some time to spare and want to get off the beaten track, trips can be arranged into the interior to see villages of tribal people who continue to follow their traditional lifestyles.

214 MALAYSIA

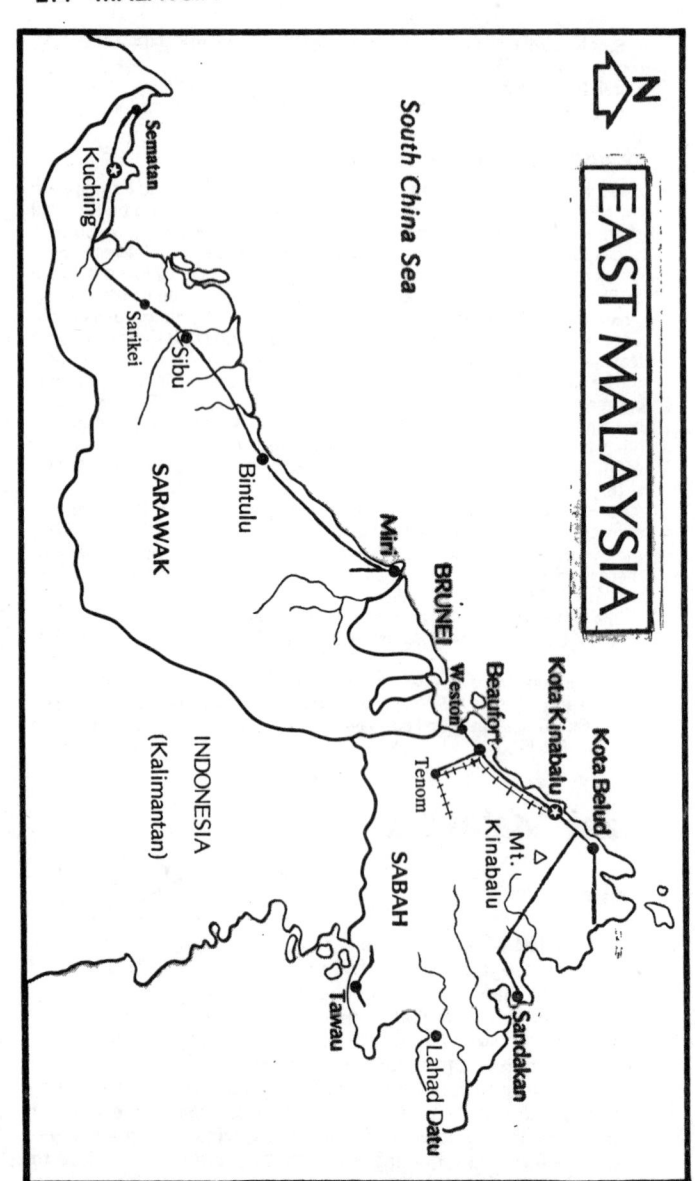

MALAYSIA 215

Arrival: MAS has daily flights to Kota Kinabalu from Kuala Lumpur and Singapore and three flights a week from Hong Kong. Most economical is the M$176 night flight from KL.

Free hotel cars which meet all incoming flights provide the best way of making the short trip from the airport into Kota Kinabalu. All the hotels listed for Kota Kinabalu under **Accommodations in Sabah** have a representative with a car waiting at the airport for potential customers. Buses into the city stop near the airport every 30 minutes (M$.40). Taxis make the trip for M$4.

Sources of Information

Sabah Tourist Association, Lot 4, Block L, 2nd floor, Sinsuran Complex, Kota Kinabalu; tel. 52424. Has brochures and maps which are useful for planning trips from the capital. Open all day Monday through Friday and until noon on Saturday.

Sabah Tourism Promotion Corporation, Lot 4-6, Block L, Sinsuran Complex, Kota Kinabalu. A new semi-governmental organization.

Exploring Kota Kinabalu

Kota Kinabalu is small enough that it can be seen best on foot. Because the city was completely flattened during World War II, almost everything is relatively new. On the drive from the airport look for the gold-domed **Sabah Mosque** which opened in 1976 and is the second largest in Malaysia. The small **Sabah Museum** on Jln. Gaya, opposite the post office, has an interesting collection of artifacts from Sabah's diverse ethnic groups. The many Chinese shops in the neighborhood are jammed with foodstuffs and housewares and are fun to wander through. During the late afternoons visit **Tanjung Aru Beach**, only a 6½ km bus ride from town.

Night life in Kota Kinabalu is fairly subdued, except for a handful of theaters and several pitch-black bawdy nightclubs.

Eating in Kota Kinabalu

The frequently crowded **Sui Sien Restaurant**, 46 Jln. Pantai, serves excellent Chinese food; try the breakfast dim sum. The **Jade Fountain** on Jln. Segama behind the Cathay Theatre is another good spot for Chinese food. The **Kung Hu** has the advantage of being on Jln. Sentosa, where the night market is held, so you can watch all the activity while you eat. Prices are a little high, but the menu includes such delicacies as bird's-nest soup and sea slugs. Good, spicy Indian curries are served at the **Restoran Taj** on Jln. Tugu and at the **Islamic Restaurant** on Jln. Papaduan. If you can afford slightly higher prices and want to try excellent Malay and Indonesian food, head for the **Rama Restaurant** on Jln. Tugu, across from the Central Hotel. The

216 MALAYSIA

least expensive meals are served in the evenings at the food stalls next to the bus station—try the satay, chicken rice and fried bananas.

Excursions from Kota Kinabalu

You can make a rigorous two-day climb on **Mt. Kinabalu**, which looms 13,455 ft (4,101 m) over huge **Kinabalu National Park**, 95 km from Kota Kinabalu. The saw-toothed peak is the highest point between New Guinea and the Himalayas in Burma. Mt. Kinabalu is sacred to the Kadazan people who live near it. The name is derived from 'aki nabalu'—revered place of the dead.

Simpangan Kinabalu, the Park Headquarters where you should check in first (1560 m) can be reached by Land Rover in a 3 hr. ride over a jaw-clattering road from Kota Kinabalu (M$8). The daily Land Rover service departs the Kota Kinabalu bus station at 8 am. The ascent begins at the Power Station (1829 m) with a graded trail joining a jungle track which is followed to the first of the shelters (2 hr.). A further walk of some 2½ hr. takes you to Pahar Laban (3,353 m), another hour's walk over rocks to Sayat-sayat (3,810 m). From here, Low's Peak, the summit, can be reached in about an hour. Visitors must have a guide for the ascent to the summit. The rates for the guide range from M$15 to M$20 per day for a normal 2-day trip depending on the size of the group. All arrangements for the climb should be made well in advance through the Park Headquarters or through the Sabah Tourist Association.

If you're not the Sir Edmund Hilary type, stay on the Park's numerous trails at the lower elevations. With luck, you might be able to find the Nepenthes raja (the pitcher plant) whose leaves shaped like pitchers hold a fluid that attracts insects. The insect is trapped and later devoured when the lid of the pitcher slams shut. Or perhaps you might come across the famed Rafflesia, a plant producing a reddish flower that is often a meter in diameter.

The **Poring Hot Springs** on the eastern edge of the Park, 45 km from Park HQ, will give tired hiking muscles the perfect place to relax. So that nature can be enjoyed while one is bathing, the seven large sunken cement tubs at the hot springs, built by the Japanese during World War II, are outside in a well-kept garden.

Tamu are weekly markets held in Sabah's major towns. On Sundays one of the most festive and colorful of these can be visited in **Kota Belud**, 75 km from Kota Kinabalu. Here Kadazan, Bajau and Chinese traders come from their villages to sell livestock, produce and craftwork. It's a good place to pick up a few souvenirs and possibly see some cockfights at the same time. Land Rovers leave Kota Kinabalu for Kota Belud every morning from near the bus station (M$7, 1½ hr.).

About 140 km south of Kota Kinabalu, in the heart of Murut country, lies the town of **Tenom**. The Murut live in longhouses, hunt with blowpipes and practice shifting agriculture. From Tenom, trips to Murut villages can be arranged through most hotels. The best way to reach Tenom is to take one of two trains from Tanjung Aru, the railway station just outside Kota Kinabalu. The first train (M$24) leaves at 6:30 am and arrives in Tenom at 9:45 am. The second train (M$10) leaves at 7:45 am and arrives in Tenom just before 3 pm.

From the bustling port of **Sandakan**, 400 km due east of Kota Kinabalu, you can make trips to fishing villages on stilts, and visit small islands populated mainly by birds and giant turtles. In town, see the Forestry Exhibition, which has flowers and plants from all over Sabah, and the Orchid House, noted for the size and completeness of its collection. Land Rovers leave Kota Kinabalu daily at 8 am arriving in Sandakan at 6 pm (M$28).

ACCOMMODATIONS IN SABAH

Unfortunately for those on modest budgets, hotels in Sabah are considerably more expensive than comparable accommodations elsewhere in Malaysia.

Kota Kinabalu:
Sea View Hotel, 31 jln. Haji Saman; tel. 54422.
Singles M$20, doubles M$37. Some rooms w/ac. Has a bar and restaurant; centrally located.
Eden Hotel, 1/2 Jln. Merdeka; tel. 53577.
Singles M$20, doubles M$28.
Hotel Asia, 68 Jln. Bandar Berjaya; tel. 53533.
Singles and doubles w/fan and shared bath M$15-25. One of the cheapest hotels in town. Many of the rooms have no windows.

Kinabalu National Park:
Fellowship Hostel, dorm beds M$3 (M$1 for students). Has a dining hall w/fireplace, kitchen w/cooking facilities. Two-room cabins (4-5 person occupancy), M$18/person the 1st night, M$4.50 after that. Fireplace w/cooking facilities provided.

Kota Belud:
Hotel Kota Belud. Singles and doubles M$20-30.

Tenom:
Tenom Hotel. Singles and doubles M$15-30. Some rooms have ac.

Sandakan:
Hotel Paris, 45 Jln. Tiga; tel. 2288/9.
Singles M$13-20, doubles M$18-28.
King Nam Shing Hotel. Singles and doubles M$15-30. Some rooms w/ac. Has a bar and restaurant.

Sarawak

Three-quarters of Sarawak's land area is covered by tropical rain forest; in the interior, tribal people live much as they have for centuries. The state's population of just over 1 million include Ibans, Malays, Chinese, Bidayuh, Melanaus, Kayans, and Kenyahs.

In 1839 an Englishman named James Brooke led the effort to put down an uprising against the Sultan of Brunei's viceroy in Sarawak. As a reward, the Sultan appointed Brooke 'rajah of Sarawak,' a title his family was to hold for three generations and 100 years. Following the Japanese occupation during WWII, James Brooke's grandnephew ceded the state to the British government, which in turn relinquished control in 1963 when Sarawak became part of Malaysia.

Arrivals: MAS has two flights daily to Kuching, the provincial capital, from Singapore, in addition to daily flights from Kuala Lumpur and Kota Kinabalu. Buses from the airport into Kuching leave every 20 min. from a stop a short walk away from the airport (M$.75). If you have much luggage, it would be easier to take a taxi for the 15-min. ride into town (M$8).

Sources of Information

Sarawak Tourist Association, Sarawak Museum Gardens, Jln. Tun Haji Openg, Kuching; tel. 20620. For information on travel throughout Sarawak, and on visiting longhouses. Open 8:30 am-noon & 2-4:30 pm weekdays, 8:30 am-noon Saturdays.

Tourist Information Counter, Kuching Airport. Run by the Sarawak Tourist Association.

Information Centre, Jln. Gambier, near the market. They can tell you what to see in Kuching. Open all day Monday-Friday and until noon on Saturday.

Exploring Kuching

Kuching, the capital of the state of Sarawak, sits on the banks of the Sarawak River, 32 km from the sea. It's a pleasant, clean city, easy to see on foot. The **Sarawak Museum**, which opened in 1891, is one of the finest in Asia and should not be missed. It has a large, well-organized collection of artifacts from northern Borneo's many ethnic groups, a traditionally-furnished longhouse taking up the entire East Gallery, and a model of the enormous Niah Caves. Open every day but Monday, 9:15-5:30 (6 on Saturday). Next to the museum is a park with an open-air aquarium.

The **Tua Pek Kong Temple** (or **Siew Sen Teng**), at the junction of Leboh Temple and Jln. Tunku Abdul Rahman, was built before 1851 (exact date not known); it's the oldest temple in Kuching and one of the most ornate. A M$.10 boat ride from Kuching's pier will take you across the river to **Fort Margherita**. The fort, built in 1879 by the second 'White Rajah,' Charles Brooke, is named after his wife. It is now a police museum, with exhibits of weapons and such tools of the underworld as counterfeit machines. Slightly upriver is the **Istana** (Palace), dating from 1870, also built by Charles Brooke. Since it now serves as the governor's residence, visitors can only look at it from the outside.

Eating in Kuching

Chinese restaurants are numerous. The **Hua Jang Cafe**, across from the Rex Theatre on Leboh Temple, has good noodle soup and chicken rice. A great variety of Chinese and Malay dishes can be sampled at the stalls across from the Electra House on Khoo Hun Yeang St.; this is a particularly lively neighborhood at night. Several Indian restaurants worth trying can be found along (where else?) India St.

Excursions from Kuching

Only by venturing into the interior and visiting a longhouse can you begin to get a sense of traditional Sarawak. Longhouses contain anywhere from 10 to 100 rooms where families live and do their cooking. All the rooms, which are under one roof, open onto a common porch which runs the length of the house and is used for meetings and entertainment. Not surprisingly, this design makes for close ties among neighbors and encourages mutual assistance.

The longhouse closest to Kuching is in **Kampung Segu**, 35 km from the capital. Take STC bus #6 from the Kuching STC Bus Station on Market St. at noon or 2:30 pm (M$2). The buses make the return trip as soon as there are enough passengers (usually around 2 pm and 4 pm). It's best to go on the first bus and come back on the second. The buses stop at a terminal a ½ hr. walk from Bunuk Longhouse. (At the village a M$1 fee is collected from each visitor.) For trips to longhouses further away from Kuching, check with the Sarawak Tourist Assn.

When visiting longhouses, take along a small bag of cookies for the children and some canned food to give in return for the meals you will be offered.

About 35 km from Kuching, near the mouth of the Sarawak

220 MALAYSIA

River, is **Bako National Park**, a great place for a picnic. To get there take a launch from the Kuching wharf; they leave at 8 am and 1 pm.

Santubong Beach is a popular resort area only 30 km from Kuching. Take the launch which leaves at 8 am daily from Long Jetty on Gambier Rd.; it returns between noon and 1:30 pm. On Saturdays and Sundays boats leave Kuching at 8 am and 2 pm and return at about 9:30 am and 4 pm. Fare is M$1.50 one-way. (Note: departure times are not fixed).

From **Sibu**, boats travel up the Rejang River, which is lined with longhouses that welcome visitors. The most interesting way to get to Sibu is overland through the jungles of the interior. From Kuching take an 8 or 9:30 am STC Express to **Simanggang**, 75 km away (M$8.40, 4 hr.). From Simanggang take a bus to **Sarikei**, leaving at 7:30 am or 1:30 pm (3½ hr.). The next morning at 7 am an express launch leaves Sarikei for Sibu (1½ hr.). The faster way to get to Sibu is by boat. An express boat leaves Kuching daily at 9 am (M$20, 6 hr.); cargo/passenger ships leave Kuching at 6 pm every Monday, Tuesday, Thursday and Saturday (M$10 deck class, 18 hr.).

Miri, 580 km up the coast from Kuching, is Sarawak's oil center; a large oil refinery is located at nearby Lutong. About 115 km southwest of Miri are the **Niah Caves**, which have a floor space of 27 acres. Major archaeological finds have recently been made here, including a 35,000-year-old skull which places the progress of Homo sapiens into insular Southeast Asia at a date earlier than previously known. To reach Miri take a boat from Kuching to Bintulu (M$35); the Tourist Association can provide boat schedules. From Bintulu take a bus to Miri (M$15); from Miri take a bus or taxi to the caves.

ACCOMMODATIONS IN SARAWAK

Kuching:
Kuching Hotel, 6 Leboh Temple; tel. 22780.
  Rooms w/common bath M$10, doubles M$13-17. Located on a noisy street but only a 5-min walk from the center of the city.
Ah Chew Hotel, Leboh Java, across from the pier.
  Rooms w/shared bath M$12. Nothing to sneeze at: nice place on a busy street.
Fata Hotel, Jln. McDougall & Leboh Temple; tel. 22578.
  Singles M$18--32, doubles M$26-46. All rooms w/private bath. A 5-min walk from the center of the city.
Mayfair Hotel, 45-47 Jln. Palm; tel. 24181.
  Singles M$20-30, doubles M$30-40.

Bako National Park:
  Two **youth hostels** in the park charge M$2/night. Bring your own bedding, food, and eating utensils. A fancier **rest house**, accommodating 7 people, rents for M$30. For reservations write or visit the National Park Office, Forest Department, Kuching.

MALAYSIA 221

Simanggang:
Hoover Hotel, 125 Club Rd.; tel. 2173.
 Singles M$20-30, doubles M$15-25.

Sarikei:
Rejang Hotel, 1 Berjaya Rd.
 Rooms for under M$10.

Sibu:
Hotel Malaysia, 8 Kampung Nyabor Rd., tel. 22298.
 Singles start at M$17, doubles at M$30.
Ambassador Hotel, 54 Jln. Repok; tel. 5264.
 Singles M$15-25, doubles M$17-35.
Rex Hotel, across from the Chartered Bank.
 Rooms for under M$10.

Batu Niah Caves:
Hotel Niah, near the caves.
 Rooms for under M$15.

Bibliography

Guide to Malaysia, Apa Photo Guide, ed. by Star Black. Gorgeous pictures, good text.

Vanishing World: The Ibans of Borneo, by Wright, Morrison, and Wong. Describes Iban lifestyles and traditions. Excellent photography.

Malaysia and Singapore, by Stanley Bedlington. Readable, informative introduction to Malaysia.

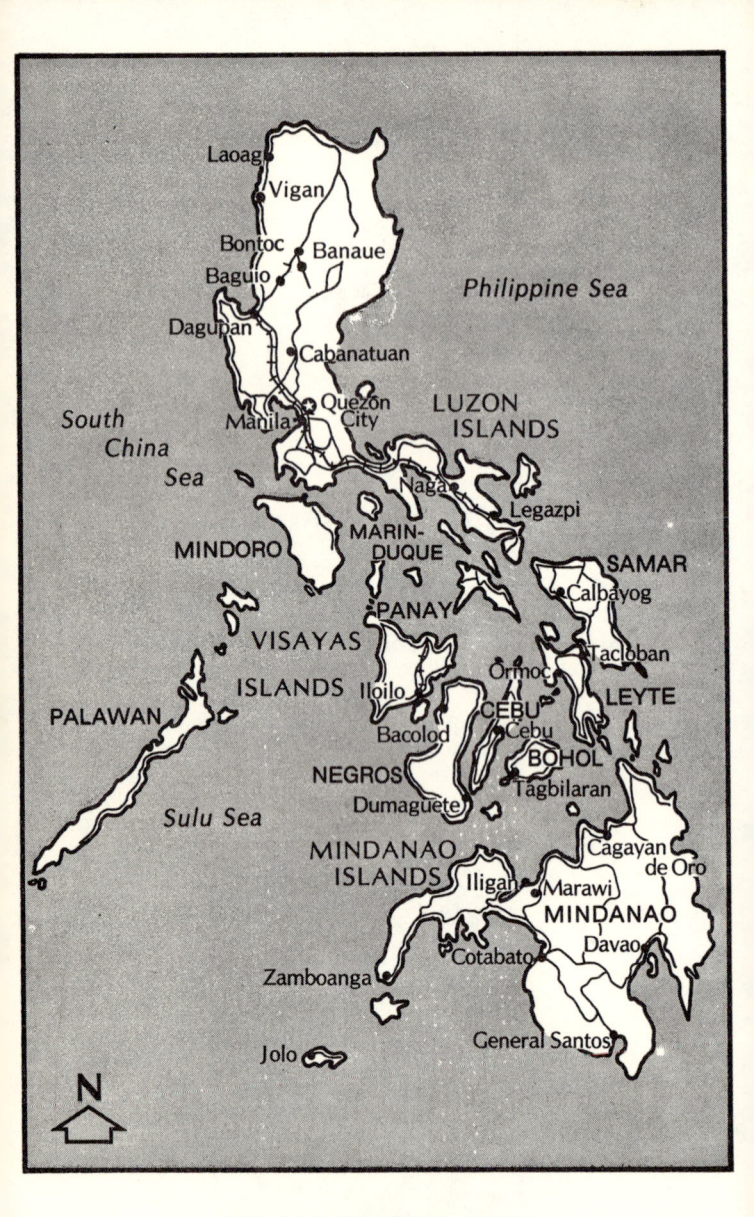

PHILIPPINES

General Information

Arrival: After immigration and customs at Manila International Airport (MIA) you will see a bank on the right where you can exchange money. Pick up a **Map of the Philippines and Manila** at the nearby Tourist Information Center (both the bank and the TIC are open 24 hr./day). From MIA a bus to Taft Ave. in downtown Manila will put you near the **Ermita** (Mabini St.) area where many of the inexpensive hotels are located. Walk out of the airport lobby and veer left (west) until you reach the traffic circle (50 m). Climb on board the California Lines bus with the 'Sta Cruz/Monumento' signboard. Get off the bus at the Philippine Women's University, and walk west down Pedro Gil St. until you reach Mabini. Buses are very frequent (P.80). Taxis from MIA to Ermita will be around P20; take one if it's rainy.

Departure: The airport departure tax is P25.

Currency: The exchange rate in November 1980 was 7.58 pesos (P7.58) to the US dollar. Keep your receipts so you can change left-over pesos back to dollars, because changing pesos in other Asian countries is difficult.

Visas: Visitors, by filling out the proper forms upon arrival, can stay in the Philippines without a visa for 21 days or up to 54 days if they have tickets for their next destination. A tourist visa allows a maximum stay of 59 days. Long-term visas are available for students and volunteer workers who register with the Bureau of Immigration within 59 days after their arrival.

Climate: Tropical. Hot and humid all year round in the lowlands. The hottest months are March-May; the rainy season is June-Oct.

Sources of Information

The main office of the **Ministry of Tourism** (MOT) is in Rizal Park on the corner of Taft Ave. and T.M. Kalaw (9-6, Mon.-Sat.). The information office is on the 1st floor; the Student Affairs Section on the 5th floor has more information on the location of new youth hostels and a library.

When you travel in the provinces, stop by the MOT field offices (addresses given in relevant sections) for maps, brochures, and advice; they're friendly folks.

YSTAPHIL (Youth and Student Travel Association of the

Philippines), 2456 Taft Ave. (across from LaSalle College); tel. 50-03-17. Ask about student discounts for hotels, restaurants and transportation; you can also apply for an International Student Identification Card (ISIC) here.

The **Mobil Travel Map of the Philippines** is the most detailed map of Manila and the Philippines; pick one up at their service stations.

Background

The energetic traveler will find a great diversity of cultural traditions throughout the numerous islands of the Philippines (7,107 in all, 11 of which make up 96% of the total land area). Along with neighboring Asian civilizations, Moslem, Spanish and American cultures have influenced the islands of the Philippines to various degrees. Islam spread through the southern Philippines during the 13th century, when traders of the powerful Malacca State on the Malay peninsula frequented the Sulus on their way from Borneo to China. The Portuguese later captured Malacca in the 16th century, and the islands of the Philippines then came under Spanish control. Miguel Lopez de Legazpi, leader of the Spanish conquistadores, provided the impetus for the colonialization of most of the Philippine Islands, but the Moslems in the islands of Mindanao and the Sulus were never fully brought under Spanish control.

During the 300 years of Spanish rule, strong Catholic missions were established throughout the central and northern Philippines. Today nearly 95% of the population in the Philippines is Christian, and one can find many old Spanish churches and forts in Luzon and the Visayas which date back to the 16th and 17th centuries. The Moslems in the southern islands have persisted in bitter struggles against foreign domination and infringement upon their trade routes, property rights and religious practices. They were forced to depend on piracy after the Spanish first took control of the trade routes in Southeast Asia, and they suffered heavily defending their land against Christians from the north during the Moro Wars of the 18th and 19th centuries. As a result of these political and religious conflicts, the economy and the educational system have not developed as rapidly on Mindanao and in the Sulus as in other parts of the Philippines.

In the 19th century Manila became more involved in international trade, and this development, among others, helped stimulate the growth of Filipino nationalism. The Philippines' most famous national hero was Dr. Jose Rizal (1861-1896), a man who, in addition to his numerous other talents, was a gifted writer. For his leadership in the reform movement and his 'seditious' novels, **Noli Me Tangere** and **El Filibusterismo**, Rizal was arrested by the Spanish government and executed. Meanwhile, the Katipunan, a secret society founded in 1892 by Andres Bonifacio, was trying to spark a true revolution. In late 1896 fighting broke out all over, though the revolutionary forces had an uphill battle against the far better equipped Spanish forces. A Declaration of Freedom was announced on June 12, 1898 (now celebrated as Independence Day), modeled on the American Declaration of Independence. But ironically it was American intervention that prevented the triumph of Filipino nationalism.

The Spanish-American War of 1898 marked the end of Spanish rule in Southeast Asia. Though Filipino revolutionaries had defeated the Spanish garrisons in most of the country and proclaimed their independence in 1898, American forces landed on the islands and accepted the surrender of the Spanish garrison in Manila. The Americans assumed control of the government in accordance with the Treaty of Paris between the U.S. and Spain. The 46 years of American rule had a far greater impact on the Philippine economy than the 327 years under the Spanish. Much American capital was invested in the country; economic resources were developed and the educational system was improved quite rapidly. By 1930, English had become the official language of higher education and government affairs. When the Philippines finally attained independence in 1946, many of its economic, educational and political institutions (including the constitution) were patterned closely after American models, though the Filipino social and cultural heritage was dramatically different from that of the U.S.

Ferdinand Marcos, president of the Philippines, was first elected in 1965 and then re-elected for a second term in 1969. Following student protests and political demonstrations of the early 1970s, Marcos declared martial law in 1972. In what he claimed was an attempt to curb violence within the nation, clamp down on the corruption of government officials, and make a new effort at land reform, Marcos had the constitution suspended by national referendum in 1973. Political opponents of the Marcos regime were silenced, independent newspapers were shut down, and many dissident activists were imprisoned. Armed conflict continues between the Muslims and the Philippine Constabulary in Mindanao and the Sulus, and there is increasingly overt opposition to the Marcos government in other parts of the country.

Culture and Customs

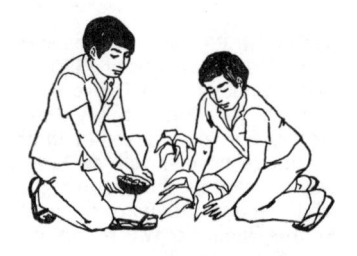

The Philippines were subject to colonial rule for over 400 years. For centuries whites held the highest positions of authority, leading Filipinos to believe that superior culture lay overseas. This 'colonial mentality' has been giving way to a renewed pride in Filipino ways of life. While Western influence has left a mark on the consciousness of the people, a distinct Filipino character within institutions has been maintained.

An indication of this has been the pervasiveness of Christianity in Filipino society. Its outward signs—huge Sunday congregations, prominent social position of priests, fiestas celebrating the Virgin Mary, etc.—attest to the influential role of Christianity. Catholicism was introduced to the Philippines in the 16th century by Spanish missionaries and has prospered into the twentieth century because of its identification with Filipino nationalism. Its nationalist character developed in the nineteenth century as a result of an internal revolt of the Church. Filipino clergy demanded Filipinisation of the clergy. Hence, considered part of the anti-colonial movement then evolving, the revolt was suppressed when three Filipinos priests were garrotted on charges of instigating a rebellion in Cavite in 1872. Within thirty years, the Philippine Independent Church was founded, a break from the colonial orientation of the Roman Catholic Church. After national independence and in conjunction with Vatican II and the World Council of Churches, politicized clergy of both Catholic and Protestant faiths have initiated community development programs emphasizing human rights and justice. Because of their firmly entrenched status, the Marcos government has been reluctant to criticize the anti-martial law stance of the churches.

Filipinos, more than any other people in Asia, are aware of the American presence in their country and throughout the world. This familiarity and special regard which Filipinos have for American culture has both advantages and disadvantages for Americans and other travelers. People will be kind and generous to you. Your strange behavior will be more quickly understood and forgiven. But likewise it will be difficult to move about in relative anonymity; especially in the provinces men and women alike will be greeted with choruses of 'Hey Joe!' Though you may travel among strangers in the Philippines, you will be the familiar foreigner wherever you go.

The diversity of cultures within the Philippines is great; the generalizations which follow should not mislead you into thinking that customs throughout the archipelago are uniform. But they may serve as a starting point for understanding certain ways of life here.

It is considered unrefined to express feelings strongly in public; well-mannered people are in control of their emotions. If you are upset over an 'unnecessary' delay, it will be counterproductive to respond with anger. It would be better to explain in an apologetic tone why you are in such a hurry. (Better yet, don't be in a hurry).

The Filipino attitude towards time is very relaxed; promptness is not highly valued. For instance, a Filipino will 'go to the movies' at any time irregardless of show times.

Filipinos are very proud of their warm hospitality, which reaches the height of its expression at fiesta time. Each household within a barrio or town prepares a feast for the many friends and relatives who circulate about visiting homes and attending the festivities in the central plaza. Even when it is not fiesta time, travelers are often invited into homes for meals or even spend the night. Such offers are sincere; however, when accepting it is best not to appear too anxious, and to refuse once or twice (pleading that it would be inconvenient for the host) before giving in. A refused offer is rarely retracted immediately.

According to Filipino custom, the host will insist on paying the full amount when expenses arise while entertaining a guest, such as the cost of eating at a restaurant or the price of admission to a movie. If you are the guest, you might offer to pay the entire amount yourself but then relent and permit the host to offer such hospitality if s/he insists. At some point you should offer at first but may eventually give in. Never try to pay for only your share of the expense—either your host pays all of it or you do.

In accepting your host's hospitality, you assume certain unspoken debts commensurate with the hospitality you've been shown. Because you're probably only staying a short while and may never see your host again, these debts usually remain forever unpaid. Your host is aware of this and his hospitality is genuine and sincere. But we recommend, if you are invited to someone's home, that you bring a small gift—ballpoint pens, bookcovers, calenders, etc. from the U.S., or cigarettes or chocolates if the gift is bought locally. And if by chance you travel elsewhere in the Philippines and then return to see your host again, it is thoughtful to bring gifts from the place you have visited (these gifts are called 'pasalubong'). Many Filipinos, for example, commute on weekends from Manila to their home provinces to visit relatives; when they return to Manila Sunday evening they are laden with pasalubong (usually food) for family and friends.

Festivals

There are always fiestas going on somewhere in the Philippines. These festivities, which commemmorate the patron saint of each particular town, are an unusual blend of local traditions, Christian pageantry, and an exuberant mardi-gras spirit. For a complete list of fiestas and holidays, see the brochure 'Exploring the Philippines, available in MOT offices.

Language

The national language, Pilipino, is based on Tagalog and is understood by about one-third of the population (mostly in Luzon). English, on the other hand, has been the language of instruction for upper level schools since the 1930s and is widely understood; the Philippines claims to be the third largest English-speaking nation in the world. Several English language newspapers are published in Manila.

The words and phrases below may come in handy in Luzon.

Good morning	**Magandang umaga (po)**
Good afternoon	**Magandang hapon (po)**
Good evening, good night	**Magandang gabi (po)**
Thank you	**Salamat po**
You're welcome	**Wala pong anuman**
Yes	**Opo, oho, oo** (different levels; **po** and **ho** are honorifics)
No	**Hindi**
City/Town	**Siyudad, lungsod/Bayan**
Street	**Kalye, daan**
Market	**Palengke**
Toilet	**Kasilyas, kubeta**
Female/Male	**Babae/Lalaki**
Island/Mountain	**Isla/Bundok**
North/South	**Hilaga/Timog**
East/West	**Silangan/Kanluran**
When?	**Kailan?**
Today	**Ngayong araw na ito**
Tomorrow/Yesterday	**Bukas/Kahapon**
Where is ——?	**Saan (nasaan) po ba ang ——?**

I want to go to ——	**Gusto ko po pumunta sa ——.**
Is this the bus to ——?	**Ito ba ang bus na pupunta sa ——?**
Stop (please).	**Para po.**
Is it far?	**Malayo po ba?**
Do you have a room?	**Mayroon ba kayong kuwarto?**
How much is it?	**Magkano po ito?**
I don't understand.	**Hindi ko po maintindihan.**

Inexpensive	**Mura na rin**
Too expensive	**Mahal naman po**
Good (fine, great)	**Mabuti, mahusay**
Bad	**Masama, hindi na bale**

One/Two/Three/Four	**Isa/Dalawa/Tatlo/Apat**
Five/Six/Seven	**Lima/Anim/Pito**
Eight/Nine/Ten	**Walo/Siyam/Sampu**
Twenty/Thirty	**Dalawampu/Tatlumpu**
Forty/Fifty	**Apatnapu/Limampu**
Sixty/Seventy	**Animnapu/Pitumpu**
Eighty/Ninety	**Walumpu/Siyamnapu**
One hundred	**Isang daan**

Food

For a filling meal try one of the small restaurants which offers **a** set lunch or dinner for P8-12. A Filipino meal includes several meat, fish, or vegetable dishes, rice and fruit; an American meal generally includes soup, two entrees, rolls and butter, and coffee or tea. Even cheaper meals may be found at cafeteria-style restaurants called **turo-turo** in which you just choose from dishes which are already prepared and pay by the dish. Filipinos eat with a spoon in the right hand, fork in the left.

Filipino foods are frequently identified by the style of cooking rather than by the major meat or fish ingredient. For instance, sinigang can be made with pork, beef, mudfish, or milkfish but the thing that makes it sinigang is the sour soup with vegetables. Sinigang made with pork is simply sinigang na baboy; adobong manok is chicken cooked adobo style.

MEAT AND FISH DISHES

sinigang — soup with vegetables and seasoned with a strained sour fruit (e.g. tamarind); different kinds made with beef, pork, fish, or shellfish

230 PHILIPPINES

adobo — anything marinated in vinegar, garlic, and pepper, then stewed (usually chicken, pork or squid)

kilawin — raw beef (na baka) or raw fish (a sort of Filipino sashimi) marinated in onion, vinegar, garlic kalamansi

inihaw — anything broiled over a charcoal fire (all kinds of meat and fish)

baboy	pork	**pusit**	squid
manok	chicken	**bangus**	milkfish
baka	beef	**hito**	catfish
hipon	shrimp	**lapu-lapu**	rock bass

kare kare — beef cooked in a spicy peanut sauce and served with vegetables mixed in a shrimp sauce

crispy pata — pork knuckle cooked in delicate spices with crisp skin (an expensive dish)

lechon — suckling pig roasted slowly over charcoal and served with a liver sauce

menudo — stew

VEGETABLES AND NOODLE DISHES

pansit — noodles (generic name, usually followed by an adjective, e.g. bijon, to indicate what kind of noodles)

pansit bijon — rice noodles, served with vegetables

pinakbet — vegetables stewed in a fish sauce

mongo — mung beans

mami — noodle soup

SNACKS (MERIENDA)

leche flan — custard

sapin-sapin — layered sticky-rice cake

halo-halo — mixture of fruit, ice cream, coconut milk, ice and beans

macupuno merinque — coconut merinque pie

suman — sticky rice wrapped in a banana leaf

puto — rice cake

bibingka — a round, flat pastry made of ground rice, coconut milk, eggs, and sugar

FRUIT

lanzones — small, yellow, round fruit; sold in bunches

suha — yellow, grapefruit-size, pink inside

atis — light green; soft fruit inside with small black seeds

durian — large, with brown spiny skin; pungent odor and unique taste and texture

saging [banana] — very cheap and more than a dozen varieties to try

DRINKS

kalamansi juice — like lemonade, served hot or cold
tuba — coconut wine
iced buko — fresh coconut milk
San Miguel beer — very tasty, made in the Philippines

Accommodations

Youth hostels provide dorm accommodations and inexpensive meals in Baguio, Banuae, Chocolate Hills, Corregidor Island, Dagupan, Kalibo, Malate, Manila, Marawi, Pagsanjan, Quezon City, San Pablo and Tiwi. Most hostels charge P15/night, P5 for breakfast and P10 for lunch or dinner. If you don't have an International Student Identification Card (ISIC) or an International Youth Hostel Federation (IYHF) card, you can still stay at these hostels for an extra P2/night. An ISIC can be obtained at YSTAPHIL, 2456 Taft Ave, Manila.

Most towns have several **inexpensive hotels** or **pensions**. A single with shared bath will cost about P20-30; singles with private bath or ac will be P45-85.

Transportation

INTERNATIONAL: Manila International Airport is the port of entry and exit for most travelers. Owing to its great natural harbor and strategic location, many shipping lines including Knutsen Lines and American President Lines have **passenger ships** cruising between Manila and Hong Kong about once a month.

INTERCITY: **Buses** are the most convenient form of transportation for overland travel outside Manila. First-class express buses have air-conditioning and reclining seats; ordinary express buses are less comfortable but almost as fast, and cost only half as much. (Consult the **Escaping Manila** section for bus company addresses.) When traveling between cities in the outlying provinces, you can choose between express buses, which leave several times daily, and local minibuses or jeepneys, which leave from the central market place as soon as they're full. The jeepneys will stop anywhere along their routes to pick up and drop off passengers and cargo. (Note: Local buses, even if scheduled to leave at a particular time, only occasionally do. They may even leave early. The drivers wait until he feels his bus or jeepney is full enough to ensure a profitable run).

If the roads are impassable due to heavy showers and you're traveling from one coastal city to another, a **banca** may be a good alternative. These motorized canoes provide regular service between many towns, and can be easily found at the pier in the early morning. Notwithstanding the endless din of their motors, bancas offer a fast, cheap way to cruise along the coastline. (Ever fantasize about being Clyde Beatty in a jungle canoe?) Bancas leave only when full.

The **Philippine National Railway** (RNP) serves only the island of Luzon: from San Fernando in La Union to Legazpi in Bicol. All trains have first-class (air-conditioned), economy, and third class. Manila's Tutuban Station is at 943 Claro M. Recto Ave; tel. 210011.

For island-hopping in Central and Southern Philippines, **shipping lines** offer incredibly comfortable and relatively inexpensive means of traveling. The MOT has a complete listing of current shipping schedules; Williams Lines, Sulpicio Lines, Sweet Lines and Negros Navigation Company offer the best rates and most frequent service. (Their addresses are in the **Escaping Manila** section below.) Buy a ticket in advance at one of their branch offices in Metro Manila. You can purchase a ticket at the pier but, like waterfronts in many Asian capitals, they tend to be quite rough especially after dark.

Transport is extremely crowded around the holidays— Christmas, New Year's, Easter, All Saint's Day and school vacations. Everyone heads back to their homes in the provinces. Be forewarned and make reservations accordingly. (Note: Though it's possible to make reservations—bus, plane, boat—in Manila and other places, these 'reservations' are conditional on the local office not having already booked all the spaces; therefore, all reservations for ongoing travel should be confirmed **immediately** upon arrival in each city along your route.)

INTRA-CITY: Jeepneys are not only the cheapest mode of transportation but certainly also the most outrageous in terms of appearance. Built from WWII US Army surplus jeeps, these vehicles have been overhauled to carry up to 14 passengers at a time. They can be seen at all hours jockeying for space in traffic, filled with passengers and cargo—perhaps even with somebody's chickens—with chrome medallions on their hoods and streamers, flags and tassles flapping in the breeze. Additional trappings reflect the inventiveness of each individual Jeepney owner. A single brightly painted jeepney may be furnished with a Chrysler bumper, Cadillac headlights, Ford chrome railings

PHILIPPINES 233

along the sides, half a dozen rear and side view mirrors, XMAS lights blinking on all sides and top, and countless small ornaments, charms and decals inside—even a occasional glowing, plastic Jesus. Signboards show the destination of the suburbs/major streets of their routes; it'll require some close inspection of your road map to figure out how to get around in Manila. Fares start at 60 centavos, increasing with the distance traveled.

Bus fares range from 60 centavos to P2.50 in Metro Manila. Several different bus companies operate in the city. The signboard states the destination of the bus, with smaller signs often giving the names of the major streets or landmarks along the route. The conductor collects the fares and hands out tickets after everyone has boarded the bus. (People make a hissing sound or rap on the roof of the bus with their knuckles when they're trying to get off a crowded bus.)

Taxis are fast and comfortable, but are expensive over the long hauls. Fares start at P2.

Tricycles (motorcycles with a passenger cab attached) provide inexpensive transportation over short distances in smaller towns and in the outskirts of larger cities; rides cost at least 75 centavos.

Love buses, which only operate in Manila, are big blue air-conditioned buses with hearts painted on their sides. The fare is P2.50 regardless of the distance traveled. They only pick up as many passengers as there are seats, so though they can be flagged down anywhere along their routes, particularly during rush hours try to board them at one of their regular stops. These are: Cubao—in the parking lot next to Ali Mall; Ayala—in the parking lot next to Rizal Theater; Manila International Airport—in the parking lot across from the Philippine Village Hotel; and at bus stops along Escolta, Santa Cruz and Monumento Streets.

A Final Tip: Efficiency isn't considered the greatest virtue in the Philippines so don't be put out if your bus arrives late or you're left stranded somewhere. Just take a deep breath, relax and poke around—people in the Philippines love to pass the time by talking; remember that unlike other Asian countries almost everyone speaks English. And if all else fails, you can retire to a cafe for a few San Miguel beers. Beer is so cheap and tasty that it simply behooves you to drink.

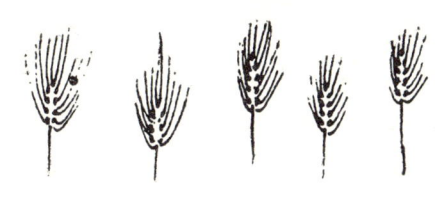

234 PHILIPPINES

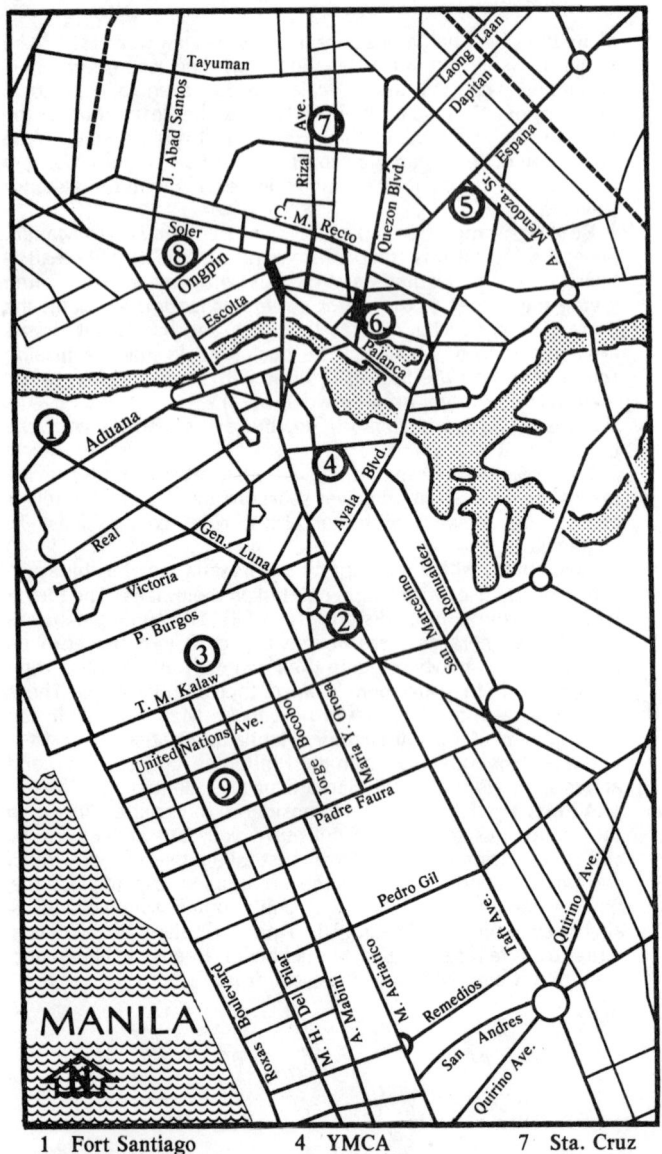

1 Fort Santiago	4 YMCA	7 Sta. Cruz
2 Min. of Tourism	5 University Belt	8 Binondo
3 Rizal Park (Luneta)	6 Quiapo	9 Ermita

Manila

At first the sheer size of Metro Manila can be intimidating—it embraces four cities and 13 municipalities, and over 4 million people. But there's no need to feel bewildered since most of the places visitors want to see are either fairly close to each other or are on major bus/jeepney routes.

Two of the nices parts of Manila are **Intramuros** and **Rizal Park**, both of which can be toured in a leisurely three-hour walk. Begin at the eastern end of Rizal Park (also known as **Luneta**) on Taft Ave., near the MOT building, and walk westward towards Manila Bay. Almost immediately there'll be a large pool surrounding a relief map representing the Philippine islands. After a heavy rain most of the islands will be submerged...and ducks will be bathing themselves in Manila Bay.

Further on is a fountain encircled by a roller skating track where skaters will be cruising along to the piped-in disco music. To the right is a small amphitheater where music and dance performances are usually held on Sundays. Across from the theater is an outdoor restaurant operated by members of the Philippine Association of the Deaf. Situated under the trees, you can munch and watch folks stroll by. As you continue towards the bay, there'll be a meticulously cared-for Chinese garden on the right.

At the far western end, facing Roxas Blvd., is a monument dedicated to the national hero, Dr. Jose Rizal (see **Background**). Rizal was shot by a Spanish firing squad in 1896 on the spot where the monument now stands.

From the monument, leave the park and walk north along Roxas Blvd., which will become Bonifacio Dr. Within a block you'll see a statue of Miguel Lopez de Legazpi and Fray Andreas de Urdaneta, two Spaniards who were in the original party which captured Manila in 1571. Continuing along Bonifacio Dr. you'll see the stone walls of the original settlement known as **Intramuros**. These walls were built in 1584 by conscript labor under the direction of the Spanish—and now they are being restored under the direction of the Marcos government. In the spirit of progress, the beautiful moat which had once surrounded Intramuros has been drained and turned into a golf course.

At Real St., turn right and enter the walled city. In the first couple of blocks you can get a sense of the former architectural elegance of Intramuros before most of it had been obliterated by bombing during World War II. At one time, Intramuros had fifteen churches, six monasteries and several hospitals and schools.

Continue on several blocks to Gen. Luna St. On the corner stands **St. Augustin Church and Monastery**, begun in 1587 and completed in 1607. Its classic facade supported by Doric and Corinthian columns has survived five major earthquakes. There is a fair-sized museum (open 8 am to 5 pm daily) with displays documenting the Christianization of the country. There are a series of oil paintings depicting determined-looking Spanish missionaries. It was in this church that the Spanish surrendered the Philippines to the U.S. in 1898.

Continue north up Gen. Luna St. and walk two blocks to the beautiful **Manila Cathedral** on the corner of Magallanes Dr. Across from the cathedral is **Fort Santiago** (open 6 am to 10 pm). Construction of the fort began in 1590 under the direction of the Jesuits, though it wasn't completed until 1739. Since that time, the flags of Spain, Britain, the US, Japan, and finally the Philippines, have flown above it. Gen. Douglas MacArther made this fort his headquarters from 1936 until 1942, when the Japanese took control of the city.

There is a two-story museum displaying many of Dr. Jose Rizal's personal possessions and writings. He was incarcerated in a cell, near the museum, before his execution.

From the fort's exit on Magallanes Dr., you can take a jeepney marked 'Taft Ave.' or walk back to Ermita.

A walk at sunset along Roxas Blvd. is a particularly nice way to end the day. If you're feeling energetic, from the Rizal Monument you can walk south on the boulevard 15 blocks to the lavish **Cultural Center of the Philippines**, built on a 21-hectare area reclaimed from Manila Bay. In the Center are several theaters, including the Folk Arts Theater, a number of galleries, a restaurant, a cafeteria, and a snack bar. You can find out what's being performed at the Center by picking up a calender of events at the Center itself, or at major hotels.

The boats **Carina I & II** make a highly recommended cruise around Manila Bay (P3.50, 1 hr). They leave everyday during the afternoon, and from March through May during the morning as well, from the former Hydrofoil Landing, Gate A, South Blvd., Rizal Park.

At the southern edge of Metro Manila is the town of **Las Pinas**, where the 150-year-old San Jose Church has a bamboo organ with over 100 bamboo reeds for the pipes. The church is on the road which the buses use, and is open all day. Las Pinas is also where the colorful jeepneys are manufactured. You can visit the Francisco Motor Co., on the main road, anytime during the working day to see how the fancy painting and decoration is done. Take the Metro-Manila Transit (blue) bus with the "Las Pinas/Zapote" signboard (they run along Taft Ave. and E. de los Santos Ave.).

Makati Commercial Center represents the newest and most modern aspect of life in Manila; in fact, it looks like concrete & glass Americana. At the eastern end of Makati, near Ayala and E. de los Santos Ave., are a series of fast food centers with every imaginable kind of short-order cuisine. In the same area a large movie theater complex offers the latest Western flicks. At the western end of the Commercial Center, on Makati Ave., the new Ayala Museum is worth a visit. As you walk through the streets of Makati, with skyscrapers on both sides, keep in mind that only thirteen years ago this area was covered by cogon grass and you'll understand some of the changes Metro Manila has undergone recently. Southern Californians will get the idea.

In **Ermita**, the so-called tourist belt, you can windowshop for a variety of handicrafts made in outlying provinces. The prices are quite high in these shops, but you should be able to get at least a 10% discount if you really want to buy something. (Prices are generally 25-50% lower outside Manila.)

Quiapo (the name comes from the waterlily that used to clog the Pasig River) is still the heartland of Manila in terms of transportation and trade. Start a tour of the area at Quiapo Church at the base of Quezon Bridge. The church is famous for its Black Nazarene, a large wooden statue of Christ bearing the cross carved by Mexican Indians in the 17th century. In Plaza Miranda, in front of the church, hawkers sell medicinal herbs and charms. Walk back under the bridge to find dozens of stalls selling handicrafts; bargains are plentiful for those skillful at haggling. If you return to Plaza Miranda and turn left onto Carriedo St., you will be on 'shoe street.'

Two of the largest **bookstores** in Manila are the National Bookstore at 701 Rizal Ave. and Alemar's at 769 Rizal Ave.;

238 PHILIPPINES

both have branches all over Metro Manila. Some of the most interesting small press material can be found at La Solidaridad Bookstore on Padre Faura, just off Mabini St.

Manila has many museums. The National Museum, on the 3rd floor of the DOT Bldg., has artifacts from archaeological excavations in the Tabon caves on Palawan Island. It's open 8-5 daily. The Ayala Museum (open 9-8 daily except Monday) displays scale model representations of 60 major events in Philippine history. It's located on Makati Ave. near Ayala Ave. (admission P3 for adults, 25 centavos for students). Nayong Filipino, near Manila International Airport, has a Museum of Traditional Cultures as well as live performances of ethnic dances; it's open 9-6 Mon. to Fri., 9-7 Sat & Sun. The Carfel Museum of Seashells, 1786 Mabini St., has a large collection of beautiful and unusual shells found in Philippine waters (open 8-7 daily).

Recreation and Entertainment

Manila has no shortage of cultural entertainment—the trick is to find out when and where. Pick up a Cultural Center calendar of events; something's happening there almost every night. The **TV Times** provides a fairly complete listing of plays, concerts, etc. on a weekly basis, while the **Daily Express** offers the best daily coverage.

The Rajah Sulayman theater at Fort Santiago has an outdoor season of **plays** in Pilipino running from December to June. Other groups concentrating on Filipino presentations include PETA (Philippines Educational Theater Assn.) and Teatro Pilipino. The Reparatory Philippines offers plays in English. Admission for all these performances is quite modest, usually P5-10. If you're interested in community theater and its role in development, visit the Teatro Kabataan on Gen. Lim St., Heroes Hill, Quezon City.

The University of the Philippines (U.P.), Diliman campus, offers a full schedule of plays, concerts, and films. It's not well publicized so check the bulletin boards in the student union or at the College of Arts and Sciences if you're on campus.

If you'd like to meet some of the people behind the recent cultural explosion in the Philippines, make arrangements at the Cultural Center to visit the National Arts Center at Mt. Makiling (see **Southern Tagalog Provinces**) or get in touch with the Heritage Art Center, 43 Hillside Loop, San Juan, Quezon City (tel. 70-08-67). The center offers workshops and programs, and serves as a weekend meeting place for local artists, authors, and poets.

Two foreign missions (U.S. and Germany) have cultural centers in Quezon City offering films, recitals, and exhibits at various times, plus libraries with recent foreign periodicals if you'd like to catch up on the news. Check with the Thomas Jefferson Cultural Center, 12 Araneta Ave. near the corner of Aurora Blvd. (tel. 59-80-11) and the German Cultural Center, Goethe House, 687 Aurora Blvd. near the corner of Gilmore (tel. 78-93-78).

Jai-alai is one of the most popular sporting attractions in Manila. Originally a Basque game, Jai-alai resembles squash, though smaller wicker baskets are used instead of rackets to hurl the ball against the wall. The Jai-alai stadium is on Taft Ave. near Rizal Park. Matches take place nightly 5:30-10:30, except on Sundays. Admission is free if you're willing to stand downstairs; it's worth it, however, to pay P2 for a seat upstairs. There are 10 separate events, one each half hour.

Filipinos are great **basketball** fans; watch games at Araneta Coliseum in Cubao or Rizal Coliseum on Vito Cruz Ave. near Taft Ave. Players are technically amateurs playing in an industrial league, but it's actually big-time basketball. Tickets are P2-15; check the newspaper for schedules.

Getting Around Town

No one in MOT has yet devised a systematic bus and jeepney route map for the bewildered visitor. You can get yourself around town fairly easily by familiarizing yourself with the key street or neighborhood names in Manila. Buses and jeepneys all have signboards listing a number of destinations. For instance, if you were standing along Taft Ave. near the MOT office, you would see a jeepney with painted signs saying 'Taft Ave., Quiapo, Espana Ext., Cubao... . The question therefore is to link up where you want to go with the appropriate signboards. If for some reason you wanted to go to the City Hall or the YMCA, and you were still on Taft Ave., then you could hop onto a jeepney that has Quiapo or Santa Cruz written on it.

Although buses aren't as numerous, they have more clearly defined routes:

Manila Int'l Airport (MIA)-Sta. Cruz/Monumento (California Bus Lines, red and gray): From MIA, the bus travels the length of Taft Ave., passing YSTAPHIL and the City Hall, and crosses the Pasig River for Santa Cruz and Monumento. At Monumento the bus turns east and runs along E. de los Santo Ave. returning to MIA via Cubao.

U.P. Balara-Quiapo (blue, red or white): From the University of the Philippines, it runs down Quezon Blvd.—past the Pantranco North Express Bus Station at Roosevelt Rd. and Santo Tomas University—before entering Quiapo. It then makes a loop near the South Harbor and Rizal Park and returns to Quiapo. You can

240 PHILIPPINES

also get to the U.P. campus by U.P. bus from Taft Ave.

Monumento-Baclaran: The bus travels the length of E. de los Santos Ave., around the outskirts of Manila proper. It stops in Cubao at the Farmers' Market (Aurora Blvd.) and in Makati Commercial Center at Ayala Blvd.

Quiapo-Buendia (red or blue): From Quiapo, this bus goes down Taft Ave., turns east on Buendia (Pasay City) and then south on Ayala Blvd. to the Makati commercial Center near E. de los Santos Ave. The reverse is the same.

Ayala-Buenida-Monumento (red or blue): This bus leaves from the Makati Commercial Center, runs down Ayala Blvd., turns west onto Buenida and then north onto Taft Ave., crosses the bridge to Rizal Ave. and follows that street to Monumento. The reverse route is the same.

Note: Try to avoid passing through Quiapo at rush hours (roughly 7-9 am and 5-7 pm). A bumper-to-bumper bummer.

Eating in Manila

There are countless small restaurants in the Ermita 'tourist belt' (around U.N. Ave. and Mabini St.), but less expensive restaurants are easy to find in Chinatown (or Binondo), Quiapo, and the University Belt—all about 15 min. from Ermita by jeepney. Full meals in these places will cost only P5-10. The restaurants upstairs in the Farmers' Market in Cubao are also recommended (40 min. by bus from Taft Ave.).

The first three restaurants listed below have branches throughout Metro Manila.

Barrio Fiesta, J. Bocobo St. near U.N. Ave., Ermita.
Outstanding selection of Filipino food; their specialties are crispy pata (P25) and kare-kare (P15).

Max's, 1207 M.Y. Orosa St., Ermita.
Specializes in chicken dishes, P15. Nice atmosphere.

Aristocrat, Roxas Blvd. & San Andres St. (near the Cultural Center)/ E. de los Santos Ave., Cubao, Quezon City (near the Farmer's Market).
Serves Filipino food; the grilled seafood wrapped in banana leaves is highly recommended. Prices start at P15.

Mabini House, 1551 Mabini St.
A small, informal restaurant which serves good Chinese and Filipino food for P7-12.

Sam Ghee's, Taft Ave. and Vito Cruz.
A good restaurant outside the tourist belt.

Paru-Parong Bukid, 1158A Mabini St.
Excellent Filipino food at moderate prices.

Tanglaw Restaurant, M. Adriatico near Padre Fauna St.
Great seafood. Try the bangus (milkfish); for P9 you get enough for two people.

Country Bake Shop, 424 U.N. Ave. & **Goldilocks**, 1907 Taft Ave. (with five other branches).

Nightlife

There is an abundance of places to spend the evening in Manila, ranging from modestly priced folk music houses to expensive nightclubs. The latter can be found along Roxas Blvd., where there are noontime and dinner shows. **Makati** is slightly less expensive and offers smaller bars and nightclubs, many of which feature full bands. The least expensive entertainment, and that preferred by the younger crowd, is in the **Mabini-Del Pilar** area. **The Hobbit**, 1801 Mabini St. (near San Andres) is one of the most unusual as well as popular folk rock clubs. It continually has a good show and there rarely is a cover charge. Up the street is the **Bodega**, 1158 Mabini St., where many of the best Manila musicians appear—usually with a cover charge. Many of the bands play Filipino folk or American '60's hits. On Padre Fauna St., just east of Mabini St., the **Espanolas Beer Garden** features rock & roll under the stars. Along Del Pilar are a score of girlie bars that cater to foreign males. Live entertainment is provided nightly in the San Mig Pubs located in the shopping areas of Cubao, Greenhills and Makati. Throughout the city, most bars have happy hours between 4 and 7 pm, when San Miguel beers are sold for as little as P2.

Slightly off-beat folks might try the bowling alley on Mabini, one block south of Pistang Pilipina. Grapefruit-sized bowling balls are retrieved and pins reset by hired hands. Dart fans will want to hang out at **Pension Filipinas**, 572 Arkansas St.

Meeting Students

The **University of Philippines, Diliman**, located in Quezon City, has a peaceful, almost rural atmosphere. **Ateneo de Manila**, near U.P., has a strong sociology department; the Institute of Philippine Culture at Ateneo de Manila is well-known for its research and publications (which are available at the Ateneo de Manila Press on campus). **Philippines Women's University**, on Taft Ave. near Pedro Gil, often hosts performances by the renowned Bayanihan Dance Troupe on Saturday afternoons. The **University of Santo Tomas**, founded in 1611, is the oldest institution of higher learning in Asia. The present campus, established in 1911, was used as a concentration camp for allied nationals during World War II.

ACCOMMODATIONS IN MANILA

Casa Pension, 1406 M.H. del Pilar St. (Ermita); tel. 59-62-65.
P30-50 for rooms w/fan and common bath. Singles w/ac P60; doubles, P70.

Congress Family Hotel, 1427 M.H. del Pilar St. (Ermita); tel. 50-96-96/7.
Singles w/fan P44; w/ac, P66; doubles w/fan, P49; w/ac, P71.

YMCA, 1068 Concepcion St.; tel. 47-14-61.
In the Manuel Camus Bldg., single w/fan and common bath P20, double w/fan and common bath P29-34. In the nicer Jose Abad Santos Blidg., single w/ac P45-60, double w/ac P55-95. Dorm beds are P19. To get to the YMCA from the airport take the California Bus Lines bus marked 'Sta. Cruz/Monumento' and get off at City Hall on Taft Ave. From the bus stop, it's a block east.

YSTAPHIL International Youth Hostel, 2456 Taft Ave. (across from LaSalle College); tel. 5003-17.
Singles P17, doubles P25. Those without hostel cards are charged slightly more. Has travel service.

Mabini Pension, 1337 Mabini St.; tel. 59-48-53.
Singles w/fan, P55; w/ac, P65; doubles w/ac P78.

Traveler's Pension, 934 Pedro Gil St., corner of F. Agoneillo St. (one block down from Taft Ave.).
Double w/fan P40.

Pension Filipinas, 572 Arkansas St., Ermita.
Singles P66.50; doubles P132. All rooms w/ac.

Escaping Manila

By Land:

Pantranco North Express, 325 Quezon Blvd. Extension, near Roosevelt Ave., Quezon City; tel. 99-70-91. For Hundred Islands, Bauang beaches, Baguio, Banaue and other destinations north of Manila.

Pantranco South Express, 2944 Taft Ave., Pasay City; tel. 80-21-50. For the Bicol region.

Philippine Rabbit Bus Lines, 819 Oroquieta St., Santa Cruz; tel. 21-69-96. For Vigan and Bauang beaches.

Batangas-Laguna-Tayabas Bus Company (BLTB), E. de los Santos Ave., Pasay City; tel. 89-47-80. For the Southern Tagalog Provinces.

Philippines National Railways Motor Service (PNR), Tutuban Station, 943 Claro M. Recto Ave.; tel. 21-00-11. For buses and trains to the mountain provinces and the Bicol region.

By Sea:

Sulpicio Lines, near the YMCA, Concepcion St., Ermita; tel. 49-82-36. (This is only one of their booking offices.)

Negros Navigation Company, 849 Pasay Rd., Makati; tel. 86-49-21/25.

William Lines, 609 San Marcelino St., corner of Concepcion St., Ermita; tel. 40-45-24 (booking office).

Sweet Lines, 416 Padre Fauna St., Ermita; tel. 50-54-12 (booking office).

China Sea Beaches

A large number of fine beaches—with white sand, swaying coconut trees, and that placid emerald sea—lie within a day's travel of Manila. The ones listed below are those most easily reached by public transportation. The months between November and May are the best for beach-hopping; during the rest of the year, occasional rain and recurring jellyfish invasions make them less than ideal.

In any case, snorkeling is excellent off many of these Beaches—you can spend hours watching schools of tropical fish swimming around in their natural aquariums of multi-colored coral. Some resorts rent snorkeling equipment, but it's cheaper to rent/buy a set before leaving Manila; check with Aquaventure or Dive Asia in the Makati Commercial Center or Bunn's Philippine Diving, corner of Pasay Rd. and Makati Ave. These stores will also rent scuba equipment to international scuba card holders.

Hundred Islands, a cluster of islets in the Lingayen Gulf north of Manila, has so far remained relatively untouched by the tourist industry. From the small town of Lucap, near Alaminos, you can hire a boat to spend a great day swimming, snorkeling, and sunbathing among these rocky offshore islands. The staff of the small hotels in Lucap will fix a picnic lunch for you if you like, and they can give you tips about what to see among the islands. Quezon Island is the most popular for swimming and sunbathing; Panacan, Cathedral, and Padre Islands have interesting coral gardens. For a beautiful sunset, head for Primicias Island. Only a few of the other islands have sandy beaches, but there are many caves, secluded coves, and coral reefs where you can hunt for shells and unusual marine life. Boats which can take up to six people make six-hour tours of the islands for a set price. In Lucap, visit the Marine Biological Museum and the Oceanographic Fishery Research Laboratory.

Lucap is just a 15-min. jeepney ride from Alaminos, where you can catch local or express buses to Manila, Baguio, or Bauang (all via Dagupan). If you stop over in **Dagupan**, take a

244 PHILIPPINES

jeepney to the nearby beaches of Barrio Bonuan or San Fabian, or over to Blue Beach (15 min.) where overnight accommodations are available at the Villa Millagrosa Youth Hostel.

Bauang, a small town further up the coast, claims to have the best beach resort in the Philippines, but the beach itself is not as nice as some of those mentioned above. Bauang's major advantage is its proximity to Baguio (see **The Mountain Provinces and Ilocos**), one hour away. The most popular beach area, which is lined with resort hotels, lies just off the coastal highway about 2 km. north of Bauang and 4 km. south of San Fernando; many jeepneys and mini-buses connect the two towns. The local DOT office is located on the outskirts of San Fernando, in the Veterans Bldg., Capitol Site (tel. 24-11).

If you're only in Bauang for the day, you can swim for free and then use the showers at one of the resorts for a small charge, P1.50-5. The Beach just south of the Long Beach Hotel is the most popular. Bring your own lunch or eat in San Fernando because the resort restaurants are expensive. The white sand beach and coral gardens are a 30-min. banca ride from the resorts, P15/hr. for 1-2 people (fixed price).

Located in Cavite Province, south of Manila, are **Amaya Beach** in Tanza and **Puerto Asul** and **Aplayita Beaches** in Ternate. All are less than a 2 hr. bus ride (P2.50) away. Take one of the mini-buses (e.g. Donna May Liners) in Baclaran, about ½ km. south of the Taft Ave. and E. de los Santos intersection; the signboards will indicate either Tanza or Ternate.

There is usually no entrance fee at these beaches, but use of the covered picnic tables will cost about P10/day, use of showers or a freshwater pump about P2. Aplayita has overnight accommodations.

Further south lie the beaches of **Nasugbu** in Batangas Province. Make an overnight trip of it so you can stop en route to the city of **Tagaytay**, about an hour from Manila. From the city's ridge at an altitude of 2250 ft. you can get a stunning view of **Lake Taal** with its island volcano, one of the most active in the world (its last eruption in 1965 destroyed an entire village). Boats can be rented in town for a trip to the island. Get back on a bus for Nasugbu before evening, though, as there are no inexpensive hotels in the area.

Two beaches lie within a 5-min. tricycle radius of Nasugbu: **Dalampasigan** and **Baybay**, both with nearby resort cottages and restaurants. The more secluded and beautiful beaches are **White Sands, Maya Maya, Tali Beach** or **Fortune Island**; take a tricycle to Wawa pier and hire a banca to any of these beaches (P150 for a roundtrip). Fortune Island has especially good coral reefs and all the beaches except White Sands have resort accommodations (P50 to P150/night).

PHILIPPINES 245

A morning bus from Manila to Batangas City and then a 2-hr. boat ride will take you to some of the best swimming and snorkeling in the Philippines at **Puerta Gallera** on Mindora (the next major island south of Luzon). Boats leave twice daily for Puerta Gallera from the Batangas City pier at around noon and 2 pm (P8). The return trips leave in the morning about 7 and 10:30, so plan on an overnight. (Chartering a boat is also an option, but at a cost of over P100 one-way).

ACCOMMODATIONS FOR CHINA SEA BEACHES

Many beach resorts have seasonal rates varying as much as 50% between March-May (the peak season) and June-Oct. (the rainy off-season). Prices may also vary between weekends and weekdays. The rates given below are averages or ranges.

Hundred Islands:

Bayside Lodge, Lucap. Single, P30; double, P60. Friendly staff who will help you plan excursions among the islands.

Kilometres 1 Hostel, 1 mile from Lucap. Single, P20. Secluded location.

Fidel Gummonry Resthouse, Lucap, single P13.

National Park House, Lucap, single P30.

Bauang Beaches:

The resorts in this area are quite expensive; it's cheaper to spend the night in Baguio, 1 hr. away. If you don't want to go that far, these two resorts are the most reasonable:

Long Beach Resort Hotel, near Cresta Ola. Doubles w/fan and private bath P170.

Lourdes Beach Resort, next to Sun Valley. Their two-bedroom cottages sleep four, P180. Fan, private bath and cooking area.

Nasugbu Beaches:

Dalampasigan Beach Resort. Three-bedroom cottages P100-180. Congenial staff and nice restaurant.

Baybay Dagat Resort. Two-bedroom cottages P85. Good restaurant.

Maya Maya Beach Resort. Cottages rent for around P150.

Linjoco Boarding House, in town. Simple accommodations; two-bed rooms P40.

Puerta Gallera:

There are several small hotels in town, all charging about P15/person. Look for **Seven Dwarfs, Virgie's Hotel, Sharon's Hotel** or **Kathy's Inn.**

TRANSPORTATION FOR CHINA SEA BEACHES

For **Hundred Islands:** Pantranco has buses hourly to Alaminos, 4:40 am-3:40 pm (P18, 5-6 hr.). Next to the bus stop in Alaminos catch a jeepney making the short run to Lucap, where the boat landing for Hundred Islands is located.

For **Bauang Beaches:** Pantranco, Philippine Rabbit and PNR all have frequent buses to San Fernando which pass through Bauang (P21). From San Fernando to Baguio it's about P10.

For **Nasugbu Beaches:** The BLTB bus company serves the Batangas area. Buses leave regularly until 7 pm (P4.25). For **Puerta Gallera**, take the Batangas Pier bus (P7, 3 hr).

Ilocos and The Mountain Provinces

The provinces of northern Luzon and the lowlands around Manila have little in common geographically. As you travel north from central Luzon, spacious fields of rice and sugar cane yield to small vegetable and rice terraces carved lovingly out of mountainsides, pine trees replace coconut palms, and the cool, fresh mountain air makes it difficult to believe you're still in the tropics. The northern provinces also offer glimpses of some of the distinctive cultures that have helped shape the present-day Philippines. Ride a calesa (horse-drawn cart) over the cobblestone streets of an old Spanish town, hike through Igorot villages to ancient burial caves, and take in the "Eighth Wonder of the World"—the Banaue rice terraces.

Baguio, a popular retreat 250 km north of Manila, is an excellent starting point for trips further into the mountains. Some 75 years ago the American colonialists made this city their summer capital during the months when Manila got too hot and humid, and Baguio is still packed with lowlanders throughout the year. The MOT office is located ½ km. east of the central market on Gov. Pack Rd.; they have considered historical and travel information on Northern Luzon.

Baguio is a city of pine-forested parks—Burnham, Wright, Mines View, Imelda Gardens—in which the dominant sport is horseback riding. Horses can be ridden for P14 an hour. A brisk walk up Dominican Hill will give you a view of the China Sea on clear days. Baguio's market, at the western end of Session Rd., specializes in fresh vegetables, flowers and strawberries—all very expensive or unavailable in lower areas. As for handicrafts, Baguio serves as a center for goods from all over Northern Luzon. The prices of these 'imported' products tend to be on the steep side so bargain fiercely. Locally-made handicrafts: St. Louis University silver shop sells all kinds of silver pieces at fair fixed prices. For woodcarvings, go to the shop/factory on Leonard Rd. above the Teachers' Camp, or to the woodcarving village off Kennon Rd. A fine selection of Igorot woven material can be found at Easter School, on the outskirts of Baguio near Pinsao Rd. After all this running around, stop by

PHILIPPINES 247

the Strawberry House—near St. Vincent's Church on the road to Asin Hot Springs—for a free sample of their strawberry wine.

The Baguio bakeries are among the best in Luzon. Holsum Bakery on Perfecto Rd. and Good Shepard Mission (featuring strawberry and Blueberry jams) shouldn't be missed. Restaurants in Baguio are by no means cheap but the Dainty Restaurant does serve good Chinese and American set dinners for P16. Despite Baguio's small size, there are numerous sources of night entertainment due to its heavy influx of students and tourists; many coffeeshops (with thumping American disco) and theaters line Abanao St.

At the Benguet Provincial Capitol in **La Trinidad**, just north of Baguio, ask to see the mummies of Kabayan, kept in the governor's office. The mummies, brought from burial caves in the northern part of the province, are believed to be many centuries old despite their remarkable state of preservation— even the skin and some hair and teeth remain intact. Throughout the mountains, corpses have been preserved this way by washing the skin with boiled water and guava leaves, then slowly drying them in the sun or by small fires.

Along the northern China Sea coast are the Ilocos provinces. This region is the homeland of the Ilocanos, the second largest ethnic group in the Philippines. It is from this rugged, marginally productive land that many Ilocanos—widely known for their industriousness—have emigrated to many parts of the Philippines and beyond.

Vigan, tucked in between the Cordillera Mts. and the China Sea coast, was the first Spanish settlement established outside of Manila (1574). The height of Vigan's prosperity came when the town was a focal point in the Asian indigo trade in the 1850's. This boom caused a rapid infusion of wealth which resulted in many Spanish homes that were built. World War II bombing raids destroyed much of old Manila, but Ilocos was spared and thus many of the original Spanish buildings still stand. Ilocos, and Vigan in particular, has retained a definite Spanish complexion that has been fading in other areas in the Philippines.

Vigan is known as the birthplace of Father Jose Burgos, a priest-patriot, who was martyred in 1872 for the Cavite Mutiny, a movement which demanded equal status among native and Spanish clergy. His birthplace, now a museum located behind the provincial capitol, displays Burgos mementos as well as a series of Villanueva paintings which depict the Ilocano revolt against the Spanish monopoly on 'basi' (a local sugar cane brew).

In the center of town is the **Vigan Cathedral**, located between two plazas, Plaza Burgos and Plaza Salcedo. Built in 1641, the cathedral has a magnificent main alter flanked by smaller side

248 PHILIPPINES

ones with centuries-old gravestones lining the walls and columns.

Take a horse-drawn celesa to ride through the sidestreets and alleys and (in the Crisologo St. area) explore what was once a strong settlement of Spanish Asia.

There are many white sand beaches in the Vigan area, ½ to 1 hr. away by jeepney. **Suso Beach**, in Santa Maria, has a small oyster farm, a restaurant, and some resthouses. **Pug-os Beach Resort**, in Cabugao, is only a few meters off the main highway. If you'd like to see more Spanish architecture in the Ilocos, head north for Bantay (½ km. from Vigan), Paoay (60 km.) and Laoag (78 km.).

About 100 km. northeast of Baguio are the famed **rice terraces** of the North. The rice terrace culture originated in either south China or Indochina and was brought to the Philippines in two waves of migration, around 2000 and 1000 BC. Although much of the farmland in this region is terraced, the most accessible and best-known terraces are those of **Banaue**.

Banaue can be reached by two routes—one fast and reliable, the other tortuous, time-consuming, and much more spectacular. Whether you use one route or the other, or both in a loop, depends on the weather, how much time you have, and how many stops you want to make (e.g. Bontoc, Sagada). The slower but more interesting route (recommended during the drier months between November and May) takes you from Baguio to Banaue via Bontoc on a winding, narrow, unpaved road. In the best of weather and with no mishaps you can make the 150-km. Baguio-Bontoc trip in 7-8 hours. Sagada is one hour west of Bontoc and Banaue is 3-4 hours southeast of Bontoc, over the same winding roads. Banaue can also be reached directly from Manila via the province of Nueva Viscaya in 7-8 hours all year round, due to a new concrete road. This is the way to go if you're pressed for time or it's the middle of the rainy season. Once in Banaue you can always ask about the condition of the road on to Bontoc and Sagada.

When you arrive in **Bontoc**, the capital of the Mountain Province, you'll quickly realize you've left the neon and glitter of Manila far behind. Much of daily life in this area has been going on in the same way for hundreds, perhaps thousands, of years. People still get around by walking and bathe in the river. The city's electric currents only run for a few hours in the early morning and evening.

The town's small museum is worth a visit. At the All Saints' Mission weaving school see how traditional Bontoc cloth is made; a small store there sells cloth and ready-made articles at fair prices. Both Bontoc and Banaue are good places to shop for

PHILIPPINES 249

handwoven materials and blankets, rattan bags, baskets, backpacks, and woodcarvings, all made in the area.

The **Maligcong** rice terraces are a steep, 2-3 hr. climb from Bontoc, in a valley northwest of the Chico River. The people of Bontoc claim these terraces are more beautiful than those of Banaue or Sagada because the terrace dikes are built with stone rather than clay. Take food and water along on the hike, plus boxes of matches and/or cigarettes for the Igorot villagers if you want to take their pictures. After an hour or so, when you're gasping for breath and your head whirls with the altitude, stop and look around; the view is magnificent. You can find a guide for this hike in Bontoc. (Guides in the mountain areas generally charge P40-50 for the whole day, proportionately less for part of the day. You're expected to provide your guide with food and water for the trip, but he'll help carry the provisions.)

The tiny town of **Sagada** nestles in the mountains only 18 km. from Bontoc. In addition to rice terraces which cover the entire side of a mountain, Sagada has several limestone burial caves, one of which (Balangang Cave) features a wide "auditorium" and a cascading waterfall. Ask in town for a guide; you'll probably also need to rent a lantern, about P5.

The rice terraces at **Banaue** are perhaps the most beautiful and certainly the largest, covering two mountainsides (400 sq. km.). It's estimated that it took the ancestors of the local Ifugao people more than 2000 years to build these terraces.

You can get a detailed map and hiking information at the Banaue Youth Hostel. Batad, one of the best lookouts, can be reached in a 2-hr. hike from the highway; take a jeepney to the starting point, 12 km. from the youth hostel on the road to Mayo-yao.

ACCOMMODATIONS FOR ILOCOS AND THE MOUNTAIN PROVINCES
Baguio:

Emerald Inn, 36 Gen. Luna St. Broom-closet rooms for P16/night in the heart of town. There are other inns on the same street.

Traveler's Lodge, 60 Lakandula St. (4 blocks from Magsaysay Rd., near the market). Singles w/shared bath P22.

Mountain View Villa, 7 Military Cut-off Rd. Dorm beds P25.

Vigan:

Village Inn, 14 Bonifacio St., P30; all rooms w/private bath and fan. Old beautiful Spanish home converted into an inn.

Grandpa's Inn, Corner of Bonifacio & Quirino Sts. All rooms w/fan, P25.

Cordillera Inn, 29 Crisologo (next to Ilocos Sur Development Bank). Singles w/private bath & fan P42; doubles w/shared bath & fan, P54.

Bontoc:

Bus Stop Hotel, facing the bus stop. Singles P10. Clean but noisy. Its 'Bus Stop Rice' has good meals for P4.

250 PHILIPPINES

Bontoc Hotel, near the bus stop too. Singles P15. Bontoc's oldest hotel but still clean.

Pines Kitchenette and Inn, a 5-min. walk from the bus stop. Singles P15; doubles P30. Some rooms w/private bath. Has a good but slightly expensive restaurant.

Sagada:

St. Joseph Resthouse, across from the hospital where the bus stops. P10/person. Meals are available (skimpy but good) for P4; friendly, well-kept place.

Banaue:

Banaue Youth Hostel, directly behind the Municipal City Hall near the fancy Banaue Hotel. P13.60 for members, P24.45 for non-members.

Valgreg Hotel, near the market. Rooms w/shared bath P10/person; w/private bath P20/person.

Wonderlodge, near the market. Dorm beds, P10.

TRANSPORTATION FOR ILOCOS AND THE MOUNTAIN PROVINCES

Baguio: Several companies cover the Manila-Baguio route; PNR and Pantranco offer the best service. Regular buses leave every 30 min., 5 am-6 pm (P33.65, 4-5 hr.). Air-conditioned buses leave a couple of times each day (P60-65). Baguio is accessible from Bauang and Hundred Islands via San Fernando; take a Pantranco bus.

Vigan: Philippine Rabbit buses from Manila leave to Laoag; all stop in Vigan (P45, 6-8 hr.). They leave hourly, 4 am-11 pm. Vigan can also be reached from Baguio via San Fernando, again on Philippine Rabbit (P22.50, 5 hr.).

The only major bus company operating within the mountainous areas north of Baguio is Dangwa Co. If you go to Baguio first, stop by the Dangwa Station on Magsaysay Rd. near the market and check on departure times. Road conditions in the area tend to make for more 'flexible' scheduling. For shorter distances you might want to take mini-buses or jeepneys, which usually leave from town markets. They are generally more frequent and more crowded.

Bontoc: Dangwa has 4-5 buses going daily between Baguio and Bontoc (P36.50, 7-8 hr.). They leave Baguio between 4:30 and 9:30 am and return from Bontoc between about 6 am and 1 pm.

Sagada: There's one direct bus from Baguio to Besao which stops in Sagada (about P30). Or take one of the Dangwa buses to Bontoc and transfer to a local bus which makes 2 roundtrips a day to Sagada (P5, 1 hr.).

Banaue: From Baguio there is a daily bus to Banaue at 7:30 am (P36.50, 8-9 hr.). Buy tickets at the station on Gov. Pack Rd. The return bus from Banaue leaves at 4:30 am. Dangwa also makes several roundtrips daily between Bonyoc and Banaue via Nueva Viscaya on a new concrete road (7-8 hr.). A regular bus leaves their Quezon City station daily around 7:30 am (P38.50); on weekends an ac bus leaves at about the same time (P76.50). If you miss the bus and still want to leave that morning, take any Pantranco bus going to Cagayan Valley and get off in Solano, Nueva Viscaya (about 5 hr.). From the market jeepneys and minibuses leave for Banaue until 2-3 pm. The return bus to Manila leaves Banaue at 8 am.

Southern Tagalog Provinces

The Southern Tagalog Provinces (Laguna, Quezon, Batangas, Cavite)—all within easy reach of Manila—are full of gorgeous lakes, rivers, waterfalls, and mountains. A visit to this popular region can be part of a trip to Bicol and beyond, or can be combined with beach-hopping south of Manila. (See the appropriate sections for details.)

By traveling directly to **San Pablo**, you can make a series of sidetrips before preceeding to the Bicol region. Beautiful San Pablo is known as the 'City of Seven Lakes'; it is nestled between the Makiling ranges and the Banahaw mountains. You can stroll around the most popular crater lake, **Sampaloc Lake**, in about an hour. The more energetic will hike for the 'twin lakes' of **Pandin** and **Yambo**, a good ½-day trip. The Sampaloc Youth Hostel can provide hiking information. While in San Pablo, taste the local brew, 'lambanog'; a whole jug of this coconut wines goes for a couple of pesos, and if you have your own container they practically give it away. Lambanog is true firewater.

Backtracking towards Manila, take a jeepney towards **Los Banos**, home of the International Rice Research Institute (IRRI) and the University of the Philippines, Los Banos. In the '60's IRRI developed what was known as 'miracle' rice varieties that spawned the so-called Green Revolution in Asia. On its experimental farms research continues on new rice varieties and small-scale farm machinery. If you'd like to tour IRRI, contact the institute's Manila office first (tel. 88-48-69) or make arrangements once you're in Los Banos at its information office. Closed on weekends.

The U.P. campus, known for its excellent College of Agriculture, is a short journey from the town's main intersection. Wander around the Philippines' most beautiful campus and meet students from all over Asia. You can have a good meal at the student union or in the SEARCA dormitory across the street. Or, stop by the Dairy Bar of the Dairy Training and Research Institute—try its quesong puti (white cheese).

252 PHILIPPINES

By taking the campus jeepney to the corner of Kanluran and Sampaloc Sts., you can walk a remaining 2 km. and enter **Mt. Makiling National Park**. While climbing the dormant volcano isn't particularly advisable due to a rainy season onslaught of leeches, ask at the boy scout camp for alternative climbing. At the camp, you can stay overnight and spend some time in its pool. Mt. Makiling is also the site of the National Arts Center which serves as a school and retreat for Filipino artists of all disciplines. Entrance to the center is restricted, but you can apply for a pass at the Cultural Center in Manila.

A short jeepney ride from Los Banos is **Pansol**, known for its hot springs. It's this area that gives Los Banos, Spanish for 'The Baths,' its name; the resorts here have large swimming pools fed by veins of hot sulphuric water. You'll be soaked for about P5. If you're shy, Lakeside Resort and Agua Caliente offer private baths for about P5/person/hour.

Further north you can take a short jeepney ride to the small town of **Calamba** sitting beneath towering Mt. Makiling. Calamba is the birthplace of the national hero, Dr. Jose Rizal. A replica of the Rizal family home contains an interesting museum; to visit it, get off the bus at the town's main intersection and walk a few blocks (there are signs showing the way). A contribution of a few pesos is expected.

West of San Pablo, take a day to visit **Hidden Valley Springs**, a remarkable resort inside a 110-acre volcanic crater. First take a jeepney to Alaminos (10-15 min.), then a tricycle (P5) or jeepney (P12) to Hidden Valley. Arrange for the driver to pick you up later in the day because resort accommodations are very expensive. Hidden Valley has three swimming pools fed by spring water, all skillfully placed in lush natural settings, excellent hiking through tropical forests, and a lovely secluded waterfall. The P50 entrance fee includes a buffet lunch and use of the facilities for the day.

Shooting the rapids at **Pagsanjan Falls**, northeast of both San Pablo and Los Banos, is a major tourist attraction. Take a bus to Santa Cruz; go right as you leave the town bus station and walk toward the market—jeepneys to Pagsanjan pass by here. Once in Pagsanjan, the jeepney will turn right at the town plaza and then cross a small bridge. Get off here and walk along Gen. Luna St. to the youth hostel (#237).

PHILIPPINES 253

Rates are fixed for the rapids boats (capacity, 3 people): P25 if you are alone, P20/person for groups. The youth hostel or nearby hotels can make the arrangements for you. Make the 2½-hr trip early in the morning to avoid traffic jams of boats later in the day. December to February is the best time of the year; during the rainy season, July-September, the river might be too fast to get to the highest rapids. The youth hostel manager can suggest nearby places for hiking and swimming.

From Santa Cruz you can complete a circle for Laguna Lake (take a jeepney to Paete and then a bus along the rugged mountain road on the north side of the lake back to Manila) or go south to Lucena City (by mini-bus).

In **Paete**, shop for handcrafted wood products and carvings. This side of the lake is particularly known for its Spanish churches, many of them hundreds of years old.

Lucena City (accessible from Manila and San Pablo) is the bustling capital of Quezon Province. It has numerous hotels and restaurants—try the Casa Arias Garden Restaurant near the BLTB station downtown—and a city park, Perez Park. **Dalahican Beach**, a popular place to swim, is 4 km. outside the city, and **Mainit Hot Springs** are on the way to Lucban (18 km.). But the main attraction in this area is **Quezon National Park**, one of the largest bird and game sanctuaries in Luzon. From Lucena, take a mini-bus going to Antimonan or Caliuag (P2.50) and ask to get off at the park resthouse. The park covers 985 hectares of protected wilderness, a refuge for monkeys, wild boars, deer, parrots, and other wildlife. The trails are well-marked (but there are no maps); if you go hiking or back-packing take along complete provisions, including water or purifying tablets.

ACCOMMODATIONS FOR THE SOUTHERN TAGALOG PROVINCES

San Pablo:
Sampaloc Lake Youth Hostel, Efraca Subdivision. Dorm beds P17-20.

U.P. Los Banos:
If there is space available in the dorms (usually between semesters) travelers may stay overnight for P10/person. On campus call Mrs. Rose Gabatin, ext. 2567.

Pansol:
Lake View Resort, Singles P40; doubles P50.

Pagsanjan:
Pagsanjan Youth Hostel, 237 Gen. Luna St. Dorm beds P20.
Pagsanjan Rapids Hotel, Gen. Taino St. Singles, P85; doubles, P100.

Lucena City:
Most of the hotels are located in **Barrio Ayam**. To get there take a Lucena-Suburbs jeepney (P.60) or tricycle (P3).

Tourist Hotel, a variety of rooms, ranging from singles w/fan, P15 to doubles w/ac & bath, P45.

The Fresh Air, singles w/fan P20, w/ac & bath P48. Has a restaurant and a swimming pool.

TRANSPORTATION FOR THE SOUTHERN TAGALOG PROVINCES

The BLTB bus company serves the provinces immediately south of Manila; so does Laguna Transit.

From Manila to **San Pablo, Los Banos**, and **Calamba**: take any of the Laguna-bound buses going via Calauan or College (2½ hr. to San Pablo, P7; 1½ hr. to Los Banos, P5). For **Pagsanjan**, take the bus to Santa Cruz (2½ hr., P7.50), then a jeepney. For **Hidden Valley**, take the Manila-Lucena City bus which goes via Alaminos (1 hr., P5). Express buses going directly to **Lucena City** take 2½ hr. (P10.50).

If you plan to do a lot of traveling in Luzon, buy a road map. The roads are good and you might save yourself time by making use of the jeepneys and mini-buses connecting many of the places mentioned. If there's a road connecting two places, you can be sure that there'll be jeepneys on it.

Bicol

The Bicol region is composed of four provinces in southern Luzon (Camarines Norte, Camrines Sur, Albay, and Sorsogon) and two islands (Masbate and Catanduanes). Its two main cities are Legazpi and Naga. Legazpi, the capital of Albay, is a good starting point for touring Bicol. It's easily reached from Manila by a combination of night train and bus.

The trick to **Legazpi** is that it is divided into two distinct districts: Legazpi Port and Albay. Many of the hotels, restaurants and theaters are in Legazpi Port while many of the government offices, including MOT, are in Albay. The MOT office, located on the northern side of Penaranda Park near the cathedral, are helpful in supplying information and maps. Incidently, these two districts are linked together by Rizal Avenue which hosts swarms of jeepneys; a ride between districts costs P55. The bus stations are in Legazpi Port and close by the BLTB station on Penaranda St. are two fine inexpensive restaurants: Peking Restaurant and Mike's Oak Room. On Rizal Ave., near Albay district, is The Magic Pan—a gourmet restaurant that has evening folk music.

Dominating Legazpi is the active volcano, **Mt. Mayon**, with its symmetrical sides soaring 2462 m topping into a near-perfect cone. Mayon adheres to a ten-year eruption cycle with its largest occurring in 1978; it continues to emit a steady stream of sulphurous smoke. Hikers can arrange with MOT to climb the cone—a trek of 1½ days. The starting point is generally the

Mayon Rest House and Volcano Observatory situated at a lofty 850 m. From the coastal town Tobaco there is an occasional minibus that makes the run up to the Rest House.

Down below, there are two particularly good areas to view the volcano. The **Cagsawa Ruins** is a belfry and crumbled masonry of a church just outside Daraga. The church was destroyed by Mayon on February 1, 1814. Molten lava flowed to the lowlands while many villagers converged in the Cagsawa Church to pray for their safety. Continuing on its mission of destruction, molten matter seeped into the church causing the death of hundreds of villagers. Following the 1814 eruption, survivors built a new church on a hilltop in what is now Daraga. **Daraga Church** was made from volcanic rock and is well-known for its exterior baroque carvings.

From Legazpi, trips can be taken by bus or jeepney to the towns and beaches along the coastline between Legazpi and Naga. Particularly well-known and somewhat overrated is **Tiwi**, a hot springs resort and beach. There is also a nearby geothermal salt-conversion plant and wells project that utilizes the hot springs to generate electricity for the Bicol region. Nearby is the Naglabong boiling lake which, according to legend, is hell itself with souls in torment shrieking during moonless nights.

Some of the best snorkeling can be found in **Santo Domingo**. Take either a jeepney or bus and get off at the church plaza. From there, take a tricycle to either the black-sand Reyes Beach or Buhatan Beach. The latter is the wreck site of an old Spanish galleon. Further north is the beach town of **Bacacay** where more snorkeling is possible. Camping is allowed on beaches. You can also hire a banca (about P30) to go to the uninhabited island of **Guinanayan**, where you can camp if you bring your own food and water.

If you plan to travel on to the Visayas from Bicol, one option is to take the ferry to **Masbate** from the town of Bulan in Sorsogon Province. There are good beaches and reasonably-priced accommodations there. However, the only ship heading south from Masbate leaves on Tuesdays and goes directly to Cebu. The more common route for traveling south goes through Matnog at the southern tip of Luzon and on to the island of Samar (see **Transportation for the Visayas** below).

If you're passing through Bicol in the early fall, stop in **Naga**, northwest of Legazpi, where the famous Penafrancia Fiesta and Fluvial Procession is held on the third Saturday of September. This is one of the largest festivals in the Philippines, as Our Lady of Penafrancia is the patroness of the Bicol region. In recent years the Fluvial Procession, which takes place on the Bicol River, has attracted 25,000 people. The Penafrancia Church, located 1 km. east of the center of town, has an interesting graveyard.

ACCOMMODATIONS IN BICOL

Legazpi:

There is an abundance of reasonably-priced hotels in Legazpi, most of them stretched along the main drag, Penaranda Ave.

Xandra Hotel. Singles, P45; doubles, P67. Has ac and private baths.
Mayon Hotel. Singles, P45-85; doubles, P60-125. Most rooms have ac.
Shirman Hotel. Singles, P47-95; doubles, P54-110. Same deal as above.
Ritz Hotel. Singles, P36-60; doubles, P42-75.

Tiwi:

Manatiel de Tiwi Youth Hostel. Singles w/fan, P50 and singles w/ac, P80. You're right, it is steep for a hostel, but the rooms are all modern, w/private shower and toilet. If you have a valid International Youth Hostel Card, you can spend the night for considerably less.

Naga:

Crown Hotel, Pearl Hotel & Gem Hotel have inexpensive rooms.

TRANSPORTATION FOR BICOL

Trains for **Naga** and **Legazpi** leave from Paco Station on Quirino Ave. From Taft Ave. and Pedro Gil St., take a 'Santa Ana' jeepney that goes near the station. At the station or at MOT you can ask for complete schedules that include slower economy trains, but the two night trains, the Mayon Limited (leaving at 4 pm) and the Mayon Limited Special (leaving at 7 pm) are recommended. To Naga (11 hr. either train) the Mayon Limited offers economy class (P25) and sleeping berths (P35-40) while the Mayon Limited Special has a tourist class (P42) and an ac deluxe (P53). To go to Legazpi you must take an additional half-hour bus ride from the end of the line at Camalig. The total trip usually takes 14 hr. You can and should purchase a train ticket that includes bus fare; Philippine National Railway buses will be waiting for you at Camalig. Total fares to Legazpi are: Mayon Limited, economy P31 and sleeping berths P42-47; Mayon Limited Special, tourist P51 and ac deluxe P65. Buy a ticket early in the day to assure yourself a seat.

Pantranco and JB lines have buses going to the Bicol region; addresses are listed in **Escaping Manila**. Pantranco offers a faster, more expensive ac bus to Naga and Legazpi (P85, 10 hr. to Legazpi), but both Pantranco and JB Lines offer regular buses that are slower and less expensive (P50, 14 hr. to Legazpi). The regular bus fare to Naga is P38 (10 hr.).

The Visayas

Samar

Samar is a relatively underdeveloped island which has been the scene of increasingly active rebel insurgency. Areas in northern and eastern Samar have been scenes of conflict between government troops and the New People's Army. Check with MOT officials about which areas may be off-limits to travelers.

The ferry from Matnog will stop in the coastal village of **Allen**. Although there are beautiful beaches near Allen, you might want to push on to **Catarman** (48 km. to the east), one of Samar's main towns and the home of the University of Eastern Philippines. **Tamburosan Beach**, 4 km. from Catarman, is the local student hang-out. From either Allen or Catarman you can ride to **Calbayog** to see the seven-tiered Darsodos Waterfalls. While you could stop in **Catbalogan** to spend time on its beaches, it's just as well to go southward to Leyte.

Leyte

Leyte was the site of one of the bloodiest battles of the Pacific War. Thousands of Filipinos, Americans and Japanese died on the beaches and hills of Leyte in the autumn of 1944. The Leyte Valley, enclosed by the towns of Palo, Jaro, Dagami, Burauen, Dulag and Tanauan, was the first line of defense of the Japanese Imperial Forces. As a result, many of the tourists who visit the Leyte Valley are Japanese coming to pay their respects to those who died here and whose bodies were never found.

The provincial capital of **Tacloban** will most likely be where you will stop first and could be the base for sidetrips. Tacloban is an unpretentious seaport town. It is a very easy town to get around in since the ferry landing, bus station and central market are all located in the same place. Down J. Romualdez St. are many small shops selling fine handicrafts—especially reed-woven products. In any of Tacloban's bakeries is the local delicacy, 'binagol'. Binagol is a mixture of gabi root, egg, coconut milk and sugar that is whipped together and served wrapped in banana leaves inside a coconut shell. Moongold Fastfood on M.H. Del Pilar St. and Asiatic Restaurant on Zamora St. serve heaping dishes of excellent Filipino/Chinese food. Except for the double-features, Tacloban nights are very quiet. People must go to bed awfully early.

258 PHILIPPINES

If Tacloban moves too fast for you, perhaps it's time for you to walk to the MOT office in Children's Park near the capitol building for suggested sidetrips. Incidently, a gaze at the capitol building will give you a sense of the pervasiveness of Western influence in Filipino culture; the base reliefs on the wall depict the first Mass at Limasawa and MacArthur's return to Palo.

Fourteen kilometers south of Tacloban near the town of Palo, is sandy **Red Beach** where Gen. MacArthur and the American forces landed on October 1944. MacArthur did indeed return and this time it's in the form of larger-than-life sized statues that immortalize his landing. The figures look particularly haunting at dusk.

Like many of the beaches in Samar and Leyte, **White Beach** (8 km. south of Tacloban) is another sandy beach which had been color code-named by the Americans in World War II. This beach is a popular site for swimming and picnicking. **Dio Island** has excellent beach facilities but there's a catch. Since the island belongs to Mrs. Marcos, you must first get written permission from the Island Development Bank on Real Street. Once permission is granted, they'll make transport arrangements for you.

North of Leyte lies the demure isle of **Biliran**. Recently, the island has been slated for tourist development. As of yet, Biliran has remained a virtual paradise: volcanic peaks and emerald waters. Caibiran has both hot springs and a natural swimming pool. From Naval you can either hike up Biliran volcano or take a moonlight cruise in a banca. **Gigantangan Island** attracts divers because of its coral gardens and rich sea life.

From Tacloban you can go directly to Cebu or you can go via **Ormoc City**. Along the 4½-hr. ride between Tacloban and Ormoc City are rice fields, sugar cane plantations and coconut palms. While waiting for a boat to Cebu, you can soak in the nearby Tungonan Hot Springs.

If you'd prefer to see more of the Leyte countryside, take a bus from Tacloban to **Maasin**. From there you can take the ferry to Surigao on Mindanao.

Cebu

When you come ashore at **Cebu** you will be entering the Philippines' third largest city, and you'll be retracing the steps of the earliest Spanish explorers. Cebu's character is determined less by its large size than by the long years of Hispanic influence. Ferdinand Magellan landed on nearby Mactan Island in 1521 and planted the Spanish flag and cross. He was soon followed by Spanish soldiers and settlers led by Miguel Lopez de Legazpi who built Cebu into the largest town of the Spanish colonial period.

Most of the restaurants, hotels, theaters, and ticket agencies are clustered along **Colon St.** Arriving from the pier it is easiest to take a jeepney (P65) or a Public Utilities (P.U.) cab (P2) bound for Colon St. Jeepney rides within the city generally range between P.50-P1 while P.U. fares are always P2 regardless of destination within the city proper.

Once checked into a hotel you can walk east past the Skyview Hotel on Juan Luna St. A couple of blocks later you will be at **San Agustin Church** which contains an image of Santo Nino (Holy Child) which had been brought by Magellan's company from Mexico. First built in 1565, the basilica has repeatedly burned down and been rebuilt; the present structure dates from 1740. On the parallel street to the south, Magallanes St., stands a centuries-old kiosk containing **Magellan's Cross** (the original that he planted in 1521 is now encased within a larger hollow cross). Further east down either Juan Luna or Magallanes Sts. is **Fort San Pedro**, a triangular bastion built as a lookout in 1738. Inside is the regional MOT office. (There's a slight catch: in order to go to the MOT you must pay admission to Fort San Pedro first.)

By P.U. cab or a jeepney marked 'Lahug' you can drive through the upper class residential areas nestled in the hills above Cebu, named oddly enough, **Beverly Hills**. Prosperous Chinese merchants live here, and amid the split-level homes are three Taoist temples.

On Gorordo Avenue, two blocks below the Cebu branch of the University of the Philippines, is a unique museum. Housed in the **Arthaus Center** is a collection of Jumalon's Lepido-Mosaic Art—impressionistic pictures made from butterfly wings. Admission is P1. Also scattered around Cebu City are private homes with extensive collections of antiques, shells, coins and rare photos. MOT has the addresses and can arrange visits.

For evening entertainment Cebu has several nightclubs. The best seem to be the **Before and After Six Club** on Jones Ave. and rock/disco folk **El Cabrito** on Ramos St. Neither has a cover charge, but charges for drinks make up for it.

From A. Pigafetta St. in front of Fort San Pedro, you can take a jeepney (P.85) to **Mactan Island** (there's a bridge). In Lapu-lapu, there is a monument honoring the Cebuano chieftain who killed Magellan. From Lapu-lapu take a tricycle (P2) to see the guitar factories in Maribago. There are several large factories, but people often mention Lilang's Guitar Factory as the best—it certainly is the friendliest. There are a number of excellent beaches with an undersea wealth of coral where you can skindive and observe marine life. Marigondon, Sogod, and Buyong are all accessible by tricycle (P2). Camping is permitted for about P10 at most beaches.

The best skindiving in the Visayas is on the western coast of Cebu. **Moalboal** is a 3-hr. bus ride originating from the South Expressway Bus Terminal (P5).

260 PHILIPPINES

Bohol

Across the straits from Cebu is Bohol, an island of pristine hills and beaches with virgin forests and foliage. Bohol is well-known as the home of the thumb-sized, bug-eyed primate, the **Philippine Tarsier**, which has a body length of 3¼-6½ inches and can swivel its head 180 degrees. Just as well-known are Bohol's **Chocolate Hills**: hundreds of bald brown domes. Legend has it that these are teardrops of the demigod giant, Arugo, whose unrequited love caused him to weep for the mortal, Aluya. Scientists however don't buy this story. They say that Bohol was once underwater and a series of volcanic eruptions caused irregularities in some areas. These irregularities were later transformed into their present shape by water currents. When the island emerged they appeared as hills.

Hiking is better in the Chocolate Hills during the dry season (Dec.-May) as trails during the rest of the year turn into something like the consistency of sticky chocolate. The Chocolate Hills are located near Carmen, 58 km. inland from the port city of **Tagbilaran**; you can stay at a resort which sits atop one of the highest mounds.

Six kilometers from Tagbilaran is the town of **Baclayon** which has the oldest stone church in the Philippines, built by the Jesuits in 1595. Three kilometers away is Laya Beach. By taking a short banca trip from Tagbilaran or Baclayon, you can get to **Panglao Island**. In **Dauis**, along the island's east coast, are the **Hinagdanan Caves**, a subterranean maze of natural springs that are ideal for swimming and bathing, and Bikini Beach. On the west coast in **Panglao** are Doljo and Momo beaches which are particularly good for skindiving. West of Panglao is a small coral-bound island named **Balicasang** which has incredible scuba diving.

Negros

Dumaguete, in southeastern Negros, is a university town. Siliman University, a Protestant school, accounts for a large portion of the 20,000 students studying in Dumaguete. That's a lot considering the population of Dumaguete is only 62,000. Periodically there are performances at Siliman's Cultural Luce Auditorium and a pause through its anthropology museum is worthwhile.

Bordering the campus is a beach resort ideal for swimming. Cottages for rent are available. Other beaches with magnificent coral formations dot the coastline north and south of Dumaguete: Kawayan (8.5 km. south), El Oriente (15 km. north) and Wuthering Heights (16 km. north)—whether or not this last beach resembles any English coastline is up to you imagination. **La Vista Mar**, 102 km. south of Dumaguete, was the site of the 1976 International Skin and Scuba Diving competitions.

Camp Look Out is a mountain resort, 14 km. west of Dumaguete, that has a panoramic view of Dumaguete City, Bohol and Cebu. There are rest houses with sleeping accommodations.

In **Bais**, 45 km. northeast of Dumaguete, is the Central Azucarera de Bais, one of the oldest sugar processing operations in the country. Tours of the Central are available.

Straddling the northwestern coast of Negros is the 'sugar capital' of the Philippines, **Bacolod**. In this city the difference between the neighborhoods of the sugar barons and those of the less-well-to-do is particularly striking.

Take a P1.70 jeepney ride north to the **Victoria Milling Company Central**, one of the biggest sugar mill and refinery complexes in the world; tours are offered. There is also a capiz shell cottage industry at the complex where you can see how they make chandeliers, placemats, etc. out of the translucent white capiz shells. You'll also probably catch a glimpse of the old steam locomotives bringing the cane to the mill on narrow gauge tracks.

Back in Bacolod the **Anaware**, **NLS**, and **Bilbao** ceramics shops turn out high quality porcelain pieces. Another interesting place to visit is the home-shop where wood-shaving flowers are made. When you stop to eat, look for a bakery that makes the Bacolod specialty 'piyaya,' a sort of flakey pancake with sesame seeds outside and a burned brown sugar filling.

Panay

Across the straits from Bacolod is **Iloilo** (ee-loh-ee-loh), the largest city on the sugar-cane island of Panay. Iloilo is known for its jusi (raw silk) and pina (pineapple fibre) cloth, and a popular woven material called hablon. Most examples of these can be found in the Arevalo District of Iloilo and in Pavia (7.5 km. north).

Iloilo has a fine museum, the **Museo Iloilo**, with exhibits of stoneage flake tools, burial coffins, ornamented teeth, relics of shipwrecks and modern art. Outside the museum are trees on fire with bright orange blossoms in spring. There is a MOT office in the Sarabia Bldg. on Gen. Luna St. nearby.

Traveling forty kilometers south, you'll be at the **Miag-ao Fortress** which had been built in 1797 by an Augustinian priest. The structure had two functions: as a place of worship and as a fortress against pirates terrorizing coastal towns of Panay. The church's twin towers are different since the first foreman-priest died before he could finish both and his successor deviated from the original plan. At the center of the facade is the statue of St. Thomas Villanova, patron saint of Miag-ao.

Thirteen kilometers further south is **San Joaquin**. In the center of town is a church with a rather violent cover. Its facade depicts Christian Spain's cavalry and infantry routing out Moorish defenders of Morocco. So explicit is the sculpture that even the pained expression of wounded soldiers is apparent.

You can catch a bus further to **San Jose de Buenavista**. There's great skindiving along the nearby coastal reefs. Take a tricycle to Madranka or Salazar Beach. On the way back to Iloilo is another fine spot for diving, **Anini-y**, at the southern tip of the island. At Anini-y, hire a boat to Nogas Island, where you can find coral sand and some unusual marine life.

A 20-min. ferry ride from Iloilo will bring you to Jordon on **Guimaras Island**. An hour south by bus is **Nueva Valencia** which is well-known for its Catiliran Cave and the snorkeling at Igang Point. At nearby Taklong Island, there are white sand beaches and underwater gardens which are ideal for swimming, sunbathing, and diving.

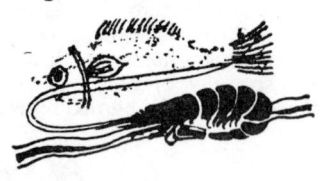

ACCOMMODATIONS IN THE VISAYAS

SAMAR

Allen: Not big on accommodations but try **Bicolano Hotel**. Electricity goes off at 10 pm, no fans, no screened windows, and wicker beds with woven mats instead of mattresses but the price is right—P5.

Catarman: All offer ordinary rooms at P10 per person.
  Larissa's Lodging House, J. Rizal St.
  Sanitary Lodging House, A. Bonifacio St.

Calbayog: Both **Hyacinth Lodge House** and **Wayside Lodging House** on Orquin St. offer rooms at P10 per person.
  San Joaquin Lodge, Nijaga St. Singles w/fan, P30; singles w/ac, P70; doubles w/fan, P40; doubles w/ac, P90.

Catbalogan: Both **Townhouse** and **Deluxe Lodging House** on Del Rosario St. offer rooms at P10 per person.
  Tony's Lodging House, Del Rosario St. Singles w/fan, P16; doubles w/fan, P34; rooms w/ac, P78. Hard to find, but its restaurant serves great food.

LEYTE

Tacloban: Benedicto Pensione, Lopez Jaena Extension. Singles w/fan, P30; singles w/ac, P65-85; doubles w/ac, P75-95. Has an excellent restaurant and disco. Friendly staff.

PHILIPPINES 263

Wander'd Lodging House, Rizal Ave. Rooms w/fan, P18; rooms w/ac, P55-70. Across from the bus stop. Has fastfood and cocktail lounge.

Tacloban Traveler's Lodge, P. Zamora St. Singles w/fan, P15; doubles w/fan, P25.

San Juanico Travel Lodge, J. Romualdez St. Rooms w/private bath & fan, P30-50; rooms w/common bath & fan, P20-30. Its fastfood is very good.

Ormoc: Pongos Hotel, Bonifacio St. Singles w/fan, P30; singles w/ac, P60; doubles w/fan, P50; doubles w/ac, P80.

Eddie's Lodge, Rizal St. Rooms w/common bath, P13; rooms w/ private bath, P15.

Naval, Biliran: Traveler's Lodge and **Naval Lodging House** on Cor. Garcia & P. Inocentes Sts. have rooms for P12/person.

Maasin: Maasin Lodging House, Cor. Enage & Garces St. Rooms P15-17 per person.

CEBU

Cebu City:

Statefair Hotel, Colon St. Singles/doubles w/fan, P18. Good restaurant downstairs.

Galaxy Inn, Colon St. Singles w/fan, P28; singles w/ac, P47; doubles w/fan, P40; doubles w/ac, P60.

Patria de Cebu, Burgos St. Singles w/fan, P20; doubles w/fan, P30. Looks like a convent, but has a bowling alley.

Dollar Hotel, Juan Luna St. Singles w/ac, P45; doubles w/fan, P27; doubles w/ac, P68.

YMCA, Jones Ave. Singles w/fan, P18-22; doubles w/fan, P16-18.

BOHOL

Tagbilaran: Tagbilaran Hotel & Dagohoy Hotel offer singles w/ac, P35; singles w/fan, P15.

Chocolate Hills: Chocolate Hills Resort, 4 km from Carmen; dorm, P15/person; cottage, P60/person.

NEGROS

Dumaguete: The **Victoria Lodging House**, Urdaneta St., has singles for P10.

Terminal Lodging House, Terminal Area Colon St. Singles, P10; doubles, P17.

Florentine Hotel. Singles w/fan, P18; doubles w/fan, P35.

Bacolod: New Pacific Lodging House. Singles w/fan, P14; singles w/ac, P24; doubles w/fan, P34.

PANAY

Iloilo: Bayani Super Inn & Night Club, Valeria-Delgado Sts.; tel. 7-26-13. Singles w/fan, P30; singles w/ac, P40; doubles w/ac, P80.

Beni-Rose Hall, Luna St.; tel. 7-51-72. Singles w/ac, P30; doubles w/ac, P40; communal rooms, P15.

Iloilo International House, J.M. Basa St.; tel. 7-47-86. Singles w/ac, P28; doubles w/ac, P38; other rooms w/fan, P10-13 per person.

Family Pension House, Gen. Luna St.; tel. 7-20-47. Rooms are P20 per person.

YMCA, Iznart St.; tel. 7-57-60. Singles w/fan, P13; doubles w/fan, P22. Non-members will be charged slightly more.

TRANSPORTATION FOR THE VISAYAS

Manila's 'Bulletin Today' carries advertisements from many shipping companies with their latest schedules and fares. Check with MOT for more complete listings. Beware of pickpockets on ships.

SAMAR

The ferry connecting Matnog, southern Luzon, with **Allen**, northern Samar, leaves Matnog daily at 8:30 am arriving in Allen at 9:40 am and returns at 2:30 pm arriving at 3:40 pm in Matnog. Fare is P14. Since the ferry leaves so early, you must take the 4 am bus from Legazpi (P17) in order to arrive in Matnog in time.

The trip from Allen to **Calbayog** by bus is 2 hr. (P5) and to **Catarman** is 1½ hr. (P3). From Calbayog, you can take a E.V. Tranco bus directly to **Tacloban** which takes 3½ hr. (P19.90) or to **Catbalongan** which takes 1½ hr. (P3). Or you can go directly from Allen to Tacloban taking 5½ hr. (P25).

An adventurous soul could take a banca from Allen to Calbayog (P25, 4 hr.) which hugs the coastline. Try to get there by 2 pm as that is the time the last bus leaves Calbayog if you're continuing to Tacloban.

LEYTE

From Catbalongan you can take a bus (P11.25, 2 hr.) to **Tacloban**.

Sweet Lines, Sulpicio Lines and William Lines run ships once or twice a week between Manila and Tacloban. Tourist class tickets are P143.50; 3rd class tickets cost P82.15. Check with MOT for exact days and times of departure.

If you're coming from Cebu, Western Samar Lines has two ships to Tacloban running alternate days of the week. The ships leave at 6 pm and arrive at 6 am (1st class, P42; 2nd class, P35).

From Cebu to Ormoc, catch the Aboitiz Line night ferry that runs daily except Sunday. The ferry leaves Cebu at 11 pm and arrives at 4 am. You are permitted however to sleep on board until dawn (2nd class, P24.50;

3rd class, P21).

From Surigao, Mindanao to Maasin, Leyte, take the ferry that leaves Surigao at noon and arrives at 5:45 pm (P20).

CEBU

Two Western Samar Lines ships leave on alternate days of the week from Tacloban to **Cebu** at 6 pm arriving in the early morning (1st class, P42; 2nd class, P35).

Aboitiz Shipping Lines has a trip every day except Sunday that leaves from Ormoc to Cebu at 10 pm and arrives in Cebu at 4 am (2nd class, P24.50; 3rd class, P21).

Sweet Lines, Sulpicio Lines, William Lines and Negros Navigation run ships once or twice weekly between Manila and Cebu leaving at 10 am and arriving at 8 am the next day (tourist class, P124; 3rd class, P89). These ships are like luxury liners.

From San Carlos, Negros, take one of three daily ferries (leaving at 6, 9:30, and 1:30) to Toledo and then take a bus to Cebu (1½ hr.). Total fare should be P21.

BOHOL

Tagbilaran can be reached by ferry from Cebu. There is a Sweet Lines ship that runs daily at noon arriving about 3:30-4 pm. The return trip begins at 11 pm and arrives at 3 am in Cebu (2nd class, P26; 3rd class, P20). Bohol is only accessible from Cebu.

NEGROS

To get to **Bacolod City** brom Cebu you must first take a bus to Toledo (1½ hr.), then take one of the three daily ferries (8, 11:30, & 3:30) to San Carlos (1 hr.). From San Carlos, take a bus to Bacolod (3-4 hr.). Total cost should be P25.

Negros Navigation Shipping Lines, as well as many others, offers transportation between Manila and Bacolod once or twice a week. Check with their office in Manila or Bacolod for the current schedule and fares.

To get to Bacolod from Iloilo, take one of the ferries which leave four times a day. The 2-hr. trip costs P10.

The George and Peter Lines serves **Dumaguete** from Cebu. There are several ships leaving at least twice a day every day except Sunday. Dumaguete to Cebu runs are frequent. Check with MOT for their current schedule. Fares start at P20.

George and Peter Lines ships also go on to Zamboanga (see **Transportation in Mindanao**).

Ceres Line buses run hourly (4:15 am-noon) between Dumaguete and Bacolod.

PANAY

If you're coming from Bacolod there is a regular ferry service (4 times a day) between Bacolod and **Iloilo** (P14, 2½ hr.).

To get to Iloilo from Manila you can take a Negros Navigation Shipping Line ship (it will stop first in Bacolod), leaving four times a week. The Williams and Sulpicio Lines also serve Manila-Iloilo and Cebu-Iloilo two or three times a week. Fares from Manila to Iloilo are P75.70 (3rd class) and P131 (tourist class).

Miag-ao and San Joaquin are on the main route to San Jose. Take the Seventy-Six Liner that departs every day from 5:30 am to 5 pm (P11) from Fuentes-DeLeon Sts.

Mindanao

Most of the Muslim peoples of the Philippines live on Mindanao (or nearby Sulu Archipelago), but they have never constituted a majority in the area as a whole. Heavy government-encouraged Christian migrations from the North has further diluted thier numbers, so that Muslims and other cultural minorities now account for only about 20% of the island's population. The Philippine government forces and the Muslim-successionist Moro National Liberation Front have been at war in Mindanao for years. For tourists the only relatively safe areas to see a dominant Muslim culture are Marawi and Zamboanga; other tourist areas are predominantly Christian. Check with MOT for the latest word on areas open to visitors.

Marawi City, one of the most Muslim of Philippine cities, lies in a cool area south of Iligan. Lake Lanao—the second largest lake in the country—lends its name to the region. The Maranaos excel in brassmaking, weaving and woodcarving. You can find their work in the Marawi market or at the non-profit shop of the artisans' co-op at Danasalen College where prices are fixed. Mindanao State University, 3 km. out of town, was founded to serve the region's Muslim population. A MOT office is located on campus at the Fort Guest House No. 2 (tel. 58-92-55). Both the campus and the city have been scenes of some of the Muslim-Government strife.

Cagayan de Oro, on Mindanao's north coast, is the center of the local pineapple industry. Stop by the MOT office on the ground floor of the GSP Bldg., Marcos Sports Center Complex (tel. 33-40), for tourist information. Take a bus headed for Butuan City but get off at Balingoan for **Camaguin Island**. Leave early in order to catch the morning ferry (P5) from Balingoan to Binone, Camaguin at 9 am (P8.50, 1½ hr.). From Binone take a jeepney (P2) to Mambajao. Within walking distance of Mambajao is Katibawasan Falls which has a nice pool for swimmng. A longer trek would be a hike to the lookout house of the Commission of Volcanology to glimpse the Hibok-hibok Volcano. White Island, off of Mambajao, is an excellent spot for snorkeling—if you don't have equipment it's useless to rent a banca since the island is just an enlarged sandbar sticking out of the sea.

PHILIPPINES 267

Davao, on the southeast coast of Mindanao, is a microcosm of ethnic diversity of the Philippines. Eighty percent of the inhabitants are migrants from other places in the Philippines with Cebuanos as the dominant group. Mixing with the 'natives,' these pioneer families have changed the character of Davao—from a sleepy town near mangrove swamps to a bustling cosmopolitan center of over 800,000 people. Look for the MOT office at the Apo View Hotel, J. Camus St. (tel. 74-86-1).

Getting around Davao: City jeepney don't follow standard routes but simply meander through the streets looking for passengers. People call out their destinations to passing jeepney drivers, who stop if they're going in that direction. If this is completely bewildering, then just flag down one of the local taxis, called mini-cars (standard fare within the city is P2).

Sample the many tropical fruits for which Davao is famous; lying outside the typhoon belt, Davao has fruits year round which are only seasonally available in Luzon and the Visayas. There's a large fruit market on Anda St., but you'll find better prices at stands along Ponciono Reyes St. near the big intersection. Try kilawin—marinated raw fish, something like sashimi—at small stalls along the waterfront, just to the left as you leave the pier area. You might try the local drink, lambanute, brewed from coconuts. It's great with lime juice, but be careful not to light a match or you'll end up on top of one of those coconut trees.

The Davao area offers good swimming and snorkeling. Though there are beaches within the city limits, better beaches can be found in **Talomo** (8 km. south), **Santa Cruz** (41 km. south), and **Digos** (59 km. south). For skin and scuba diving, head to **Palma Gil Island** (which is a 45-min. motorized banca ride from Davao City). The well-known Aguinaldo Pearl Farm has pretentiously changed its name to the Agro-Seafoods Corporation at Kaputian on **Samal Island**. There are demonstrations of pearl culture and a beach suited for skin and scuba diving as well as caves which had been used as burial places for the Kalagan and Isamal trives. The boat to Samal Island leaves only on weekends which is fine since the Farm is only open then. Leave from St. Ana pier at 8 am (P15). Rather than stay at the expensive hotel (P120/night) there, it's best to stay for the day and return to Davao at 3 pm.

If you are the adventurous sort, Davao will be your first stop on your way to the top of **Mt. Apo** (9696 ft.), the tallest peak in the Philippines. About a four-day journey up and back, the Mt. Apo climb will take you through moss-covered forests and volcanic areas of steaming springs and bubbling mud. The trip can be made at any time of the year but the drier months, March-May, are best. No special gear required (you can improvise on everything you need); the MOT office will provide

268 PHILIPPINES

itineries plus information on transport, hiring guides, etc.

Zamboanga, the 'city of flowers,' offers travelers a chance to learn something of the culture of the seafaring Muslim tribes. Check in first with the MOT office at the Lantaka Hotel on Valderoza St. (tel. 39-39). For local handicrafts, visit the Zamboanga market behind the City Hall, where you can bargain for cloth, brassware, mats and bamboo products. The Rocan Shell Shop has marvelous shells; there's a tourist outlet in the city but go to the factory itself on the outskirts of town.

A popular resort, 7 km. outside of Zamboanga, is **Pasonanca Park**. The park gardens are full of brightly colored tropical flowers. If you check in at the mayor's office you might be able to spend the night in a treehouse in the park. Just outside the city you can also visit Fort Pilar, built in the 17th century, and the nearby Muslim village of Rio Hondo. For swimming and snorkeling, head for **Santa Cruz Island**, not far from the city; take your own food and water. There is a Badjao cemetary just off the beach where the 'sea gypsies' come ashore to bury their dead and string up white cloth to ward off spirits. Bancas can be rented for the trip to the island (bargain after first asking around about prices).

ACCOMMODATIONS IN MINDANAO

Marawi City: There is a youth hostel at Mindanao State University (P15/night).

Cagayan de Oro: The Ambassador, D.A. Velez & Yacapin Sts. Single, P35; double, P56.

Casa Filipina, J.R. Borga St. (across from Gala Theatre). Single, P38; double, P56.

Mambajao, Camaguin Island: Mrs. Tia's Lodging House. No sign for Mrs. Tia's, just ask someone. P12 for a bed. Has good food.

Davao: Men Seng Hotel, San Pedro St. Single, P28; double, P44.

Lam Seng Lodge, San Pedro St. Single w/fan, P12; single w/ac, P30; double w/fan, P30.

Martinez Lodge, San Pedro St. Single w/fan, P12; double w/fan, P18-30.

Sta. Ana Lodge, R. Magsaysay Ave. Single w/fan, P10.

Zamboanga: Imperial Inn, Pura Brilliantes St. Single, P24; double, P45.
Old Astoria, Barcelona St. Single, P20; double, P35.
Bayview Hotel, Gov. Lim Ave. Single, P20; double, P35.

TRANSPORTATION FOR MINDANAO

Iligan, Cagayan de Oro, Davao and Zamboanga can be reached by ship from Manila and various ports in the Visayas. Below is a list of some of the possible combinations:

Manila-Cebu-Davao: The Sulpicio Lines ship leaves every Sunday at 10 am for Cebu. It then leaves Cebu every Monday at 11 am for Davao. The return trip leaves Wednesday at 8 pm (tourist class, P247; 3rd class, P149).

Manila-Zamboanga-Davao: William Lines has ships leaving 7 am every Thursday arriving in Zamboanga Friday noon. It reaches Davao early Saturday morning. Manila-Zamboanga: P216; Zamboanga-Davao: P129; Manila-Davao: P281.

Cebu-Cagayan De Oro: Sweet Lines has frequent ships. P58-75.

Iloilo-Zamboanga-Davao: Williams Lines has ships leaving Iloilo on Saturday at 7 pm which arrive in Zamboanga early Sunday. It departs from Zamboanga Sunday at 4 pm and arrives in Davao Monday at 5 pm. The return trip starts on Tuesday at 1 am, and arrives in Zamboanga on Wednesday at 8 am. From Zamboanga it departs at 4 pm on Wednesday and returns to Iloilo at 10 am on Thursday.

Check with MOT or at the shipping line offices for details (for instance, in Davao all the offices are on Alvarez St.).

Good roads link Davao with Cagayan de Oro via Butuan City (10-11 hr.). You could also take a bus from Surigao and go to either Cagayan de Oro or Davao. All the Davao bus stations are located near the large public market.

Bankerohan, Bachelor Express, on E. Quirino Ave. between Mt. Apo and San Pedro Sts., and Surigao Bus Lines, corner of Pichon and E. Quirino, both have buses leaving hourly for Butuan (P45). Mintranco Bus, next to Bachelor Express, has buses serving destinations to the south and west (Mt. Apo and the beaches).

Bibliography

The Philippines, by Onofre Corpuz. General background reading. Corpuz is president of the University of the Philippines, Diliman; a highly respected man.

Philippines—A Past Revisited and **A Continuing Past**, by Renato Constantino. Gives an enlightening interpretation of Philippine history. The second volume picks up where the first leaves off (the beginning of WWII).

Tarong: An Ilocos Barrio in the Philippines, by W. & C. Nydegger. One part of a six-culture series on socialization processes in different cultures.

Roger's Do-It-Yourself Tours, by Roger Olivares. Written primarily for Filipino families and foreign residents. Though it sometimes assumes you have access to a private car, it covers Luzon's main attractions in great detail.

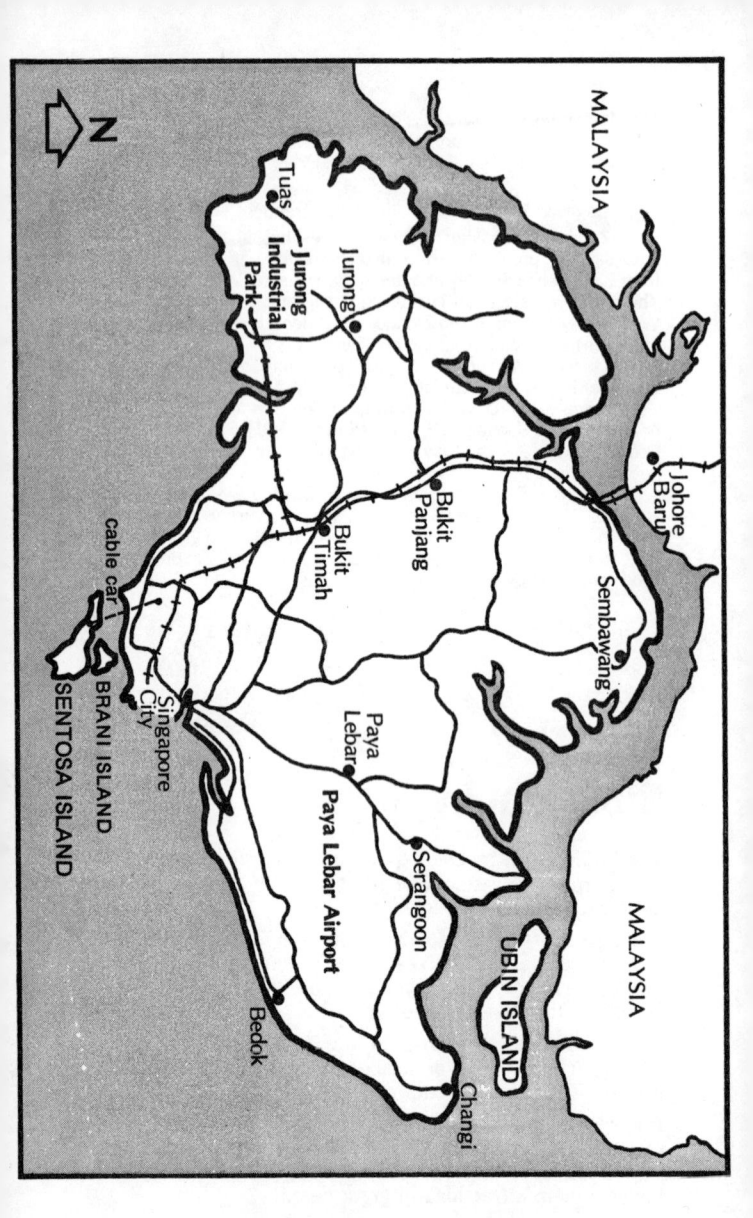

SINGAPORE

General Information

Arrival: If you arrive by plane, stop at the airport's STPB Information Counter for maps and pamphlets. From the airport at Paya Lebar, 10 km from downtown Singapore, take bus #92 (Jln. Besar, Bencoolen St., Orchard Rd., Penang Rd.) or bus #91 (Beach Rd., Connaught Dr., Shenton Way, Prince Edward Rd.). The buses leave roughly every 15 min., 6 am-11:35 pm (bus #92 runs until midnight), from the bus stop in the parking lot across the street from the terminal (S$.70). Taxi fare from the airport is about S$5, plus a S$1.50 surcharge (for all taxis hired from the airport). [Note: A new international airport is scheduled to open at Changi, on the east side of the island, in mid-1981. Travelers arriving there can find out how to get into town by public transportation at the airport's information center.] If you arrive at the train station on Keppel Rd., on the southern edge of the city, take bus #20 (Cecil St., Empress Place, St. Andrew's Rd., Stamford Rd., Victoria St., Middle Rd., Selegie Rd.), bus #146 (Cecil St., Empress Place, St. Andrew's Rd., Stamford Rd., Orchard Rd., Selegie Rd., Serangoon Rd.), or bus #176 (Robinson Rd., Empress Place, St. Andrew's Rd., Stamford Rd., Victoria St.). Taxis from the train station to various parts of the city cost S$3-4.

After getting settled, head for the nearest bookstore to buy a Singapore Bus Guide (S$.50).

Departure: The airport departure tax is S$10, or S$4 if you're flying to Malaysia.

Currency: The exchange rate in November 1980 was 2.1 Singapore dollars (S$2.10) to the U.S. dollar. There are lots of money changers in Singapore, especially near the intersection of Chulia and Market Sts., but in summer 1980 many of them were refusing to change travelers' checks.

Visas: Visas are not required for Commonwealth citizens or nationals of the Netherlands and Switzerland. Citizens of the United States, Japan, and many West European countries may visit for up to three months without a visa; they're given permission to stay 14 days on arrival, and can get extensions of 3 to 4 weeks at a time from the Immigration Office at Empress Place. Nationals of most other countries may stay in Singapore up to 14 days without a visa.

Climate: Tropical; hot and humid year round. No defined wet and dry seasons, but more rain Oct.-Feb.

Sources of Information

Singapore Tourist Promotion Board (STPB), 131 Tudor Court, Tanglin Rd.; tel. 2356611. Pick up their free publications: "Welcome to Singapore," and the "Singapore Weekly Guide" (a map is attached inside the back cover). Open 8-5 daily, except Sundays and holidays.

STPB Information Counter, Airport Arrival Hall; tel. 888321, ext. 565. Open 6 am-10 pm daily.

Background

The Republic of Singapore consists of one main island (only 42 km long and 22½ km wide) and 54 much smaller ones. Except for the central plateau, most of the island of Singapore is low-lying and originally was covered with swamps and jungle; it's connected with Johor Baru, Malaysia by the Johore Causeway. The city of Singapore sits on the island's southern edge. This tiny nation of 2.4 million people, completely devoid of natural resources, has had to rely on free trade and its strategic location for its existence, and has thrived. Singapore boasts the third largest port in the world, and the third largest oil refinery.

You can tell that Singapore is unusual as soon as you start heading into town. There are so many well-tended trees and shrubs that parts of the city look like manicured parks. Everything is so organized—cars and taxis obey the traffic lights, pedestrians cross in the crosswalks, and the streets are immaculate.

There's a price for all this tidiness. In contrast to some countries, the energetic Singaporean government enforces its laws with a singular thoroughness and impartiality; littering carries a fine of up to S$500, as does smoking in public places (buses, theaters, etc.). A particular vision of Singaporean society is also promoted by hortatory campaigns; in mid-1980 posters all over the city urged people to go "Into the 1980s with Determination and Fortitude," and to "Make GENUINE SMILE our Way of Life." Campaigns in the last decade have ranged from "Garden City" and "Gracious Living" (disparaging a single-minded money orientation and urging more aesthetic sensibility) to "Use Your Hands" (encouraging students not to look down on manual labor) and "Two is Enough" (family planning).

SINGAPORE

Singapore is unique in that over 95% of its population is urban. While the majority of the people in neighboring Asian countries are engaged in agriculture, this island nation must import its entire food supply. Singapore's thriving economy is built on commercial, manufacturing, and financial activity. It's one of the world's largest oil refining and distributing centers, a leader in shipbuilding, and a major world supplier of electronic components. More than 200 shipping lines use its port.

Given Singapore's urban nature, it's not surprising that housing is a major concern. The government decided two decades ago that it needed to deal with the problem in a systematic fashion, so it set up a Housing and Development Board (HDB). New towns and housing estates were constructed during the following 20 years, and by early 1980 70% of Singapore's population was living in government-subsidized HDB housing. In spite of the speed with which these estates are being built, they can't keep up with the demand; thousands of people are on waiting lists to buy or rent flats. Much HDB construction work is going on in downtown Singapore as well as in the new towns; most of the older, more traditional sections of the city, like Chinatown, are scheduled to be razed.

Singapore's extensive contact with neighboring Asian civilizations and western colonial empires can be traced back to the 14th century, when this 'seatown' was established at the western entrance to the trading routes of the South China Sea. At one time a Malay capital of the Srivijaya Empire, Singapore came under the control of the Siamese for a short period before the arrival of western colonial powers. The roots of British influence in Singapore were firmly established in 1819, when Stamford Raffles of the East India Company concluded a treaty here with Sultan Hussein Mohammed Shah and Temenggong Abdul Rahman, authorizing the establishment of a company trading post at the mouth of the Singapore River. By 1826 Malacca and Penang had joined Singapore (then collectively called the "Straits Settlements") to become important bases for British seapower and international trade.

Except for a short period of Japanese occupation during WWII, the British administered Singapore from 1824 until 1959, when the island became an independent state. The large Chinese population of present-day Singapore is descended from the great number of Chinese merchants who settled here during the 19th and 20th centuries. Singapore joined Malaya, Sabah, and Sarawak as a member state of the Federation of Malaysia in 1963, but later seceded from the Federation to become an independent republic in 1965. Singapore is governed by the People's Action Party, headed by Prime Minister Lee Kuan Yew.

274 SINGAPORE

NOTE: Singapore is not the place to take chances with drugs. The death penalty is mandatory for anyone trafficking more than 15 grams of heroin or morphine, and even tiny quantities of hash can get you expelled or hit with a heavy fine.

Culture and Customs

Singapore's population is 76% Chinese, 15% Malay, 7% Indian, and the rest European or others. "Nonya" and "baba" are terms for Straits-born Chinese who have adopted the indigenous language and lifestyle.

In general, Chinesé are Buddhist, Taoist, or Confucian; Malays and Pakistanis are Moslem; Indians are Hindu or Moslem, and Europeans and Eurasians are Christian.

Each culture has its own customs and traditions in the home, but it's becoming more difficult to maintain ethnic identities in fast-changing Singaporean society. The government-subsidized housing projects are creating new patterns of life for the majority of Singaporeans; distinctive cultural communities are gradually disappearing.

But a rich variety of traditions are still observed in this bustling city. Hardly a week passes without a ceremony or celebration of some kind, whether it be a Chinese clan procession, a Hindu rite, or a Moslem holiday. Since these festivals do not follow the Gregorian calendar, check with the STPPB for the dates of upcoming celebrations (see the "Singapore Weekly Guide").

Language

Most Singaporeans are bilingual, and many speak three or four languages and dialects. While Malay is the national language, English is the language of business and administration and is widely understood. Mandarin, formerly the dialect of the Imperial Chinese court and scholars, is the official Chinese language, but the majority of Singapore Chinese speak Hokkien as their native dialect. Other Chinese dialects include Cantonese,

Teochew, Hakka, Hamanese, and Foochow. However, the government is now trying to eliminate dialects; only Mandarin is taught in schools. Tamil, widely spoken in southeast India, is the official Indian language; other languages used by the Indian and Pakistani communities include Telegu, Urdu, Malayam, Punjabi, Gujerati, Hindi, and Bengali.

Food

Adventurous gourmets will have a field day in Singapore. Distinctive versions of Malay, Indian, Chinese, and European dishes are widely available at reasonable prices; there's also an intriguing local cuisine called nyonya cooking.

Nonya cooking is frequently overshadowed by the immense variety of Chinese cuisines. It features Chinese ingredients—such as pork, dried mushrooms, and soy sauce—cooked Malay style, with lots of coconut milk, scented roots and grasses, spices, and chili. Nonya dishes are often sold at food stalls; look for **sambal** (a spicy prawn stew served with rice), **mee siam** (very thin rice noodles fried with vegetables and topped with a bean curd or peanut gravy and slices of hardboiled egg), and **laksa** (noodles in a spicy coconut sauce sprinkled with herbs).

Noodles (mee) will be the mainstay of the budget traveler's diet. There's a great variety to choose from, including wheat noodles (yellow) and rice noodles (white, either threadlike or in flat strips), fried or cooked in a soup with different types of meat and vegetables. A lunch for two in a noodle shop might include two bowls of noodles with fish balls, green onions, meat, and prawns (a Singapore specialty), and a plate of fried black noodles with clams, bean sprouts, and chili—all for S$4-5. **Hokkien mee** is another standard Singaporean noodle dish, made with pork and prawns; **mee goreng** (Indian-style noodles) consists of fried egg noodles cooked in chili sauce with egg, vegetables, and whatever else is available; **mee rebus** (Malay-style noodles) features noodles in a spicy gravy garnished with bean sprouts and slices of hardboiled egg and soybean cake.

A big local favorite is **chicken rice** (kai fan), a Hainanese dish: boiled or roast chicken served with rice cooked in chicken stock. Simple and filling, it usually costs S$1.50-2, depending on the amount of chicken.

Rojak, the Singapore version of a tropical salad, consists of cucumber, bean sprouts, pineapple, soybean cake, and turnips, served with a tangy dressing made of shrimp paste, tamarind juice, sugar, crushed groundnuts, and chili. Give it a try.

All the dishes described above and many more are available at **food stalls**, usually for S$1-3. All stalls are licensed and

276 SINGAPORE

inspected by the government, so you don't need to worry about hygienic standards. They used to be dispersed throughout the city, but in recent years the ever-efficient government has taken to rounding them up into official clusters, usually referred to as hawkers' centres. The list below is far from exhaustive:

- **Newton Circus**—one of the most popular hawker's centres, located on the northwest edge of town at the intersection of Clemenceau Ave. and Bukit Timah Rd.

- **Telok Ayer Market**—over 100 stalls selling Chinese, Malay, and Indian food (fried oysters, S$1.50). Located in the financial district, on Robinson Rd. and Cross St. Only open during the day; local office workers eat lunch here, so go early to get a seat.

- **Capitol Food Centre**—behind the Capitol Shopping Centre on North Bridge Rd. just south of Stamford Rd. (Turtle soup S$1.50, satay S$.20/stick, fresh watermelon juice S$.50.)

- **Cuppage Rd.**—a scaled-down version of the once famous, now disbanded Orchard Rd. Carpark Hawker's Centre. On the north side of Orchard Rd. (Try the turtle soup.)

- **The Satay Club**—has a good selection of Malay and Indian dishes. On Queen Elizabeth Walk overlooking what was once a harbor and is now reclaimed land. Open evenings only.

- **Rasa Singapura**—a Tourist Promotion Board Project; the 29 stalls are said to have been chosen as Singapore's best. Prices may be slightly higher than those at other centers. Located behind the STPB office, next to the Singapore Handicrafts Centre.

- **Empress Place Food Centre**—a large collection of stalls on the banks of the Singapore River, just off the waterfront. Watch the tugs and barges chug up and down.

- **Boat Quay Food Centre**—across the river from Empress Place.

- **Glutton's Corner**—on the bottom floor of the Tanjong Pagar Shopping Complex at the corner of Tanjong Pagar and Keppel Rds. (near the railway station). The Jubilee Cafe & Restaurant has a branch here.

- **Botanical Gardens Food Centre**—opposite the Botanical Gardens on Cluny Rd. Try the fruit drinks.

- **Hong Lim Food Centre**—on Upper Hokien St. between North and South Bridge Rds.

- Not all hawkers' centres are formally organized and named. You can still find plenty of unofficial ones if you keep your eyes open. The financial/business district, between Chinatown and the harbor, is a good hunting ground because hawkers give good value in order to attract regular customers among local office workers. Here's two to get you started: the alley off McCallum St. between Robinson Rd. and Cecil St. (huge helping of chicken beriyani, S$2.20) and the alley off Chulia St. between Market and Philip Sts.

The sidewalks of **China St.** in Chinatown overflow nightly with one-person restaurants; comparatively few travelers eat here. More famous (and thus more expensive) nighttime food stalls attract throngs of tourists on **Albert**, **Hokkien**, and **Bugis Sts**.

Singapore has some excellent **seafood restaurants**. A string of great ones with outdoor tables can be found on Changi Rd. in the Bedok area, on the east side of the island (take buses #10,

11, 12, and 14, among others), and along Ponggol Rd. (bus #82 or 83) on the northeast side. They're moderately priced; a dinner of the famous local dish—**chilli crab**—costs S$10-12 for two, including beer (check price when you order). Ask for some bread to sop up the sauce after you finish the crab meat. As with all Chinese meals, it would be best to go in a large group (cheaper and more variety).

Indian cuisine can be roughly divided into northern and southern varieties. Northern Indian dishes are milder, often eaten with wheat bread; try **tandoori chicken**. Southern Indian food is more heavily seasoned, usually served with rice; **chicken beriyani** is a typical dish.

Consult the "Singapore Weekly Guide" for more details on eating in Singapore.

Restaurants

Komala Vilas, 76/78 Serangoon Rd.

Excellent South Indian vegetarian food. Open 5:30 am to 10 pm. In the evening (after 7)—you'll be served 5 or 6 curries, rice, chutney and poppadum (a kind of bread) on a banana leaf with small bowls of yogurt and 'pepper water' on the side—a very filling meal for only S$2.50. Eat with your right hand (never the left) like everyone else; there are sinks where you can wash up before and after.

Rendezvous Restaurant, on Bras Basah Rd. across from the Cathay Cinema (1 block up from Bencoolen St.).

A popular spot serving Padang dishes (beef rendang, egg sambal, etc.) and Malay curries. Choose what you want to eat at the front counter before sitting down; S$4-6/person.

Jubilee Cafe & Restaurant and **Islamic Restaurant**, a block apart on North Bridge Rd. (771/773 and 795/797 respectively), just north of Arab St.

Both specialize in Indian Muslim dishes. Fine curries, beriyani, chapati. Chicken beriyani at the Jubilee, S$3; mutton mysore, S$2.20.

Yaohan Dept. Store, in the Plaza Singapura near the foot of Orchard Rd.

Lots of cheap snack bars in the basement, including Chinese and Japanese 'delis' and two bakeries. They're next to the grocery store, said to be one of the largest in Southeast Asia.

Song Heng Wee, at the corner of Middle Rd. & Bencoolen St.

A traveler's hangout serving a wide variety of dishes; huge menus are posted on the wall. Prawn fried rice, S$2-4; toast, butter, & marmalade S$.70; fried vegetables w/abalone, S$6-10.

278 SINGAPORE

Jockey Pub, 2nd floor, Shaw Center, Scotts Rd. (just off Orchard Rd.; entrance is on side facing Holiday Inn, on Claymore Hill Rd.).

The pub's attractions are not food (too expensive) but beer and entertainment. Jazz workshop every Sunday, 3-6 pm, no cover, beer costs S$3.40.

Ginivy Restaurant & Lounge, ground floor, International Bldg. (next to Lido Cinema), Orchard Rd. (near intersection w/Scotts Rd.).

Live country western music every night; no cover, but the price of a beer goes up from S$3.10 to S$4.15 when the music starts. Specializes in Mexican and Italian food (not too expensive if you order carefully): spaghetti S$6-7, 2 enchiladas S$6.50. Open til 1 am every night except Sunday, when it's open til 11 pm.

Accommodations

Low-cost accommodations are getting harder to find in Singapore, especially in the central part of the city. Even in those well-known hunting grounds for cheap hotels—Bencoolen St. (between Bras Basah Rd. and Albert St.) and Beach Rd. (between Bras Basah Rd. and Rochor Rd.)—urban renewal is making inroads, the hotels are often full, and prices have been climbing sharply for several years. The accommodations listed below are loosely grouped by area in order to make it easier for you to find alternatives if the first place(s) you go to are full. Especially for the Ys it is worth the effort to make reservations in advance.

NOTE: Most 'single' rooms have double beds.

Northeast Area:

To get to these hotels (and other hotels similar in style and price nearby) take bus #92 from the airport. From the train station, take bus #146 and get off on Serangoon Rd. at Petain Rd. or Lavender St. and walk southeast (to the right). Serangoon Rd. is parallel to and 1 block northwest of Jln. Besar, which is a 1-way street.)

Palace Hotel, 407 Jln. Besar (just south of intersection with Lavender St.); tel. 2583108.

Single S$14, double S$16. Airy, spacious rooms.

Singapore Island Hotel, 315 Jln. Besar (at corner of Jln. Besar & Petain Rd.); tel. 2583337.

Single S$14; double S$16, w/ac S$18.

International Hotel, 290 Jln. Besar (two blocks south of Lavender St.); tel. 2583347.

Single S$20; double S$22, w/bath S$26. All rooms w/ac. Has a restaurant downstairs.

Bencoolen St. area:

Near the middle of the city. Take bus #92 from the airport or bus #125 or #176 from the train station.

YWCA, 6/8 Fort Canning Rd. (near intersection of Bencoolen St. & beds/room). Single S$20, w/ac S$23; double S$24, w/ac S$32, w/bath & ac, S$35. Has hot water.

YMCA, "A" Orchard Rd. (just above intersection w/Bencoolen St.); tel. 3377638.

Men only. Single w/bath S$18, double w/bath S$28. A more expensive, out-of-the-way Y, the **YMCA Tanglin Centre**, at 60 Stevens Rd. (near the Botanic Gardens—a 15-min. walk from Orchard Rd.), offers rooms w/bath, ac, & TV. Double S$40-48 (single occupancy S$5 less), triple S$50-58.

Tiong Hoa Hotel, 6 Prinsep St. (near intersection w/Bras Basah Rd., one block inland from Bencoolen St.); tel. 3384522.

Double S$31, w/ac S$35-S$37. (All w/shared bath.)

South Asia Hotel, 12 Bencoolen St.; tel. 3370034.

Single S$18-20, w/bath S$22, w/bath & ac S$27; double S$26, w/bath S$28, w/bath & ac S$33; triple w/bath & ac S$35.

San Wah Hotel, 36 Bencoolen St.; tel. 2362428.

Single S$22, double S$24, w/ac S$28. Quiet, set slightly back from the street.

Peony Mansion, 46/52 Bencoolen St., 5th floor, #50E.

Dorm bed S$5, room w/2 beds S$6. Clean, fairly quiet. Take the elevator at the back of the building.

Kian Hua Hotel, 81 Bencoolen St.; tel. 3383492.

Single S$15, double S$18-22.

Nam Hai Hotel, 166 Bencoolen St.; tel. 3375395.

Single S$14, double S$16, triple S$21.

Bencoolen Street Service Apartment, 173D/175D Bencoolen St. (opposite the Nam Hai Hotel); tel. 323914.

Dorm bed S$7, double S$16-24. If rooms are full, you can sleep on a mattress on the floor for S$5. Also has lockers. Friendly management. Take the elevator at the back; the manager's office is on the 4th floor.

South East Asia Hotel, 190 Waterloo St. (near intersection w/Rochor Rd.); tel. 3382394/6.

Single S$28, double S$34. All rooms w/bath & ac.

Beach Rd. area:

Beach Rd. is parallel to Bencoolen St. and five blocks nearer the harbor; take bus #91 from the airport or bus #20 from the train station.

Hai Chew Hotel, 35 Beach Rd. (corner of Purvis St.); tel. 3380578.

Single (1 person) S$16, double S$22, triple S$28.

Shang Onn Hotel, 37 Beach Rd. (corner of Purvis St., opposite Hai Chew Hotel); tel. 3384153.

Single S$16, double S$18.

Hai Hin Hotel, 97A Beach Rd. (corner of Liang Seah St.); tel. 3363739.

Single S$16-17, double S$20. Nice rooms.

New 7th Storey Hotel, 228/229 Rochor Rd. (between North Bridge Rd. and Beach Rd.); tel. 3370251/4.

Single S$34, w/bath S$43; double S$44, w/bath S$53. A large hotel with restaurant and bar.

280 SINGAPORE

Southwest area:

This area is very near the train station. From the airport take bus #91 to Prince Edward Rd., parallel to & 1 block north of Palmer Rd. From Prince Edward Rd. walk 1 block south on Shenton Way and turn left onto Palmer Rd.

YMCA International Centre ("Metropolitan YMCA"), 70 Palmer Rd; tel. 2224666.

Single w/shared bath (men only) S$13, w/ac S$18; double w/bath & ac S$30 (single occupancy S$25); triple w/bath & ac S$40. From the train station walk east on Keppel Rd. until it deadends. Turn left, then right onto Palmer Rd. A 10-min. walk.

Station Hotel, Railway Station, Keppel Rd.; tel. 2221551.

Single S$24, double S$34. All rooms w/bath & ac.

Transportation

INTERNATIONAL: There is excellent **bus** service between Singapore and Malaysia. Buses to Johor Baru, just across the causeway, leave roughly every 10 min. from the Rochor Centre at the corner of Waterloo St. and Rochor Rd. (S$.80). The main terminus for express buses bound for other Malaysian cities is located in the New Bridge Road parking lot ('car park') on the southwest side of the city near the intersection of New Bridge and Neil Rds. Buses leave daily: for Butterworth/Penang at 7 pm (14 hr.; S$28, ac only), for Kuala Lumpur at 9 am and 9 pm (8 hr.; S$13, or S$16 ac), for Kuantan at 9 am, 10 am, and 10 pm (7½ hr.; S$11, or S$15 ac), for Kuala Trengganu at 8 am and 8 pm (12 hr.; S$17.50, non-ac only), and for Kota Bharu at 7:30 am, 5:30 pm, and 7:30 pm (14 hr.; S$23, or S$27 ac). The ticket office is open every day, 7:30 am-8 pm; tel. 2216601/3. Buses to Malacca start from in front of the Malacca-Singapore Express Bus office at 23 Beach Rd. (tel. 326337), leaving at 8, 9:30, 11 (ac), 2 and 3. Fare for the 5+ hr. trip is S$8/S$11 (ac). For all express buses, it's advisable to book a day or two in advance.

To take **shared taxis** to various destinations in Malaysia, you must first go to Johor Baru. Take the bus (mentioned above) or a taxi from the Rochor Centre; Taxi fare is S$4.

Six **trains** connect Singapore with Kuala Lumpur daily, the speediest of which are the Expres Rakyat (People's Express) and the Ekspres KTM. The former leaves Singapore at 8 am and arrives in KL at 2:30 pm, the latter leaves at 1:15 pm and arrives at 7 pm; on either train the fare is S$15.50 (or S$26 for an ac coach). The other four trains are slower and slightly cheaper 'ordinary' and 'express' trains. The most convenient train for those going to Butterworth (the station serving Penang) is again the Ekspres Rakyat, which leaves KL after a half hour stopover and arrives in Butterworth at 9:15 pm. The fare is S$27.60 (or S$46 for an ac coach). Berths are available on express trains (all kinds) for S$4 (upper)/S$6 (lower) in second class or S$7.50 (ordinary)/S$15 (ac) in first class. Three times a week you can make connections through to Bangkok, by changing in Butterworth to the Ekspres Antarabangsa (International Express) which leaves Mondays, Wednesdays and Fridays at 7:55 am. For more details, see the **International Transportation** section of the Malaysia chapter. Singapore's railway station is on Keppel Rd., on the south side of the city (tel. 2225165).

It's possible to travel cheaply if not comfortably to Jakarta or Medan, Indonesia, by **ship**. All the fares listed below include a 5-6 hr. boat ride from Singapore to the small island of Tanjung Pinang and a 15-min. sampan ride from the island to the KM Tampomas (Indonesia's Pelni Lines). Deck-class fare to Jakarta is S$106, while second- and first-class cabins cost S$138-157. The ship leaves from Tanjung Pinang for Jakarta every Saturday at 5 pm (local time, 30 min. less than Singapore time), arriving Monday morning. Deck-class fare to Medan is S$111, and cabins cost S$141-177. The ship sails from Tanjung Pinang for Belawan (the port serving Medan) every Wednesday at 6 am (local time), arriving Thursday afternoon. For more details and bookings, contact German Asian Travels (PTE) Ltd., Straits Trading Bldg., 1303/4, 9 Battery Rd. (near Empress Place); tel. 435466 or 91516/7. German Asian Travels can also provide information about other Pelni routes and schedules, and can even sell tickets for the Pelni ship which connects Padang and Ujung Pandang via Jakarta.

INTRA-CITY: Singapore **bus** service is fast, reliable, and cheap. It will be worth your time to take a few minutes to figure out how to use it effectively. First buy a Singapore Bus Service (SBS) guide—only S$.50, available at most bookstores. The guide includes a detailed map with a very helpful index on one side. Keep in mind that many of Singapore's streets are one-way. These are the main arteries (listed in opposite direction pairs): Orchard Rd. and Orchard Blvd./Penang Rd., Bencoolen St./Jln. Besar and Selegie Rd./Serangoon Rd., Victoria St. and North Bridge Rd., New Bridge Rd. and South Bridge Rd., and Anson Rd./Robinson Rd. and Shenton Way. Several different kinds of buses operate within the city—the red and grey buses are the ones run by the SBS. (Bus stops sometimes have more than one sign listing the numbers of buses which stop; the white numbers on red boards are for SBS buses.) Many SBS buses still have ticket sellers, and fares are charged according to distance traveled (S$.30-S$.70), so have a destination in mind. 'Oneman-operation' (OMO) buses, however, charge a flat fare, usually S$.70—it will be clearly posted outside the bus and on the coin box. Pay with exact change. Buses run from 6 am to 11:30 pm or midnight.

SBS bus service is supplemented during much of the day by a variety of smaller private shuttle buses, usually yellow or blue. They have signs on the side listing the main roads of their routes; fares are usually S$.30-.60.

Catch **taxis** at marked taxi stands, or anywhere double yellow lines are painted on the edge of the street. Taxi fare is S$1 for the first mile (S$1.20 for air-conditioned taxis) and 20 cents for each additional half mile. There is an extra 10-cent charge for each passenger in excess of two, plus 10 cents for each piece of luggage. From 1 to 6 am, a 60% surcharge is added to the fare. If the meter is 'out of order,' look for another taxi.

Exploring Singapore

In Town

Thieves Market fills the small streets just east of the intersection of Jln. Besar and Weld Rd. every day from mid-afternoon until late at night. Years ago you could shop here mid-day for things stolen from you the night before. Today you can buy fake antiques, watches, pirated cassette tapes (not the best quality but quite cheap), radios, silver and brassware, army surplus gear, walking sticks, motorcycle parts, and handicrafts. Bargaining is mandatory, of course.

The **National Museum & Art Gallery** at Stamford Rd. and Bencoolen St. exhibits porcelain, jade, and Indonesian and Malay crafts, as well as an extensive art collection. Also has displays on the history of Singapore. Open 10:30 am-7 pm daily.

The bulldozers are always busy in Singapore, thanks to nonstop urban redevelopment, but they haven't yet completely flattened **Chinatown**, the heart of the traditional Chinese community. It's centered in the area between South Bridge Rd. and New Bridge Rd., where markets and food stalls still line many of the alleys between streets. The Singapore River, which winds its way through Chinatown's warehouses and tenements, is an important artery of the 'old life.' Workers still haul 100 lb. sacks of rice from lighters to godowns, and families which have been controlling the longshoring for generations still maintain their riverside houses and temples. Look on Telok Ayer St. for the Thian Hock Keng Temple, the city's oldest Buddhist temple. Old people come to stay in Sago Lane 'death houses' because death in a home brings bad luck. (Mr. Lim Kim Guan, a guide who can be reached at 641-733, gives excellent tours of Chinatown and the riverfront area, 3-4 hr. long; S$4.)

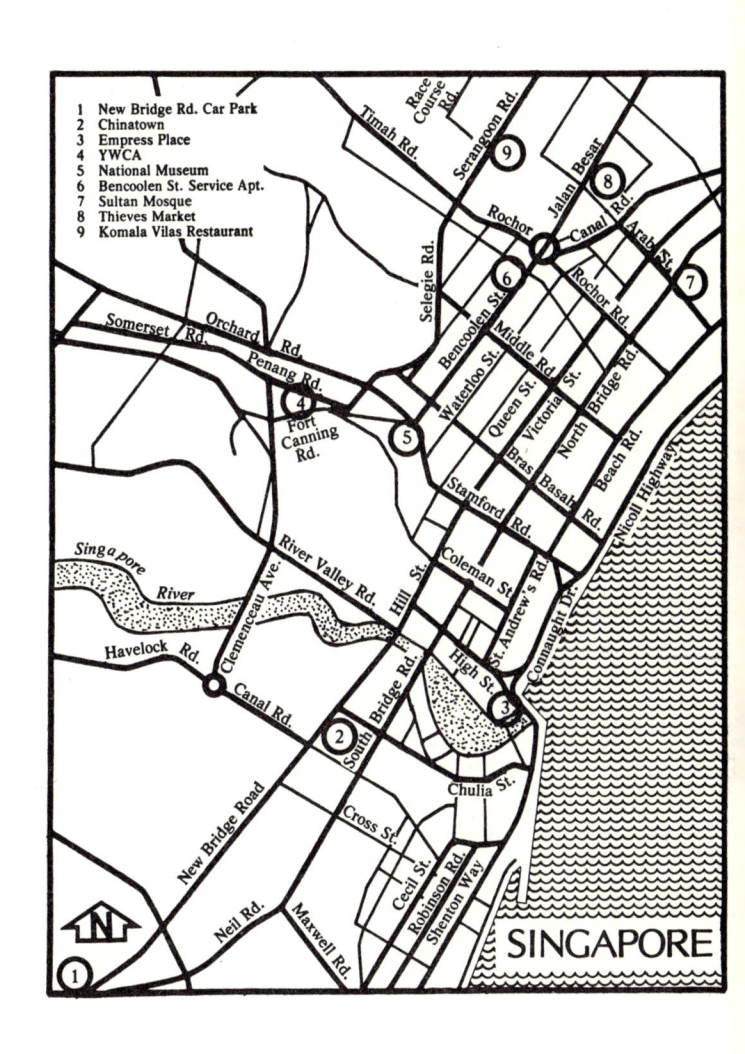

SINGAPORE 283

1 New Bridge Rd. Car Park
2 Chinatown
3 Empress Place
4 YWCA
5 National Museum
6 Bencoolen St. Service Apt.
7 Sultan Mosque
8 Thieves Market
9 Komala Vilas Restaurant

One of Singapore's most lively Indian communities can be found in the area around **Serangoon Rd.**, where vegetarian restaurants, Hindu temples, and sprawling markets serve several thousand Indian Singaporeans. The streets are lined with the shops of dealers in tea, joss, and madras textiles, and scents of curry, incense, and flowers (sold for offerings) fill the air.

The **Arab Street** area, one of the oldest districts in the city, was once the hub of a much larger Malay and Indian community. At Arab St. and North Bridge Rd. stands the **Masjid Sultan** (Sultan Mosque), Singapore's largest, built in accord with Moorish tradition though it was designed by the firm of Swan & MacLaren. Moslems come from all over the city to worship here at midday on Friday. Nearby there are lots of small shops and cloth stores.

The **Sakya Muni Buddha Gaya Temple** (Temple of a Thousand Lights), on the northern side of the city at 366 Race Course Rd., houses a huge seated Buddha. Follow the story of Buddha's life in panels around the base; a much smaller Buddha reclines in a small chamber at the back, below the seated Buddha. The **Srinivasa Perumal Temple** is close by, at 397 Serangoon Rd. On the other side of town, visit the **Sri Marriamman Temple** on South Bridge Rd.—built in 1827. This temple, dedicated to a goddess who cures epidemic diseases, is the site of fire-walking and flesh-piercing rituals several times each year.

Details on the Van Kleef Aquarium, the House of Jade, and other popular tourist spots can be found in the "Singapore Weekly Guide."

Outside the City

You can trek around in primary jungle in the **Bukit Timah Nature Reserve**, half an hour north of downtown Singapore. Unfortunately, the drumming of the cicadas, the twittering of birds, and other familiar jungle sounds are punctuated at certain times of day by blasting in the quarries which lie in or near the reserve. An inexpensive pamphlet with a map is sold at the main gate describing the reserve and suggesting 4 hiking routes (ranging from 1 to 2½ hr. roundtrip); the trails are well-marked. The entrance to the reserve is at the 7½ milestone (11 km) on Upper Bukit Timah Rd. Take bus #172, 180-2, or 193 and get off opposite the Gala Theatre at the Bukit Timah Shopping Centre, then walk a few hundred meters further till you see a sign on the right. Turn in and walk about 1 km to the main gate.

The 80-acre **Botanic Gardens**, on Cluny Rd. off Napier Rd. on the northwest edge of the city, have ornamental plants, orchids, etc., as well as magnificent trees. At dawn watch Chinese practicing tai chi chuan near the still lake. Open 5 am-10 pm daily. (Bus service: #7, 95, 106, 112, 174, 188, 190, and 191.)

Quite different but at least as famous are the **Tiger Balm Gardens**, on Pasir Panjang Rd. on the south side of the island. Founded by the family which made and makes millions from Tiger Balm all-purpose medicine, these 'gardens' are more like fantasy in lavender, turquoise, and fluorescent pink: scenes from Chinese folklore and myths, sometimes with little morality lessons, plus other tableaux that defy easy classification. Take bus #10, 30, 143, 145, 146, or 192.

If you're partial to pelicans or fond of pheasants, the **Jurong Bird Park** in the industrial town of Jurong on the west side of the island is a must. There are more than 7,000 birds in this large park, many of which look like they flew out of the pages of a Dr. Seuss book. It's open from 9 am till 6:30 pm on weekdays, till 7 on weekends and holidays; admission is S$2.50. To get there take bus #10, 30, 183, 196, 197, or 198 to the Jurong Interchange and switch to bus #250 for the 3-4 min. ride to the park.

While you're in the area, visit the **Chinese Garden** (Yu Hwa Yuan) and the **Japanese Garden** (Seiwaen) on Yuan Ching Rd., only a short hop by bus from the Jurong Interchange; take bus #240, 242, or 246. Both are open 8 am to 7 pm daily (but no admission after 6 pm) and charge small admission fees. For S$2 you can visit both, located within easy walking distance of each other.

Traditional Malay communities can still be found at the edges of Singapore Island, particularly in the Sembawang area to the north and in the fishing villages on the east coast near **Changi**. Pulau Tekong, an island a short ferry ride from Changi, has nice beaches, a small village, and a few small rubber holdings and tapioca plantations.

The Port of Singapore Authority (PSA) operates several remarkably cheap **cruises** around Singapore Harbor and small neighboring islands from the World Trade Center (WTC) Ferry Terminal. Two-hour cruises through the harbor's busy boat traffic, with a stop at Sentosa Island, start at 10, 12:30 and 3

Monday through Saturday (S$1). An 'evening cruise' around Kusu and St. John's Islands starts every day at 7:15 (S$2). Or, take the Kusu and St. John's Ferry, which leaves at 9, 11:20, 2 and 4:20 Monday through Saturday (S$3 roundtrip); more frequent departures on Sunday. The WTC Ferry Terminal is west of the city, on Telok Belangah Rd.; take bus #10, 20, 30, 61, 125, 143, 145, 146, or 176.

Ferries also shuttle regularly between the WTC Ferry Terminal and **Sentosa Island**, a short trip to the south. Sentosa is a resort with a roller skating rink, swimming lagoon, canoes for rent, a golf course, a coralarium with seashells from all over the world, etc. The ferry service operates 7:30 am-11 pm daily (though most of Sentosa's attractions close at 6 pm—but not the roller skating rink). The roundtrip fare is included in the resort's 'Ticket II' S$2 admission ticket, which is good for everything except the coralarium.

You can also get to Sentosa Island by **cable car**. It runs from the top of Mt. Faber to Jardine Steps (next to the World Trade Center), then to Sentosa. Roundtrip fare is S$4, and cable cars operate 10 am-6:30 pm Monday through Saturday, 9 am-6:30 pm Sunday. For a treat eat at the restaurant on top of Mt. Faber; nice view.

Given Singapore's success in developing housing estates, it might be interesting to visit one of these self-sufficient communities. Queenstown, just west of downtown Singapore, is the oldest estate, built in 1960-65; it has a population of 150,000. Toa Payoh, in the center of the island, houses 190,000 people in five neighborhoods. Telok Blangah, in the foothills of Mt. Faber, was the third new town to be constructed. Large towns are currently being developed at Woodlands, Bedok, Ang Mo Kio, and Clementi among other sites, and many more are in the planning stages.

Night Life

The cool evenings are pleasant for strolling and sampling new dishes in the ubiquitous clusters of food stalls. Kung fu films and censored western imports are popular local entertainment. Movie seats are reserved; buy tickets in advance at the theater. Colorful wayangs (Chinese street operas) last until midnight at various locations in the city. You can see spectacular views of the city at night from the top of Mt. Faber, from the Sentosa Cable Car, and from the top of the Mandarin Hotel. **Bugis** Street, once the scene of all sorts of nocturnal activity, is now rather subdued. It's still packed with stalls selling clothing, fruit, watches, sugar cane juice, and pirated cassettes, but local transvestites are no longer allowed to gather here.

The National Theatre often has music or dance performances. The National Stadium hosts football matches and various exhibitions from time to time. For details on current schedules, admission fees, and locations of various events, check the "Singapore Weekly Guide".

NOTE: Bus service stops between 11:30 and midnight.

Shopping

Singapore offers tax-free bargains on watches, cameras, records, tapes, and electrical appliances; it's also a good place to look for handicrafts. The STPB publishes "A Guide to Shopping in Singapore" with some helpful tips. The People's Park Centre off New Bridge Rd. in Chinatown is popular with locals; be sure to bargain. Most of the largest and fanciest shopping complexes are on Orchard Rd. Bras Basah Rd. has a variety of small bookstores. The MPH Bookshop, 71-77 Stamford Rd., is Singapore's largest; it has several branches around the city. Indian goods can be found on Serangoon Rd. For Indonesian and Malay batiks and handicrafts, look along Arab St. At Change Alley, Thieves Market, and night markets in Chinatown, you can bargain for all kinds of odds and ends—ancient coins, incense burners, door chimes, opium pipes, masks, etc. The huge Yaohan Dept. Store, in the Plaza Singapura on Orchard Rd., has everything from groceries to books spread out over five floors.

High quality handicrafts, with prices to match, can be found at the Singapore Handicrafts Centre, next to the STPB office at the corner of Tanglin and Grange Rds.

Meeting Students

The student union at the University of Singapore, on Kent Ridge Rd. off Ayer Rajah Rd. on the west side of the city, is the best place to meet students. Nanyang University, on the west edge of the island near the Jurong Industrial Estate, is another large university.

Bibliography

Guide to Singapore, Apa Photo Guide, ed. by Star Black. Beautifully photographed; good general background reading.

Singapore in Southeast Asia, by Ian Buchanan. Deals with economic and political developments from Raffles to the People's Action Party in a detailed fashion.

Saint Jack, by Paul Theroux. Offers a glimpse of Singapore's rowdy seatown past, vestiges of which still survive behind the city's clean, green exterior.

Malaysia and Singapore, by Stanley Bedlington. Informative and readable.

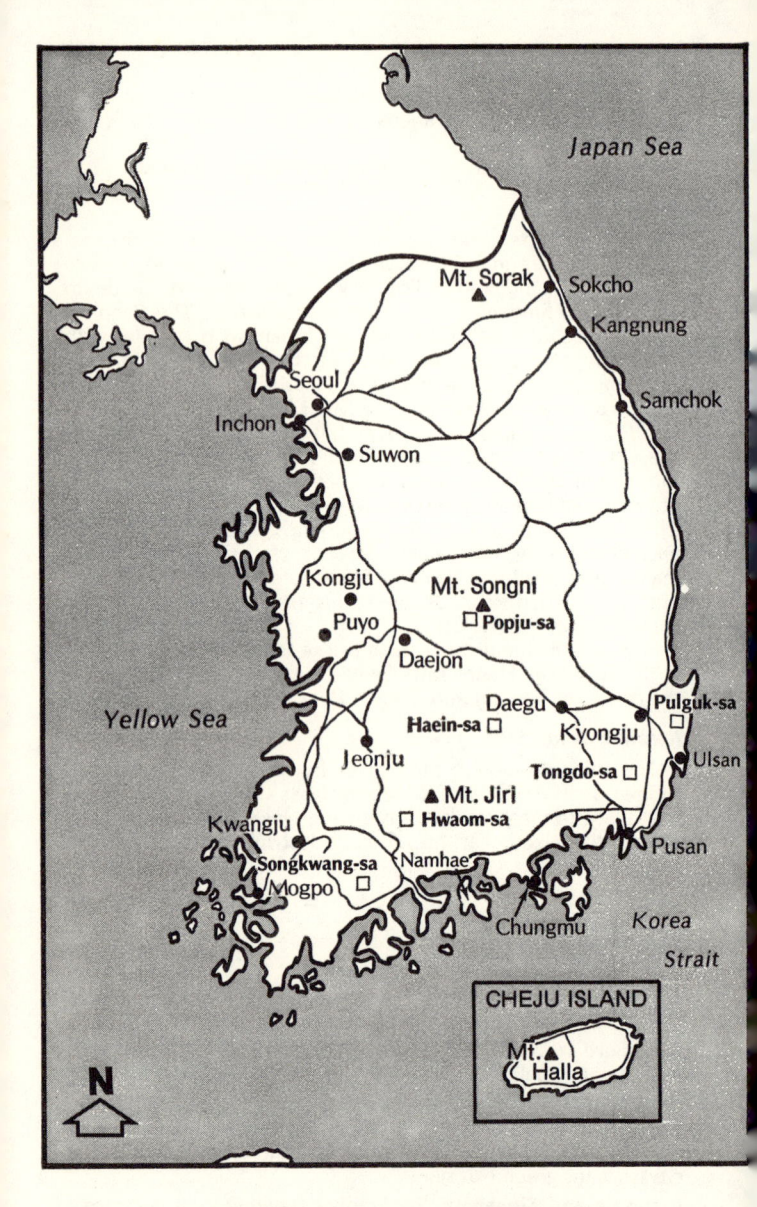

SOUTH KOREA

General Information

Arrival: If You arrive at Kimpo International Airport, 25 km outside of **Seoul**, stop by the Tourist Information Center in the lobby after customs; they can help arrange for a place to stay in the city as well as provide maps of Seoul and Korea. Taxi fare should be W2800. But the most reasonable method is taking the airport bus (**Walker Hill Express**) which stops at major hotels and strategic points along the way for W500. Get off at the Plaza Hotel which is across from the City Hall and Deogsu Palace. From there it is a 5 minute walk to Kwanghwa-mun where many of the cheaper hotels are located.

If you arrive in **Pusan** by ferry from Japan, the TIC is on the main street which passes in front of the ferry terminal. As you leave the building, turn left and walk out to the street. Continue up this street, then turn right onto the main street; the TIC is located next to the Tongnae Hotel on the right side of the road.

Departure: The airport departure tax is W1500.

Currency: The exchange rate in November 1980 was 623 won (W623) to the US dollar The airport gives a good rate. Save your receipts so you can convert extra won into US dollars upon leaving South Korea; it's difficult to find a favorable exchange rate outside the country.

Visas: Visas are not required for travelers staying 120 hrs (5 days) or less if they have confirmed, on-going plane tickets. Tourist visas are granted for up to 60 days.

Climate: Four distinct seasons. Spring and fall are warm and dry, summer is hot and humid, winter is cold and dry. Rainy season: June-Aug. Cheju-do, the large island off the southern coast, has a milder climate than the rest of the country.

Sources of Information

Seoul Tourist Information Center, 31 Taepyong-no, 1-ka, Chung-ku, Seoul (tel. 72-5765), is across from the Bank of Tokyo and just behind the City Hall. This office is the most useful source of information for budget travelers. They can provide train and bus schedules and fare information for travel anywhere in the country; train and domestic airline tickets are sold here as well. In addition, they can arrange visits with Korean families and offer a free tour of Seoul daily in a TIC minibus.

Korean Tourist Bureau (KTB), a private organization, has an office in the Koreana Hotel (9th floor) on Sejong St. between City Hall and the Kwanghwa-mun intersection in downtown

Seoul. In Pusan, the KTB office is on the 1st floor of the New Port Hotel in front of Pusan's train station. KTB offices throughout the country can help you buy train or plane tickets and sometimes give you information on local transportation.

Korean National Tourism Corp., #198-1 Kwanhoon-dong, Chongno-ku, Seoul (C.P.O. Box 903); tel. 261-7001. They publish the "Tourist Map of Korea," "Topical Tours to Korea," "Welcome to Korea: Pearl of the Orient," and other brochures which are also available at TIC offices.

Royal Asiatic Society, Jongno 5-ga, Rm. 901, Christian Building, Seoul (C.P.O. Box 255); tel. 29-5483. They offer tours (including visiting artists in their studios) and have a large library in English on Korea.

Background

South Korea has a great variety of attractions—mountains, temples, beaches, islands, and ancient palaces—but few of them have been packaged for the international tourist. While other countries boast about their 'exotic' cultures and assorted scenic wonders, South Korea has till now taken a more humble approach in its promotion of tourism. As a result, visitors are often surprised and impressed with the country's great natural beauty and rich cultural heritage.

The roots of Korean traditions go back to the early dynasties of the Three Kingdoms period (57 B.C.-676 A.D.). The Koguryo Kingdom, which encompassed the lands of present-day southern Manchuria and North Korea, defended the small peninsula from the expansion of the Chinese Empire during the Han Dynasty. The Paekje Kingdom, occupying the central Han River basin, adopted Confucianism and Buddhism as early as the 4th century and passed on many facets of Chinese culture to the island empire of Japan. The Silla Kingdom, based in the southern part of the peninsula, conquered its two neighboring kingdoms and unified the Korean peninsula for the first time in 670 A.D. You can still see vestiges of this early Korean civilization in Kyongju, once the capital of the Unified Silla Dynasty.

The influence of Chinese culture remained strong throughout Korea's early history. Following the decline of the Unified Silla Dynasty, Buddhism became the state religion during the Koryo Dynasty (935-1392). Buddhism was later banished during the Yi Dynasty, when Confucianism prevailed as the dominant ideology of Korean culture. Under King Sejong, ruler of the Yi Dynasty from 1397 to 1450, a phonetic alphabet (called Hangul) was devised which dramatically increased literacy among the population and further facilitated the diffusion of Confucian

SOUTH KOREA

ideals. Seoul, the capital city of the Yi Dynasty, became the center of Korean civilization during the 15th century. The ancient royal palaces and large fortresses now hidden in the heart of modern Seoul offer the 20th century traveler a glimpse of the days of Korea's most prosperous dynasty.

Japan first launched major attacks upon Korea in the latter part of the 16th century. The armies of Shogun Hideyoshi weakened the country considerably but were unable to capture the capital of the Yi Dynasty. After Japan emerged victorious from the Sino-Japanese War of 1894-1898 and the Russo-Japanese War of 1904-1905 it was finally able to annex Korea in 1910. The Japanese military occupation of Korea lasted until 1945, when the Japanese surrendered to the American forces in Seoul at the end of the war.

Unfortunately, Korean dreams of a unified, independent nation were not realized after the war. The Russians had occupied the northern half of the peninsula at the same time that the American forces defeated the Japanese in the south. An artificial dividing line was drawn at the 38th parallel, originally for military purposes during the disarmament of Japanese forces. The U.S.-U.S.S.R. Joint Commission failed, however, to reach an agreement on the unification of Korea. In 1947 the United Nations resolved to supervise general elections in order to form a unified Korean government. The Communist government in the North rejected the U.N. resolution and prevented elections from being held there. The elections in the South resulted in the establishment of the Republic of Korea government, which was recognized by the U.N. as the legitimate government of Korea in December, 1948. War broke out in 1950 and the North Koreans captured the city of Seoul. Three years of fighting ensued as United States and U.N. forces came to South Korea's aid. The armistice finally signed on July 27, 1953 has maintained the division of North and South Korea at the 38th parallel to the present day.

Park Chung Hee came to power through a military coup in 1961. Constitutional government was re-established two years later and Park assumed the presidency. Having won his third term made possible by a special referendum which allowed him to run, Park declared a national state of emergency in 1972 in an apparent effort to strengthen the government's defense against threats from North Korea and to silence local opposition to the Park regime. Civil liberties which had been guaranteed by the constitution, such as freedom of speech, press, and assembly, were radically curtailed.

In contrast to its political developments, South Korea has made remarkable economic advances, transforming its once agricultural-based economy into an emerging manufacturing economy bent on global export. This transformation has caused a shift from rural to urban orientation thereby creating a discontented urban middle class. While in a sense these better-off urban dwellers are the recipients of economic prosperity, they have also become in recent years the agitators for political reform.

Only fragments of outward political opposition were expressed during the Park regime until his assassination on October 26, 1979 by the then director of the KCIA. For the next few months there was a fragile peace between the military and the newly-aroused dissidents. The caretaker government of Choi Kyu Hah removed most of Park's restraints on civil liberties and this in turn inspired a further liberalization on a whole range of social and political activities. For awhile urban workers could organize for better wages and conditions and politicians could mount open criticisms of the government without fear of reprisal. The fragile peace was shattered in May 1980 as student demonstrations in Seoul and Kwangju were met by brutal military reprisals.

The Choi Kyu Hah government soon fell apart and was replaced by the head of the military, Chun Doo Hwan. With his rule, martial law has returned which has in effect eliminated the political opposition as well as its leader, Kim Dae Jung, who has been sentenced to death as of September 1980.

Culture and Customs

When you meet Koreans, keep in mind that older people are always treated with special respect; people stand up for them and greet them first with a slight bow.

As a foreign traveler you may be offered very warm hospitality; it is polite to refuse at first, but in some cases you might insult your host if you didn't accept.

Korean names consist of three syllables; the first syllable is the family name and the last two syllables together make up the given name. People usually address each other by family name or full name followed with the honorific term "sonsaeng" (for example, Kim Sonsaeng or Pak Ji Soo Sonsaeng). Only friends within the same peer group call each other by their given names.

Industrialization has had a tremendous impact on social customs and lifestyles in Seoul, but Korea's traditional heritage is much in evidence outside the city. Some of the older men still wear traditional clothing—a loose jacket and wide, baggy trousers. The material is usually white, indicating that these patriarchs have retired from active life where they might soil their hands and garb. Traditional clothing for women consists of a short, flared blouse (chogori) and a high-waisted skirt (chima).

SOUTH KOREA 293

Korean culture has been strongly influenced by Chinese religion and thought. Confucian ethics were introduced during the Three Kingdoms period and Buddhism became the court religion of the Koryo Dynasty. Traditional Korean medicine, called Han Yak, also has its roots in ancient imperial China.

Old-style Confucian funerals, which have gradually been simplified, were once elaborate ceremonies involving solemn processions and the wailing of hired mourners. Grave sites were selected with the help of a fortune teller who found an auspicious location for the future good luck of the family. Old-fashioned wedding ceremonies, with the elaborately costumed groom riding to the home of the bride in a sedan chair, are now very rare. Instead, in the cities and towns wedding halls are rented for a brief half-hour ceremony. The old system whereby families arranged marriages through matchmakers has given way in recent years to an increasing number of 'marriages of love.'

If you have a chance to visit a traditional-style home during the winter, you will experience a unique Korean invention called the 'ondol' (a radiant heating system). Underneath the baked clay floor, a system of stone flues carries heat from the kitchen fire or from ground-level grates accessible from the outside. The warm floors heat the room most efficiently, since people generally sit on the floor and sleep on quilts laid out on the floor at night. (Incidentally, don't forget to remove your shoes before entering most Korean homes).

Most Korean festivals are related to the seasonal farming cycle and are celebrated according to the lunar calendar. Four are of special interest and shouldn't be missed if you are in the country at the right time. **Lunar New Year's Day** is more festive than the solar new year. Residents of Seoul and other urbanites return to their villages for family celebrations. **Buddha's Birthday** (the 18th day of the 4th month) is celebrated with a grand procession at Chongye Temple in Seoul (for which the curfew is lifted) as well as at temples throughout Korea. **Tano**, a festival which marks the end of spring planting (the 5th day of the 5th month), is a time when families make food offerings to their ancestors and pray at local shrines. Traditional dancing and games can be seen in the rural areas. You can also hear performances of traditional dance music at Korea House in Seoul during the festival.

Of the seven festivals in October, the **Silla Festival** is the most lively as there are parades, folk dancing and music in Kyongju, the ancient capital of the Silla Kingdom.

For a complete list of Korea's festivals, check with the TIC.

Language

During the Yi Dynasty (1392-1910) a group of scholars were commissioned by King Sejong to devise a simple phonetic alphabet for the Korean language. In 1443 they presented the 24 phonetic symbols which now comprise the Korean alphabet (known as the Hangul). You can learn this alphabet in just two hours, and you'll find it well worth the effort in order to be able to sound out place and food names; Korean is not a tonal language, so once the alphabet is mastered, pronunciation is fairly systematic. Grammatically Korean is similar to Japanese. Regional dialects exist, but they are not divergent enough to really hamper communication.

The romanization of Korean words is frequently confusing, partly because two different romanization systems are still in use. The McCune-Reischauer System is used in most tourist publications and in this guide, but street signs and some maps still use the Ministry of Education system. In regard to consonants, you'll find that **k, t, p, ch,** and **r** are often interchanged with **g, d, b, j,** and **l.** With vowels, romanization is even less consistent. One Korean vowel can be romanized as **eo, o,** or **u.** Usually **eo** and **o, oo** and **u,** and **u** and **o** are interchanged in the two romanization systems. With so many variables, the different renderings possible for a single name can be disorienting, to say the least. For instance, 'Seolag-san' and 'Sorak-san' refer to the same mountain, 'Gyeongju' and 'Kyongju' are the same place, and 'Puyo' can also be spelled 'Buyeo.'

The following Korean phrases (phonetic pronunciation given) may come in handy.

Hello	(AHN-nyung HAH-shim-nee-kah)
Goodbye (to someone who is not leaving)	(AHN-nyung-HEE KYEI-sei-yoh)
Goodbye (to someone who is leaving)	(AHN-nyung-HEE KAH-sei-yoh)
Thank you	(KAHM-sah HAHM-nee-dah)
Excuse me	(SHIL-lei HAHM-nee-dah)
I'm sorry	(MEE-AHN HAHM-nee-dah)
Yes	(nei)
No	(AH-nee-yoh)
I don't understand.	(MOH-lah-yoh)
Where is ?	(OH-di ei EE-sum-nee-kah?)
Train station	(yuk)
Bus	(bus)
Inn	(yoh-gwahn)
Public bath	(MOHG-yohk-tahng)
Toilet	(PYUN-soh)
Is it far?	(MOO-roi-yoh?)
Do you have a room?	(BAHNG-ee EE-soi-yoh?)

SOUTH KOREA 295

How much does it cost?	(UL-mah IM-nee-kah?)
It's good (or simply **good**)	(CHOH-ah-yoh)
This is delicious.	(MAH-shi EE-soi-yoh)
This is too hot!	(NOH-moo MEH-woi-yoh)
Water	(mool)
Give me some water, please.	(MOOL JUM JOO-sei-yoh)

Korea has two different numbering systems. The following system is used for won, but you can use it to count anything, knowing that even though you'll occasionally be using it inappropriately you will still be understood.

1	(eel)	14	(ship-sah)
2	(ee)	23	(ee-ship-sahm)
3	(sahm)	100	(behk)
4	(sah)	568	(oh-behk-yook-ship-pahl)
5	(oh)	1000	(chun)
6	(yook)	7500	(chil-chun oh-behk)
7	(chil)	10,000	(mahn)
8	(pahl)	23,600	(ee-mahn sahm-chun yook-behk)
9	(goo)		
10	(ship)		

* * * * *

In Korean, the words for mountain, temple, island, etc. are attached like suffixes to proper names:

mountain	san	(sahn)	Jiri-san = Mt. Jiri
temple	sa	(sah)	Haein-sa = Haein Temple
island	do	(doh)	Cheju-do = Cheju Island

These ''suffixes'' will also be useful to know:

village (within a city)	dong	(dohng)
district (within a city)	gu	(goo)
street (within a city)	ro*	(roh)

*Exception: when a street name ends with ''ng,'' then ''ro'' becomes ''no.'' Thus Eulji St. is Eulji-ro, while Sejong St. is Sejong-no.

Food

Both Korean and Chinese food can be found throughout the country. Do-it-yourself meals and snacks can be bought from small bakeries and local food stands; fruit should be peeled or washed thoroughly. Noodles make a good, inexpensive lunch. Chinese food is generally less expensive than Korean food and not as peppery.

296 SOUTH KOREA

The two most famous Korean dishes are kimchi and bulgogi. There are over 15 varieties of kimchi, but basically it consists of a vegetable (cabbage, radish, cucumber, etc.) which has been pickled with red peppers, garlic, and onion. It's served with all Korean meals. You'll often see kimchi stored in large ceramic pots placed near the front doors of traditional homes. Bulgogi is similar to the Japanese dish, sukiyaki: marinated beef cooked over an open flame, served with vegetable side dishes and, naturally, rice.

Except for the meat dishes, which cost W1200-1800, the dishes listed below cost W300-1000 and make for quite filling meals.

NOODLES

u-dong (OO-dohng) — noodle soup w/chopped vegetables and meat
kuk-su (GOOK-soo) — soup w/thin noodles
ra-myun (RAH-myun) — factory-made (processed) noodles in soup w/egg and scallions
ja-jang-myun (JAH-jahng-myun) — noodle dish w/dark vegetable paste of fried onions and squash (Chinese)
naeng-myun (NEHNG-myun) — cold, spicy buckwheat noodles w/vegetables (a summer dish)

SOUPS

kuk-pap (GOOK-pahp) — boiled rice soup w/meat and vegetables
mul-man-du (MOOL-mahn-doo) — dumpling filled w/onion, egg, meat, sesame and chives served in a soup
so-long-tang (SOH-lohng-tahng) — beef, rice and chives soup

RICE

po-keum-pap (POH-kum-pahp) — fried rice w/vegetables and diced meat
pee-pim-pap (PEE-pim-pahp) — boiled rice w/vegetables, eggs, pieces of meat and/or fruit, and hot sauce, all mixed together
jap-chae-pap (JAHP-cheh-pahp) — rice w/seasoned noodles and vegetables
paek-pan (PEHK-pahn) — a bowl of rice w/a variety of vegetable side dishes

MEAT

bulgogi (BOOL-goh-gee) — marinated beef cooked over an open flame, served w/vegetable side dishes
kal-bi (KAHL-bee) — same as above, made w/spare ribs
tong-talk (TOHNG-dahk) — roast chicken
tang-su-yook (TAHNG-soo-yook) — sweet and sour pork

Accommodations

Most Korean travelers stay in **yogwan** (yoh-gwahn), inns which can be found throughout the countryside; they're marked by the sign of 여관. The rooms tend to be compact with no furniture; quilts and bedding are laid out at night. Sometimes a mosquito net is provided but bring either insect repellant or mosquito coils. A pyonso (PYUN-soh)—squat latrine—and an outdoor washing area are shared by everyone staying at the inn. (Bring your own toilet paper.) Breakfast and dinner are served for an extra charge of W500-600. Both meals consist of rice, soup, and a half-dozen spicy side dishes, including kimchi and fish. Occasionally even Western meals are available. The cost of one night without meals ranges between W2500 and W3400, sometimes slightly less in more remote areas. In every city or town mentioned in this chapter there are many yogwan; they are by far the most convenient places to stay. Though the Accommodations section will give addresses only for youth hostels, you can take it for granted that there will be yogwan wherever you turn up.

Youth hostels have begun to be popular in Korea. The Korean Youth Hostel Association (KYH) lists 16 hostels, the majority of which are located in the northwestern and southeastern corners of the country. If you haven't got an International Youth Hostel card you can get one at the KYH office, Rm. 407, Seoul Youth Center, #27-1, Soopyo-dong, Chung-ku (tel. 266-2896). The office is near the well-known Pan Korea building. If you have two photos and W5400 in hand and fill out a small application in the morning, the KYH will give you your card that afternoon.

Youth hostel rates range from W1500 for dormitory accommodations to W2750 for semi-private rooms. Breakfast and dinner will be W800-1000 more. Reservations are not necessary except for groups of more than four.

Some yogwan and youth hostels provide a Korean-style bath. Those which don't will provide a bucket at the water pump in the central bath area. Some hostels will provide hot water even though there is no bath. Any small town will have a public bath called mog-yok-tang (MOHG-yohk-tahng), recognizable by the sign ♨ . The cost is usually W550 and sometimes towels are provided for an extra charge. Proper etiquette requires that you rinse off by pouring water over yourself before you sit in the bath. It is allowable, however, to soak in the bath before you actually soap up and rinse off—**outside** the bath. Never dirty the water with soap because you will ruin it for folks who follow.

Korean travelers frequently **camp out** on mountains and at beaches, and unless it is a military-controlled area foreign travelers should not hesitate to follow their lead.

Transportation

INTERNATIONAL: A number of **airlines** serve Seoul from Tokyo, Taipei, Hong Kong, Osaka, Fukuoka, Honolulu and Los Angeles. A comfortable and less expensive way to Korea is on the **Kampu Ferry** which links Shimonoseki, Japan and Pusan, South Korea. Third class (or what they refer to as 'ordinary 2nd class') fare is US$32 for the 8-hr trip; a 20% student discount and 10% round-trip discount are offered. (Note: 10 kg of baggage may be carried free of charge; each additional 5 kg costs US$1.) Blankets and pillows are provided for sleeping on the raised, carpeted floor and a Japanese-style bath is available. The boat leaves Shimonoseki on Monday, Wednesday and Friday at 5 pm (the pier is about 200m from the bus and train stations). It leaves Pusan at 5 pm on Tuesday and Thursday and at 10 pm on Saturday.

INTER-CITY: Trains offer a safe, inexpensive and relatively fast way of getting around Korea. There are four different services: slow (wan-haeng), express (tuk-gup), luxury express (u-deung). New Village express (sae-ma-ul u-deung). The slow trains run quite frequently and are the cheapest, but are usually very crowded. The express is recommended for longer journeys since reserved seats are available. You can avoid long lines and language problems by buying tickets through TIC or KTB offices.

Buses connect all towns and cities throughout Korea. They run more frequently and are a bit faster than trains, but they are slightly more expensive. There are three services: slow (wan-haeng), express (chik-haeng) and highway bus (ko-suk). Slow buses are often crowded and somewhat uncomfortable on unpaved roads, but they do offer the best means of seeing the countryside. Highway buses are air-conditioned but rather expensive.

Seoul recently consolidated the many private bus companies at one large express bus terminal in Kangnam-ku, south of the Han River. The Kangnam Express Bus Terminal (KOH-sohk terminal) can be reached by buses #16 (from the railway station), #1-1 (from Sinseoldong) and #42 micro bus (from the Shinseyge Dept. Store). Other cities usually don't have centralized express bus terminals, so when doing inter-city travel which requires bus changes, it may be necessary to take a local bus from one express terminal to another. The same is true when switching from buses to trains or vice-versa.

Hitchhiking is a relatively convenient way to travel along the major highways. Given Korea's small size, you can almost hitchhike anywhere within a day.

INTRA-CITY: A ride on a Seoul bus with more standing than sitting room costs W90 if you pay on the bus; otherwise it's W80 if you buy tokens ahead of time. Tokens can be purchased at snack shops, cigarette booths and stalls displaying a yellow sign which reads 'Bus Tokens.' Bus stops are clearly marked and the bus numbers are written on front, right and rear windows but the destinations and routes are written in Korean. A new transportation map has just been published and is available at TIC.

Another possibility is using Seoul's **subway** system. Check with TIC for the subway's routes and fares.

Taxi fares are W500 for the first two kilometers and W50 for every additional 400 meters.

Seoul

When Yi T'aejo overthrew the King of Koryo in 1392, he established a dynasty which lasted 518 years and a capital which endures until today. Seoul, with 8.5 million people, is a sprawling, bustling city of contrasts. There is still evidence of Taejo in the ten-mile wall he had ordered built in 1396 and the ancient palaces he occupied. Superimposed over this ancient capital are broad boulevards flanked by towering glass and steel skyscrapers.

At the turn of the century Seoul was a thatched-roof town of about 150,000. Seoul began to expand rapidly up until 1953 when four invasion armies left the city in rubble. Seoul has returned from the ashes and has emerged as one of the most modern cities in Asia.

Exploring Seoul

To explore Seoul on your own, first get a detailed map at TIC, KTB or the airport. Seoul can be confusing.

The center of the city, bordered by Nam-san to the south and the Kyongbok Palace complex to the north, stretches out along an east-west axis, as do Seoul's major streets Jong-no and Eulji-ro. Sejong-no is the main north-south street; it runs from the old capital building in front of Kyongbok Palace down through Kwanghwa-mun intersection, past City Hall and on past Namdaemun (South Gate) to Seoul's railway station.

Changdok Palace was originally constructed in 1405 and is one of the best preserved of Seoul's five palaces. The original palace had been burned by the Japanese Hideyoshi invasion of 1592, but was re-built in 1611. By 1907 it was renovated and at present the Villa of Naksonjae is the residence of Princess Yi Pangja. Behind the palace lies the **Secret Garden**(BEE-won in Korean), more accurately described as a small forest with ponds, pavilions and gardens. Here members of the privileged class once withdrew within its splendor. Today guided tours (W200) in English at 10:40, 1:10 and 3:40 give you a sense of how Korean royalty once lived.

Located behind the old capitol building at the end of Sejong-no is **Kyongbok Palace**. This palace was completed in 1396 in spite of T'aejo's chief advisor who had predicted that the palace would be destroyed in two hundred years. Sure enough the Hideyoshi invasion (and the subsequent levelling of the Palace) coincided with the prophesy. Left in ruins for 270 years, the palace was rebuilt in 1867 using the old palace plans and foundation stones.

Also on the palace grounds are two museums. One is the **National Museum** which offers a visual history of the country spanning thousands of years of Korean history and artistry. Collections of gold and silver jewelry, brassware, bronze implements and beautiful ceramics are on display. The other is the **National Folklore Museum** which has impressive exhibits of traditional handicrafts. Admission to either museum is W150; both are closed Mondays.

Many Seoul people find relief by climbing above the city's constant buzz. **Nam-san** peak is a 30 minute walk south from the downtown area. An alternative way is to ride the cable car up the northern slope. Another popular area is **Changgyung Gardens** (adjacent to Secret Gardens but with access from the east side), which contains a botannical garden, a zoo and an amusement park.

A walk through downtown, especially if you venture off the main streets and into the back alleys which are home for many people, is a good way to catch a glimpse of everyday life in Seoul. With a good street map in hand, you might start by walking through Namdae-mun market, up Nam-san, back down to Myong-dong district and across to the antique shops behind Jong-no. From there, you could walk to either Kyongbok or Chandok Palace.

For those with an ear for music there are two places to drop by: **Korea House** and the **National Classical Music Institute**. Korea House, located just off Twoegye-ro near the Astoria Hotel, is an old-style Korean mansion which provides foreigners with a view of Korean culture free of charge. Every Saturday and Sunday afternoon, there are free performances of dance and music as well as inexpensive Korean food. The National Classical Musical Institute (now located in the National Theatre Complex) lies on the east side of Nam-san near the Silla Hotel. The Institute's aim is the preservation and development of traditional Korean music. There are regular monthly performances, but tickets are difficult to obtain. Inquire at the TIC.

Getting Around in Seoul

As mentioned above, you can easily get around the downtown area by walking. A tourist agency or a friend can provide bus

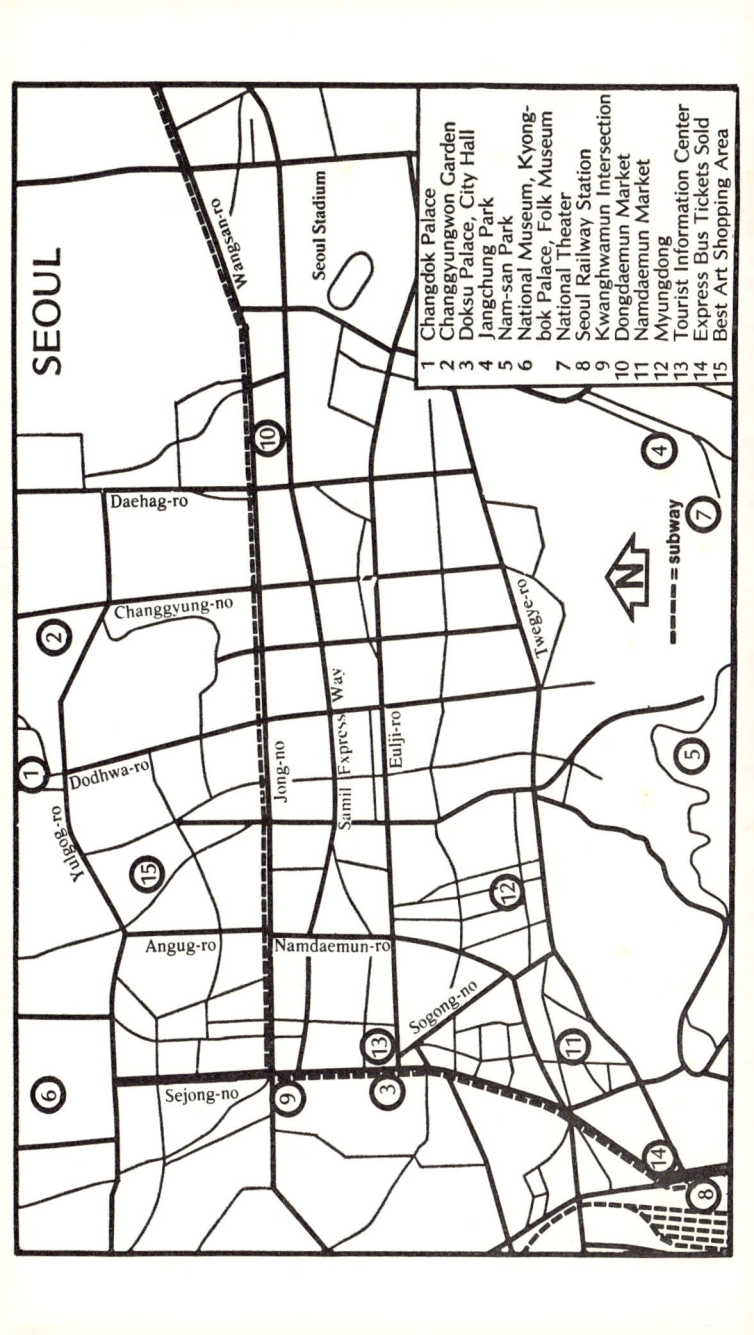

SEOUL

1 Changdok Palace
2 Changgyungwon Garden
3 Doksu Palace, City Hall
4 Jangchung Park
5 Nam-san Park
6 National Museum, Kyongbok Palace, Folk Museum
7 National Theater
8 Seoul Railway Station
9 Kwanghwamun Intersection
10 Dongdaemun Market
11 Namdaemun Market
12 Myungdong
13 Tourist Information Center
14 Express Bus Tickets Sold
15 Best Art Shopping Area

----- subway

302 SOUTH KOREA

numbers and describe stops for covering longer distances within the city. Within the downtown area buses **#9** and **#20** travel the same route in opposite directions, stopping at Changdok Palace/Secret Garden/Changgyung Gardens, the capitol building (behind which stand the Kyongbok Palace complex), Kwanghwa-mun, Doksu Palace, Deoul Railway Station, Namdae-mun and its market, the entrance to Myung-dong, and Twoegye-ro (for a walk to Nam-san and to Korea House).

Seoul has a major subway system which runs between the Railway Station and Chungyang-ni, a village in eastern Seoul. The subway passes City Hall and runs down the entire length of Jong-no, stopping at Kwanghwa-mun and every other block thereafter until Dongdaemun; the subway is particularly convenient for avoiding bus congestion in the downtown area.

Eating in Seoul

For low-budget meals try the numerous food stalls in the back alleys of the city. In the area near Jong-no and Sejong-no you'll find a great number of small restaurants with good, inexpensive meals. The market areas, especially at Namdae-mun and Dongdae-mun, offer an impressive array of meals for those with adventurous stomachs: onion pancakes, blood sausage, cooked or raw squid, octopus, steamed mussels, raw oysters, barbequed sparrows, etc.

Nightlife

The night entertainment seems to revolve outside the luxury hotels in the Myung-dong area. There are numerous Western-style bars and beer halls with booming stereos. The cheapest beer hall could just well be the **Green Villa**, up the alley opposite the Kolon building (one block directly behind the City Hall. Beer costs W2-3000 a bottle; wine is about W6000. 25 meters past the Green Villa is the bizarre **San Soo Gap San** (or the Classic Music Beer Hall)—yep, it's a rowdy beerhall that has live classical music. At 9 pm the waitresses all go on stage and sing together. You could also go to **Heart-to-Heart** and chummy up to a maccoli (50 proof rice wine) and listen to soft rock. There are a number of maccoli houses in the area and occasionally one can hear live, traditional music.

Movies provide another alternative as many Koreans are enthralled with Hollywood flicks. There is the midnight-to-4 am curfew. Although it doesn't apply to foreigners, buses and taxis literally disappear (turning presumably into pumpkins) which could leave you stranded.

Shopping

Myong-dong is the center of the fancy shopping district with expensive boutiques and fixed-price department stores. For cheaper prices, a course in the art of fearless haggling must be pursued in either of these three market areas: **Dongdaemun** (East Gate Market), **Namdaemun** (South Gate Market), or **Insadong** (also called Mary's Alley). **Gwanhung-dong** remains the best area for pottery, watercolor painting, calligraphy, and woven straw goods. To get there jump on board a bus to Jong-no 3-ga and walk north into the streets between the YMCA and Pagoda Park. If you're apt to buy older art items, be sure you'll be able to take them out of the country. The government has been trying to halt the drain of Korea's valuable art treasures and antiques.

Good selections of **books** can be found at Chongno Book Center (on the 2nd floor of a Bible society store across from the YMCA). Paperbacks are also sold at Pan Korea Bookstore, just west of the Kwanghwa-mun intersection, and in small bookstores several blocks west of the YMCA on Jong-no. Another possibility is at the Royal Asiatic Society at Jongno 5-ga for books on Korea.

Meeting Students

Students generally get together in tea rooms (tabang) and maccoli houses near the universities, where customers can stay as long as they please, listening to music in a relaxed atmosphere. Tabang are common all over the country, but only in cities are they filled with students.

ACCOMMODATIONS IN SEOUL

The area around Kwanghwa-mun in particular has many well-kept **yogwan** which charge about W3000/night.

Daiwon Inn, 26 Dagju-dong, Jongno-ku; tel. 74-5300.

W3000/night or W2000 if you share a room. A popular traveler stop. If you're taking the #42 bus, transfer to the #8 bus at Seoul Station for Kwanghwa-mun. From there walk west on Jongno to the first alley; it'll be 50 meters up on the right. Good restaurants in the area.

Dae-ji Inn, next door to Daiwon Inn, with similar prices. Tel. 73-4650.

Bando Youth Hostel, 60-13 Yoksam-dong, Songdong-ku, Seoul; tel. 57-2141.

Rates range between W2200 to W2750 for shared rooms w/o bath. The hostel is new and clean, but the location is somewhat out of the way and room rates are relatively high compared to other youth hostels. TIC can tell you how to get there.

Chungang Youth Hostel, 67 Chung-ro 1-ga, Seodaemun-ku; tel. 73-2485.
Yogwan-style, W2300 w/two meals. 20 minutes from downtown.

YMCA. Jongno 2-ga, near Jongkak subway station; tel. 72-8291-8.
Single W7502, double W8470-W12,100. All rooms w/private bath.

One-Day Trips from Seoul

For the time-pressed traveler anxious to get a quick glimpse of Korean life outside of Seoul, there are several one-day trips which are easy to make.

Kanghwa-do (GAHNG-hwah-doh), an island off the coast just west of Seoul, offers mountain climbing, a historically significant temple, and a trip through Korean farmland. Kanghwa-do is famous for its legendary Mani-san (MAH-nee-sahn), the mountain on top which the mythological creator of Korea, Tangeun, established an altar for worship in 2333 B.C. a strenuous hike will put you on top of Mani-san in an hour. Eight kilometers from Mani-san is Jeondeung-sa (JUN-deung-sah), the temple where the 80,000 wooden printing blocks of Buddhist scriptures now kept at Haein-sa were originally commissioned during the late Koryo period. (Lodging is available at yogwan in Onsu near Jeondeung-sa for W800-1000.)

Inchon, Seoul's port city to the west, is a relief from Seoul's congestion and confusion. At the town pier, octopus (GOHL-doo-gee), eel (BEHM-jahng-awe), and sea cucumber (HEH-sahm) can be bought and eaten.

Only an hour's ride south from Seoul by bus or subway is **Suwon** (SOO-wun), a fortress town still enclosed within a wall linking elegantly designed gates and watchtowers. Nearby is the **Korean Folk Village**, a real community in which families are following the ways of old Korea. You can observe artisans at their trades and get a sense of classical folk entertainment, which includes mask dramas, puppet plays, and rhythmic music played on percussion instruments. A full day can easily be spent enjoying the diversity of activities in this village. Admission is W1500.

Near Onyang, south of Seoul on the Janghang train line, is **Hyunchungsa** (HYUN-choong-sah), a national monument erected in memory of Admiral Yi, the heroic naval commander who designed iron-clad, turtle-shaped ships to defeat a Japanese invasion in the late 1940s. This peaceful, tucked-away monument includes a small museum with a model ship and a shrine honoring the national hero—an interesting display of Korean pride.

Onyang is also the home a famous hot spring which has been converted into a public bath house in the middle of town. A visit (W550) is guaranteed to be relaxing.

Further south on the same train line you can disembark at Sabgyo for a side trip to **Sudeog-sa** (SOO-dug-sah), a temple set on a forested mountainside, and **Deogsan** (Dug-sahn) **Hot**

SOUTH KOREA 305

Springs, several kilometers from Sudeog-sa. Both places can be easily reached by bus from Sabgyo Station. (There is a youth hostel at Sudeog-sa.)

Further west from the temple, you can relax at secluded **Mallipo**, a beautiful beach on the Yellow Sea. A bus will take you there via the towns of Seosan and Taean.

TRANSPORTATION FOR ONE-DAY TRIPS FROM SEOUL

Kanghwa-do: Express buses leave from just west of Shinchon's rotary (in western Seoul) every 10 minutes for Kanghwa City (W700, 1¼ hr.) and Jeondeung-sa (W840, 1½ hr.) to Kanghwa-do. From Onsu, the village at Jeondeung-sa, you can catch a local bus for Hwado, the village at the base of Mani-san (W80, 20 min.).

Inchon: Can be reached by subway in just under an hour (W240).

Suwon/Korean Folk Village: Take a subway to Suwon from anywhere along the subway line, including the Seoul Station stop (W260, 1 hr.+); from Suwon Station catch a local bus going to the Folk Village.

Onyang/Hyunchungsa: Onyang is 2½ hr. from Seoul by express train on the Janghang Line (W1000). From Onyang's train station, buses leave every 10 min. for the 10-min. ride to the shrine.

Sabgyo: 3 hr. from Seoul by express train on the Janghang Line (W1290); a slow train is much cheaper (W570) but, especially in the summer, may not be worth the savings. (The sign in the station will say 'Sudeog-sa' rather than 'Sabgyo.')

Sorak-san and the East Coast

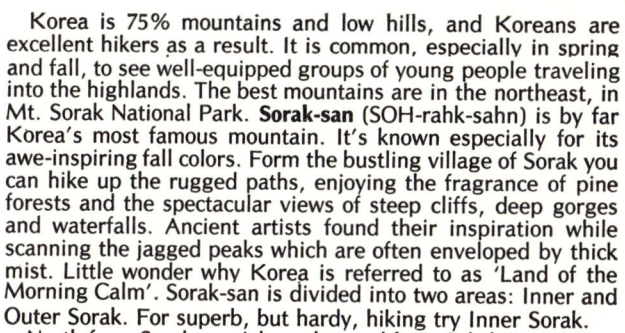

Korea is 75% mountains and low hills, and Koreans are excellent hikers as a result. It is common, especially in spring and fall, to see well-equipped groups of young people traveling into the highlands. The best mountains are in the northeast, in Mt. Sorak National Park. **Sorak-san** (SOH-rahk-sahn) is by far Korea's most famous mountain. It's known especially for its awe-inspiring fall colors. Form the bustling village of Sorak you can hike up the rugged paths, enjoying the fragrance of pine forests and the spectacular views of steep cliffs, deep gorges and waterfalls. Ancient artists found their inspiration while scanning the jagged peaks which are often enveloped by thick mist. Little wonder why Korea is referred to as 'Land of the Morning Calm'. Sorak-san is divided into two areas: Inner and Outer Sorak. For superb, but hardy, hiking try Inner Sorak.

North from Sorak-san (along the road from Sokcho) are some of the most impressive beaches in Korea; **Hwajingpo Beach** is quite popular.

306 SOUTH KOREA

The stretch of east coast from Samchok (Samcheog) down to Pohang (north of Kyongju) is the least traveled area of the country. Only in late 1978 was the coastal road paved making travel much quicker and less rugged. There is a steady stream of buses up and down the east coast (starting and ending in Taegu and Kangneung). With the rugged Taebaek mountain range running north-south along the coast there isn't much room for towns to develop. Most of the settlements are sleepy fishing villages along the alternately sandy and rocky coast in what is for Korea a sparsely populated region. There is virtually no advanced industry or commerce; consequently, the lifestyle is slow, simple and traditional. About midway between Samchok and Pohang is a large town of Uljin (OOL-jin) which is noted for its Mangyang Pavilion and the Songryu Cave. (Note: without any knowledge of Korean, travel on the east coast will be more difficult than other areas in Korea).

ACCOMMODATIONS FOR SORAK-SAN AND THE EAST COAST

Sorak: The village has yogwan for W4000-5000.

Samchok: Hamtai Youth Hostel, Sodo-Ri, Jangseong-Up; W2200.

TRANSPORTATION FOR SORAK-SAN AND THE EAST COAST

Sorak-san: No train service. Express buses from Seoul's Kangnam Terminal leave for Kangneung (Gangneng) every 15 min. (W2710, 4 hr.). From Kangneung express buses up the coast leave regularly. Or, take one of the five direct buses to Sokcho daily. They leave from Dongma-jang terminal at 6:30, 9:10 and 11 am & 1:45 and 2:20 pm (W3070, 6 hr.). From Sokcho buses leave frequently for the village of Sorak (W180).

Kyongju and the Southeast Corner

For a thousand years the capital of the Silla Dynasty (57 BC-935 AD), **Kyongju** is today the richest repository of Korean historical and cultural landmarks. This old city, located in the southeast, contains many tombs and relics, an ancient astronomical observatory (called CHOHM-sohng-deh) and a branch of the National Museum (displaying a collection of Silla sculptures, implements, and ornaments). Ancient burial mounds can be seen in the hills surrounding the city, along with fortresses once used by Silla kings. Just 12 km south of Kyongju is the famous temple **Pulguk-sa** (POOL-gook-sa), noted for the five-story pagodas which flank it on each side; its delicately painted,

SOUTH KOREA

colorful caves are another striking characteristic. To get to Pulguk-sa, take a local bus from Kyongju. **Sokkuram** (SOHK-kool-ahm) **Grotto**, a half-hour ride over the hill from Pulguk-sa, is a stone cave hermitage containing a large stone Buddha surrounded by ten disciples carved in relief. The Grotto faces east, and most Korean tourists rise before dawn to walk there and watch the sunrise illuminate the cave.

Midway between Kyongju and Pusan lies Korea's largest temple, **Tongdo-sa** which consists of 35 buildings along with 13 hermitages. It was founded in 647 AD.

In sharp contrast to Kyongju's antiquity and Tongdo-sa's grace is the nearby industrial complex of **Ulsan** (OOL-sahn). Ulsan represents the rapid advances of modern Korean development; the shipbuilding yard of the Hyundai Group and large petrochemical complex stand out as impressive examples of Korean enterprise. Tours are given daily at some of the plants in Ulsan.

ACCOMMODATIONS FOR KYONGJU AND THE SOUTHEAST CORNER

Kyongju: Kyongju (Gyeongju) Youth Hostel, 145-1 Kujung-dong; **tel.** 2-991. Bunk rooms W2000/night.

Tongdo-sa: You can stay at the hermitages, or else in either Kyongju or Pusan.

Ulsan: Plenty of local yogwan.

TRANSPORTATION FOR KYONGJU AND THE SOUTHEAST CORNER

Kyongju: The express bus from Seoul (W3710, 4½ hr.) is the quickest way to get there. Alternatively, you could take a train to Dong Daegu and then take the express train (W2870) to Kyongju. Kyongju as well as Tongdo-sa can be reached from Pusan by express bus (W740).

Tongdo-sa: Accessible from either Kyongju or Pusan by bus (W350).

Ulsan: 45 min. by bus from Kyongju (W370).

Songni-san and the Southwest

In the central highlands is Mt. Songni National Park; the peak of **Songni-san** (SOHNG-nee-sahn) affords a panoramic view of craggy slopes and verdant valleys. **Popju-sa** (pup-joo-sah), the 1400 year-old enclave considered revered ground by Korea's Buddhists, contains the tallest Buddha image in the country. Once the site of large Buddhist gatherings, Popju-sa still holds elaborate ceremonies on Buddhist holidays. A lantern parade highlights the celebration of Buddha's birthday in the fourth month of the Lunar Year. Songni-san and Popju-sa offer a dual attraction to Koreans, and their proximity to Seoul means numerous visitors each year.

Puyo (POO-yoh) or Buyeo, the last capital of the Paekje Kingdom, is today a quiet country town located along the Keum River in west-central Korea. Its 123-yr. history as a royal city is evident from the substantial number of impressive tombs and relics. **Puso-san** was at one time the capital's fortress and many of the ancient pavilions have been reconstructed. Nakhwa-am is the famous bluff from which 3000 court ladies plunged to their deaths rather than submit to their conquerors.

Kongju, near Puyo, served as the Paekje capital until almost the mid-6th century. Besides housing a branch of the National Museum, it has recently attracted visitors following the discovery of the tomb of King Muryong (501-524), which was found completely undisturbed; the tomb is now open to the public.

On the way to Kongju, stop a while at Mt. Kyeryong National Park. **Kyeryong-san** (GYEI-ryohng-sahn) is famous as the home of many of Korea's shamanistic religions, which gathered here because of the mountain's mystical qualities. **Kap-sa**, a well known temple founded in 424 A.D., is also located here.

Further south lie **Mt. Deogyu** and **Mt. Gaya National Parks**. Both are noted for their hiking trails that run through lush forests dotted with caves, castles, old shrines and waterfalls. Near Gaya-san is the center of Korean Buddhism today. **Haein-sa** is one of the three temples where monks practice Zen Buddhism. The buildings have been restored to show the intricate designs of the original paintings and architecture. Haein-sa contains the Pal-man-dai-jang-kyung, a library of 80,000 wooden printed blocks of Buddhist scriptures.

Towards the southern coast lies **Mt. Jiri National Park**. **Jiri-san** is South Korea's second highest peak (behind Halla-san on Cheju-do) and thus attracts its share of visitors. Its network of hiking trails is more extensive than that of Sorak-san because

SOUTH KOREA 309

it is not as steep or rugged. On the slopes on Jiri-san, **Hwaom-sa** is one of Korea's most famous temples. Situated high in a boat-shaped valley, the temple's two five-storied pagodas symbolize a ship's masts. The ship is often used as a symbolic vehicle to transport Buddhist souls across evil waters into the realm of Nirvana.

Mt. Naejang National Park, in Korea's southwestern corner, offers a view of one of the country's most beautiful waterfalls. With its complement of temples and dramatic scenery, **Naejang-san** (NEH-jahng-sahn) is a popular stop for southern dwellers.

ACCOMMODATIONS FOR SONGNI-SAN AND THE SOUTHWEST

Songni-san: There are yogwan in Songni village for W3400. An hour's hike up the mountain is the 'Piro Sanjang' villa. A new hostel called **Sokri-san** at 820-2, Nesokri, Beoun-kun has just recently been completed. Bunk rooms are W1900.

Puyo & Kongju: Stay in yogwan.

Haein-sa: Stay in hermitages.

Jiri-san: There are yogwan in Gurye. Also, on top of the mountain there is a hiker's lodge.

Naejang-san: There are yogwan in Jong Eub.

TRANSPORTATION FOR SONGNI-SAN AND THE SOUTHWEST

Songni-san: Express buses leave Seoul every 10 min. for Chingju (W1400, 2 hr.). From Chongju, switch to a local bus for Songni-san (about W800, 1½ hr.).

Puyo & Kongju: Express buses from Seoul's Kangnam Terminal go directly to Puyo (W1660) and Kongju (W2390).

Kyeryong-san: Local or express bus from terminals in either Puyo or Kongju (W500).

Haein-sa: Take a train from Seoul (W2870, 4 hr.) or Pusan (W920, 1½ hr.) to Dong Daegu. From the train station catch local bus #1 to the bus terminal for Haein-sa buses, 5 km away. From the terminal you can take a fast bus to Haein-sa (W800, 1½ hr.), or a slow bus (W700, 2 hr.).

Jiri-san: Express trains run from Seoul to Gurye on the Honam Line (6 hr.). From the Gurye Station take a bus into town; from there you can walk to Hwaom-sa.

Naejang-san: Accessible by local bus every hour from Jong Eub, a stop on the Kwangju train line. From Chongju, there are 6 trains daily and several express buses from the terminal (W2450).

Pusan and the South Coast

Pusan has historically been the gateway to Korea from Japan. It is the country's second largest city with over two million people. See **General Information** above for the addresses of Pusan's TIC and KTB offices.

Pusan has little to offer in the way of historical or cultural attractions, but it does have fine weather and there are numerous beaches and parks. **Haeundae** (HEH-oon-deh) **Beach** is Pusan's most famous beach. Popular **Taejongdae** (Teh-johng-deh) is a hilly park along the waterfront on the nearby island Yong-do. In Pusan's fish market, the fourth largest in Asia, many of the kinds of raw fish popular in Korea are sold. Pusan Tower, located downtown, provides a great view of the city, mountains and harbor.

The **Tongnae Hot Springs** are a common stopping place on the way out to **Pomosa**. This temple is situated at the head of a river valley in the forested mountains near Pusan. Take bus #18 or #19 from downtown.

The **South Coast** is unlike any other in Korea, with its spectacular seascapes, picturesque islets and secluded beaches. Between Pusan in the east and Mogpo in the west, there are countless offshore islands, the most famous of which are **Geoje-do** (GAWE-jei-doh) and **Chungmu** (CHOONG-moo). This area in general is referred to as the **Hallyosudo Waterway**.

Geoje-do's claim to fame, besides its gorgeous mountain scenery and luscious farming valleys, is a natural monument off its southern tip called **Haegeumgang** (HEH-geum-gahng), a towering slab of rock with crevices that run through it enabling boats to enter one side of the monument and puff their way out in tune with the ebb and flow of the water. Boats can be rented on an hourly basis at Haegeumgang village, a very out-ot-the-way fishing town that is accessible from Chung-mu by bus. The bus ride between Haegeumgang to Jangseunpo (another fishing town up a few peninsulas) is one of the most exciting in Korea; the bus rambles its way down a bumpy dirty road, skirting isolated beaches, rocky cliffs and through a well-forested part of the island.

Chungmu is a bustling town in comparison to Geoje-do. It has fancy yogwans, an endless array of seafood restaurants, and public baths. Historically, it is known for being the headquarters for the national hero, Admiral Yi Sun-Shin, who brilliantly defeated the Japanese at sea during the Hideyoshi invasion in 1592. There are several shrines honoring him in the city itself. However, the most beautiful one lies just beyond the Chungmu harbor and it is easily reached by boat (W135, 20 min.); **Jae-seung-dang** (Che sung dang) shrine lies on a hill overlooking a tiny inlet on Hansan-do. The shrine is composed of a number of traditional Korean pavilions. There are several beaches in the area, the best of which is Bijin-do.

Midway between Chungmu and Mongno is **Songkwang-sa** (SOHNG-gwahg-sah). It is considered to be one of the three greatest monasteries of Korea, the others being Haein-sa and Tongdo-sa. The temple is still known to be the center of Zen Buddhism in Korea. It is relatively remote and can only be reached by bus over dirt roads from Suncheon.

ACCOMMODATIONS FOR PUSAN AND THE SOUTH COAST

Pusan:
   Aerin Youth Hostel, 41. 1-ga, Bosu-dong; tel. 42-8959. Dormitory accommodations, W2000. To get there from Pusan Station, take bus #86 and get off in front of the Aerin Orphanage.
   Nam Kwang Youth Hostel, Mt. 15 Nopo-dong, Dongae-ku; tel. 52-4063.

Geoje-do:
   Geoje-do Nongjang Youth Hostel, Jisepo-ri, Ilun-myun.
   Aekwang Youth Hostel (beach), Mt. 64-8 Jangseungpo-ri, Jangseungpo-up.
   Aekwang Youth Hostel (mount), Mt. 110 Gucheon-ri, Dongbu-myun.

Haegeumgang, Jae-seung-dang & Chungmu: Stay in yogwan.

Songkwang-sa: Stay in the hermitage next to the temple.

TRANSPORTATION FOR PUSAN AND THE SOUTH COAST

Pusan: About 5½ hr. away from Seoul by train—W3900, W5920, or W8480, depending on which type of train you take.

Chungmu and the South Coast: High-speed hydrofoils ply the waters along the South Coast between Pusan and Yosu, stopping in Chungmu, Samcheonpo and Namhae. Because the seating areas on these fast boats are completely enclosed, it is a frustrating experience. A passenger can see the seascapes only through a blurry window. For those who are not out to save time and do want to save money it is recommended to take an ordinary boat or ferry. From Pusan, there are boats to Chungmu daily at 10 am and 3:30 pm (W930, 3rd class). There are several buses to Geoje-do daily.

Songkwang-sa: Can be reached by bus from Kwangju (W690, 1½ hr.) or from Suncheon on the southern coast.

Cheju-do

South Korea's best known island, **Cheju-do**, enjoys a warm, windy climate that offers a paradise atmosphere to its visitors. Although tourist authorities have highly touted Cheju-do as a resort, you must be forewarned that little has been done to implement any plan to do so; consequently, accommodations tend to be simple and spoken English nonexistent.

The starting point will be inevitably Cheju City; a tour of tis Folk Museum (Min Sok Pammulgwan) is rewarding as it is rich in the folklore of the island. Shortly thereafter, most folks head for **Halla-san**, an extinct volcano which is often snow-covered throughout the year. There are craters, lava-tube cave, and waterfalls exploding into the sea. From Yongsil, hike along the path to the crater and return via the Kwanumsa Temple on the lower slopes of Halla-san. There are shelters for hikers to sleep but you must bring your own food as nothing is sold along the way. Start the climb in the wee hours.

Agriculturally, Cheju-do boasts tangerine orchards and dairy farms, which help support an economy based on fishing. The island is known for its hardy women drivers who can hold their breath for several minutes while swimming underwater to catch fish in nets. Korea's best tropical beaches dot the perimeter of the island: be sure to visit **Hamdok, Hyopje** (HYUP-jei) and **Jungmun** beaches in particular.

It's easy to get around on Cheju-do's many buses—some circle the island in both directions, others criscross the island between Cheju City and Sogwipo.

TRANSPORTATION FOR CHEJU-DO

Boats leave daily from Pusan (W7590, 12 hr.) at 7:30 pm and from Mogpo (W5090, 6 hr.) at 5 pm. Also there is a ferry from Yeosu (W6020, 4 hr.) at 4 pm.

Bibliography

Through a Rain-splattered Window, by Michael Daniels. An excellent source.

Virtues in Conflict: Tradition and the Korean Woman Today, ed. by Sandra Matielli. Fascinating accounts of Korean women's lives, plus good historical background.

Korean Works and Days, by Richard Rutt.

SOUTH KOREA 313

Some Korean Journeys, by Dorothy & William Middleton. Essential for travel outside of Seoul.

Kyongju Guide, by Edward Adams. Well worth the price because it's more than just a guide; includes dozens of folk tales, art history, etc.

In This Earth, In That Wind, by Lee. A series of essays about different aspects of life in Korea.

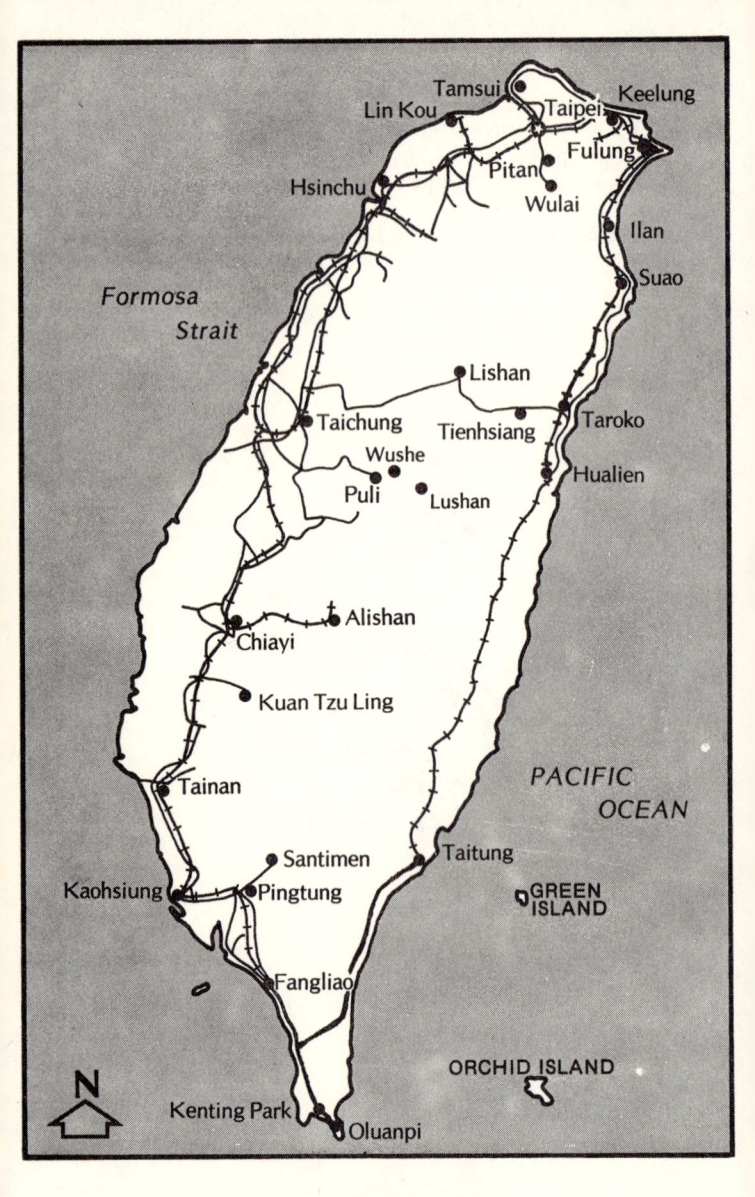

TAIWAN

General Information

Arrival: After landing in Taiwan's new Chiang Kai-shek International Airport (40 km southwest of Taipei in Taoyuan), you will want to leave as quickly as possible by way of the air-conditioned highway Express buses (NT$30, no baggage racks) or Chung Hsing Limousine buses (NT$50, w/baggage racks) which leave from in front of the arrival lobby every 10-20 min. until 10:30 pm (Express Bus) or 11:30 pm (Limousine Bus). The buses make three stops in Taipei before they reach Sungshan Airport, Taipei's domestic airport. The second stop (corner of Minchuan West Rd. and Chungshan North Rd.) is in Taipei's central business district and is 10 min. and NT$5 by bus from the Taipei Bus/Train Station 台北車站. From this station, buses run to all parts of the city and to other cities in Taiwan; the station is also close to many budget accommodations.

The Tourist Service Center is located in the middle of the greeter's lobby, just beyond the customs area. Stop there to get maps and information. Inquire about bonding baggage at the airport.

Departure: Catch bus #23 across the street from the train station (see map, p.331; it will take you to Taipei's Sungshan Airport used only for domestic flights. From here catch another NT$50 highway bus directly to "Departures" at the Chiang Kai-shek International Airport. The whole trip takes about 1¼ hr. The airport departure tax is NT$150.

Currency: The exchange rate in November 1980 was 36 New Taiwan dollars (NT$36) to the U.S. dollar. Keep your receipts when changing cash or traveler's checks so you can convert extra NT back into U.S. dollars before leaving Taiwan.

Visas: There are two kinds of tourist visas; Tourist A permits a one-month visit with two one-month extensions possible; Tourist B allows a two-month stay which can also be renewed twice (usually a reason for renewal is needed such as a certification proving one is attending school at one of the government-approved language schools). Japan, Hong Kong, and the U.S. (along with other nations which have broken official ties with Taiwan) no longer have embassies of the Republic of China, but visas can be obtained from trade and travel associations. Japan: Association of East Asian Relations, 2nd floor, Heiwado-Boeki Bldg., 1-8 Higashi Azabu, Minato-ku, Tokyo (tel. 583-8030). Hong Kong: Chung Hua Travel Service, 1009 Tak Shing House, 20 Des Voeux Rd., Central District (tel. 5-225639). United

States: Coordination Council for North American Affairs, 210 Post St., Suite 705, San Francisco, CA 94108 (tel. 415-989-8677).

Climate: Subtropical. Warm and humid summer (May-Oct.), cool winter (Jan. & Feb.). Brief spring and fall. Most rain falls April-Aug.; July-Sept. is typhoon season.

Sources of Information

Ministry of Communication Tourism Bureau, 9th floor, 280 Chunghsiao E. Rd., Sec. 4, Taipei; tel. 721-8541. The information desk provides maps and brochures. The Tourism Bureau also operates an information counter at the airport.

China Travel Service (CTS), 16 Lin Sen North Rd., Sec. 1 林森北路一段 16 號 (tel. 551-5933) in Taipei; 188 Chung Cheng 4th Rd. 中正四路 188 號 (tel. 232131) in Kaohsiung; Tienhsiang Lodge (tel. '0') in Tienhsiang. CTS is a large travel agency which specializes in group tours, but the friendly staff will also help individual travelers. They publish a variety of pamphlets.

American Institute in Taiwan, 7 Lane 134, Hsingi Rd., Sec. 3 (tel. 752-6040 and 708-4151). Serves as liaison office between Taiwan and U.S. governments. Provides information on visas, duties, and travel in Taiwan.

The Taiwan Visitors Association and a private group publish "This Month in Taiwan," which lists some train and bus fares along with basic travel information and maps of Taipei, Taichung, and Kaohsiung. Free at hotels and the airport tourist service center.

Detailed maps of Taipei, Taichung, Tainan, and Kaohsiung are sold at Nan Hua Publishing Co., No. 7 Lane 278, Kang Ting Rd., Taipei.

For telephone numbers and directions to places in Taipei, call the city's English-language **information number**, 311-6796.

Background

Taiwan, located less than 160 km off the southeastern coast of the Chinese mainland, serves as the seat of the Nationalist Government of the Republic of China. This small, mountainous island has endured a long history of struggles against foreign powers and broken ties with the Chinese government on the mainland.

The earliest inhabitants of the island were of Malay stock, and their descendants (approx. 200,000 'aborigines') live primarily

TAIWAN

in the remote mountain areas of Taiwan. The ancestors of the majority of the Taiwanese people came from Fukien Province on the coast of the Chinese mainland after the 15th century. Portuguese mariners were the first foreigners to land on the island in 1517, and the Dutch and Spanish later fought for control of Taiwan during the early 1600s. Koxinga (or Cheng Cheng-kung), a famous Fukien-born warrior of the Ming Dynasty, drove out these foreign powers in 1661 and used the island as a base for an unsuccessful attempt to recapture the Chinese mainland from the Manchu Dynasty. The Manchus incorporated Taiwan into the Chinese Empire as a part of Fukien Province in 1682, and during the next 200 years a great number of people from Fukien emigrated to Taiwan, bringing their dialect and their cultural traditions with them.

Taiwan became a separate province within the Chinese Empire in 1885, but the island was ceded to Japan after the Sino-Japanese War of 1894-95. The Japanese crushed Taiwanese attempts to set up an independent republic and ruled the country for 50 years. The impact of the Japanese occupation was greatest in the economic sector; highways, railroads and communication networks were established throughout the island in a very successful effort to develop and exploit Taiwan's natural resources.

Japan returned Taiwan to China at the end of World War II. However, as the Communist revolutionaries began to take control of the Chinese mainland, Chiang Kai-shek and his Nationalist army retreated to Taiwan, hoping to recapture the mainland from the Communists in the future. By 1947 nearly one million Chinese Nationalists had fled to Taiwan, where they started to take over control of the economy. The Taiwanese rebelled against the 'mainlanders' in February 1947, but Nationalist troops quashed the revolt. Most of the outspoken proponents of an independent Taiwan were killed. Chiang Kai-shek established the Republic of China on Taiwan in 1949, and the island has been ruled under martial law ever since.

The position of Taiwan's government has weakened considerably in recent years—Taiwan was ousted from the U.N. in 1971 and most nations have now recognized the People's Republic of China (including the U.S. in December 1978)—but Taiwan's economy continues to prosper. Generalissimo Chiang Kai-shek, head of the Kuomintang (Nationalist Party) since 1926 and president almost continuously since 1948, died in 1975. His son, Premier Chiang Ching-kuo, took over leadership of the Kuomintang, and became president himself in 1978. The last two years have seen opposition parties banned, dissidents arrested and jailed, and several newspapers closed down by Chiang's government. But in spite of the political tensions which persist today, the life of the people on Taiwan seems to remain somewhat detached from the irregularities of national politics and international diplomacy.

You will doubtless hear or read about the recently completed 'Ten Modernization Projects' of which Taiwan is so proud. These construction ventures, costing over US $8 billion, include the new Chiang Kai-shek airport, an electric railway from Keelung to Kaohsiung, a nuclear power plant near Taipei, and a railway along the rugged east coast from Suao to Hualien. The country is now working on twelve more development projects, not as grand in scale as the original 'ten.' They are just the finishing touches to Taiwan's remarkable transformation in the last 35 years into a thoroughly industrialized nation.

Travelers merely making a stopover in Taipei will not discover why the 16th century Portuguese mariners exclaimed "ilha formosa!" (beautiful island) when they landed on the east coast of Taiwan. Taipei has all the modern conveniences imaginable for 20th century tourists, but if life in rainy cities dampens your spirits then escape immediately. For spectacular mountain scenery you can travel down the east coast on the Suao-Hualien 'cliff highway,' then hike through the famed Taroko Gorge on the Cross-Island Highway. Mountain villages with natural hot springs provide restful (and inexpensive) retreats for adventurous travelers, and if you obtain a mountain pass before leaving Taipei you can hike on the remote trails in the Central Mountain Range. The west coast of Taiwan is heavily populated and more developed than the rest of the island. Though the scenery is less spectacular, as you pass through the lush agricultural areas, coastal fishing villages, and the rapidly growing industrial cities you can get a first-hand feeling for different Chinese lifestyles and traditions.

Culture and Customs

Several age-old customs still thrive in Taiwan. Chinese hospitality, for example, is formidable to this day. Polite scuffles over who will pay the bill are common between hosts and guests, or even casual acquaintances meeting for lunch. Travelers who intend to stay in Taiwan for any extended period of time are advised to arm themselves before arriving with a supply of small gifts from their home country for doing battle in the ever-raging war of hospitality on the island.

This hospitality is often extended to visitors who seem sincerely interested in the local culture and in getting to know people. As a foreigner and a guest you will be at a severe

TAIWAN

disadvantage; you may be puzzled by what seems like excessive generosity and not know how to return favors or express gratitude properly. Here are a few guidelines: First, refuse everything at least once to be polite. Second, enjoy yourself once you have 'given in'—your friend will be most pleased just to see that you're happy. Third, try to find an opportunity to reciprocate by treating your friend; if this isn't possible before you leave, take pictures and send them later, and keep in touch by letter. A fourth custom to keep in mind regards gift-giving—always bring a small present (a special food, imported coffee, candies, cigarettes, liquor, etc.) when you visit a Taiwanese home.

As in other parts of Asia, the concept of face underlies many aspects of social relations. People go to great lengths to avoid shaming or insulting others. Communication may be very indirect when disagreements arise, since smooth interpersonal relations are generally valued more highly than frankness. Foreigners who have lived in Taiwan for a while remark that Chinese rarely say "no"; instead they say "maybe," which can be interpreted as a negative response.

Although there are few 'pure' religious sects in Taiwan (most temples enshrine gods of all types) most people at least pay respect to their ancestors. An altar is usually found in one room of a home, flanked by pictures of the family's deceased grandparents. On holidays such as New Year's, offerings are left here for the spirits to feast on.

Dress neatly if you want to meet people. Although fashions are changing fast, women wearing dresses and blouses with sleeves rather than halter tops, and long pants as opposed to shorts, are looked on more favorably. Men should not walk around without a shirt on. Shoes and sandals are acceptable if they have a strap or something that covers your heel. Always take off your shoes before going in the front door and put on a pair of slippers that your host will probably point out to you. Also, some houses have a separate set of slippers to be worn in the bathroom.

Final hints: carry a handkerchief to mop your damp forehead; keep a small supply of toilet paper, beacuse it's seldom supplied in public restrooms; bargain when shopping, especially at night markets (but not in department stores); picture-taking, sketching, and painting are prohibited at most beaches and several mountain parks; the import of PRC goods is also prohibited, so don't flaunt clothing, etc. newly purchased in Hong Kong's PRC department stores. Public displays of affection are not common; in fact, contact between young men and women is kept to a minimum. Boys and girls must attend separate high schools. Members of the same sex often walk arm in arm or hold hands, especially classmates.

320 TAIWAN

English language is required from junior high school on, so if you have a question, your best bet is to direct it to someone who looks approximately college age.

Festivals

Like most Chinese, people in Taiwan celebrate the Lunar New Year, the Dragon Boat Festival, and the Mid-Autumn Festival (see the **Culture and Customs** section of the Hong Kong chapter for details). On Confucius' Birthday (Sept. 28), all teachers are honored in ceremonies throughout the island. Tickets are required for the 6 am festivities; ask your friends or your hotel about how to get them. Parades celebrate the establishment of the Republic of China in 1912 on Double Tenth Day (Oct. 10). During Ghost Month (usually in June or July), you can see tables of food set out on the sidewalk. These are offerings to the gods and spirits—of course, what isn't eaten by the ghosts is later consumed by the family. Paper money is also burned as an offering to the gods.

Language

Mandarin has been taught in the schools for the past 20 years as the official national language. Approximately 80% of the people on Taiwan (the descendants of Han Chinese who migrated to Taiwan from Fukien Province over the last four centuries) speak a Taiwanese dialect in the home. Many of the people over the age of 50 can speak Japanese well, since they were educated during the Japanese occupation between 1895 and 1945.

The phonemes of Mandarin Chinese are limited, unlike the endless combinations of vowels and consonants in English; thus Mandarin evolved as a language using four tones to differentiate between the similar phonemes which make up the language. The tones are: (1) even (—), no change in pitch; (2) rising (✓); (3) falling-rising (ᴗ); and (4) falling (✎). A first tone sounds much like a word whose pitch is extended with no change in intonation. A rising tone resembles the intonation at the end of a question in English. The third tone falls deep into one's throat before rising to finish like the second tone. The fourth tone falls like the intonation at the end of a statement in English.

bùhǎo yìsz	an expression used to thank someone for a special favor or gift
sỳe sỳe nǐn	thank you
dwèi bùchǐ	excuse me

TAIWAN 321

méiyǒu gwānshì	never mind, it's nothing
ni hǎo ma?	how are you?
hén hǎo	very good
–––dzài nǎr?	where is –––?
hwǒ chē jàn 火車站	train station
chì chē jàn 汽車站	bus station
wǒ yàu dàu–––chyù.	I want to go to–––.
lyǔ gwǎn 旅館	hotel
dzài jyàn	goodbye
syè chē	I want to get off the bus
dwō shǎu chyán?	How much is it?
bù kéchì	You're welcome

Food

In order to thoroughly enjoy Chinese food, you must put western eating habits completely out of your mind. Do as the Chinese do, and you may discover why the Chinese have the world's most varied and delicious cuisine.

For the Chinese, food is much more than just fuel for the body; it is the focal point of most social interactions as well (the traditional greeting between friends, "You meiyou chr ba le?" means "Have you eaten?").

After mastering the art of using chopsticks, forget Western table manners; let nothing interfere with the pleasure of eating. Slurp your hot soup (no need to burn your tongue), belch softly after a hearty meal if it feels good, raise your bowl to your mouth to avoid spilling rice into your lap, and learn to put bones onto the table rather than back into your soup. But do eat slowly, savoring each dish. More often than not, a meal is an excuse for friends to share an hour or more together, so the pace is very relaxed. Your 'napkin' (the damp handcloth) may be used to clean your hands before and during the meal, but it should stay on the table rather than in your lap.

Chinese usually eat in a group, sharing a six- or seven-course

322 TAIWAN

meal which may include appetizers, a meat dish, a vegetable dish, soups, seafood, and a sweet curd or assorted fruit dish at the end. If you ever have the good fortune to be invited to a party or celebration, be prepared for a feast. The guests will be urged to eat as much as humanly possible (but it's polite to leave a little food on each dish). Eating is also a major part of Chinese entertainment, as you will find out if you explore Taipei's unique (and expensive) night life.

Breakfast

There are two kinds of Taiwanese breakfast to try. The less expensive version consists of hot soybean milk and various kinds of deep-fried bread, served early in the morning in open-front shops and food stands. At hotels and restaurants, the standard breakfast is boiled rice with a salty egg, bean curd, peanuts, pickled vegetables, and dried, shredded beef or pork. If you don't care for either of these breakfasts, you can buy milk and bread at a bakery to eat with fruit, but it will be much more expensive.

you tiao 油條	long bread stick
sao bing 燒餅	flat bread wrapped around you tiao
dan bing 蛋餅	flat bread deep-fried with egg batter
do jang 豆漿	soybean milk, served hot ('tyan de' means 'sweet')
syi fan 稀飯	boiled rice porridge
syan dan 鹹蛋	boiled salty egg
rou song 肉鬆	dried, shredded meat
ping gwo 蘋果	apple (expensive)
syang jyau 香蕉	banana (inexpensive)
pu tao 葡萄	grapes
mang gwo 芒果	mango
lyou ding 柳丁	orange
mu gwa 木瓜	papaya
jyudz 橘子	tangerine
syi gwa 西瓜	watermelon
shr dz 柿子	persimmon

Lunch

The food shops near the central market areas in most towns and villages are recommended; the atmosphere may be a little noisy and crowded, but the food is good (in Taipei during the summer months you may want to stick to cleaner restaurants

TAIWAN

with doors). Or find a small hotel restaurant and order 'ke fan' (guest meal); the fixed menu will include a soup, a dish or two, and all the rice you can eat.

To cool off during the hot afternoon, try a delicious fruit **nyounai**—these blender-mixed drinks combine fruit and milk with ice. Especially good are **feng li** (pineapple), **mu gwa** (papaya), **syang jyau** (banana), and **syi gwa** (watermelon). Just look for signs advertising '500cc.'

RICE DISHES

Curried rice 加里飯
Fried rice 蝦仁炒飯
Fried rice w/eggs 蛋炒飯
Fried rice w/poached egg 蛋包飯
Fried rice w/sliced pork 排骨飯
Fried rice w/seafood 三鮮炒飯
Barbecued fish w/rice 炸魚飯
Combination rice 什錦魯飯
Quick lunch 快餐

NOODLE DISHES

Shrimp noodles 蝦仁麵
Shredded pork noodles 肉絲麵
Seafood noodles 三鮮麵
Fried noodles w/shrimp 蝦仁炒麵
Fried noodles w/shredded pork 肉絲炒麵
Fried noodles w/seafood 三鮮炒麵
Fried rice noodles w/shredded pork 肉絲炒米粉

SOUPS

Seafood soup 三鮮湯
Scrambled egg soup 蛋花湯
Cabbage and bean curd soup 白菜豆腐湯
Oyster soup 蚵仔湯
Lily flower and shredded pork soup 金針排骨湯

QUICK LUNCHES

Shwei jyau (steamed dumplings) 水餃
Gwo tye (fried dumplings) 鍋貼
Baudz (steamed bread w/meat inside) 包子
Mien tang (noodle soup) 麵湯
Mi fen (rice noodles w/meat and vegetables) 米粉

324 TAIWAN

Dinner

Look for inexpensive cafeterias, often patronized by college students (but be careful to pick a clean one—cases of hepatitis have been reported recently in university areas). You can choose the dishes that look good, and the rice and soup are sometimes free with the meal. Most larger restaurants have Chinese and English menus.

You can also eat well in the night market found in almost every town. Wander around until you see or smell something good, then sit down and point it out to the waiter. Seafood is the best bargain—it's usually all fresh.

PEKINESE FOOD, the cuisine of North China, is hot and salty, also oily because much of it is deep fried. Some kind of bread (baked, steamed, or fried) usually accompanies the meal, because wheat rather than rice is the staple grain in that area. This cuisine is noted for its variety of dumplings and noodles, its barbecued meats, and, of course, Peking Duck.

 Peking Duck 北京烤鴨
 Duck with bean sprouts 鴨肉炒豆芽
 Duck soup 鴨架子湯
 Fried pork balls 乾炸丸子
 Chicken with egg 芙蓉雞片
 Dumplings 餃子
 Beef noodles 牛肉麵
 Spring rolls 春捲
 Steamed bread with stuffing 包子

Most **SHANGHAINESE FOOD** is fried in sesame oil. Liberal use is made of ginger, garlic, soy sauce, and those hot little red peppers. Vegetables and meats are cooked for a long time so that they absorb the flavor of the spices. Good seafood.

 Sauteed mushrooms with bamboo shoots 炒三冬
 Fish simmered in soy sauce 紅燒魚
 Eel 鱔魚糊
 Shrimp ball 蝦球
 Simmered meat ball, 紅燒獅子頭

CANTONESE CUISINE is the kind of Chinese food most foreigners are familiar with; it tends toward the sweet side and isn't too spicy. Most Cantonese dishes are steamed or quickly fried in a light oil in order to retain juices and natural flavors. Usually served with white rice. (For a great treat, try 'dim sum'; see the description in the Food section of the Hong Kong chapter.)

 Sweet and sour pork 古老肉
 Beef with oyster sauce 蠔油牛肉

TAIWAN 325

Minced quail 鴿鬆
Pot beef 紅悶牛腩

TAIWANESE FOOD generally uses little salt or seasoning; the delicious soups contain a great variety of ingredients.

Fried meat 卜肉
Assorted firepot 什錦火鍋
Prawns 紅燒大蝦
Glutinous rice dumplings 粿粽
Fried fish with bean oil 豆油魚
Fried oyster 蚵煎
Boiled fish with vegetables seasoned with sauce 五柳枝
Old-fashioned simmered pork 嚕肉

HUNANESE and **SZECHWAN CUISINES** feature hot, peppery dishes, heavy on the noodles and bean curd. You can order it 'men hung' (minus the red pepper) if you like.

Ant on the tree (chopped beef sauteed with vermicelli) 螞蟻上樹
Diced chicken 公保雞丁
Mrs. Ma's bean curd 麻婆豆腐
Pork sauteed in red pepper oil 魚香肉絲
Fish in soy paste 豆瓣魚

Accommodations

In most cities you can find fairly inexpensive hotels within a few blocks of the train or bus station. Westerners will often be given western-style rooms; ask if they have less expensive tatami-style rooms. In these the bedding—several thick quilts with sheets—is laid out on the floor in the evening; you may find this more comfortable than some of the old, saggy beds.

The China Youth Corps (CYC) operates 15 **youth hostels** and seven **activities centers**. Prices vary somewhat, but the cost of dormitory-style lodging at these places is always reasonable. Hostels provide only board and lodging, while the activities centers offer boating, swimming, etc., depending on their location. There's a hostel and a center in Taipei, and hostels in Taichung, Tainan, and Kaohsiung; the rest are located in scenic areas around the island. As the CYC hostels are set up for groups, it's advisable to phone ahead for reservations if you're not part of a pre-arranged tour. For more information, check with the CYC headquarters, 219 Sungkiang Rd., Taipei; tel. 5513294.

Transportation

INTERNATIONAL: Several **airlines** have daily flights to Taipei, and China Airlines has daily flights from Kaohsiung to Hong Kong. Keelung in the north and Kaohsiung in the south are the two major ports. Information on **shipping lines** connecting Taiwan with Hong Kong, Japan, and other Asian countries is difficult to obatin; check with the lines directly for current schedules and fares.

INTER-CITY: Express trains and highway buses provide reliable access to all parts of the island, except during the typhoon season (July-Sept.), when landslides frequently disrupt service to mountain areas. It's best to buy train and bus tickets one or two days in advance, especially on weekends during the summer months and around Chinese New Year. Hotels will often buy tickets on request, for a small service charge. Pick up a **Travel Gazette**, which includes most details on train and bus schedules, at the Taiwan Tourist Bureau or the China Travel Service in Taipei. "This Month in Taiwan" lists some of the more expensive train and bus routes. For train reservations, call 312-2233 in Taipei; 289608/9 in Taichung; and 221-4721 in Kaohsiung.

TRAINS   Taipei-Taichung Fare

Tzu Chiang 自強 , deluxe, electrified, ac, express, 2-2½ hr.	NT$224
Chu Kuang 莒光號 , deluxe, ac, express, 2½-3 hr.	NT$186
Dwei Hau Kwai 冷氣對號車, ac, limited express	NT$153
Kuang Hua, fast express	NT$122
Dui Hua Kwai 對號車	NT$119
Ping Kwai 平號車 , ordinary express, fan, no reserved seats	NT$119
Pu Tung Che 普通車 , ordinary train	NT$99

Trains provide excellent service along the recently electrified route from Taipei to Kaohsiung. At present the Dwei Hau Kwai (limited express) is the best train to take for longer journeys if you want a reserved seat. Your car and seat number will be listed on the back of your ticket (put the ticket in a safe place because it will be collected at the end of the trip). We also recommend trains for trips from Chiayi to Alishan, Taipei to Hualien via Suao, and Hualien to Taitung. You get a special treat on Taiwanese trains—hot tea! The train attendants will fill your glass several times during the trip.

In Taipei, the office where you can buy tickets in advance is separate from the train station. As you approach the entrance to the station turn left towards the adjacent building in front of the bus station parking lot (see map, p.331). Be sure to get in the correct line for morning or afternoon trains. Most other train stations have their ticket offices all in one area, but check the signs above the windows.

Highway buses serve most parts of the island; they are slightly less expensive than trains, and usually faster. A new highway between Taipei and Kaohsiung, completed in 1978, speeds up bus travel on the West Coast (Taipei to Kaohsiung in less than five hours). Bus tickets to Tainan and Kaohsiung can be purchased in Taipei one or two days in advance; tickets to Taichung cannot be bought in advance, so expect to wait in line. Buses depart frequently from stations next to the train depots in most cities. The Suao-Hualien 'Cliff Highway' and the Cross-Island Highway are especially thrilling because the roads are windy, narrow, and literally carved out of the steep mountainsides.

INTRA-CITY: You won't have any problem flagging down a **cab** in this land of the ubiquitous taxi; the drivers will be looking for you, at almost any hour of the day or night. The fare is NT$22 for the first kilometer and NT$4.50 for each additional 500 meters. Be sure to make your destination quite clear to the drivers, especially those serving airports and train stations. The taxis at the stands near the train stations, incidentally, are usually looking for long-haul passengers (i.e. to nearby towns). If you're just heading for a nearby hotel, walk down the street and hail a local taxi.

You will have to get explicit directions from a hotel or travel information center to master the **bus** system in most cities. Buses usually run regularly on scheduled routes—with route numbers written on the front of each bus. Bus maps are available but the destinations are written in Chinese. Even if you know which bus number you want, make sure you use the right bus company. Different bus companies use the same numbers for entirely different routes.

We recommend that you always have the Chinese characters for your destination written down in advance when you use taxis and buses. On most buses the bus attendant will tell you when to get off if you have shown her your destination (provided of course it isn't rush hour).

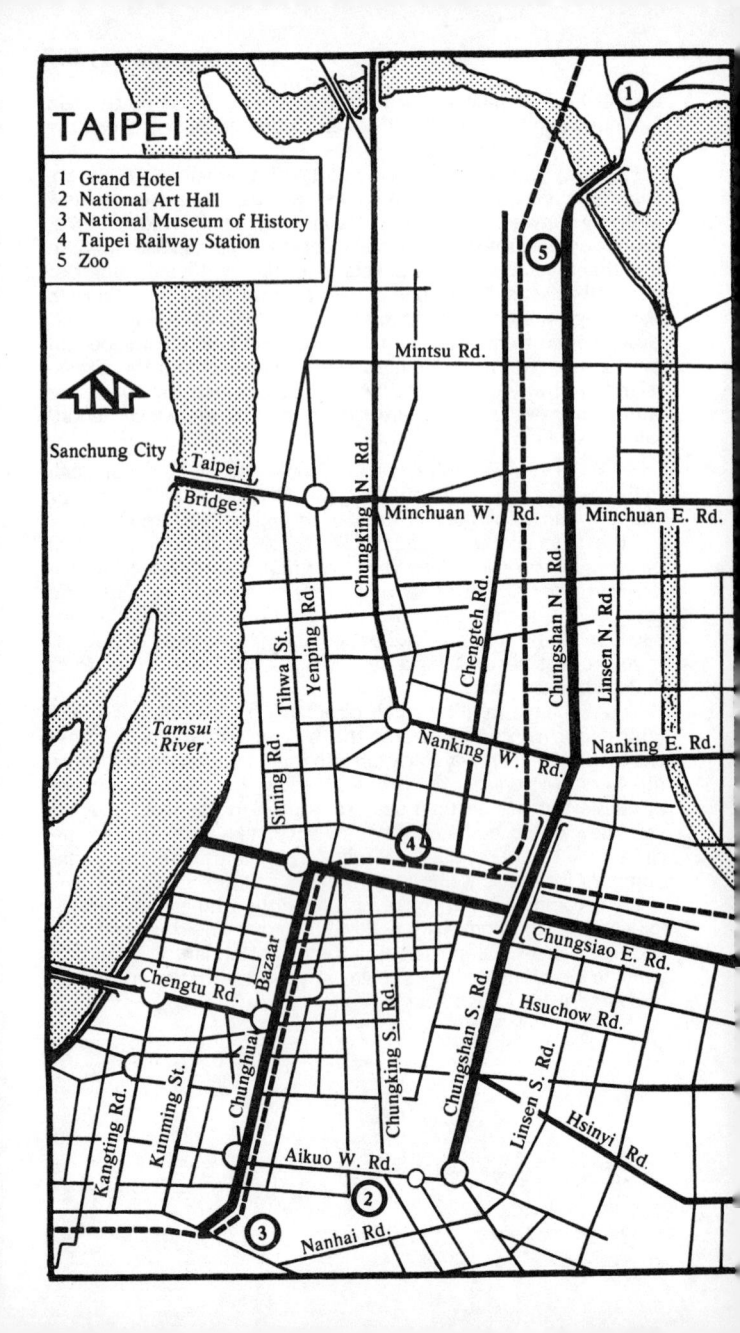

TAIPEI

1. Grand Hotel
2. National Art Hall
3. National Museum of History
4. Taipei Railway Station
5. Zoo

Taipei

Exploring Taipei

The **National Palace Museum**國立故宮博物院, nestled in the mountain suburbs of Taipei, contains a vast collection of art treasures and frequent special exhibits. In addition to the 10,000 pieces on display there are upwards of 200,000 more stored in the air-conditioned caves behind the museum. English-language tours are given at 10 and 3 daily; lectures (in English) on various aspects of Chinese culture are given Tuesday and Friday 10-12 am. After looking at the exhibits, walk around in Wai Shung Hsi, near the museum grounds; the scenery is gorgeous.) The museum is open 9-5 daily. From the train station take buses 17, 218, or 246 (see map) to Yuan Shan (Grand Hotel 圓山) bus stop and transfer to #213, #210, or #304 which all go to the museum on a 2-ticket ride.

If you have time after touring the museum, bus #213 continues from the museum bus stop on up the mountain to a stop overlooking the museum. From there take a short walk up the hill until you see a small stone path on your right. This path will take you up in an easy ½-hour climb to the top of the mountain overlooking Taipei. It's a cool, quiet retreat from Taipei's noise and smog.

Lungshan Szu (Dragon Mountain Temple) 龍山寺, 211 Kuang Chou St., is the oldest and most famous Buddhist temple in Taipei. Kuan Yin (Goddess of Mercy) birthday celebrations take place here in March or April each year. The temple is located in Wan Hua, a very old section of the city. Two interesting night markets—one for food and one for all kinds of discounted merchandise—are nearby. Take bus #218 to the last stop, then walk about two blocks further to the temple. Buses #7 or #18 also go to Lungshan Temple.

The **Botanical Gardens** 植物園, 54 Nan Hai Rd., include the **National Museum of History** and the **National Art Hall**, both of which have good displays. From downtown (see map), bus #7 goes near these places. Ask the bus girl where to get off. At the stop, across the street is the 'American Cultural Center' which includes a library, a cool haven of mostly non-fiction books plus all sorts of English language newspapers and magazines.

New Park 新公園, one block from the Presidential Building, provides another refuge in the middle of the city. The park surrounds the Taiwan Provincial Museum, which has a small natural history collection. Exhibits include life-size statues of members of Taiwan's many aboriginal tribes and handicraft displays. Closed Mondays.

Confucian Temple 孔子廟, Chiu Chuan St., is within walking distance of the zoo at the north end of Chung Shan Rd. Its simple style differs from that of most temples you see in Taiwan. If you happen to be in Taipei on Sept. 28, inquire about getting a ticket to see the traditional ceremonies for Confucius' birthday; the places to call for tickets are the temple's management office, 592-3934, or the information department of the Taipei city government (541-5351). Compare the Confucian Temple's style with that of nearby **Pao An Taoist Temple** (61 Hami St.), a 230-yr.-old structure.

National Taiwan University 國立台灣大學 (or Tai Da) is a good place to meet students. Take bus #251 or #236 from in front of New Park to the corner of Hsin Sheng Rd. where you can see the palm tree-lined entrance.

Getting Around in Taipei

Downtown Taipei is small enough to be explored on foot; walk off the bustling main roads to the more quiet side streets where the people live and discover delicious cheap neighborhood restaurants. Use the train station as a base and landmark. One and a half (1½) blocks east of the station is Chungshan Rd., a large thoroughfare running from the Grand Hotel in the north, over the railroad tracks on Fushing Bridge, to the downtown area in the south. Chungshan Rd. is divided into sections 1, 2, 3, and 4, with 4 being the section furthest north. A major east-west street is Chungsiao Rd., located directly across from the railroad station. Helpful maps written in English are available for NT$30 from any street corner in the downtown area.

Buses are recommended for travelers who don't mind getting lost or confused periodically (there are no English signs on the buses or at bus stops). Public and private bus lines were united into one system in 1977, so buses in operation come in a variety of colors. Individual bus tickets can be purchased in small booths located next to major bus stops for NT$5 (ticket prices are due to rise again soon). If you don't have a ticket, the bus attendants will accept a NT$5 coin. Tickets can also be bought on punch cards in bunches of 10, 20, or 40 tickets. Route numbers are written on the front of each bus. Routes numbered 0-99 always cost one ticket (or 'ride'); 100-199 cost one or two tickets, depending on the distance traveled; 200-299 cost up to three tickets. (A single ticket covers most bus trips in Taipei proper.)

Bus stops are designated by round signs with route numbers and a list of the stops each makes; have your destination written down in characters so you can compare them with those on the signs.

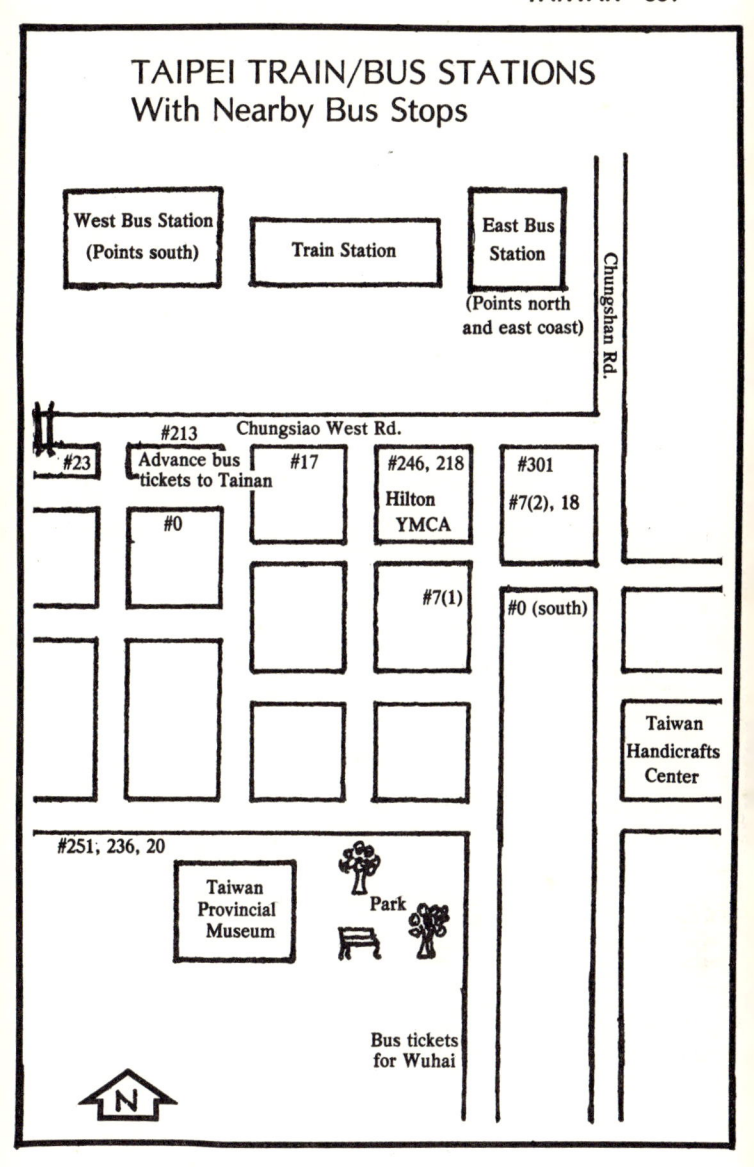

TAIPEI TRAIN/BUS STATIONS
With Nearby Bus Stops

- West Bus Station (Points south)
- Train Station
- East Bus Station (Points north and east coast)

Chungshan Rd.

Chungsiao West Rd.

#213
#23
Advance bus tickets to Tainan
#17
#246, 218 Hilton YMCA
#301
#7(2), 18
#0
#7(1)
#0 (south)

Taiwan Handicrafts Center

#251, 236, 20

Taiwan Provincial Museum

Park

Bus tickets for Wuhai

N

332 TAIWAN

Sungshan Airport to train station	#23
Train station to International House	#20
International House to Chungshan North Rd., terminating at the zoo	#211
Zoo to National Palace Museum	#213
Train station to Botanical Gardens	#7 & #262

If you get lost or can't figure out which bus to take, just hail a passing **taxi**.

Eating in Taipei

For inexpensive restaurants look near Taipei's universities and colleges. Short-order food shops serving dumplings, fried rice, noodle dishes, and soups are easy to find almost anywhere. You can also get inexpensive meals in small cafeterias where you choose from the assortment of dishes that have been prepared.

Restaurants

Aranda Marga Yoga Jagrti (Yoga Vegetarian Happiness Center), 257 Roosevelt Rd.
This cafeteria serves a variety of delicious and inexpensive vegetarian Chinese dishes. Located on the 2nd floor of a yoga institute.

Old Fatty Chou's Noodle House, 53 Han Chung St.
Great Peking food: dumplings, baudz, and soups.

Ruby Restaurant, 135 Chungshan North Rd., Sec. 2.
Excellent Cantonese dim sum. Choose dishes from the pushcarts which are wheeled through the restaurant; your bill will be figured by the number of empty dishes on the table at the end of the meal.

International House, 18 Hsin Yi Rd., Sec. 3.
Clean and inexpensive cafeteria. Dinner (NT$60) includes three dishes, soup, rice, and a drink. Good place to meet students, and other travelers.

Cheng Ch'i Sz Han 成吉思汗, 176 Nanking East Rd., Sec. 3.
Mongolian barbecue. You prepare your own dish and have the chef barbecue it for you. Best to stick to one kind of meat (mutton); mix with vegetables, add sauce as follows: 4 spoonfuls soy sauce, 2 water, 4 sesame oil, 1 wine, 1 ginger water, and a dash of pepper oil. A great place for a splurge.

The Real Beiping 真北平, 37 Chunghua Rd., Sec. 2, 2nd floor; near the clock circle.
An expensive but delicious introduction to the wonders of Peking duck. In addition to other dishes, order a duck (size depending on the number of people in your party). The duck comes in four parts; the first two, meat and skin, should be placed on a crepe, liberally smeared with onions and the sumptuous sauce before being rolled up in the fashion of a taco. Guests are even given a look at their duck before the cutting. The meal will cost in excess of NT$300 but is well worth it.

On Nan Yang St. near the Hilton are two small, inexpensive restaurants. One of them, 廣東大仁餐廳, serves Cantonese food at reasonable prices. Their hui tan is especially recommended. Across the street at the **Hsiao Syin Hsin** 小欣欣 you can find ke fan (客飯). In the mornings they serve good do jang and you tiao.

Taiwan Shiau Dau Restaurant, Chungshan North Rd., Sec. 2, no. 71, 9th floor.

Taiwanese style food and live traditional Chinese music. Prices are expensive, but the music and atmosphere put you right in the heart of old China. Take bus #246, 218 or 17 to the second stop, get off and walk north; it's on your right.

Night Life

China Bazaar, an eight-building complex on Chunghua Rd. near North Gate, is an intriguing place for nighttime walking and window-shopping. There's always plenty of activity; in front of some shops salesmen use small microphones to shout out their discounts as they stand amid tables piled with merchandise.

A trip to Taipei would not be complete without visiting one of the many **night markets**. You can get just about anything here: clothes, beautiful pottery (both the fake and the genuine kind), fresh oyster omelete, roasted Chinese chestnuts, hot and sour soup, etc. If you dare, try some of the foods prepared from snakes; wash it down with a little snake blood (it's supposed to increase one's vigor and prolong one's lifespan). The Wanhua area, between Chunghua Rd. and the Tamsui River, is the oldest district in Taipei and abounds in night markets. Shr Lin Night Market 士林夜市, though not as exotic as Wanhua, is as least as large and in some cases offers a better selection of goods. Take bus #216, #217, or #218 from the train station or from any stop along Chungshan North Rd.; get off at the Yangming Theater.

Sun Yat Sen Memorial Hall 國父紀念館, a sprawling complex commemorates the founding father of the Republic of China. Chinese and Western cultural events are performed daily in its huge auditorium. Prices usually range from NT$100 for seats in the rear to NT$400 for front seats. Take a bus NT$ from the train station (20 min.); ask at the information window at the train station for the correct bus number.

334 TAIWAN

The **movie district** beckons from further down Chunghua Rd., near the 'clock circle.' Some of the latest Western movies (as well as some of the earliest) are often shown in these theaters.

Many young people go to **coffee shops** at night. The atmosphere is relaxed—with music, air-conditioning, dim lighting, and large soft chairs to lounge in. Coffee shops usually have an English menu.

The **World of Today Recreation Center** 今日世界娛樂中心 at 52 Omei St., one block north of the movie district, is a large, fancy entertainment facility. Compare it with the so-called 'poor man's theater' at Yen Ping North Rd. near the Taipei Bridge, where you can see afternoon or eveining performances of Chinese opera.

If you're tired out from walking the streets all day, buy some Taiwanese beer or wine and return to the peace and quiet of your hotel room to play 'fingers,' a Chinese drinking game. At some point you may see men engaging in this contest after a dinner party at a restaurant. First set up glasses filled with wine or beer. Then two people simultaneously hold out from zero to five fingers and call out the number they guess will be the sum of both their hands. This is repeated with a particular quick rhythm until one person correctly guesses the total of their fingers, and then the other person must drink ("Gan bei!", literally "Dry glass!"). Warning: Taiwan wine is quite potent. Shao Hsing wine is popular, plum wine is tasty, and Kaoliang wine is nasty.

Shopping

Scrolls, paintings, dolls, jade and pearl jewelry, handmade flowers, wood carvings, pottery and marble products are sold in many Taipei shops. Handwoven rugs, antiques, teakwood furniture, and intricately carved screens are also special bargains for those on substantially higher budgets. Unless you speak Chinese it's probably best to shop on Chungshan North Rd., but you can also look for bargains at the China Bazaar, night markets, and the large department stores. Always bargain vigorously (except in department stores) or at least ask for a student discount. See the 'Bargaining' section in the **Before You Go** chapter for tips on bargaining. The displays at the Taiwan Handicraft Promotion Center (see below) will give you some idea of fixed retail prices.

Taiwan Handicraft Promotion Center, 1 Hsu Chou (Hsuchou) South Rd. (see map).

Displays handicraft from all over Taiwan.

Mei Hwa Handicrafts, 178 Chungshan North Rd., Sec. 3.

Small selection from church-related self-help projects for aborigines.

TAIWAN 335

Far Eastern Department Store, Chung Hsu South Rd., near the clock circle.

Far Eastern has stores all over the island. In addition to discounted merchandise the stores have relatively inexpensive dim sum restaurants on the top floor.

Ting San Iou, 12 Chungshan North Rd., Sec. 1.

Wide selection of hiking and camping gear.

Caves Bookstore, 99 Chungshan North Rd., Sec. 2.

Excellent selection of English-language books. Other bookstores one and two blocks north and south of Caves offer equally large selections of books in English (many of them pirated) and current cassette tapes. (Incidentally, be discreet about bringing pirated books into your own country.) Take bus #218, #17, or #246 from the train station to Taiwan Cement Corporation—the third stop on Chungshan North Rd.—and walk north or south on the same side of the road. Caves also sells tickets to concerts and other cultural events being held at the Sun Yat-Sen Memorial Hall.

ACCOMMODATIONS IN TAIPEI

Taipei Hostel 錦州街4巷5號二樓 , 2nd floor, #5, Lane 4, Chin Chow St.; tel. 541-2025.

Four rooms w/four beds each, NT$60/person. Take bus #23 from Sungshan Airport and get off on Chungshan North Rd., Sec. 2, at the 100 block. The hostel is on an alley directly behind the Caves Bookstore, 99 Chungshan North Rd. A good place to get travel information for the whole island. From the bus/train station take any bus that goes to Chungshan North Rd. and get off at Taiwan Cement Corporation, the third stop.

Chientan Youth Activity Center, 16 Chungshan North Rd., Sec. 4; tel. 593-1904.

Dormitory accommodations; prices similar to Taipei Hostel. Much more expensive private rooms also available.

Taipei YMCA Hotel, 19 Hsu Chang St. (one block south of the train station); tel. 3113201, 3312924.

Offers 100 clean, well-kept rooms, all w/ac, private bath, and telephone. Singles NT$440-600; doubles NT$610-770. NT$100 for an extra bed. Discounts available for students, educators/teachers, and YMCA members.

International Hotel 國際大旅社, located in Yang Ming Shan Park; tel. 861-6022.

Tatami rooms w/o bath start at NT$275/night; add NT$55 for every extra person. Tatami rooms w/bath start at NT$550; add NT$110 for each extra person. More expensive Western rooms also available. Discounts available for longer periods of a week or more. Though Yang Ming Shan is far from downtown (1 hr. by bus) it's only a 20 min. bus ride from the Grand Hotel, and is an interesting, more quiet area of town.

336 TAIWAN

International House 信義路四段16號, 18 Hsin Yi Rd., Sec. 3; tel. 707-3151.

Single w/private bath NT$350; double w/bath NT$450. Special rates for students (males only): single w/o bath NT$150, dorm accommodations (four beds/room) NT$100.

New Mayflower Hotel, 1 Chungking South Rd.; tel. 361-4171.

Single w/bath & ac NT$303, double w/bath & ac NT$424; single w/shared bath NT$300; NT$100 for an extra bed.

Liberty House, 16 Ai Kuo Rd. 愛國路16號 ; tel. 311-9987.

Singles w/ac NT$410; doubles w/ac NT$550-600. Located near the Botanical Gardens (see map); from the train station take bus 0 (zero) south to Ching Bei Dzung Bu

NOTE: Most accommodations listed above add a 10% surcharge to the bill.

Escaping Taipei

Highway buses leave from the East and West Terminals next to the railway station (see map). If you take the train, remember to buy tickets one or two days in advance.

Yang Ming Shan 陽明山 is a nice mountain park; go on a weekday if possible to enjoy the flower gardens and blossoms. Catch bus #301 across the street from the railway station or along Chungshan North Rd. If you get off the bus partway up the hill and walk the rest of the way to the park, you can get a flavor of rural Taiwan from the numbers of small farms tucked into various nooks of the Yang Ming Mountain Valley. **Walking in Taiwan** (see **Bibliography**) lists 9 easy hikes around Yang Ming Shan and other areas in and around Taipei.

Yeh Liu 野柳, north of Taipei near the port city of Keelung, is famous for its unique coral rock formations. **Chin Shan** is a popular beach near Yeh Liu Park, good for swimming. From the East Bus Terminal take the Keelung Express, then from Keelung take a bus to Chin Shan; return to Taipei through the small town of Tamsui.

At **Pitan** (Green Lake) 碧潭 row boats, swim, or cross the suspension bridge and enjoy the view from the cool mountain park. From the small bus station at 3 Kaifeng St., catch a highway bus to Hsindian, which is within walking distance of Pitan.

Wulai 烏來 is a touristy but beautiful retreat in the mountains. From the bus station walk up the hill, cross the suspension bridge, and continue climbing. An aboriginal village display sits halfway up the hill on the left, and further up a ropeway crosses high over the ravine to the 'Dreamland' complex above the waterfall. Dreamland includes an aquarium, a roller skating rink, lakes for fishing and rowing boats, electric bumper cars, and a swimming pool. Go on a weekday; you can stay overnight inexpensively in a tatami room in one of the hotels.

Fulung Beach 福隆 is one of the finest beaches in Taiwan. Good snorkeling can be found by walking south along the main road of Fulung for ½ km. Following a path to the beach you'll reach a coastline of flat rocks from which you can snorkel, sunbathe, and swim in relative privacy. For details on transportation and accommodations check with the Information Service Center at the Taipei Railway Station, where you can make reservations on the crowded morning express train (1½ hr.). Or take a bus to Fulung from Taipei (via Keelung); the trip takes 1¼ hr.

The East Coast

The completion of the new railway from Suao through 15 tunnels and over 91 bridges to Hualien was a major transportation breakthrough for Taiwan's East Coast. Costing US$200 million, the railway is one of the most difficult engineering projects ever undertaken in Asia. Transportation by train is now possible from Taipei to Hualien in less than 2½ hrs. The Coastal Highway from Suao to Hualien, clinging to precipitous cliffs the length of the 4-hr. bus trip, offers some of the most breathtaking scenery in Taiwan. Be sure to sit on the ocean side of the bus and bring extra film.

Suao 蘇澳, once a quiet coastal town, is now a busy industrializing city thanks to the new railway and the construction of a huge port there (along with the new railway, one of Taiwan's Ten Development Projects).

Hualien 花蓮, with its small but busy international port, still has a small town atmosphere (though that is sure to change with the new railway). Tourists fly here to see the folk dances of the Ami aboriginal tribe. Most hotels offer free transportation to the performances, held daily at 2:30 pm, 7 pm, and 8 pm. Tickets cost NT$80; discounts are available through your hotel.

Tienhsiang 天祥 and **Taroko Gorge** 太魯閣, less than a couple of hours from Hualien by bus, should not be missed. Taroko is a tiny village on the coast north of Hualien; from Taroko the narrow highway follows the gorge created by the rapid Li Wu River up to Tienhsiang. The scenery is truly spectacular. Get off the bus at the marble bridge about 10 km below Tienhsiang and hike the rest of the way. This section of the road runs through many tunnels carved out of the steep sides of the gorge. The landscape is reminiscent of ancient Chinese scroll paintings, with mist rising from the rushing river

338 TAIWAN

and sharp peaks jutting straight up into the sky. Stay overnight in Tienhsiang. In the morning, hike up from the town to a small waterfall and pool in the mountains across the large suspension bridge.

Taitung 台東, noted for its pottery (esp. tea sets and plateware), lies further down the East Coast. The train ride from Hualien to Taitung offers some fine views of the inland valleys. Buses run from Taitung to Fengkang on the west coast.

Lan Yu Island (Orchid Island) 蘭嶼島, less than 80 km. southeast of Taitung, is a volcanic island inhabited by approximately 2000 aborigines of the Ya-Mai tribe. Lan Yu is less visited by foreign tourists than other areas of Taiwan and careful preparations should be made beforehand. It can be reached by plane or boat (though boats must have 40 passengers before they'll sail). For complete information on transportation and exit permits, etc., contact the travel agency directly across from the train station in Taitung or the Huang Chia Luhsing She Travel Agency in Taipei, 10th floor, 82 Chung Shan North Rd., Sec. 1.

ACCOMMODATIONS ON THE EAST COAST

Suao:
Several small hotels with tatami rooms are located near the train station. Walk one block east from the station and turn right to find the **Golden Swallow Inn**—inexpensive rooms w/bed & fan.

Hualien:
Youth Hostel, 84 Chungshan Rd. (½ block to the left as you leave the train station). Tatami rooms in back for 2 or more, NT$80/person; Western singles w/fan NT$150. Not particularly clean.

Teachers' Hostel, near the fire station. Inexpensive rooms on the 2nd floor. From the train station walk up the hill past the Tung Ching Pagoda, then downhill past the police station and Main Gate, and turn left at the first big intersection; the hostel is one block past the fire station on the right. Across from the hostel is a bus stop for the Hualien-Taroko route.

Representatives from various hotels in Hualien will often meet travelers at the Hualien New Station with pictures and broken but recognizable English to describe their hotels. They usually provide free transportation to their hotel and a choice of rooms which you can see before you decide. Prices start at around NT$400 for a double and go up from there. Hotels also provide special services such as reduced tickets to aboriginal dancing performances.

TAIWAN 339

Tienhsiang:
 Catholic Youth Hostel, up the hill west of the bus station. Tatami and Western-style rooms, NT$50-150. Ask for information on good hikes in the surrounding mountains.
 Government Youth Hostel, further up the hill from the Catholic Hostel (look for the signs). Offers a variety of prices and rooms. Dormitory accomodations (each tatami room fits 8 persons) NT$100/person; doubles w/bath NT$400; 4 persons in one room w/bath NT$600. Very modern, clean, and spacious.

Taitung:
 Turn right as you come out of the train station to find several inexpensive hotels offering rooms w/beds, fan, and shared bath (NT$100); nicer rooms cost up to NT$400.

Lan Yu:
 Lan Yu Hotel. Has tatami rooms, but it's expensive. Inquire about staying at a Catholic church or sleeping in a school.

TRANSPORTATION ON THE EAST COAST

The following is a partial list of train schedules and fares from Taipei to Hualien. Check with a travel agency or at the information window at the Taipei train station for details. Make reservations one or two days in advance if possible.

	Southbound		Northbound	
Train	Lv. Taipei	Ar. Hualien	Lv. Hualien	Ar. Taipei
Dwei Hau	0700	1016	0745	1250
Chu Kuang	0740	1210	1040	1440
Dwei Hau	0935	1345	1234	1715

Several buses leave Hualien daily for Taroko Gorge and Tienhsiang (NT$29). It's not necessary to go all the way to Hualien from Suao in order to get to Tienhsiang; you can get off the highway bus in Taroko and catch a bus or hike (several hours) up the gorge. Or walk down after an overnight in Tienhsiang for an easier hike. You can also take a bus from Tienhsiang, then get off halfway to the gorge and walk the rest of the way.

Taitung can be reached from Hualien by train. The Dwei Hau leaves Hualien at 8 am (NT$120, 4 hr.). There are also four daily Chu Kuang trains on the same run (NT$154).

If you are stranded in Hualien by landslides on both the Hualien-Suao Highway and the Cross-Island Highway, you can take a ferry from Hualien to Keelung (Taipei's port). Buy tickets at the ferry company office across the street from the train station. One ferry 花蓮輪 makes the return trip to Keelung each night at 10:30 (and leaves Keelung every morning at 9). Fares: reclining seat, NT$300; student, NT$240; for a sleeping berth add NT$120 to the basic fare. Sometimes the boats don't sail due to heavy fog.

The Central Mountains

A **mountain pass** is required for hiking on the Cross-Island Highway, the Lushan-Hualien Powerline Trail, and in other remote areas. It's best to get a pass in Taipei and then register with the county police headquarters in the area where you'll be hiking; mountain passes can also be obtained in other cities but the applications must be sent to Taipei, which means waiting several days. In Taipei, call or visit the Consul of the US Embassy, Passport and Citizenship Office, 87 Nanking East Rd., Sec. 2, for a letter to the city's Provincial Police Headquarters endorsing your travel plans. In addition to this letter of reference, you'll need several photos, NT$10, and your passport when you fill out the application at the Foreign Affairs Office of the Provincial Police Headquarters on Chung Hsiao Rd. (see tourist map).

The **Cross-Island Highway**, winding and climbing its way through the rugged Central Mountain Range, provides access to some challenging hiking trails and remote villages. The highway itself was literally carved out of the mountainside by thousands of workers, many of whom lost their lives during the half decade of construction. The two-way traffic is carefully regulated, but occasionally buses narrowly miss each other as they round the sharp curves, horns blaring, high above the winding valleys. Refer to the book **Walking in Taiwan** (see **Bibliography**) for details on trails in this area and elsewhere.

The hiking trail from **Wushe** 霧社 to **Tayuling** 大禹嶺 passes over Hohuan Mountain 合歡山, a ski resort during the winter. From Wushe (the site of a 1930 uprising against the Japanese) it takes three hours to hike up to the ski lodge at Hohuan, and another three hours to Tayuling on the Cross-Island Highway. The ski lodge, which is open all year round, has inexpensive tatami bunks downstairs. Meals are offered at set prices—a bit expensive but quite filling.

NOTE: For these and other hiking trips in the mountains be sure to bring gear appropriate for rainy weather and steep trails. Also be aware that Taiwan has many poisonous snakes; be especially careful when hiking at dusk. If you're bitten by a snake, identify it by color and size immediately (better yet kill it if possible and take it along to the doctor, should you by any long chance be near one), apply a loose tourniquet, remain calm to avoid quick absorption of the venum, and obtain an antivenom serum as soon as possible. (It would be a good idea to get descriptions of the island's snakes before you start your hike; inquire at the Tourism Bureau.) Also note that drinking water should be boiled for at least 20 minutes.

TAIWAN 341

The **Lushan**蘆山**Hualien**花蓮**Powerline Trail** takes you into the wilderness of Taiwan. Apply at least 3 weeks ahead of time to the Taiwan Power Company (39, Hoping East Rd., Sec. 1), Taipei for permission to use the trail and houses along the trail. If you start from Lushan (famous for its hot springs), the trip takes about three days of fast walking down a fairly easy trail, but if you come up from Hualien plan on at least four days of rugged hiking. Free houses are maintained along the trail by the Taiwan Power Company, but it is imperative to bring wine, cigarettes, or food for the workmen who let you stay in them. Blankets are provided, but bring your own food and water (some water is available, but bring some along just in case).

Hiking East on the Powerline Patrol Road

1st day (15 km)
12:00 Lushan
      1391 m.
16:00 Yun Hai
      2340 m.
18:30 Tyan Chi
      2860 m.

2nd day (20 km)
7:00 Tyan Chi
8:00 Tyan Chi
    sky pool
10:00 Tyan Chi
    north peak
16:00 Chi Lai
    1126 m.

3rd day (29 km)
7:00 Chi Lai
8:00 Tyan Jang
    cliff
9:30 Pan Shr
    1048 m.
14:00 Shwei Lin
    385 m.
16:00 Tung Men
    165 m.
18:00 Hualien

ACCOMMODATIONS IN THE CENTRAL MOUNTAINS

Wushe:
Stay at the Catholic Youth Hostel.

Lushan:
The Lower Lushan Hot Springs area has reasonably-priced hotels near the suspension bridge. If you plan to hike the Powerline Trail with a group you may be able to arrange to sleep in the school further up at Lushan Town, right at the start of the trail.

Tayuling:
Try the government **Youth Hostel** up the steps near the bus station. (It may be crowded on weekends during the summer months.)

TRANSPORTATION IN THE CENTRAL MOUNTAINS

Buses leave for the trip over the Cross-Island Highway from Taichung Train Station at 7:15 and 7:55 am, and from Hualien at 7:20 and 8:20 am (9 hr., NT$173 one-way). For shorter trips along the Cross-Island Highway, and from Taichung to Puli, Wushe, or Lushan, local buses leave two or three times a day.

The West Coast

Those who have an interest in Buddhism should visit the temples at **Shihtou Shan** (Lion's Head Mountain) 獅頭山, near Hsinchu. At this major Buddhist center travelers are welcome to stay overnight and eat vegetarian meals prepared in the temples. (Leave a donation of NT$110-120 for tatami room and meals.) When you get off the bus at Shihtou Shan, walk up the steep stone steps and follow the path to the temples (the nicest ones are at the top of the mountain). Spend a day hiking cliffs; if you hike all the way over the mountain you'll reach the town of Omei, where you can catch a bus back to Hsinchu.

Taichung, 台中, the starting point for trips on the Cross-Island Highway, is a provincial capital and major college town. Parts of the city are quite modern, but traditional markets are still easy to find. The **First Market** 第一市場 is a sight not to miss; to get there walk straight out from the train station, cross the canal, and enter the first block on the right (there's a narrow alley on the corner which leads into the center of the block). As you wander through the network of passageways, look for a group of shops selling dishes of mixed fruit and shaved ice for NT$15-20 a plate (it's called 'bing,' and though it can be found throughout the island it's particularly famous in Taichung). Another specialty of Taichung found in the First Market is the sun cake, 'tai yang bing,' 太陽餅 NT$5 each.

For a brief respite from the traffic and noise, visit Taichung's main **city park**, a 10-min. walk from the train station. Walk straight out the main entrance of the train station for 3 blocks; turn right at the intersection with a large department store on your right and a bank on your left; this is Tzu Yui Rd., Taichung's main shopping street. Walk along this street for 3 blocks; the park is ahead of you. The park has a large central lake with benches for resting and paddle boats for rent. Shan Shi Kwan Restaurant, 4 blocks from the park, on Shr Fu Lu Rd., offers, northern Chinese food for NT$125-200 a person. To get there, leave from the main park entrance; bear right on Kuang Yuan Rd. The first street on the left is Shr Fu Lu Rd.

Other points of interest in and around Taichung include **Pa Kua Shan**, the large Buddha at Changhua (16 km south of the city); a new **Confucian temple** on Shuang Shih Rd., across the street from the city's main outdoor stadium; the **Giant Smiling Buddha** on Chien Hsing Rd., which features a good folklore museum inside the 60-ft. Buddha; **Taichung Chung Shan Park** 中山公園, on Gung Yuen Rd., where you can see Chinese martial arts, folk-dancing, and disco dancing from 6 to 9 am daily; and the **Night Market** on Chung Hwa Rd.

Chitou Park, a university forest research area open to the public for hiking, is only two hours from Taichung by bus. Beautiful bamboo, pine-covered misty mountains; you can hike from here to Alishan in about 12 hours. Catch the bus (NT$48) to Chitou Park at the Taichung Bus Station, behind the railroad tracks (cross the pedestrian bridge). Lu Kang, 鹿港, 30 km south of Taichung, is Taiwan's second oldest city, and is still very traditional with narrow streets, many older buildings, and a fine folklore museum.

The only way to get to Alishan (except by hiking) is by train from **Chiayi** 嘉義. We recommend staying overnight in Chiayi and getting a reserved seat on the Chiayi-Alishan Forestry Railway's early morning train. You can ride the ordinary diesel train down; you may have to stand, but it's less expensive. Chiayi has a night market that stretches for five blocks along Wen Hua Rd. Kuan Ying Pubu 觀音瀑布 is a series of waterfalls located in the green mountain outside of Chiayi. It's a cool respite from the city heat. Take the bus from the station next to the train station, then hike for an hour up the trail to the main waterfall. A good place for a picnic and splashing in the water.

From Chiayi you can also go to **Kuan Tzu Ling**, 關子嶺, a popular hot springs resort. Soak away your troubles, if not your chronic minor ailments, in the muddy-gray waters.

Alishan 阿里山 is one of the most beautiful mountain retreats easily accessible to travelers. It can get quite cool, but the cherry blossoms in spring, the sunrise over a sea of clouds, and the mountain mists are stunning. The town of Alishan is quite small, and there are many paths nearby for short hikes. (Almost all the Taiwanese travelers get up at 4 am to hike up the road to watch the sun rise.)

Tainan 台南, one of Taiwan's oldest cities, was the seat of the provincial government when Taiwan was officially a part of China. The city's old buildings, temples, and markets can be toured easily on foot.

An Ping Fort (also known as Fort Zeelandia), built by the Dutch in the 16th century, is on the outskirts of the city in the An Ping district. Enclosed by a 100-yard wall, all that remains today of the original fort, this military stronghold was where the Dutch

344 TAIWAN

surrendered to Koxinga, after a nine-month siege. The tower and the main buildings that cover the ruins of the original fort were built by the Japanese. Look for the traditional Chinese houses in this area, some of which are over 100 years old. Across from the fort is a temple built by the fishermen of An Ping in honor of Matsu, the goddess of the sea.

Chih Kan Tower (called Fort Providentia by the Dutch), 212 Min Tsu Rd., was the administrative center of the Dutch colony and the seat of Koxinga's government after he defeated the Dutch. A memorial to this Fukien-born warrior is located next to the Tainan historical museum on 152 Kai Shan Rd.

There seems to be a temple on almost every city block of Tainan. **Confucius Temple**, 2 Nan Men Rd., is the oldest temple of its kind in Taiwan. Built in 1666, it is the site where Teacher's Day celebrations take place on September 28, Confucius' birthday. **K'ai Yuan Temple**, on K'ai Yuan Rd., is the largest temple in Tainan. Frequently families clothed in white and sackcloth can be seen mourning a relative's death. This temple also supports the hospital that stands next to the grounds. **Great Queen of Heaven Temple**, 18 Yung Fu Rd., honors the sea goddess Matsu. The temple carvings are reputedly the finest on the island.

At the end of the day, try relaxing in the dim sum restaurant on the top floor of the Far Eastern Dept. Store on Min Tsu Rd. (just down the street from Fort Providentia). Great dim sum at moderate prices. The night market that runs along Min Tsu Rd. offers local specialties; if you're really daring, try a bowl of snake meat/blood (NT$40). At the end of Chong Cheng Rd. there is a roofed maze of stalls referred to as the 'saw-caw-lee-bah', famous for inexpensive saefood dishes. Cafeterias behind the train station near the local university also serve meals at moderate prices.

For a good side trip from Tainan, take a bus up to the **Tsengwen Reservoir**, a beautiful artificial lake in the mountains, and an essential source of power and water for all of central western Taiwan. Stay overnight at the Tsengwen Youth Activities Center.

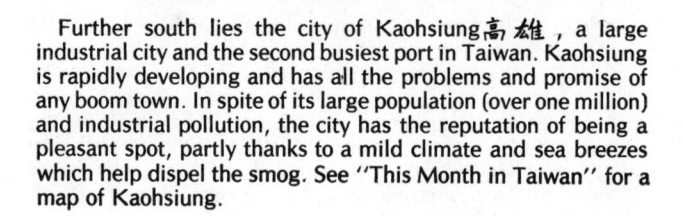

Further south lies the city of Kaohsiung 高雄, a large industrial city and the second busiest port in Taiwan. Kaohsiung is rapidly developing and has all the problems and promise of any boom town. In spite of its large population (over one million) and industrial pollution, the city has the reputation of being a pleasant spot, partly thanks to a mild climate and sea breezes which help dispel the smog. See "This Month in Taiwan" for a map of Kaohsiung.

For a good tour of the city, take bus #1, starting from the train station. The bus crosses Love River and passes a large circle with a statue of Chiang Kai-shek, then stops near the large Tah Shing Dept. Store. Eventually it terminates at the city's crowded wholesale fish market, where large junks unload tons of fish in the early morning.

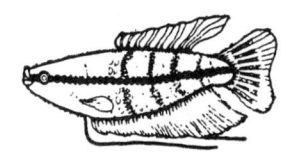

Next to the fish market is the landing ferry to **Chi Jin Island**. Take a fascinating ride across Kaohsiung Harbor (only NT$5) to a sleepy fishing village where you can buy fresh crab on the street for NT$25-30. Walk down the major road past the police station to find a public city beach. On the Kaohsiung side of the harbor is another beach, Hsi Tzu Wan, which was once Chiang Kai-shek's private retreat. Walk under the tunnel on the other side of the pier from the ferry landing to get there.

From the fish market area you can also take a bus to the village of Tung Kang, from which boats depart for **Hsiao Liuchiu Yu.** Known as 'little Okinawa,' this small island off the coast of Kaohsiung is dotted with traditional fishing villages. (Catch the bus to Tung Kang at about 7 am from the train station; about NT$30.)

For those interested in Taiwan's economic development, both the China Shipbuilding Co. and the China Steel Corp. give tours. The largest ship-wrecking operation in the world is located in Kaohsiung's 'Second Harbor'; watch huge tankers being sliced apart, so the steel can be recycled.

Shoushan Park, the hill on the western edge of the city, offers an excellent view of the city, the harbor, and the ocean.

Taiwan's main Buddhist college is located near Kaohsiung; **Fou Kuang Shan** is known for the hundreds of golden Buddha images lining the paths on the college grounds. Vegetarian Chinese food is available in the college's restaurant. To get to Fou Kuang Shan take a bus from the Kaohsiung Bus Station.

A visit to **San Ti Men**, an aboriginal village not too far from Kaohsiung, would be another interesting day trip. The village architecture is quite distinctive; the houses are made of stacked slate. Highway buses leave frequently from the Kaohsiung Station.

If you're really hankering for a hamburger (NT$60-75) or for a dish of good ice cream (NT$20) on a hot afternoon, Foremost Restaurant is the place to go. It's located in Jung Shan 1st Rd. right next to President (Ta Tony) Dept. Store.

346 TAIWAN

From Kaohsiung you can make a three- to five-day hike on the old **Southern Cross-Island Highway**. You'll need a mountain pass and you must register with the Kaohsiung County Police in Feng Shan (near Kaohsiung City). There are inexpensive hostels along the highway, which is no longer passable by car due to a partially collapsed tunnel. The new Southern Cross-Island Highway connects Kaohsiung with Taitung on the SE coast of Taiwan; the bus trip between these two cities passes through Fangliao, and takes the whole day.

In its stark, almost arid beauty, **Penghu** 澎湖, (the Pescadores), halfway between Taiwan and the mainland, is an interesting contrast to the subtropical lushness of Taiwan. Noted for strong winds, sun, and beautiful beaches, Penghu seems largely unaffected by the outside world. Take a 1½-hr. bus ride from the main town of Makung 馬公 to Wai An 外垵, a fishing village at the end of a 3-island chain; an old fortress is 20 min. away by foot. Shr Li 時裡, is a beautiful beach (except on Sundays) cove with soft white sand and aqua blue water; rarely visited on weekdays.

Oluanpi, at the island's southern tip, has the most beautiful beaches and coral reefs in Taiwan. **Kenting Tropical Park**, in the same area, has excellent botanical gardens.

TRANSPORTATION ON THE WEST COAST

Shihtou Shan: Take a train to Hsinchu from Taipei or Taichung. Turn left as you leave the Hsinchu Train Station and walk to the bus station several blocks down on the right side of the street. Buses for Shihtou Shan leave regularly.

Chitou Park: Buses leave hourly from the Taichung Bus Station (about NT$48, 2 hr.).

Chiayi & Tainan: Take the Taipei-Kaohsiung bus or train; get off at Chiayi or Tainan.

Alishan: Take a Chiayi-Alishan Forestry Railway train. The Chung Shiu Express (reserved seats) leaves Chiayi twice a day, at 7:40 am and 1:30 pm, arriving in Alishan at 11:30 am and 5:10 pm; NT$122.50. Roundtrip reservations can be made, but are only good for return the very next day. The Kuan Gu Express leaves Chiayi at 8 am and 2 pm, arriving in Alishan at 12:10 and 6:04 pm. A very crowded ordinary train makes one run a day, leaving at 8:50 am and arriving at 2 pm; NT$107 one way.

TAIWAN 347

Kuan Tzu Ling: Take a country bus from the station at Zhong Shan Rd. in Chiayi.

Kaohsiung: From Taipei by highway bus (Kuo Kuan Hao), 4-5 hr., NT$348. By night bus from Taipei (1st departure 9:07, last departure 11:30), NT$348; buy ticket same day after 2 pm. Several limited express trains (Dwei Hau Kwai) also connect Taipei and Kaohsiung daily (4-5 hr.). From Tainan, buses to Kaohsiung are cheaper than trains and leave more frequently; Chin Lung buses leave at 20- to 40-min. intervals, Chin Ma buses leave every ½ hr.

Penghu: Boats leave from Kaohsiung from pier 1 at 8 am, arriving in Makung at 1:00 pm. The boat returns from Makung at 8:30 am the next day, arriving in Kaohsiung at 1:30 pm; another boat leaves Makung at 3 pm. Buy tickets in advance at pier 1 from 8:30-11:30 am or 2-5 pm; NT$155 (no seat) and NT$276 (with seat). Boats run about every other day. For complete information contact the Taiwan Navigation Corp., 136 Chien Kuo 4th Rd. (tel. 553730 or 563866).

Kenting & Oluanpi: Chin Ma highway buses leave Kaohsiung at 7, 7:35, 8:45, and 9:30 am; 1-1½ hr. Chin Lung buses leave every morning at 8. You can also take local buses (about 2½ hr.), but you may have to stop at Hengching and take a taxi to Kenting (no more than NT$20/person).

ACCOMMODATIONS ON THE WEST COAST

Shihtou Shan:
Temple lodgings; NT$90-100 for tatami room, breakfast, and dinner.

Taichung:
Taichung CYC Youth Hostel 救國團, 262-1 Lishing Rd.; tel. 348291. NT$60 for dorm accommodations. This place seldom has rooms during summer and winter school vacations so it's best to call ahead and check.

Wan An Lyu She 萬安旅社, Cheng Kung Rd., Lane 128 #8; tel. 224173. Tatami rooms for NT$180 (add NT$30 for each additional person). From the train station, walk up Chung Cheng Rd. to the 2nd stoplight and turn right. Just past the Far Eastern Dept. Store and another stoplight are some food stalls; the hotel is in a courtyard behind these.

Mei Du Hotel 美都, 1 Chung Cheng Rd., near the train station; tel. 223046-9. Rooms w/double beds NT$342. Rooms w/twin beds NT$432 for 2 people, NT$680 for 4. All rooms have ac and color TV.

Chitou Park:
Dormitory operated by National Taiwan University, tel. (049) 612345. NT$50/person for tatami bunks. Nearby restaurants and food stalls are somewhat expensive; save money by packing in your own food. Also several hotels w/doubles for NT$550 w/ac and TV.

Chiayi:
Hotel Northwest 嘉義市仁愛路192號, near the train station; tel. (052) 223331. Tatami rooms NT$80/person, singles NT$250.

Formosa Hotel 嘉義市仁愛路244號; tel. (052) 272366. Tatami rooms NT$70/person, doubles NT$120/person, singles NT$200.

348 TAIWAN

Alishan:
Kaofeng Cottage高峯山莊, 9 North Alishan. Tatami rooms NT$180 (room NT$80, breakfast NT$30, dinner NT$70). They'll be flexible if you want to make other eating arrangements. Alisa or Fey Chen meet most of the trains and gather up the foreigners who descend looking bewildered. They can tell you about the great hiking trails in the area.

Kuan Tzu Ling:
There are several excellent Japanese-style inns with hot spring baths and meals.

Tainan:
Tainan Christian Academy Hotel, 274-2 Ching Nien Rd.; tel. (062) 379-464. Dorm accommodations NT$80, w/tatami or western bunk beds and common bath. Visitors must arrive by 5:30 pm. Ask at the Tainan Theological Academy in the same compound for information on interesting things to do in Tainan.

Kaohsiung:
Try any hotel around the train station; most range from NT$270 to NT$350 for doubles. **Hotel Duke**, 233 Lin Sen 1st Rd., a few blocks from the train station, is in this category.

Penghu:
Teacher's Hotel. 3 blocks from the harbor on the main street, next to the library. Dorm rooms NT$60/person w/common bath; private rooms NT$180 w/private bath and ac (2-3 people can stay in one room).

Oluanpi:
Guest House, located 20 min. from the last bus stop, near Oluanpi's lighthouse. Western rooms w/fan. Walk from the bus stop past the military gate; the guest house is off to the left at the very end of the road.

Kenting:
Kenting Hotel, close to the park gate; tel. (088) 892333. Tatami rooms NT$60/person.
Beach Hotel, also near the park gate; tel. (108) 244 or 264. Tatami rooms NT$60/person.
Catholic Youth Hostel, on the right side of the main road just past Kenting on the way to Oluanpi. Tatami dormitory rooms for large groups.

Bibliography

Chinese Stories from Taiwan, 1960-1970, ed. by Joseph Lau. Short stories in translation.

The House of Lim, by Margery Wolf. A study of a Chinese farm family.

Chinese Religion: An Introduction, by Laurence Thompson. Comprehensive, easy to read.

Formosa at Your Fingertips: Guide to Taipei and all Taiwan, by Joseph Nerbonne. Available in southern Taiwan.

Woman and Family in Rural Taiwan, by Marjorie Wolf.

This Month in Taiwan, free tourist publication with information on current events.

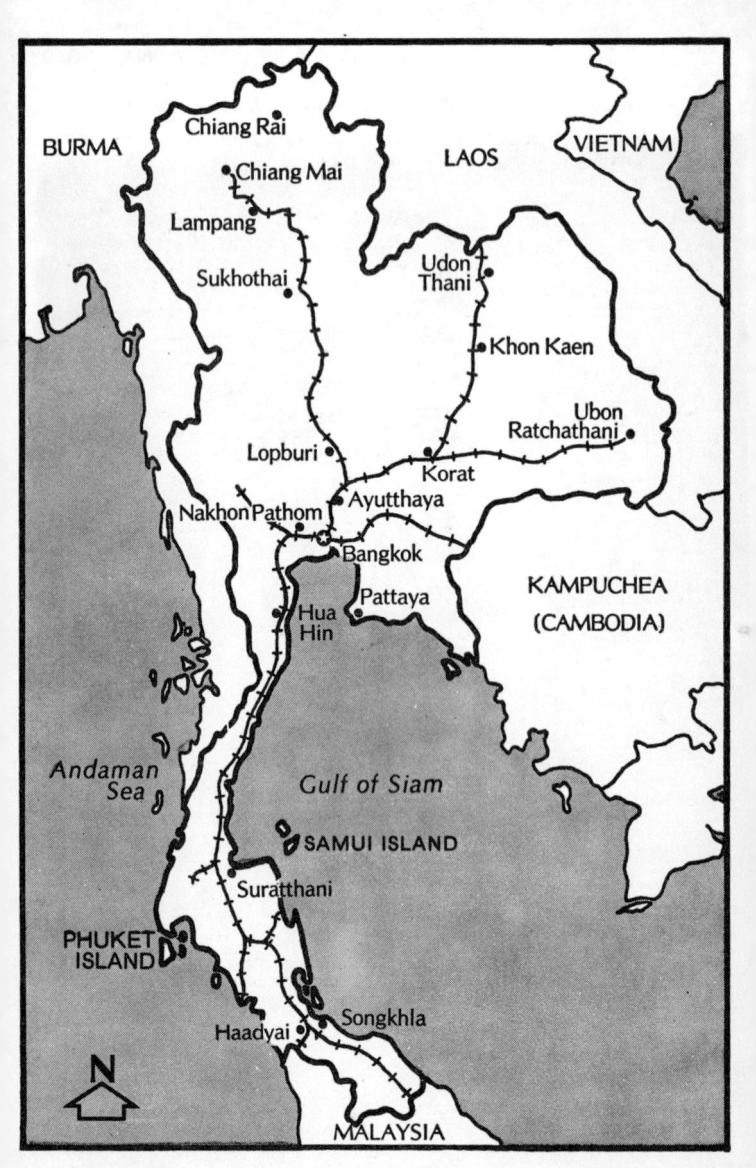

THAILAND

General Information

Arrival: The cheapest transportation for the 29 km trip from Don Muang airport to downtown Bangkok is the bus which stops on the highway in front of the airport: #29 and #34 go to the Bangkok railway station and #39 to Pramane Ground (a central area to catch other buses). The fare is B5. An air-conditioned bus (#4) leaves from the same place for Silom Rd., which is within walking distance of the YMCA, YWCA and the Malaysia Hotel (B15). These buses have no baggage racks.

By far the handiest means (and the one we recommend) is the airport transport service which, for B50, takes you directly to your hotel. Their counter is just outside the customs area. Taxis require bargaining; the airport-downtown fare should be about B150 regardless of the number of passengers. For three or more people, a taxi ride would cost less than the airport transport service. Allow at least one hour—possibly two during rush hour—from airport to hotel. (You'll collect Bangkok traffic stories during your stay).

Departure: Give yourself plenty of time to get to the airport, so that heavy traffic won't cause you to miss your flight. The airport departure tax is B50.

Currency: The exchange rate in September 1980 was 20.35 baht (B20.35) to the US dollar. One baht = 100 satang (pronounced s'tung). Thai coins can be confusing since they don't use Arabic numbers. Take a few minutes to figure them out. Size corresponds roughly to value. Starting with the smallest coin: 1) gold-colored 25 satang piece (also called salung), 2) gold-colored 50 satang (only slightly larger than the 25 satang coin), 3) silver 1 baht piece (confusion here stems from the fact that two slightly different coins are minted), 4) silver 5 baht pieces are substantially larger than 1 baht pieces and are minted 'sandwich' style, i.e. copper band in the middle.

The British/Hong Kong banks in Bangkok have recently been charging a B10 'postage fee' or 'service charge' when changing travelers' checks. All banks in Thailand must collect B1 per check for revenue stamps, but to avoid these additional charges change your money at a Thai or American bank.

Visas: Transit visas allow a stay of eight days with no extension; tourist visas permit a two-month stay with no extensions. Getting a non-immigrant visa involves complicated paperwork and usually must be carried out through the Thai Embassy in your home country. Any passport-holder whose country has diplomatic relations with Thailand may now enter

352 THAILAND

the Kingdom for a stay of up to 15 days without a visa, provided that upon entry s/he can show confirmed passage out of the country by air or ship of over 500 tons (this type of entry permit cannot be extended). According to official TAT publications (see below), this privilege will soon be extended to all travelers, regardless of transportation, but as of this writing the policy has not yet changed.

Climate: Very hot and humid. There are three seasons: 'hot' (read 'sizzling'), March-May; 'wet,' June-Oct.; 'cool' (read 'less hot'), Nov.-Feb.

Sources of Information

Tourist Authority of Thailand (TAT), Mansion 2, Ratchadamnoen Nok Ave.; tel. 2218151. Provides a helpful **Travel Handbook** which includes bus and train schedules, and numerous duplicated sheets with travel and accommodation information for various destinations. Pick up a copy of 'Where', a free newspaper distributed in conjunction with the Thai Hotels Association which features articles on unusual attractions (available at hotels as well). Also, buy a map (B10 at TAT, B20 in bookstores). This newest one, which includes both regular and ac bus routes, is called **The Latest Tour's** (sic) **Guide to Bangkok and Thailand.**

For those arriving from Malaysia by train, there is a TAT office in Haadyai at 9 Prachatipat Rd., next to the Sukhontha Hotel. Other branches are in Phuket, Kanchanaburi, Korat, Pattaya and Chiang Mai.

Trad Travel Service, Viengtai Hotel 42 Tanee Rd., Banglumpoo; tel. 2815788. Offers discounts on hotels and tours to ISIC holders.

Siam Society, 131 Soi Asok (Suhkumvit Soi 21); tel. 3914401. An organization established to encourage interest in Thai culture, history, arts and science. The Society has a library, publishes a quarterly journal of Thai history (in English), and conducts a film series.

Background

The first glimpse most travelers will have of this Buddhist nation will be Bangkok, a sprawling metropolis with enormous palaces, hundreds of temples, lots of commercial activity, and incredible traffic jams. But if you're interested in Thailand's history and indigenous traditions, you must look beyond Bangkok to the countryside. Eighty percent of the country's population of 44 million are involved in agriculture. Chiang Mai, the cultural center of the north, has preserved traditional arts and crafts, and home industries. The ancient capitals of Ayutthaya, Lopburi, Sukhothai, and Nakhon Pathom contain fascinating vestiges of Thailand's early kingdoms.

Ethnic Thais make up about 80% of the population; 10% are Chinese, 4% are Malay, and there are small groups of Khmers, Lao, Mons, Burmese, and Indians. About 20 tribes of seminomadic people (Meo, Akha, Yao, Karen, etc.) live in the mountains of the north, along the Burmese and Laotian borders.

The city of Nakhon Pathom was the center of early settlements of the Mon people. The Khmer Kingdom (Kampuchea) conquered the Mons well before the 10th century, establishing their capital at Lopburi. During the 13th century, Thais, Laotians, and Burmese fled from southeastern China as Kublai Khan and his Mongol forces conquered this region. The Thais pushed back the forces of the Khmer kingdom and settled in the Chao Phraya river valley, establishing the first capital of the integrated Thai kingdom at Sukhothai.

In 1350 the Thai capital moved to Ayutthaya, where the most impressive historical ruins may be seen today. Much of the damage to this ancient capital city was caused during the war with Burma, which became an archenemy of Thailand. The Burmese completely destroyed Ayutthaya in 1767, forcing the Thais to move their capital to Thonburi. The Thai capital was later moved across the Chao Phraya river to its present location in Bangkok.

The current king of Thailand, Bhumibol Adulyadej (Rama IX), descends from the first king of the Chakri Dynasty which established the capital in Bangkok in 1782. The political power of the king has diminished since the bloodless revolution in 1932, which established a constitutional monarchy. During most of the years since then, the military has had effective control of the nation through successive generals who served as premiers of the Thai government.

In an effort to tighten military control of the government, Field Marshal Thanom dissolved the Cabinet, abolished the Parliament, and suspended the Constitution in November, 1971. Thanom was later driven from power by massive student demonstrations in Bangkok following the arrest of prominent student leaders in October, 1973. The King subsequently appointed a new Prime Minister who produced a new Constitution and organized the first national elections, which brought M.R. Kukrit Pramoj to the Prime Minister's role in the spring of 1975. In April 1976, bickering among the factions in the Parliament led to the fall of his government and then new elections. Thanom's return from exile in September—supposedly to visit his dying father and enter the monkhood—sparked violent clashes which culminated when police and right-wing students stormed the Thammasat University campus on October 6; at least seventy were killed in the bloody siege and related incidents. Thailand's three-year experiment with parliamentary democracy thus forcibly gave way to a military-dominated 'civilian' government. In October 1977, when the civilian ministers apparently became too independent, the military officers took over in a bloodless coup. On a more optimistic note, in the Spring of 1980, one general replaced another as Prime Minister, strictly following the parliamentary procedures laid out in the present Constitution.

Since 1975, successive waves of both land (from Laos and Kampuchea) and boat (from Vietnam) refugees have sought asylum in Thailand. Although the expense of caring for the refugees is met largely through funding from the United Nations and private agencies, the social and political cost of harboring these people has been a considerable burden for the Thai nation. The influx of Kampucheans in the fall of 1979 seemed to insure that the refugee problem will continue to make Thailand an unwilling focus of regional and world politics.

Culture and Customs

Buddhism—the religion embraced by more than 90% of the population—plays a central role in Thai daily life. Monks (phra) are highly respected; if you get up early enough in the morning you'll see them walking the city streets, solemnly accepting alms of rice, cakes, fish, and fruit from the people. **Wat**—a temple, monastery, or combination of the two—are considered sacred places. (A **bot** is the main shrine in a wat, usually with a Buddha image, where the devout come to pray and make offerings, and where public ceremonies take place. The bell-shaped structure, related in design to stupas and pagodas, is a **chedi**.) In addition to the great number of wat, you will see small 'spirit houses' everywhere; at these shrines people make offerings to local spirits who protect a certain area or piece of property.

Dress neatly when visiting a wat; men should always wear shirts. Take your shoes off before entering a temple building.

Women should keep an important Buddhist practice in mind: they may not touch a monk or hand things directly to him. If a woman wishes to give a monk something, she should place it on a piece of his saffron robe which he will spread on the ground, or else put it on a handkerchief and place the handkerchief in front of him. In order to avoid physical contact with women, monks customarily sit in the rear seats of city buses (or the front seats of highway buses); when a monk boards a bus, it is expected that those in the rear will make room for him. (Traditionally all young men are supposed to become monks for at least a three-month period—and most still do.)

Buddha images, whether inside a wat or outdoors among the ruins of ancient capital cities, must be treated with respect regardless of size. If you buy a small Buddha image at a wat, don't put it in your pants pocket, because contact with the lower part of your body defiles it. (Feet, especially, are considered low and dirty; pointing at or touching another person with your feet is an insult. The head, believed to be the dwelling place of the soul, is considered sacred; Thais don't touch others on the head, especially small children.)

Several years ago there was a missionary who underestimated the importance of Buddhist customs in Thailand and climbed on top of a large Buddha at Ayutthaya to have his picture taken by a friend. The film store which developed the picture sent an extra copy to a Bangkok newspaper. His picture—straddling the neck of the large statue with his feet dangling below the Buddha's face—appeared the next day on the front page of the paper, causing a national scandal. The two missionaries were sentenced to six months in jail.

When visiting mosques in southern Thailand, women should be well-covered, with slacks or a long skirt, a long-sleeved blouse buttoned to the neck, and a scarf; men should wear long pants and a shirt with a collar. Take your shoes off before entering.

Although the King is no longer a figure of great political importance, Thais, especially in the rural areas, regard the Royal Family with reverence. You will notice that virtually all shops and houses display pictures of the members of the Royal Family. If by chance you go to an event at which a member of the Royal Family is present, you must follow the behavior of the people around you. At movies you should stand when the national anthem, written by the King, is played.

If you're invited to a Thai home, take your shoes off before entering. (A Thai host will always tell visitors, especially foreigners, "don't bother taking your shoes off" out of politeness, but you should still shed your footwear. It's fairly easy to see if there are piles of shoes from other members of the family around the doorway or not.) Don't sit with your legs crossed and avoid pointing at anyone with your feet. If you sit on the floor, you can tuck your legs beneath you. Use your right hand for eating and giving and receiving objects; to be very polite, cup your left hand under your right forearm when giving or receiving.

The traditional form of greeting is called the wai, in which hands are pressed together in a gesture similar to the Christian posture for prayer. The position of the hands indicates the social status of the two people greeting each other. The lower person must always wai first and raise her or his hands higher. Foreigners generally don't initiate the wai, but if someone greets you with a wai be sure to respond in kind.

If you do something wrong and wish to apologize, say "khau thode" (excuse me).

Some foreign ways which disturb Thais: public displays of affection between women and men, and losing your temper.

Thai Buddhist festivals are celebrated according to the lunar calendar. **Visakha Puja**, one of the most important festivals, commemorates the Lord Buddha's birth, enlightenment, and death. **Songkran** (Water Festival), held in April, features elaborate processions in the streets of Chiang Mai and the sprinkling of perfumed water on the hands of monks, elders, and Buddha statues. In practice, this custom has also been extended to include the wholesale dousing, with buckets of water, of passerbys—**especially** foreigners. There is absolutely no advantage in losing your temper if this happens to you, particularly since the culprits are children. Best to join in the spirit and laugh it off. Another special festival is **Loy Krathong**, celebrated on the full-moon night of the 12th lunar month. People use banana leaves and styrofoam to construct a krathong (small boat), which is decorated with candles and flowers in thanksgiving for the waters of the season. Then they make a wish as they set these boats afloat on rivers, canals, and ponds; it is believed that if the boat sails out of sight without sinking the wish will come true. For more information, see the "Events" pamphlet published by the TAT.

Language

Begin learning Thai by mastering the phrase 'mai pen rai', which translates roughly as 'never mind' or 'that's the way it goes'. It's the unofficial motto of Thailand.

Thai is a tonal language usually assigned to the Sino-Tibetan linguistic group, though some scholars have recently suggested that in fact it belongs to the Malayo-Polynesian family. The Thai alphabet, similar to Cambodian and Lao, was originally derived from Sanskrit.

Each of Thailand's four main regions has its own distinct dialect: Nothern Thai, Northeastern Thai (Lao), Central Thai (with several subdialects), and Southern Thai. Standard Thai—a synthesis of central dialects—is the official language of education and government. English is widely spoken in Bangkok as an administrative language.

Pocket Thai-English dictionaries can be purchased at the larger bookstores (i.e. Asia Books).

Hello (general greeting)	**Sawad-dii**
Please/thank you	**Prode/khaub khun**
Excuse me	**Khau thode**
Yes/no	**Khrab/Plaaw mai**
Town	**Muang**
Street/Lane	**Thanon/Soi**
Bus/Bus station	**Roht mai**
Train/Train station	**Rotfai/Sathaanii-rotfai**
Airport	**Sanaambin**
Boat	**Rya**
Hotel/Room	**Roangram/Hong**
Restaurant	**Raan-aahaan**
Market	**Talaad**
Post office	**Praisani**
Temple	**Wat**
Island/Mountain	**Koh/Phuukhao**
North/South	**Nua/Tai**
East/West	**Tawan-org/Tawan tog**
Inexpensive	**Thook**
Too expensive	**Phaeng pai**
Good/Bad	**Dii maak/Mai dii**
Where is —?	**— yuu thii nai?**
I want to go to —.	**Yaak pai thii —**
Is this bus to —?	**Roht kan ni pai thii —?**
Do you have a room?	**Hong mii mai?**
Where do you live?	**Yoo tii nai?**
What do you call this in Thai?	**Phasa thai ii riak waa arai?**
How much is it?	**Raakhaa thawrai?**
When?	**Mua-rai?**
Today/Tommorrow	**Wan nii/Prung nii**
Yesterday	**Mua wan nii**

1	Nung	11	Sib-et
2	Saung	22	Sib-saung
3	Saam	20	Yii-sib
4	Sii	21	Yii-sib-et
5	Haa	30	Saam-sib
6	Hok	40	Sii-sib
7	Jet	100	Nung roi
8	Paed	200	Saung roi
9	Kaw	1000	Nung phan
10	Sib		

To be polite, women should end greetings, requests, etc. with the syllable 'ka', men with the syllable 'krap'.

To make yourself understood, you'll have to practice these with a Thai friend. Tones are tricky for the untuned Western ear, and all systems of romanizing Thai script incorporate spellings that are deceiving to the uninitiated. (The difficulties in transliterating Thai are partly related to the fact that the Thai alphabet has 44 consonants and 24 vowels.) There is so little consensus that romanized Thai words usually appear in a variety of spellings. The 'Hat Yai' on train and bus schedules is the same city as the 'Haadyai' mentioned in some books and found on many maps; 'Ayutthaya' and 'Ayudhya' are the same place.

Food

After a Thai greets a friend, the first question will be: 'Bai nai?' (Where are you going?). The second inevitably will be: 'Ghin kao rue yang?' (Have you had rice yet?).

Thai cuisine, like the language, shows strains of Indian, Malay and Chinese influence (most restaurant owners are in fact Thai Chinese). Inexpensive, often open-fronted, restaurants are almost everywhere though English menus, outside Bangkok and Chiang Mai, are practically nonexistent. Upon entering the ubiquitous noodle shop which has the ingredients shown in the glass case, just point to the thin or thick noodles, bean sprouts, chopped onions, or whatever, and spice it with an appropriate key word to indicate what kind of meat you'd like:

chicken	**kai**	pork	**moo**
beef	**neua**	shrimp	**goong**

If your gesticulations prove useless, there are several dependable standbys: fried rice (kao pat), usually with fried egg on top; Thai omlette (ky jee-o); and curry (gang gully plus the word for whatever meat you want) served with white rice (kao plow).

Most foods are highly spiced—uninitiated Western faces turn a fine shade of rose. You can adjust gradually by picking out the chilis and following especially robust mouthfuls with a quick scoop of white rice or piece of fruit. Eat with fork in the left hand, spoon in the right.

Thais often finish their meals with fruit, for their country is richly blessed with a wide variety, including:

banana	**kluey**
pineapple	**supparot**
orange	**som** (both green and yellow)
papaya	**malagor** (squeeze lime over it)
watermelon	**teng-mo**
mango	**mah-muong**
jackfruit	**ka-noon**
durian	**durian** (peculiar smelling and expensive, considered a delicacy)
mangosteen	**mang-kut**
rambutan	**ngow** (grape-like taste; thick, red, hairy skin)

Avoid drinking unboiled water. Most restaurants serve a very weak iced tea (just enough tea to show that the water has been boiled). Fresh squeezed orange juice (nam som) and lime juice (nam manao) can be found in almost every restaurant and food stall. Thais, however, are quite fond of adding salt to these drinks which give it a Gatorade taste (you'll understand why folks prefer it this way once you start thinking about the tropical sun). If you'd rather keep your fruit juice sweet, say to the vendor: **mai sai klua** (don't add salt).

BREAKFAST

kao tom moo — mild rice soup with pork
pa tong go — fried bread, Chinese style

SOUPS

gang gai — hot curry with chicken
gang neua — hot curry with beef
gang liang — soup with vegetables
gang oh nam — wonton soup
tom yum kai — soup with chicken and spices
tom yum goong — soup with shrimp and spices

NOODLES

kwee teo nam — noodle soup
kwee teo hang — noodle dish
kwee teo pat — noodles fried with vegetables and sweet and sour sauce
bah mee gai — yellow noodles with chicken

RICE

kao pat — fried rice (usually tasty and cheap)
kao moo daeng — rice with sliced roast pork and soy sauce
kao man gai — rice with sliced chicken and soy sauce

SPECIAL THAI DISHES

pahtse yu — fried thin noodles with greens, broccoli, and pork; add condiments—lampa (brown sauce), vinegar, sliced peppers—and sprinkle sugar on top
gai yang — barbequed chicken with spicy sauce
yam goong/neua — a spicy shrimp/beef salad
kao nyou mah-muong — sticky rice and mangoes (for those fortunate enough to be in Thailand during the mango season, April-June)
sang kaya — fruit pie

DRINKS

karfay dumlorn — coffee
karfay lorn — coffee with mild and sugar
oleang — iced coffee with sugar
karfay yen — iced coffee with milk and sugar
nam chalorn — tea (hot)
chalorn — tea with milk and sugar
nam yen — cold water
nam keng — ice
Amarit, Singha — superb Thai beers

Accommodations

Bangkok offers travelers a wide choice of budget accommodations, and Chiang Mai boasts reasonably-priced hotels and guesthouses. A town of any size will have low-cost (B60-90 singles and B70-120 doubles) Chinese hotels, usually near the train and bus stations. They offer spartan rooms with overhead fans and a thin mattress on the bed. Baths have a shower or a dipper arrangement.

The wat in many rural areas will accept a small number of male travelers to sleep on the floor. If you stay the night at a wat, be careful to respect the religious customs—no smoking, no drinking, etc. (see Culture and Customs).

There is a system of youth hostels operated by the Ministry of Education, but the hostels are rarely used by foreigners because they are difficult for non-Thai speakers to locate. The TAT does provide a list for those who might want to check out those possibilities.

Transportation

INTERNATIONAL: Bangkok is one of the busiest crossroads in Asia. From here you can travel overland to Malaysia and Singapore—and by air to almost anywhere.

There are daily connections by train from Bangkok to **Malaysia** and **Singapore**. On Monday, Wednesday and Saturday, the International Express (1st and 2nd class only) goes directly to Butterworth (the station serving Penang) on Malaysia's west coast; it leaves at 3:40 pm and arrives at 5:45 pm the next day. Other days you can board an express (1st and 2nd class) from Bangkok to Haadyai and then change to a diesel railcar (a slower, local train) from Haadyai to Butterworth. There is also daily service from Bangkok to Butterworth via the slower 'rapid' trains (2nd and 3rd class), though this requires a change in Haadyai. If you are in a hurry to continue, all of these connections arrive in Butterworth in time to make connections for the various trains that run overnight to Kuala Lumpur and Singapore (see Transportation in Malaysia and Singapore). However, there is an advantage of buying a Bangkok/Butterworth ticket since it allows a stopover in Southern Thailand, such as Haadyai (for the beaches at Songkhla) or Surat Thani (for Koh Samui).

The 2nd class fare from Bangkok to Butterworth is B305; Bangkok/Singapore is B712. For the express trains add a B20 surcharge, and berths from Bangkok to Butterworth and Singapore are B20 respectively; the rapid train surcharge is B10. (Since a seat in a second-class car is almost twice as expensive as 3rd-class, while they are often part of the same rapid train, it only seems worthwhile to spend the extra money if: 1) you're in a hurry and want to take the express, which is 1st and 2nd class only; 2) you want a berth; 3) you don't enjoy crowding in 3rd class).

The trains described above will take you to Malaysia's west coast, but you can also enter the east coast from Haadyai via Sungai Golok (near Kota Bharu) by train or bus.

INTER-CITY: Thailand boasts fine **train** service. Four main trunk lines: northern, northeastern, eastern and southern—span the country. Schedules and fares are listed in small pamphlets which are available at most train stations. Berths are available on express trains only; 1st class provides compartments that turn into beds, 2nd class has two-tiered berths on either side of the aisle (upper berth is cheaper than lower), and 3rd class doesn't have berths.

Note that trains from Bangkok leave on time. Don't expect, as in some Asian countries, to arrive at the station two minutes after scheduled departure, thinking it will be delayed.

All tickets are sold for a particular time and date; if you miss your train, you must get a refund within three hours of departure. Train tickets in Bangkok can be booked at the Advance Booking Office, Bangkok Railway Station, west end of Rama IV Rd.; tel. 2817010. Book tickets at least 3-4 days ahead of departure.

Public buses (run by the government-owned Transport Co.) offer a good way to see the countryside in the company of locals. They tend to be less safe than trains since they are regularly involved in high-speed crack-ups—especially in the short-haul routes between cities in provinces. While these rides might be viewed as 'exciting' in lieu of the drivers' Grand Prix tactics, take the precaution of at least sitting in the safest seats which are in the middle on the driver's side.

Three main terminals serve Bangkok. The Eastern Terminal (for Pattaya, the Ancient City) is located on Sukhumvit Rd. near Soi 42. The Southern Terminal (for Nakhon Pathom, Kanchanaburi, Hua Hin, Phuket, Surat Thani, and Songkhla) is on Charan Sanitwong Rd. near Phrannok Rd. in Thonburi. The Northern Terminal is on Phahon Yothin Rd. Check your Latest Tour's map for city bus routes to these terminals.

From Bangkok you can reach virtually any major city by overnight **tour bus**. Several private tour companies operate these luxury buses with air-conditioning and reclining airline-style seats, but the most central location to find tour buses is the tour bus division of the Transport Co. An advantage of the Transport Co. is that in the event of a breakdown they guarantee another bus to pick up the passengers and continue. With some private firms, you may find yourself stranded until the bus is repaired. In addition, the Transport Co. offers a daytime AC bus on many of their routes. In Bangkok the central ticket office and starting point for most Transport Co. buses (check your ticket) is in the Air Coach City Terminal, 465/1 Si Ayutthaya Rd. near Phayathai Rd. (half a block west of the Florida Hotel).

For any tour bus, government or private, buy tickets a few days in advance, especially on such routes as Chiang Mai and Phuket. The ticket price includes a snack upon departure and a light meal at a stop.

INTRA-CITY: Once you have purchased a Latest Tour's bus map, it is fairly easy to get anywhere in Bangkok. Fares within the city are B1 for a regular **bus** and B5 for an air-conditioned bus (no transfers are given). The #2, 11, 17, 35, and 71 buses will take you to most of the places you want to go. Most buses stop running around 11:30; only a few of the major bus routes run all night.

For faster trips, there's the ubiquitous **taxi**. Fares must be bargained for; they usually start at B20. Since the majority of taxi drivers don't speak English, it's best to have your hotel write down the destination in Thai (as well as a fair price). Bargain with gusto.

Samlors (three-wheeled cabs) provide transportation for the short hops (fares generally start at B10). You must bargain with the samlor driver and this will usually require considerable haggling and sign-language.

Song-taos (Datsun minibuses with two bench seats in the rear cab) operate on the outskirts of towns. They don't always follow a fixed route; they may go in the direction of the first passenger they pick up and then stop anywhere along the way to pick up or drop off passengers. In Bangkok, song-taos follow the bus routes. In that case, the route number is usually clearly displayed.

364 THAILAND

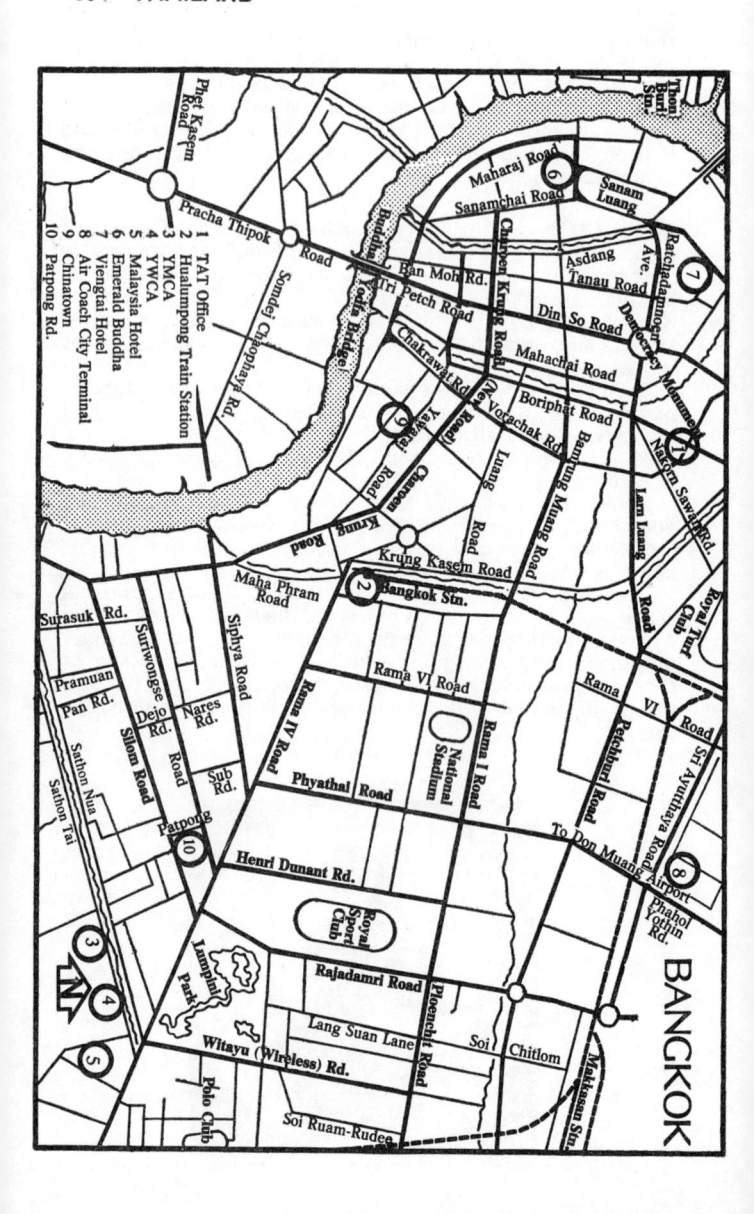

Bangkok

After Ayutthaya fell to an invading Burmese army in 1767, the Thais managed to oust the Burmese, and the new king, Taksin, selected for his capital Thonburi on the Chao Phraya River across from the bustling town, Bangkok. By 1782, Taksin was succeeded by King Rama I, the founder of the current Chakri dyansty, who set about recreating the glory of Ayutthaya in his new capital, Bangkok.

The city's history is one of haphazard growth—factories, fields, houses, offices and wat line the streets in random fashion—and therein lies part of the charm of Bangkok. It's delightfully (and at times frustratingly) unpredictable. Once reputed to be the 'Venice of the East' with a network of canals, called khlongs, lacing the cityscape, Bangkok has lost this image as the many waterways have been filled in and replaced by roads.

With approximately 5 million residents, sprawling Bangkok is home to 10% of Thailand's total population, and that figure is expected to swell to 8 million by 1990. As the only metropolis in Thailand (40 times larger than the second largest city, Chiang Mai), it continues to draw rural people in search of a new prosperity.

The system of numbering streets and buildings in Bangkok may need some explanation. A 'soi' is a lane off a larger road, usually identified by the name of that larger road plus a number. The soi are numbered consecutively, with odd numbers branching off one side of the street and the even from the other. What is confusing for the newcomer is that the different sois do not always progress at the same rate. For instance, Sukhumvit Soi 63 is opposite Sukhumvit Soi 42.

Exploring Bangkok

To get a sense of the former glory of Bangkok, take a tour of the floating market. The easiest way is to line yourself up at the pier at the Oriental Hotel before 7 am. Bargain to join one of the tourist boats for about B40 or if you are in a group of four or more, you can hire a boat at the pier for B180. This tour, however, has been criticized for its crass commercialism and pollution.

366 THAILAND

An alternative is the floating market at **Damnern Saduak** (84 km southwest of Bangkok). Being located on the Mae Klong River, the town is interlaced with a maze of khlongs. Climb on board a six-seater 'long tail' boat and float through khlongs which are filled by hundreds of small boats laden with fruits and vegetables. The main khlong of Damnern Saduak has the proportions of a river, but was dug around 120 years ago by thousands of laborers.

Every half-hour there is bus service to the Damnern Saduak floating market starting at 6 am from the Southern Bus Terminal. It takes two hours to reach the pier where the local boats can be hired (B180-250) to take visitors to the market area.

Surrounded by immense white walls, occupying an area of about a square mile, lies the **Grand Palace**. It was built in 1782 and consists of several buildings with highly decorated architectural designs. On these grounds is **Wat Phra Kaeo** which houses the Emerald Buddha—the most sacred Buddha image in Thailand. Fashioned from a single piece of jasper, the Emerald Buddha was discovered in Chiang Mai in 1436 when a crack appeared in a large plastered Buddha image. The Emerald Buddha was hidden inside. It was kept in Chiang Mai until 1552, then taken to Vientiane for protection from the Burmese who were ransacking Thailand at the time. Chao Phraya Chakri, who ascended the throne as King Rama I installed the Emerald Buddha in Wat Phra Kaeo. The admission fee of B20 covers entrance to the palace as well as the wat, but you are expected to dress 'respectfully'. On Saturdays and Sundays entrance to the compound is free, but the interior of the palace is not open. On numerous official holidays when the Royal Family uses the wat and palace, the area is closed to visitors.

Across the street from the Grand Palace is **Pramane Ground** (Sanam Luang) which was once the Royal Cremation Ground. It's noted now for its **Weekend Market**. Vendors and merchants from Bangkok and outlying provinces come to sell their wares on the weekend. Items range from fabrics to fruits, animals, handicrafts and books. Sanam Luang is also used in the windy months between February and April for kite-flying contests.

Facing Sanam Luang on the west is the **National Museum** on Naphrathat Rd. The museum features Thai art and archeological finds ranging from neolithic times to contemporary Bangkok. Open daily except Monday, Friday and holidays, 9-12 and 1-4. Free on Saturdays and Sundays; B5 other days. English language tours start at 9:30 am on Tuesday (emphasizing Thai culture), Wednesday (Buddhism), and Thursday (Thai art). A new **National Gallery** has been opened across Chao Fa Rd. (the street going over the bridge) from the National Museum, offering smaller exhibitions that change regularly. Hours are the same as the museum's. Free.

Located at the southeast corner of Sanam Luang is **Lak Muang**, the City Post Shrine, with its Thai dancing and folk opera. Erected by King Rama I in 1782, it houses the guardian

THAILAND 367

spirit of the city. Each day people come to give offerings and release doves bought there. Free too.

South of the Grand Palace is one of the most extensive temples in Bangkok, **Wat Pho**. It was built by King Rama I nearly 200 years ago and houses the immense Reclining Buddha. The image is 46 meters in length and 15 meters high and the soles of the feet are beautifully inlaid with mother-of-pearl designs. Enter the wat on Jetupon Rd. on the south side (B5 entrance fee). Many fine, and inexpensive, temple rubbings can be purchased within the grounds.

Wat Arun (Temple of Dawn) lies on the Thonburi bank of the Chao Phraya River. Despite its name, the most impressive view of it can be seen from the Bangkok bank at sunset.

Built on an artificial hill is the Golden Mount of **Wat Saket**. The wat should be climbed in time for the sunset. **Wat Benchamaborpit** (Marble Temple) is on Si Ayutthaya Rd. near Chitlada Palace. At the end of Yaowarat Rd. (close to the Bangkok Railway Station) is **Wat Traimit** which houses a huge golden Buddha image. Further information on these and other wat are available from TAT; see their 'Seven Wat in Bangkok'.

Jim Thompson's Thai House, at the end of Soi Kasemsan 2 across from the National Stadium on Rama I Rd., is endowed with art treasures. Jim Thompson, who disappeared in Malaysia in 1967, started the Thai silk industry. His house, now a museum, is open weekdays, 9:30-3:30 (B50). Located in a quiet compound off Si Ayutthaya Rd. (near Phaya Thai Rd.), the **Suan Pakkard Palace** is the residence of Princess Chumpot of Nagara Svarga, one of Thailand's leading art collectors. The complex of five traditional teak pavilions are richly furnished with Thai antiques and works of art. Open daily 9-4, except Sundays (B50).

The Pasteur Institute's **Snake Farm** produces serum for snake-bite treatment. You can watch pit vipers, cobras, and banded kraits milked for venom and fed at 11 each morning (except on holidays). The Snake Farm—the world's second largest—is located on Rama IV Rd. at Henri Dunant Rd., one block northwest of the Dusit Thani Hotel (B10).

The use of elbows, knees, fists and feet is permitted during the rowdy bouts of **Thai Boxing**. Lumpini Stadium near Lumpini park has fights Tuesday, Friday and Saturday at 6 pm.

368 THAILAND

Ratchadamnoen Stadium (next to the TAT office) has bouts Monday, Wednesday, Thursday and Sunday at the same time. Admission ranges from B40 to B150. Check with TAT or the Bangkok Times for schedules of boxing, soccer and other sporting events.

Yawaraj (Chinatown) is the throbbing heart of Bangkok's merchant community. When King Rama I decided to move his capital across the river to Bangkok, he chose for his palace a site already occupied by a larger Chinese trading community. The Chinese moved to this newer site just under 200 years ago. Take bus #1, 11, or 40 to the middle of Chinatown.

The **#17** bus is an easy way to explore Bangkok on your own. For the bus route and the exact location of the places listed below, refer to your city bus map. The #17 route includes: Lumpini Park, the Vishi Shrine (where people come to pray and burn incense throughout the day), Pratunam (a popular shopping area), Suan Pakkard Palace, Wat Benchamaborpit, the Dusit Zoo, Ratchadamnoen Boxing Stadium, and Wat Sraket. The route ends near Sanam Luang, within walking distance of the National Theater, the Emerald Buddha, the Grand Palace, Thammasat University, and the National Museum.

Eating in Bangkok

Noodle shops and inexpensive restaurants abound in Bangkok. Out of the thousands of possibilities, here are a few starters:

Sukol Tros Bakery, 14 Silom Rd. (one block from the Dusit Thani).
Vietnamese spring rolls w/fresh vegetables B10, beef w/tomato in gravy on rice B8, coconut ice cream B3. Great pastry.

Saladaeng, Silom Rd. (almost next door to the Sukol Tros Bakery).
Many dishes in the B20-25 price range. Kampong fish w/tomato sauce and white rice is tasty.

Wang Hsiou Nan, Sukhumvit Soi 8 (next to Patana Medical Clinic).
No English sign distinguishes this small shop from the others on the street, but you can pick it out by the high-backed wooden booths that line up against the wall. Serves every imaginable combination of noodles and several other delicious Thai/Chinese dishes. Proprietress speaks English.

Sorn Daeng Restaurant, 73 Ratchadamnoen Rd. (near Democracy Monument).
Famous among Thais for serving excellent, authentic Thai food at reasonable prices.

Baan Thai, 7 Sukhumvit Soi 32.
Very expensive but excellent food served in traditional Thai house. At 9 pm, Thai classical dancing begins. Prepare for a B200 dive.

American University Alumni Center (AUA), 179 Ratchdamri Rd.
Inexpensive, usually filled with students. Closed on weekends.

For international lunches at moderate prices, try the Patpong area which loses its vibrant atmosphere during the day. **The Barrel** offers huge club sandwiches or a set lunch (usually B45); the **Tien Tien** serves dim sum; the **Seafood Restaurant** offers a seafood buffet for B60; and **Bobby's Arms** specializes in fish and chips. The **New Fuji Cafe** and the **See Saw** serve inexpensive Thai/Chinese food.

Night-owls will want to pursue the various cheap late-night restaurants in Chinatown. Perhaps more convenient is the collection of all-night food stalls behind the row of shops on the south side of Petchaburi Rd., just west of the intersection with Ratchaprarop Rd. (near the Indonesian Embassy). The seafood there is delicious; no menus and little English spoken.

Night Life

For Westerners, the center of attraction in Bangkok after dark is the area east of Rama IV Rd. bounded by Silom and Suriwongse Rds. broadly known as **Patpong**. Here two narrow roads are lined with literally scores of establishments offering a variety of vices. Some bars have hostesses and subdued music, others boast go-go dancers and pounding disco. Most bars offer reduced prices during an early-evening happy hour; after 7 pm the prices go up as the night staff comes on duty. Then mixed drinks are usually B40; Thai beer goes for B30-35.

The bars in Patpong cater almost exclusively to foreign men, so at night there will be persistent hustlers advertizing 'sex shows' which involve lewd sexual gymnastics—it's a waste of time to deal with them.

If your dancing shoes have gotten a little flat during your trek through Asia, Bangkok will give you the chance to put some life into them. Many of the second-line hotels on Sukhumvit between Soi 3 and Soi 21 (Soi Asoke) have clubs where live bands blare out disco hits. Generally there is no cover charge (especially weekdays); a beer or cocktail should cost around B65. Some suggestions: the **Club Manhattan** at the Manhattan Hotel (Sukhumivit Soi 15); the **Love Club** at the Nana Hotel (Sukhumvit Soi 4; or the well-known sleaze **Grace Hotel** (Sukhumvit Soi 3). And there are countless more.

Due to a prohibitive tax on imported films, Western movies are few and far between. The **AUA** (American University Alumni Center) periodically screens American film classics (check the papers). The **Cock and Bull** (between Sukhumvit Soi 17 and 19) shows a different double feature every night. There is a minimum charge of B60; the quality of food and movies varies.

In Patpong there are a few places like the **Grand Prix** which offer video presentations of recent movies and football games.

370 THAILAND

(On Sunday afternoons, starting around 2 pm, the **Napoleon** shows a double feature, no cover charge, followed by two hours (6-8 pm) of live swing/Dixieland/jazz. Admission for the latter is B20.)

Shopping

Foreigners must bargain vigorously in most places (with the exception of department stores) and for most things (with the exception of books and some daily necessities, see Introduction, p.13). The fair price may range anywhere from 120% to 300% of the fair price, depending on how naive or wealthy you look. When bargaining, keep your sense of humor handy.

Good investments include Thai silk, antiques, silver, jewelry, and handicrafts. Bear in mind that prices tend to be considerably higher in Bangkok than in the northern provinces.

Those especially interested in shopping with the locals, or just in observing Thai markets, might want to buy Nancy Chandler's **Market Map** (available at bookstores mentioned below). Though somewhat outdated and expensive for a map (B30), it is drawn in an attractive manner and is very detailed; this is the only map that gives the stops for the Chao Phraya water bus drive.

On the first Saturday morning of the month, September through June, there is a **hilltribe crafts sale** in the International School of Bangkok gymnasium, Sukhumvit Soi 15. A good selection; prices are not cheap but are comparable with other places in Bangkok for similar handicrafts. Proceeds beyond expenses go to a scholarship for tribal children. Get there early because it's always crowded.

The **Central Department Store**, 306 Silom Rd. and on the corner of Ploen Jhit Rd. and Soi Chit Lom, stocks what is doubtless the most complete selection of English language paperbacks in Thailand. The **D.K. Bookstore** in Siam Square (directly behind the Lido Theater) and **Asia Books** (between Sukhumvit Soi 15 and 17) also have excellent selections of the classics and academic titles in paperback. For used books that cost about B10 look through the book stalls across from the Weekend Market on Ratchadamnoen Rd.

Meeting Students

Thammasat University and the food stalls across from Sanam Luang are among the best places to meet students in Bangkok. The campus sits on the banks of the Chao Phraya River just west of the National Museum. Directly south of Thammasat is Silpakorn, the fine arts university. Chulalongkorn University straddles Henri Dunant St. and Phaya Thai Rd. halfway between Rama I and Rama IV Rds.; check out the Student Union and the Information Collection Library.

The AUA has language classes in Thai and English, a library of American books, and a low-cost cafeteria; it's another good place to meet Thai students who can speak English. The Center is centrally located on Ratchdamri Rd. between Lumpini Park and the Erawan Hotel.

ACCOMMODATIONS IN BANGKOK

Bangkok abounds in reasonably-priced hotels; many were built for GIs on leave during the Vietnam War. Although there are many possibilities, we've listed a variety of hotels below:

Rama IV/Sathon area (from the Bangkok Railway Station take either #4, 46 or 100 buses):

Malaysia Hotel, 54 Soi Ngam-Du-Phli, off Rama IV Rd. (near Lumphini Stadium); tel. 2863582.

Single or double w/bath & ac B140-160. Popular stop for international travelers. The bulletin board next to the elevator is famous for its collection of travel tips and other assorted information. Even has a pool.

Rose Hotel, 118 Suriwong Rd.; tel. 2337695.

Single B340, double B440 all w/bath and ac. A moderately priced hotel squeezed in between the luxury mammoths: the Sheraton and Montien.

Bangkok Christian Guest House, 123 Saladaeng Rd., Soi 2; tel. 2336303.

Single B220, double B385, all w/bath and ac. Price includes breakfast, lunch and dinner (home-style cooking) available for around B50. Service charge of 10% added to total bill though. Right in the hub-bub of things.

Swiss Guest House, 30 Convent Rd.; tel. 2343729.

Single B200-250, double B230-300, plus 10% service charge. All rooms with bath and ac. Price includes continental breakfast and laundry service. Doors close at midnight. Not quite as nice as Bangkok Christian.

YMCA, 27 Sathon Tai Rd.; tel. 2861542.

Single B160-240, double B220-250-280. 10% discount for members. Has big pool, restaurant and English-speaking staff.

YWCA, 13 Sathon Tai Rd.; tel. 2861936.

Single B85-200, double B300, plus 5% service charge; includes ac. Women only.

Sukhumvit area (from railway station take #25, 40 or #1 air-conditioned bus):

Crown Hotel, 503 Sukhumvit Soi 29; tel. 3910511.

Singles and doubles are B178. Relaxing location w/restaurant and swimming pool.

Atlanta Hotel, end of Sukhumvit Soi 2; tel. 252608-9.

Single B70-180. Off hectic Sukhumvit. Has a pool.

Starlight Hotel, Sukhumvit Soi 22; tel. 3913644.

Singles and doubles B50-60. A bit hard to find.

Sanam Luang/Ratchadamnoen area (take #53 or 7 air-conditioned bus).

Viengtai Hotel, 42 Tani rd.; tel. 2815788.

Single B400, double B520. For students carrying ISICs, buy a voucher at the Trad Travel Service office in the hotel.

Royal Hotel, 2 Ratchadamnoen Rd. (across from Sanam Luang); tel. 2813644.

Single B300, double B360. All rooms are air-conditioned, w/dining room and pool. In the thick of downtown activity—and traffic.

Day Trips from Bangkok

In a day—or an overnight—trip, you can explore the ancient capital of **Ayutthaya**, 85 km north of Bangkok. Once a prosperous trading center on the route between India and China, it served as Thailand's capital for over 400 years until it was razed in 1767 by the Burmese. The city was built at the junction of three rivers, and the addition of a canal made it an island fortress. Most of the principal ruins are in the vicinity of the old royal palace of Wang Luang. While you can rummage around in the ruins, remember that there is an alternative method: a circular river tour. Though it will hit you in the pocketbook, tours can be arranged at the landing stage in modern Ayutthaya to reach some of the more isolated sites. Ayutthaya can be reached by train from Bangkok's Hualampong Station between 4:45 am and 8 pm (B15, 1½ hr.). Buses leave every ½ hr. from the Northern Bus Terminal (B14, 2 hr.); last bus from Ayutthaya is at 5 pm. A river excursion from Bangkok to Ayutthaya leaves from the pier of the Oriental Hotel, but there have been problems in the past with people being overcharged, stranded, etc.

You can combine a trip to Ayutthaya with one to **Bang Pa-in Palace**, 47 km to the south. The palace has been Thai royalty's summer retreat for the past few centuries. While the Royal Pavilion set in the lake reflects pure Thai architecture, other buildings borrow from the Chinese, Italian and Victorian styles. Buses leave for Bang Pa-in every ½ hr, 6 am-6 pm, from the Northern Bus Terminal (1hr, B12). Last bus leaves for Bangkok at 6 pm.

While there are no places to stay overnight in Bang Pa-in, Ayutthaya offers two inexpensive hotels: Thai Sena Hotel at 268 Sena-Navin Rd. (B50) and the Cathay Hotel, across from the post office (B60).

Two hours from Bangkok (or one hour from the floating market at Damnern Saduak) is **Nakhon Pathom**, the oldest city in Thailand and the place where Buddhism was first introduced to the country. Towering 380 ft over the city, the golden-tiled Phra Pathom Chedi is the tallest Buddhist monument in the world. From the Southern Bus Terminal take bus #83 (B10). (The well-publicized Rose Garden, midway between Bangkok and Nakhon Pathom, is an attraction geared mainly towards tour groups which you can safely skip). If you'd like to spend the night in Nakhon Pathom, perhaps going to Kanchanaburi the next day, try one of these budget hotels: the Mitsumphan on Luangphra Rd. or the Siri Chai at 37-41 Saiphra Rd. (rooms at each start around B50).

Opportunities to really explore the River Kwai in **Kanchanaburi Province** are usually limited by lack of reasonable accommodations, but one definite possibility is the **River Kwai Farm**. At this 'resort' at a remote site directly on the riverbank, you sleep under a mosquito net on a bamboo raft or in a bamboo & thatch cottage. Since the Farm is rather isolated, the price includes all meals, which are prepared with fresh produce grown right on the spot. In addition to fishing, canoeing, and swimming in the river and walking in the forest, various excursions—ranging from half-day to ten-day raft trips up to Burma—are available at reasonable prices. A standard two-day program including meals, lodging and short trips in the immediate area costs B360-400 per person. For information on how to get there (B22 by train which crosses the bridge over the River Kwai) and reservations (which are essential since there's nowhere else to go if the Farm's full), contact the M.E.I. Travel Service at 68/2 Sathon Nua Rd., Bangkok or the TAT office on Saeng Chuto Rd., A. Muang, Kanchanaburi.

To fully appreciate the **Ancient City** (Muang Boran), you ought to have some previous knowledge of Thai history and architecture or else go with someone who does. This 'outdoor museum' located 33 km southeast of Bangkok is a collection of replicas of historical monuments, buildings, and wats from all parts of Thailand. Unfortunately, there are virtually no explanation signs in English. The park tends to be touristy. To reach the Ancient City take a bus from bay no. 5 in the Eastern Bus Terminal (B5). To get back you may have to take a series of local buses since highway buses don't like to pick up passengers so close to Bangkok.

Fifteen years ago **Pattaya** was a sleepy fishing village; now it's a slick beach resort. Pattaya, 154 km southeast of Bangkok, offers a considerable array of sea sports: wind-surfing, boating, skin and scuba diving, etc. The beach itself at Pattaya is nothing to rave about, but the southern beaches near the Royal Cliff Hotel (accessible by song-taos, B30) are magnificent for sunset swimming. The mechanical sea toys must be bargained for: water-scooters, B140-200 per hour; boats to nearby islands, B800-1200 per day; diving equipment, B500-1500 per day. If you're weary of the water, bargain for motorcycles (B150-180 per day) to zoom up and along the coast. As soon as the sun dips below the horizon, 'the Strip' in South Pattaya starts to light up. Much of the night entertainment revolves around this narrow corridor of outdoor marine bars and restaurants. Prices for food and accommodations near the Strip tend to be quite high, but once you step a block or two away, prices drop considerably. Hotel rooms can be found for under B200. Check the TAT office on 171 Pattaya Beach, Chaihat Rd. for more complete information. Buses leave from Bangkok's Eastern Bus Terminal for Pattaya (B45).

Northern Thailand

If experienced travelers head straight for **Chiang Mai** (pop. 120,000), it's probably because this city is cooler and more relaxed than chaotic Bangkok. Chiang Mai, though, is rapidly becoming a tourist center swelling with souvenir shops and tourist hotels. Still, Chiang Mai seems to have maintained its charm; the city boasts a fine array of handicrafts and a number of historic wats. The city is located on a fertile plain at an elevation of about 300 meters. Looming steeply to the west is the lower end of the Himalayas.

Chiang Mai has an impressive history dating back to when King Mengrai ruled a Thai kingdom in the North. Following Kublai Khan's invasion of the Pagan area in 1287, King Mengrai, allied with the rulers of Sukhothai, founded the independent kingdom of Lanna Thai. By 1296, Chiang Mai was built to serve as the capital for King Mengrai. Chiang Mai remained independent, though at times there had been both Burmese and Siamese domination, until 1774 when it became incorporated into the Thai Kingdom.

The oldest section of Chiang Mai is surrounded by a moat. Within these parameters stands the city's first temple: **Wat Chiang Man.** It was built and inhabited by King Mengrai. Close by is **Wat Phra Singh** which was erected in 1345 by King Phayu. Inside the chapel is one of the most venerated Buddha images in the North; it is claimed to be over 1500 years old and brought over from Sri Lanka. A few blocks to the east is **Wat Chedi Luang.** The 90 meter steeple was toppled by a violent earthquake in 1545; it hasn't been repaired since. For a number of years this temple housed the Emerald Buddha. Outside of the moat's protection is **Wat Suan Dok** which was built in 1383. The numerous chedis here house the remains of several generations of the Royal Family of Chiang Mai. And high upon Doi Suthep overlooking the entire plain is **Wat Prathat.** This temple was also started in 1383 and still hosts a large number of devout pilgrims.

When you arrive in Chiang Mai and check into a hotel or guest house, stop by the TAT office near the Nawarat Bridge at 135 Praisani Rd. Grab a city map and one of the Northern area. The map will designate the four bus routes that circle around Chiang Mai for a B1 ride. Chiang Mai is small enough that you

CHIANG MAI

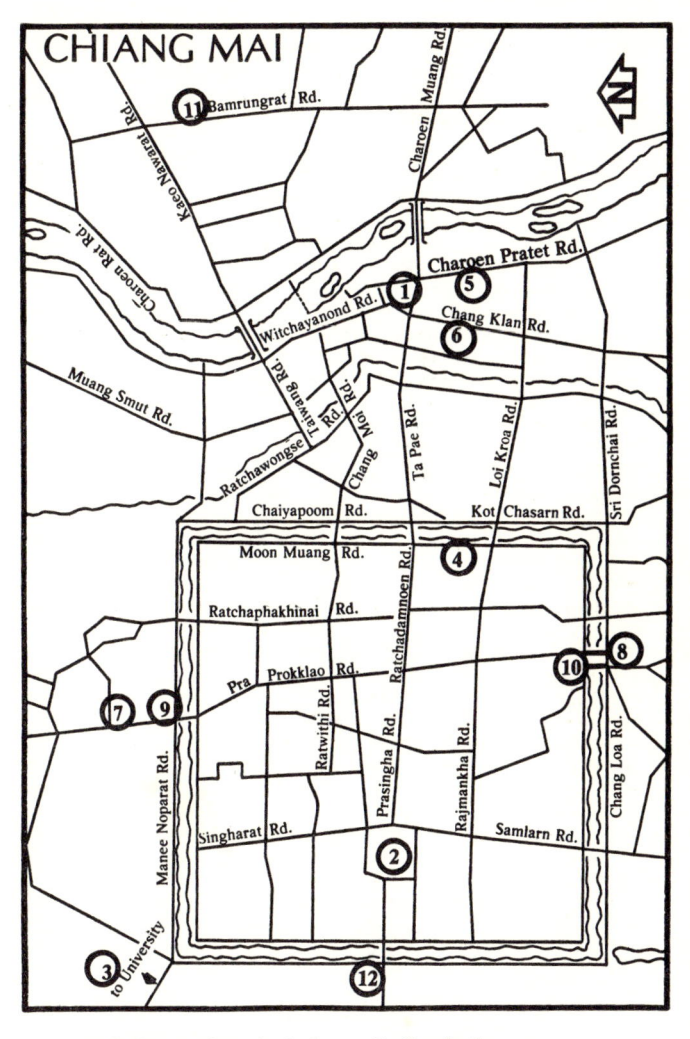

1. TAT (Tourist Organization)
2. Wat Phra Singha
3. YMCA
4. Saitum Guest House, Thai-German Dairy Restaurant
5. Pornping Hotel
6. Night Bazaar
7. Bus Station
8. Woodcarving Shops
9. Elephant Gate
10. Chiang Mai Gate
11. Thai Tribal Crafts
12. Suan Dork Road—to border crafts, vegetarian restaurant

376 THAILAND

just might want to walk or bike around. If you choose the latter, a bike can easily be rented for about B20 a day. Don't worry about trying to find bike rentals; they're located near all the popular guesthouses and hotels.

Either by bus or bicycle you can wander around the outskirts of town. For instance, south of the moated Chiang Mai are several neighborhoods specializing in particular crafts (ride a #1 bus). Silverware can be found along Wualai Rd., while lacquerware is located on the road to Chom Thong. Much of the woodcarving is sold on Raj Chiang Rd. and Wualai Rd. East of the city, past the railroad station (take either a #1 or #3 bus) on Charoen Muang Rd., are areas where silkweaving and umbrellas are available. Another place to explore is the non-profit **Thai Tribal Crafts** at 208 Bumroongat Rd. There is also a bustling night market on Chang Klan Rd. where you are expected to bargain with gusto.

While shopping for souvenirs, you'll probably be shopping for your stomach as well. Eating poses no problem since there are a large number of restaurants that have sprouted up all over--and most have English menus. If you crave a Western meal you can drift into the **Thai-German Dairy Cafe** on Moon Muang Rd. There are many more, and some like the the restaurant in the Pornping Hotel even offer a nightly floor show (nothing to rave about though). For vegies, there is an inexpensive **Vegetarian Restaurant** on Suan Dork Rd. about ¾ km beyond moated Old Chiang Mai.

While Chiang Mai can't offer a Bangkok nightlife, there are a few places for drinks and dancing--most notably the Karen Hut Bar (in the Prince Hotel). Drinks though are expensive--B50 for a beer. Sip and slide on the dance floor.

There are numerous side-trips from Chiang Mai that are worth pursuing. Either buses or motorcycles are available. A motorcycle can be rented for about B150 to B200 a day depending on size and use of the bike. The only reliable place to rent a bike is across from the Suriwongse Book Center near the night market. Be sure to check out the bike beforehand--if it's the rainy season, buy a poncho.

The mountain **Doi Suthep**, rising 3500 feet above sea level, overlooks the Chiang Mai plain. About two-thirds of the way up the mountain is **Wat Prathat**. Five kilometers beyond the Wat is the King and Queen's residence at Phuping. From the White Elephant Gate, you can jump on a bus to Doi Suthep and rise 12 km on a switchback road to the Wat.

Situated 26 km from Chiang Mai is Lamphun—take a white #4 bus which leaves every fifteen minutes across from the old wooden bridge just east of Narawat bridge. **Lamphun** was once the capital of the Haripoonchai kingdom. Where the palace once was now stands Wat Prathat Haripoonchai. It remains one of the most beautiful and best preserved wat in Thailand. If you are interested in cotton weaving, go 11 km further down the road to Pa Sang. There are reputed to be 2000 hand-looms still in use here.

With a car or motorcycle, you can get to **Mae Klang Falls**, southeast of Chiang Mai toward Chom Thong. From there head straight to **Doi Ithanon National Park**, named after the highest peak in Thailand (2596 meters). Check with park authorities at the front entrance before starting a long hike.

Due east of Chiang Mai lies **Bor Sarng** where several hundred families still pursue their village craft of umbrella-making. Unnumbered red buses leave the Chiang Mai bus station every half-hour until 5 pm. Thirteen kilometers further is **San Kamphaeng** which is famous for its hand-weaving industry.

To get a sense of hill-tribe village life, join a three- to five-day trekking tour offered by scores of tour companies in Chiang Mai. It's recommended that you visit the TAT office first to check on the various tours; the best seem to be Orbit, Manit and S.T. These tours go north into Shan, Lahu, Karen and Akha villages as well as a KMT village (remnants of the Chinese nationalists who are now involved in the opium trade). The cost of tours vary between B400-B500 which includes accommodations, transportation, and most meals. Bring your passport, mosquito repellent, good walking shoes, and small gifts. Most of these tours allow the option of ending up in Chiang Rai after a five-hour ride of the Kok River.

If you're not one to follow tours, you can take a bus from the Chiang Mai bus station up the northern route. About 50 km beyond Chiang Mai the scenery turns from farmland to jagged mountain slopes and on a clear day Chiang Dao peak will be visible. At the town of **Chiang Dao**, you can get off and walk (5 km) or ride to the **Chiang Dao Caves**—there are a number of Buddha images inside which are either lighted by thin cracks in the ceiling at the entrance of the cave, or when you're deep within the mountain, by a kerosene lamp. B20 donation insisted. From Chiang Dao it is another 80 km to the rough and ready town of Fang. Nine kilometers west of the town is a series of sulfuric hot springs in the foothills. Tricky to find so ask for clear directions at the TAT Chiang Mai. Another 24 km northward and you're at the border town of Tha Thon, where you can climb aboard the noon boat to Chiang Rai (B60).

Chiang Rai may serve as a base for a short trip to Chiang Saen where there are some archaeologically significant wats. From Chiang Rai you may return by bus to Chiang Mai costing B40 or B65 depending on whether you prefer air-conditioning. For a quick exit, B180 on a Transport Co. bus will go directly to Bangkok.

Another way to rub elbows with hilltribe people is to take a bus to **Mae Sariang**, a small market town in the high misty mountains near Burma. Buses leave twice daily from the Chiang Mai Gate (B30) and go south to Hot and then west following roller-coaster roads twisting through the mountains to Mae Sariang. From the Mae Sariang market you can jump on another bus to **Mae Hong Son** (108 km). Mae Hong Son is very secluded and it has been reputed to be 'a place where people were posted to if their superiors didn't want to see their faces for any reason.' (Hudson's Guide to Chiang Mai and the North). You can return to Chiang Mai via Mae Taeng, but check road conditions before you leave.

If you are returning to Bangkok, stop at **Sukhothai**, the first capital of Thailand. Noble ruins in various stages of restoration indicate the past grandeur of the Thai civilization. Sukhothai was founded in 1238 and flourished until 1365. King Ramkhamhaeng is regarded as the most famous Sukhothai king. It was he who adapted the Khmer alphablet which is still, more or less, in use today. Ramkhamhaeng promoted a good deal of Thai art and culture—many of the ruins now seen in Thailand are attributed to the adapted Khmer models which were conceived during his reign. There is much to see, so plan on a lot of hiking. To make sense of the area visit the Ramkhamhaeng Museum first (open daily except Mondays and Tuesdays) and ask for a guidebook published in English.

From Chiang Mai, take a bus to Tak (B45). Tak is tranquil—not much to do other than watching the river flow at sunset. If you are stranded, stay at the Tak Hotel; otherwise climb on board another bus (B15) to Sukhothai. Accommodations are in New Sukhothai, 13 km away from the bus station.

Generally, there are relatively few travelers touring the Northeast area of Thailand. While the scenery may not be as picturesque as other places in the North, there are significant Khmer ruins, most notably in Pimai near **Korat** (Nakhon Ratchasima). These tumbled-down monuments were built by the Khmers in the 11th and 12th centuries when Pimai was a vassal state to the Khmer Empire and a center of Mahayana Buddhism and Hinduism. There is another reason why the Northeast receives few travelers: it is a politically sensitive area which has been the scene of guerilla-government clashes.

ACCOMMODATIONS FOR NORTHERN THAILAND

Chiang Mai: Arriving in Chiang Mai by either bus or train no doubt you will be met by throngs of rickshaw drivers handing out various cards advertising hotels. Best to head to any of the accommodations below:

Chiang Mai Guest House, 91 Charoen Prathet Rd. Single w/common bath B80; double B100 w/common bath, B140 w/private bath. Probably the nicest place to stay in Chiang Mai for the low-budget traveler—always full. Excellent location overlooking the river.

Je T'Aime Guest House, 268 Charoen Rad Rd. Rooms run between B45 and B50 with private bath. Although location is somewhat far from center of town, the rooms are clean and comfortable.

Prince Hotel, 3 Tai Wang Rd. Single B107 w/fan, B240 w/ac; double B220 w/fan, B300 w/ac. A step up from the guest houses both in terms of service and price. Even has pool, restaurant and bar. Helpful staff.

Saitum Guest House, 21 Ratmanka Rd., off Moon Muang Rd. near Thai-German Dairy Cafe. Single B50 w/fan; double B60 w/fan. Although remotely resembles a Motel 6, the guest house is cozy and centrally located.

Pao Come Guest House, 9 Old Chiang Mai Rd. Soi 3, near Prince Hotel. Single B50 w/fan; double B80 w/fan. Common bath. Difficult to find this gem, but in a great neighborhood.

Manit Guest House, 84 Charoen Rad. Single B40-50 w/fan; double B40-80 w/fan. Secluded location east of the river.

Sumit Hotel, 198 Rajapaknai Rd. Single B100 w/fan, B120 w/ac; double B120-140 w/fan, B140-160 w/ac. Sterile, mid-size hotel.

Porn Ping Hotel, 46-48 Charoen Prathet Rd. Single B130-175 w/ac; double B175-210 w/ac. Classy hotel on tourist row.

YMCA, 2/4 Sanititham Santisook Rd. Dorms B40; single B60-80; double B100-120.

Chiang Mai Hostel, 302 Manee Noparat Rd. Single B30-40, double B60-80. IYH members receive 10% discount. Boasts cafeteria, basketball & tennis courts and free transportation from the railway station each morning.

TRANSPORTATION FOR NORTHERN THAILAND

Chiang Mai now receives weekly flights from Hong Kong on Thai International (other airlines are expected to follow suit) as well as four flights daily from Bangkok on Thai Airways. Trains leave Bangkok at 6 pm while the return trip leaves Chiang Mai at 5:20 pm daily. The train takes about thirteen hours; fares on the basic 2nd class are B190 (add B20 for express train and B50 for an upper berth—lower berth is B75). There are also many bus companies which serve the Bangkok-Chiang Mai line. These buses are air-conditioned (freezing) with reclining seats and food. prices range between B160-200. Many of the bus companies take off from larger hotels in Bangkok; or you can just go to the Northern Bus Terminal (see **Transportation** section) and take a non-ac bus between 5:25 am and 10 pm eleven times daily. Low fare and lots of locals.

Southern Thailand

As you go further south you begin to notice a series of differences in landscape, religion and language. Large rubber estates tend to become more dominant than rice paddies. A gilded minaret of a mosque will replace the flaming dragon roofs of a wat. Malay phrases begin to become interchangeable with Thai. These differences have become the roots of conflict between the South and the rest of Thailand.

Perhaps the greatest influence has been Islam which arrived in the 13th century. The Arab, Persian and Indian traders gradually intermarried with the local Thais and, by the 17th century, the southern Thai states became an Islamic entity. The area had always been a peripheral region between Thai kingdoms and the various Malay states. Even when it was dominated by one or the other, it managed to maintain a considerable degree of internal autonomy until at least 1901 when it became incorporated within Thailand. During the 1930's and 40's, the Thai government tried forcibly to assimilate the Thai-Malays and met with considerable resentment. In 1948, the Thai-Malays petitioned the UN for southern secession. Though this movement was suppressed by the Thai government, changes in the Thai hierarchy brought a more liberal policy to improve relations. One might say that this was 'too little, too late'. Secessionist guerilla activities reached a peak in the 1960's and since then there has been sporadic fighting.

The word about **Koh Samui** (Samui Island)—32 km off Thailand's eastern coast near the city of Surat Thani—is that it will be promoted by TAT as a fancy-dancy tourist resort, but that seems to be only on the drawing boards. Koh Samui is a beautiful tropical retreat geared for the slightly adventurous traveler. Accommodations tend to be simple, and it takes a bit of effort to get here. You might find yourself all alone with gorgeous waterfalls and sandy beaches.

A more popular, and likewise more accessible, spot is the island of **Phuket** on the western coast. Phuket is known for having some of the most idyllic tropical beaches in Thailand; it is ideal for swimming, snorkeling, boating or just basking in the warm sun. The best beaches are Surin Beach on the western coastline and Rawaii Beach on the southern tip of the island. Try the several small islands in Phangnga east of Phuket. There are several caverns containing primitive drawings. For further information, visit the TAT office at 73-75 Phuket Rd. (behind the Pearl Hotel).

Many of the island's hotels have moderately-priced restaurants. A B4 taxi ride outside of town is the Koa Siray Sea Food Restaurant; its tables are on the beach beneath coconut trees. As you watch the sun dip below the horizon, the tides will change and the lamps of the tin mining boats blink as if in a procession. Near the Pearl Theater on Phangnga Rd. are two excellent Thai/Chinese restaurants: the Tai Fah Restaurant and the Jack & Joy Restaurant.

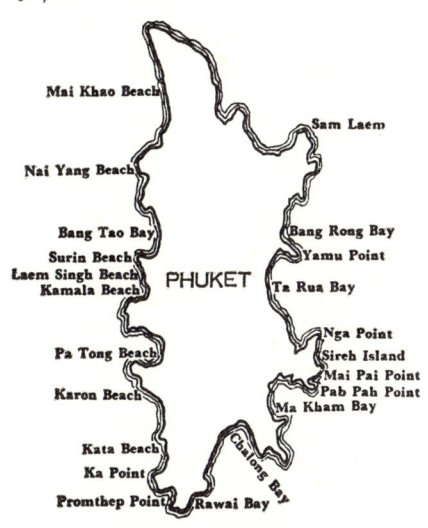

[Map of PHUKET showing: Mai Khao Beach, Sam Laem, Nai Yang Beach, Bang Tao Bay, Bang Rong Bay, Surin Beach, Yamu Point, Laem Singh Beach, Kamala Beach, Ta Rua Bay, Nga Point, Sireh Island, Mai Pai Point, Pa Tong Beach, Pab Pah Point, Karon Beach, Ma Kham Bay, Kata Beach, Ka Point, Chalong Bay, Promthep Point, Rawai Bay]

Haadyai is the thriving commercial center in the south. If you're taking the train from either Bangkok or Butterworth, you'll inevitably stop here. Visit the TAT office at 9 Prachathipat Rd. (next to the Sukhontha Hotel) for useful local travel information.

The TAT folks can tell you when the next **bullfight** will be held. Unlike the Spanish version, two bulls stand in the ring facing each other—no middle-man matadors here. The heavy gambling action is half the excitement.

On the edge of Haadyai, near Songkhla University is the Rubber Research Plantation where you can observe tappers extract latex from rubber trees and see various methods of rubber processing. Visit in the morning after 8:30. Free.

Wandering around Haadyai isn't bewildering since street signs have been romanized and most pedicab and Datsun drivers know enough English to get you where you want to go (fares to any point within the central city should be below B5). If you do not know where to go, at least duck into one of the many Thai, Chinese and Muslim restaurants. Few restaurants have English menus. The best food stalls open in the evening along Niphat Utid 3 Rd. across from the movie theater. Lights and crowds point the way.

Haadyai has a fairly bustling nightlife, most of which is centered around the Sukhontha Hotel which features live folk music nightly in its Jade Room Restaurant; the hotel also has a bar and a nightclub. Prices aren't cheap.

Thirty km east is **Songkhla** which offers a peaceful alternative to Haadyai. Songkhla is well-known for its white sandy beaches; Laem Soan and Laen Samila are the best. Also of interest is Songkhla Lake, almost 500 square miles in area. Actually it does have a narrow entrance into the Gulf of Thailand, so it's a saline lake, making it excellent for fishing. Hire a boat for B10-20 to tour the lake and visit the fishing village on the lake's large island. Scattered in the Songkhla area are wat ruins dating back to the Daravadi and Ayutthaya periods, when the town was a prosperous settlement. Most notable among these is Majimawat Temple, which is over 400 yrs. old, and now houses the National Museum of the South. The temple is located on Sraiburi St. and can be reached on foot from the bus stop.

ACCOMMODATIONS FOR SOUTHERN THAILAND

Seaside Hotel and **Sri Samui**, both in the town of Hna Ton. Rooms B40-60.

First Bungalow, Chaweng Beach, 23 km from Hna Ton. Rooms B40.

Phuket:

Imperial Hotel, 52 Phuket Rd., Tambol Talat Yai. Single B90, w/ac B110; double B110, w/ac B130. Centrally located.

Paton Beach Bungalow, c/o Southern Tour, 127 Talang Rd. B70-90. Located on one of the most popular beaches.

Siam Hotel, 13-15 Phuket Rd. Single B55, double B80. Some rooms w/ac B90. One of the least expensive hotels in town.

Thavorn Hotel, 74 Rasada Rd. Single B90, w/ac B125: double B90, w/ac B135. Modern 5-story hotel in the heart of town w/pool and restaurant.

Haadyai:

Cathay Hotel, 93/1 Nipat Utid 2 Rd. Single B70, w/ac B120; double B90, w/ac B185-200. Located in the center of town.

King's Hotel, 126-134 Nipat Utid 1 Rd. Single B100, w/ac B140; double B120, w/ac B160. Has a restaurant and a tour service.

Railway Station Hotel, Railway Station. Single B97, w/ac B141; double B119, w/ac B163. Clean rooms w/restaurant and bar.

Songkhla:

Suk Soomboon, two of them--one, on Petch Kiree Rd., the other, on Saiburi Rd. Rooms in the B50-180 range.

Narai Hotel, 12/2 Chaikhon Rd. Single B60, double B80-100.

TRANSPORTATION FOR SOUTHERN THAILAND

Koh Samui: Take a bus bound for Nakhon Si Thammarat (leaving

Bangkok's Southern Bus Terminal at 8 and 10 pm) and get off in Ban Don, the port of Surat Thani (B100, 11 hrs). From Ban Don to Koh Samui there are two boats daily; a ferry leaves at noon (6 hrs.) and a speed boat leaves at 12:30 pm (3 hrs). Tickets cost B30 and B38 respectively. The speed boat returns from Koh Samui at 7:15 am, the ferry at 11 pm.

If you take the train to Surat Thani (see transportation information for Phuket), you'll have to catch a local bus from the station to Ban Don (B20).

Phuket: Five buses leave daily from Bangkok's Southern Bus Terminal between 3 and 10 pm (12 hrs, B107). Transport ac buses leave Bangkok at 6:40 pm and 7:30 pm (one-way B200, round-trip B350) at Ratchadamnoen Klang Rd. (in front of the Mercedes Benz showroom); tel. 2229489.

Five trains make the 12 hr trip from Bangkok to Surat Thani daily. The 'no frills' 3rd class rapid train costs B89; for B213 you can get an upper berth on the 2nd class express. From Surat Thani it's a 2½ hr, B45 bus ride to Phuket.

From Haadyai, you can go by bus to Phuket 4 times daily, with departures between 5:45 and 9:30 am. Three buses cost B63; one has ac and costs B100. The trip takes 7-9 hrs. Buses leave from the Haadyai Station on Chuemrat Rd. The Phuket/Haadyai service is similar.

Haadyai: Three trains run daily from Bangkok and Haadyai and vice-versa (18 hrs). The 'budget' fares vary between B276 (2nd class with upper berth) to B106 (3rd class, rapid train).

The 20 hr bus ride costs B155-265, depending on whether you take the regular public bus from the Southern Bus Terminal or the ac bus from the Air Coach City Terminal. For each, there are several departures daily.

Haadyai can also be reached from Butterworth & Penang by train, bus or taxi (4-5 hr).

Songkhla: Buses leave Haadyai for Songkhla from in front of the market on Montri Rd. every 15 min., 6 am-8 pm (45 min., B6). Six 3rd class trains also make the trip daily (1 hr, B5). From Songkhla any of the small Datsun minibuses can take you to the beaches for under B5.

Bibliography

Thailand, Apa Guide, ed. by Charles Levine. Expensive but well-written and thorough with fantastic photogaphy.

Essays on Thai Folklore, by Phya Anuman Rajadhan. A Thai cultural history.

The Politician and Other Stories, by Khamsing Srinawk. A collection of short stories by one of Thailand's best contemporary writers.

Thailand: A Complete Guide, by William Duncan.

Little Things, by Prajuab Thirabutana. Village life as seen by a young girl.

Hudson's Guide to Chiang Mai and the North, by Roy Hudson. Out of print, but copies may still be floating around.